When a Heart Turns Rock Solid

When a Heart Turns Rock Solid

THE LIVES OF THREE PUERTO RICAN BROTHERS ON AND OFF THE STREETS

Timothy Black

Pantheon Books

New York

Copyright © 2009 by Timothy Black

All rights reserved. Published in the United States by Pantheon Books, a division of Random House, Inc., New York, and in Canada by Random House of Canada Limited, Toronto.

Pantheon Books and colophon are registered trademarks of Random House, Inc.

Library of Congress Cataloging-in-Publication Data
Black, Timothy.
When a heart turns rock solid / Timothy Black.
p.   cm.
Includes bibliographical references and index.
ISBN 978-0-307-37774-6
1. Puerto Ricans—Massachusetts—Springfield.
2. Puerto Ricans—Massachusetts—Springfield—Economic conditions.
3. Puerto Ricans—Massachusetts—Springfield—Social life and customs.
4. Urban poor—Massachusetts—Springfield.
5. Springfield (Mass.)—Social conditions. I. Title.
F74.S8B53 2009
305.38'87295074426—dc22   2008042273

www.pantheonbooks.com
Printed in the United States of America
First Edition
2 4 6 8 9 7 5 3 1

*In memory of Katherine and the innocent
smile of a seven-year-old girl*

CONTENTS

INTRODUCTION

SOME MEMORIES DON'T FADE with time. Sixteen years ago I returned home from the university in the inattentive manner that accompanies daily routine, pushed the message button on my answering machine, and began shuffling around the kitchen to start dinner. As I peered into the refrigerator, the third message rolled up, "Tim, it's Fausto, I fucked up, I'm in jail, come see me."

Fausto Rivera was among a group of young men I had met three years before, in 1990, while evaluating a school dropout prevention program in Springfield, Massachusetts. Very rapidly, our relationship spilled out of the schools and onto the basketball courts and neighborhood streets of Springfield, where we spent hours talking about our lives. Fausto was engaging and inquisitive—qualities that seemed to stand in sharp contrast to his inability to read or write. The determination of this fifteen-year-old boy was expressed one spring afternoon: "We got a saying in Spanish, '*La fe mueve las montañas.*' It means hope moves mountains."[1] One year later, Fausto left school and became more deeply involved in Springfield's underground drug economy. At eighteen, addicted to heroin, he went on a ten-week robbing spree that ended in a failed bank heist and a ten-to-twelve-year prison sentence.

Fausto's life carves out a unique pathway; after all, it is *his* life, based upon a series of events, choices, and contingencies. Yet, despite the particulars of Fausto's story, many others have taken similar paths—their lives exist within the social grooves that are created and reproduced through public policy, economic opportunities, social institutions, and cultural practices.[2] These pathways developed within the context of Springfield's deepening crisis for Puerto Rican youth in the early 1990s. The number of Puerto Ricans in Springfield nearly doubled in the 1980s and the median age of the population was merely twenty-one (twelve years younger than the white population in Springfield). The Puerto Rican school dropout rate in the late 1980s was around 50 percent, as was Springfield's Hispanic poverty rate.[3] And *then* the recession hit. At the height of the 1991 recession, the formal unemployment rate in Springfield reached 10 percent, dimming future job prospects for Puerto Rican youths and prompting one Springfield leader to refer to Fausto's cohort as the "lost generation."[4] Not surprisingly, street activity escalated during this period and exploded into gang warfare in 1994. Fausto was just one of many. By the time Fausto was released from prison in 2000, the Massachusetts inmate population had more than quadrupled in the prior twenty years and Latinos were being incarcerated at more than six times the rate of whites.[5]

Of course, the social currents that shaped the lives of young Puerto Ricans in Springfield did not deposit Fausto's entire generation in Massachusetts jails. In fact, the economic recovery that began in 1991 and lasted for a decade eased oppressive conditions in Springfield. Some of the men, including Julio Rivera, Fausto's older brother, left the street economy and found jobs in the expanding labor force. In 2007, Julio had been driving a tractor-trailer for more than ten years and had secured a unionized job that paid nearly $20 an hour, while his wife worked as a bank teller. As testimony to their success, they became homeowners in 2006, albeit two years before their variable interest rate jumped and they joined the millions of homeowners trying to hold on to their homes amidst the subprime mortgage crisis.

Getting to this stage in Julio's life, however, had not been easy, nor had it followed a straight trajectory. In the early 1990s, out of work and desperate, Julio held a gun to the head of a novice drug dealer and robbed him of $5,000. In the heat of Springfield's gang wars, he was made "godfather of the Warlords" by the street gang La Familia. His transition from the streets to working-class stability depended on a number of contingent factors, including his access to job information about the trade from an informal network of men who hung out nightly on "the block," the deregulation of the trucking industry in 1980, which opened up more driving jobs for Latinos, and the tight labor market in the late 1990s.

Also no stranger to "the block," the youngest and most street-involved of the Rivera brothers, Sammy, negotiated these circumstances in Springfield somewhat differently. Foundering in schools in Yonkers, New York, during their court-ordered school desegregation initiatives in the 1980s, Sammy gravitated to the streets at an early age, escaping the radar of his parents and brothers. By the time the Riveras reached Springfield, Sammy had already acquired a delinquent identity that provided peer status and respect in a world lacking in these opportunities. Living in one of Springfield's most ethnically isolated and neglected neighborhoods, Sammy made street connections quickly and his budding street identity was nurtured by one of Springfield's drug kingpins, who would become his mentor. Heroin-addicted and gang-involved in the early 1990s, Sammy ironically managed to avoid prison until he had begun to "age off" the streets in his late twenties.

Today, Sammy's life straddles the streets and the low-wage economy. He completed a three-year prison stint in 2005 for a drug arrest, after which he moved back in with his partner and their child. Upon release and branded with a felony conviction, Sammy looked unsuccessfully for work for months. Finally he threw down the gauntlet, insisting that if a manager of an assembly plant didn't hire him, he was "going back to do what I know best." In 2007, he had been working at the plant for nearly two years, where his salary had increased from $8 to $11 an hour, but without employee benefits. His partner, more stably employed, helped create a family environment where Sammy spent more time with Sammy Jr. and less time on the streets.

THIS BOOK ILLUSTRATES the interplay of political, economic, and cultural dynamics that shape the lives of the Rivera brothers, their family, and a network of mostly Puerto Rican men, and examines the strategies that they adopt to negotiate their social conditions. To understand the circumstances through which the drama of their lives unfolds, however, we need to consider the political and economic changes that occurred in the latter part of the twentieth century and particularly the backdrop that jobs and prison created in their lives.

SOCIOLOGICAL STORYTELLING

While this book tells the stories of three brothers, their family, and their friends, the storytelling is sociological. Indebted to the work of C. Wright Mills, the stories connect the inner life of individuals to larger social-historical structures. As Mills put it, "The biographies of men and women, the kinds of individuals they variously become, cannot be understood without reference to the historical structures in which the milieux of the everyday life are organized."[6]

THE RIVERA BROTHERS' lives are shaped by many social forces, some more concrete and discernible than others. For instance, the schools they attended, neighborhoods they live in, and resource networks that they and their families have access to are more tangible parts of a social science analysis. But less tangible and more abstract social forces are just as important. The Rivera brothers are Puerto Ricans whose lives have been shaped by the colonialist policies of the United States reaching back to 1898, when the island was acquired as a spoil of war. Migration and employment patterns are part of this history, as are the ways in which Puerto Ricans were received in U.S. cities, like Springfield. Julio's, Fausto's, and Sammy's lives are inextricably situated within this history. Moreover, the historical period in which the drama of individual life plays out is also an important part of the sociological story. The reference to a "lost generation" is a historically embedded observation in which declining job opportunities, Puerto Rican migration patterns, school neglect, and deepening poverty culminate to produce specific circumstances that will impact the lives of a generation of Puerto Rican youths.

The challenge to sociological storytelling is to see the social-historical currents that are running through individuals' lives. As individuals, most of us are too busy navigating the currents to see the larger social forces that are generating them. The sociologist's craft is to move from the concrete events that characterize individual lives to the abstract social forces that shape them, and subsequently to offer a more socially textured understanding of individual be̶ and experience. The movement from the concrete to the abstract, however, can be daunting and can tax the sociological imagination, but it is an important exercise that can deepen our understanding of the social world. There is perhaps no better example of this than drawing the connections between the political and economic transformation that began in the late 1970s and the daily lives of the Rivera brothers in the 1990s. These larger structural dynamics are far removed from and yet essential to understanding the men and women in this book.

In the late 1970s, saturated world markets and effective social and political movements created a crisis in overall profitability that forced political and economic elites into action.[7] Federal Reserve Bank chairman Paul Volcker led the charge in October 1979 when he adopted policies that were intended to wring out inflation irrespective of the negative effects on employment. This was a significant departure from postwar policies that targeted full employment as a central objective. This "draconian shift," as David Harvey described it, would force factory closings throughout the United States and weaken labor unions.[8] Under the leadership of President Jimmy Carter, the United States had also begun to deregulate parts of its economy as a response to spiraling inflation, but it was the election of Ronald Reagan in 1980 that provided the full political backing for what economists would call the "era of structural adjustment." Reagan wasted no time in reappointing Volcker, leading an attack on labor unions, decreasing taxes on the wealthy, retrenching welfare, expanding industrial deregulation, and relaxing environmental and workplace safety standards.[9]

The effects were dramatic. The 1981–83 recession was the worst since the Great Depression. As intended, the subsequent recovery reduced inflation, while unemployment remained high and deindustrialization accelerated. Income shifted upward between 1979 and 1993, with the bottom fifth of wage earners losing 15 percent of their income and the top fifth gaining 22 percent. Accordingly, the rate of poverty increased from 11.6 to 15.1 percent during this period, while the minimum wage pegged close to the poverty line in 1980 fell 30 percent by the end of the decade.[10] The era of structural adjust-

with the past and a new direction in U.S. eco-
would be described as neoliberalism. The term is
...ding because it does not refer to liberal policies at
...to a new state agenda to minimize state interference in
pry open worldwide markets and coerce competition,
...he power of labor unions, decrease taxation, and retrench
s... ...elfare.

The Democratic presidency of Bill Clinton did little, if anything, to reverse this trend. In 1994, Clinton significantly reduced the barriers to trade and investment in North America and stimulated capital mobility when he signed NAFTA, the North American Free Trade Agreement. In that same year, his administration passed the Violent Crime Control and Law Enforcement Act, which furthered the growth of prisons and expanded guard labor throughout the United States to manage the lives of the structurally unemployed. No bill signified shifting state formations more than the Personal Responsibility and Work Opportunity Reconciliation Act of 1996, which ended public assistance as an entitlement, capped welfare spending, and flooded the labor force with low-wage workers. When Clinton signed this bill, he essentially announced the end of an era of social-democratic reform begun under the New Deal in the 1930s and expanded under the War on Poverty in the 1960s. Finally, before leaving office, Clinton also repealed the Glass-Steagall Act of 1933, further deregulating finance capital and signifying the transformation from an economy based upon material production to one dominated by speculative global economic activity.

But how are these political and economic dynamics relevant to the concrete day-to-day lives of the Rivera brothers? These changes altered the nature of work at the bottom of the labor force by destabilizing industrial cities, decreasing wages, increasing underemployment and off-the-books jobs, and decreasing the safety net for the unemployed. Further, as drug dealing filled the abandoned economic spaces in urban areas, the use of concrete walls and barbed wire to incarcerate and subdue growing numbers of black and brown young men, displaced from the labor force, was expanded. Living in the dying industrial city of Springfield, Massachusetts, the Rivera brothers and their social networks were dramatically affected by these systemic changes.

Unavoidably, jobs and prison became the focus of my study, the two primary social forces shaping the lives of Puerto Rican men on the margins of the labor force at the turn of the twenty-first century. I did not set out to study jobs and prison when my work began in 1990. Instead, these men showed me how and why the employment landscape and the era of mass lockup were central to their lives—they took me through the slice of the labor force where low-income work, off-the-books jobs, and the drug economy are interchangeable, and they took me into and out of the state prisons. It is through their individual life struggles that the larger social world became clearer to me.

The saliency of jobs and prison is reflected in the time line of my study beginning in 1990. The changing political and economic terrain described above affected everyone, but it did not affect everyone equally. I met the Rivera brothers in the beginning of the 1990–91 economic recession and only six years after the warning of the lost generation had been issued in Springfield. The first two years of the economic recovery were tepid, but in 1993, the economy rebounded on the heels of the booming information technology industry. The recovery lasted an unprecedented ten years, largely because of deepening corporate and household debt that kept the economy humming. By 2001, the prospects for even young men like the Rivera brothers had improved. Family income increased from 1993 to 2001 by 17 percent, and for blacks and Latinos, by 33 percent and 24 percent respectively. The unemployment rate dropped from 7 to 4 percent, while poverty receded to 11 percent. Moreover, for blacks, the poverty rate dropped to a historic low of 23.6 percent in 1999 and the black unemployment rate fell beneath 10 percent to 7.3 percent for the first time since the Bureau of Labor Statistics began reporting unemployment rates by race in 1972. For Hispanics, unemployment reached a low of 5.7 percent.[11]

This was the good news of the 1990s; however, while conditions improved for the working classes, the neoliberal turn that had occurred in the 1980s was evident in the 1990s economic recovery—

it revealed the bedrock of social inequality that neoliberal policies had created. Despite the gains made by the working classes and by racial minority groups, in the last four years of the recovery, 1997 to 2001, nearly one-half of all income gains went to the top 10 percent of income earners and nearly one-fourth to the top one percent.[12] Further, by 1998, the latter part of the expansion, the distribution of wealth had reached a level of inequality not seen since 1929 just before the stock market crash.[13] And digging further, we see that from 1993 to 2000, during the largest period of sustained economic growth in U.S. history, the federal and state prison populations grew from around 900,000 to 1.3 million inmates, a 44 percent increase.[14] In other words, even in the best of times, inequality was increasing.

These figures represent a changing social landscape. My efforts to understand the lives of the Rivera family and their social networks required that I exercise a sociological imagination that enabled me to move between the lives of individuals and these broader social forces. Tracking the lives of the Riveras and their social networks illuminated the social and economic dynamics that were playing out seemingly behind their backs—the dynamics affecting jobs in the so-called new economy and the growing number of prison inmates. On the ground, however, the consequences were clear: some of the men in my study were going to work, while others were going to prison.

Unlike most ethnographic studies, this book is not about a community, it is not bounded by geographical space, nor is it about a particular topic or a sociological theory. It is about an eighteen-year journey . . . and as that journey unfolds, we will see how Fausto ended up addicted to heroin, emerging from his self-destructive patterns from time to time to take stock of his life, before plunging again into his addiction routines. We will see how his brother Sammy, despite occasional cocaine binges and continued street involvement, adopted a life of low-wage work organized around fathering. We will see how their older brother, Julio, ended up driving an eighteen-wheeler, making a union wage, and buying a home. But we will also see how the plunging economy in mid-2000 has affected Julio as he struggles to pay increasing gas prices to keep his truck on the road and as he and his wife, Clara, brace themselves for the looming spike in their variable mortgage interest rate. Further we will examine the life of Jorge Rodríguez, a successful, charismatic drug dealer, who has had to adjust to working in a furniture warehouse after a five-year bid in federal prison. Among others, we will also consider the lives of two of Jorge's brothers—Mundo, a street maven when my study began, who took advantage of employment opportunities to leave the streets and to become the father that his father was not, and Alexander, one of Springfield's drug kingpins, now doing twenty-five years in prison for murder.

This book tells the life stories of marginalized Puerto Rican men I have known for nearly twenty years. I have changed their names and some identifying information to protect their confidentiality, especially given the criminal nature of some of their activities. The book is driven by the journey, and even though the journey teaches us about the twists and turns of individuals' lives, at the same time, it illuminates the social world we live in at the turn of the twenty-first century.

URBAN POVERTY STUDIES

My study is indebted to a social science tradition of urban poverty scholarship. It is both shaped by as well as a response to this field of research. A brief description of some of this work will help to illustrate its influences on my study, as well as my contribution to it.

Many scholars studying post-1970s urban poverty trace their work back to William Julius Wilson's 1987 seminal book, *The Truly Disadvantaged*.[15] Wilson's book was a critical response to scholarship that had provided an intellectual rationale for the political turn to the right during the Reagan administration, celebrating the social benefits of economic capitalism and advancing a critique of civil rights gains and War on Poverty reforms passed in the 1960s. Specifically, Wilson was responding to Charles Murray and Lawrence Mead, who attributed urban social problems, like teen pregnancy, violent crime, single parent households, welfare dependency, and male unemployment, to misguided liberal welfare policies.[16]

Wilson argued that urban problems were related to broader economic and demographic changes that were having a disproportionate impact on poor urban areas—particularly deindustrialization and the mobility of the middle class, including the black middle class, to the suburbs.[17] While Wilson's book fell short in explaining the politics driving the neoliberal economic transition, he nonetheless identified the damaging effects that deindustrialization was having on Midwestern and Northeastern cities, and argued that a "tangle of pathology"—a term borrowed from Kenneth Clark and Daniel Patrick Moynihan—had taken hold in neglected, socially isolated areas of concentrated urban poverty, producing an urban underclass.[18]

Wilson's argument accounted for economic dynamics and historical racial discrimination, but it was Douglas S. Massey and Nancy Denton who articulated in their 1993 book, *American Apartheid,* the central importance of current racial segregation in understanding black urban poverty. Specifically, they showed how a history of racial discrimination, especially in housing policies, employment practices, and urban renewal efforts, had created a current institutional framework that geographically privileged whites and disadvantaged blacks.[19] As such, racial segregation, along with post-1970s economic restructuring, further entrenched black urban poverty.

Both of these books identified important systemic changes that were affecting the black ghetto, but neither provided original fieldwork to document how these changes were impacting the daily lives of the urban poor.[20] Nonetheless, the authors theorized about the cultural adaptations that the black urban poor were making toward the harsh conditions of social isolation and resource deprivation, and attributed these cultural adaptations to burgeoning urban problems. Wilson referred to a "ghetto-specific culture" while Massey and Denton, relying largely on the work of Elijah Anderson, described a "culture of segregation." Wilson associated the ghetto culture with a "tangle of pathology" that ensued because of the social and economic isolation of black urban communities, while Massey and Denton emphasized that an "alternative status system" had developed in opposition to the social mainstream that contributed to problems like teen pregnancy, school dropout, and street crime.

These two books established a theoretical foundation from which a plethora of urban poverty studies ensued. One set of studies attempted to fill in theoretical ground by focusing on community adaptations to broader political and economic changes. For example,

Mercer Sullivan's *Getting Paid* focused on three communities in Brooklyn—white, African American, and Puerto Rican—to examine how community dynamics mediated the relationship between economic opportunities and crime.[21] Narrowing the scope, Sudhir Venkatesh's *American Project* examined how a tenant organization created "community" in America's largest public housing project, the Robert Taylor Homes in Chicago, by mediating between the policies of the Chicago Housing Authority and the needs of residents, and then showed how larger structural changes, such as job loss, welfare retrenchment, prison policies, and gang control of the drug trade, altered these dynamics.[22]

A second set of studies was undertaken to show that poor urban communities were not simply comprised of broken families, tangled pathologies, ghetto-specific culture, or a culture of segregation. Mitchell Duneier's *Slim's Table* exposed respectable, hardworking, family-oriented black working-class men who had become invisible in mainstream media and social scientist accounts of poor urban communities. Elijah Anderson's *Code of the Street* demonstrated that despite an entrenched street culture, most residents in poor black ghettos had internalized mainstream values and routines, and lived "decent" lives. Katherine Newman's *No Shame in My Game* and later *Chutes and Ladders* illustrated that many young black and Latino fast-food workers eschewed urban street culture and pursued social mobility through circumscribed job opportunities, and that some achieved success in a tight 1990s labor market. Finally Duneier's second book, *Sidewalk*, showed how a network of homeless men adopted social and cultural routines that fostered a modicum of social and individual stability that challenged public stereotypes.[23] Together these authors described how socially and economically marginalized urban minority populations pursued more socially acceptable forms of status and respect despite depleted job opportunities in the 1980s and 1990s and an entrenched street culture.[24]

Few of these studies, however, addressed the effects that the 1990s economic recovery and the growing prison population simultaneously had on urban minority populations. In terms of the former, most of the above studies were conducted before the economic expansion occurred, especially given that the benefits of the tight labor market did not reach these communities until the latter part of the expansion, circa 1997–98. As such, most took as their starting point the loss of jobs in socially isolated urban communities, as the title of Wilson's book *When Work Disappears*, published in 1996, suggested.

Katherine Newman's second book on her study of fast-food workers in Harlem, New York, is a notable exception. In *Chutes and Ladders*, published more recently in 2006, Newman tracked a group of minority youths and developed three categories to describe the patterns of their mobility during the tight labor market at the turn of the twenty-first century: the high flyers, the up but not out, and the low riders. Even though she observed that some of the low riders were unable to acquire jobs due to their prison records, leaving them "bumping along the road," she did not analyze the effects of mass incarceration, which were occurring at the same time that many in her sample were going to work, or even the small contribution that inmate growth made to decreasing unemployment rates. Newman's focus was largely on urban youth who had eschewed street life, which most likely explains her lack of attention to the U.S. imprisonment binge.

Two earlier ethnographic studies—Jay MacLeod's *Ain't No Makin' It* and Philippe Bourgois's *In Search of Respect*—were key in advancing an understanding of marginalized populations.[25] MacLeod's study, published the same year as *The Truly Disadvantaged*, disentangled social class and racial oppression by showing how educational, housing, and employment dynamics reproduced poverty among white and black youth irrespective of personal aspirations and motivations. Bourgois focused on the burgeoning drug trade in Spanish Harlem. He described the postindustrial decimation of a poor urban community and how a hyper-masculine street culture, derived from alternative pursuits of personal dignity and respect, led to self-destructive practices in which "individuals shape the oppression that larger forces impose upon them."[26] These studies were invaluable in delineating the effects of structural oppression on individual lives, but both took place in the 1980s before the 1990s economic recovery, and neither examined the relationship between street culture, the U.S. War on Drugs, and the growing prison population.

Finally, many criminologists and sociologists have contributed to an understanding of mass incarceration and its effects on families, communities, and young minority men. The work of James Austin, John Irwin, Jeremy Travis, Joan Petersilia, Bruce Western, Mark Mauer, and Elliot Currie, to name a few, has documented well the extraordinary growth in the prison population, its relationship to the War on Drugs, its consequences, particularly for racial minority families and communities, the elimination of prison rehabilitation practices, the symbiotic culture that has developed between the streets and prison, and the civilian penalties associated with having a prison record along with other trials and tribulations of prisoner reentry. With the exception of John Irwin's study inside a California prison, however, these studies are quantitative analyses, and have not therefore examined directly how mass incarceration affected street youths in their daily lives.

When a Heart Turns Rock Solid draws on this extensive literature. Like Bourgois, I focus on a network of Puerto Rican men living on the social and economic borders. Since 1980, income and educational attainment have increased among Puerto Ricans on the mainland, poverty rates have declined, and a professional middle class has grown. Still, intra-group inequality among stateside Puerto Ricans has increased and a large segment of this population has suffered the effects of deindustrialization and remains mired in deep pockets of poverty in Northeastern cities.[27] In 2006, a quarter of all stateside Puerto Ricans lived in poverty, the highest poverty rate of all Latino groups in the United States, with the exception of Dominicans, and about the same rate as African Americans.[28] Moreover, compared to other Latino groups, Puerto Ricans have the highest rate of residential segregation and are more likely to live in inner cities.[29] This book is about the most impoverished and marginalized segment of the stateside Puerto Rican population and therefore should not be generalized to the larger, more diverse Puerto Rican population scattered throughout the U.S. mainland.

This is not, however, a study of the barrio, or of any given community. Instead I track a network of men across institutions (schools, work, prison, drug rehabilitation) and across cities (Springfield, Hartford, and towns in western Massachusetts), even though an important part of the study does take place at "the block," a local gathering place in a Springfield neighborhood where young men (and some women) organize a drug distribution ring, party, and socialize. My study would be better characterized, though, as research in motion—I let the men take me into the places that would comprise my study and show me the social forces shaping their lives.

Most important, my study moves the social science conversation into the end of the 1990s and the beginning of the new century. It provides an account of a network of Puerto Rican men coming of age during this time, some of whom successfully negotiated expanding job opportunities and left the streets, while others remained mired in risky and self-destructive routines. But it is my intimate involvement with the Rivera brothers for more than eighteen years that is the foundation of my book. Ethnographic studies of poor urban communities often give media-driven two-dimensional characters a third dimension—their humanness. They demonstrate through empathetic constructions of individual lives how decisions are made and identities formed, how trajectories are created and interrupted, and how the ambiguity of everyday life is experienced. More important, they often bring moral outcasts into the human fold, as anthropologist Merrill Singer describes in his life history of a heroin addict, by presenting them as people "with heartfelt hopes and fears, struggling to make it in a world that is often harsh, regularly indifferent, and at times life threatening."[30]

My profiles of the Rivera brothers, their family and social networks, are intended to give them a human dimension—to expose their vulnerabilities, humor, anger, loyalties, resentments, and personal commitments—but to do so without minimizing the social and economic forces at work.

How We Know What We Know

In January 1990 I stood before a group of eight African American and Puerto Rican young men in an aging classroom where desks, bolted into the hardwood floor, required that they sit obediently facing the front of the room. I met weekly with these men, who were identified as potential school dropouts, and led discussions on topics of their choosing.[31] My objective was to learn about the lives of urban minority youth, who were likely to join the large number of black and Latino youth leaving the Springfield schools each year, to explore their worldviews, their future hopes and dreams, their frustrations and disappointments, as well as their family lives, peer networks, and neighborhoods. This all made sense when reading the ethnographic sections of research textbooks, but standing in front of these youngsters it was a tall order—I was twice their age, white, and didn't speak Spanish and had to somehow convince them that they should take an interest in my academic agenda. I bumbled along for four months talking about school, part-time jobs they had been assigned to through the school's dropout prevention program, and their post-school hopes and dreams. I found a few points of connection, but none as powerful as basketball. I had played two years of small college basketball and found that we could speak a more common language on the local courts—and, as chance would have it, in the very city where the game had been created. At the end of the school year, I had become close enough to three young men to continue meeting with them throughout the summer—Fausto Rivera was one of them.

Knowledge derived from ethnographic studies is rooted in relationships, and as relationships change, what we know also changes. The eighteen-year breadth of my study has made this clear to me. I was thirty-one when I met Fausto, he was fifteen; in 2008, I turned fifty and Fausto thirty-four. Defining incidents in Fausto's life (and to some extent mine) changed the nature of our relationship over the past eighteen years and what I learned about Fausto changed as well. Of course, the same is true of others I engaged in the course of my work. To understand what I know about these men, it is therefore worthwhile to consider briefly the key events that shaped my study and to consider how they changed my relationships.

The first was Fausto's incarceration. By the time this occurred in 1993, I had known Fausto for three years and had observed his efforts to stay in school and play school sports, his decision to drop out of school and pursue a GED, and his growing involvement in the drug economy. My study pivoted when Fausto went to prison. I began making regular trips to the state prison facilities where Fausto was placed, which triggered my interest in mass incarceration and life behind bars. Moreover, I often made these long drives with Fausto's older brother, Julio, which deepened our relationship. At this time, I decided to write a book about Fausto and his family.[32] Both Fausto and Julio consented to the project, so I began writing field notes and tape-recording some of the conversations with Julio in the car. During this period, Julio's life caromed from high school graduation to community college, to fatherhood, to living-wage work followed by prolonged unemployment, and finally to the street drug economy and, for a short period of time, one of Springfield's Latino street gangs. In the evenings, Julio was hanging out on the block, and in the spring of 1996, he agreed to take me there and introduce me to the men.

My acceptance on the block was, to an extent, predetermined by my friendship with Julio—the men cautiously extended themselves to me as an act of respect toward him. But my access to the drug economy and to street life was largely dependent on Jorge Rodríguez's acceptance of me. In his late twenties, Jorge was at the center of nightly activities. He ran the drug business that employed several of the men on the block and financed the nightly parties. Jorge bought the beer consumed on the block and at the bar later in the night, as well as food for everyone after the bars closed, and paid the fee to get into the after-hours parties. Jorge reservedly accepted me on Julio's word, but expected me to comply with his nightly routines. Too many questions annoyed him, as did early departures—if I started the night with the guys, I was expected to end the night with them as well, a feat that I simply could not always live up to.

Nonetheless, over time, Jorge became more comfortable with me and our relationship evolved. Jorge became supportive of my book project and enjoyed showing me his world—how the streets worked, how he adeptly managed relationships, his masterful skills on the pool table and dance floor, and his masculine prowess in seducing young women. My research again pivoted. My intention to write a book about the Rivera family was broadened to include a growing network of Puerto Rican men with whom I was becoming more involved. I became a regular on the block for two years (especially in between university semesters), expanded my list of pseudonyms to more than fifty, and recorded copious field notes. My access to street life and the drug economy was made possible by Julio and Jorge.

Respect is the main currency on the street and, wherever I went, men paid their respects to me because I was with Julio and Jorge. One night at an after-hours party, I was cornered by a guy who became belligerent and accused me of being a DT, an undercover detective. When Julio intervened and explained who I was, the young man was terrified that he had disrespected not just me, but the entire group I was with that night. He spent the next hour apologizing profusely to all of us, bringing me drinks and food, telling me what cool guys Julio and Jorge were, and letting me know that if anything happened that night, he would "have my back."

The field research context worked well for me because it was relatively close to my home in Hartford, Connecticut, and because neither Julio nor Jorge used illicit drugs—in fact, Jorge had never used any illicit drugs, even though he made his living dealing them. Both Julio and Jorge were avid beer drinkers, and Jorge consumed gallons of Budweiser daily. Growing up in white rural poverty, I was no stranger to Budweiser, and drinking (as well as playing basketball, pool, and dominoes) became a medium through which my relationships with Julio, Jorge, and others on the block evolved. Of course, doing research on the streets did expose me to an increased threat of violence. The threat was somewhat mitigated by the protection that Julio provided. All three of the Rivera brothers are big men and experienced fighters—all have trained as boxers—but Julio is the biggest. Just over six feet and tipping the scales between 250 and 300 pounds, Julio is a southpaw nicknamed "One-Punch Julio" on the streets because he never had to hit a guy twice in a fight. Julio was my sponsor on the streets and he took that responsibility seriously.

During this time, my relationship with the youngest Rivera brother, Sammy, also developed. Within two years, Sammy stepped up his involvement in the drug trade and was partnering with Jorge. While Sammy is the smallest of the three brothers, what he lacked in size, he made up in charisma, skill, and aggression. Sammy kept a careful distance from me on the streets, not because, as I would later learn, he lacked trust in me, but because he felt that showing me his street lifestyle was an act of disrespect toward me (a good example of internalized racism). Still, he was probably the most protective of me when we were in public—he always had an eye out for me, whether in a bar, an after-hours party, or standing around on the streets in the North End eating pinchos and drinking beer. Sammy moved me around like a traffic cop: "Stay over here, Tim"; "Go over there and wait for me"; "Don't pay no never mind to that guy over there." Whenever I went to the bathroom at a bar, I could almost always count on Sammy being close by—either outside the door and sometimes inside if there was a lot of activity going on. One time, I walked up on Sammy berating Julio for not knowing where I was; he turned to me, "Stay close tonight, there's a lot of shit happening in here. Don't go anywhere without Julio or me."

Because I was white and older, I always stood out wherever the group went. To many in the group, I was "the professor" or "the writer" or just a "friend of the Riveras," but to others my whiteness suggested I might be a DT, a social worker, or even a drug user. One night, we went to the bar we regularly attended, usually our first stop after leaving the block. The bar served mostly Puerto Ricans and had a reputation for being a "coke bar" (a bar where one does not primarily use the bathroom to urinate). Any whites in the bar were likely to be there to buy drugs. The bar employed two uniformed Springfield police officers on the weekends who frisked everyone coming in, sat at the bar through much of the evening, and on rare occasions made a pass through the bathroom. It appeared their presence was intended to decrease violence in the bar and to manage, rather than eliminate, the drug use. One of the officers was a large, middle-age African American cop, the other an aging Irish cop. I never saw the white cop doing anything other than work the door and sit at the bar. The black cop, on the other hand, was more vigilant. They both knew Jorge and his crew, and they apparently assumed I was one of his customers. On this particular evening, I noticed that the black cop was watching me. After a few beers I went to the bathroom—for its more conventional purposes. Standing in line at the urinal, the door was thrown open and in stormed the black cop, his eyes fixed on me.

OFFICER: What you doing, white boy?
TIM: I'm standing here waiting to take a piss.
OFFICER: You and I both know that that's not why you in here.
   Now what you doing in here?

TIM: I told you, Officer, I'm standing here waiting for this guy
    to get finished so I can take a leak.
OFFICER: Let me tell you something—you either in here to
    snort a little powder or else you trying to get a good look at
    that guy's dick.

Dismissing his taunting behavior, I replied: "Believe what you
want, I told you the truth."

Shoving his finger into my chest, he countered, "I didn't get you
this time, but I will before the night's out." The officer departed, no
one said anything to me in the bathroom, and I decided not to make
an issue of it with Julio.

Later in the evening, I again made my way to the bathroom.
Sammy and one of Jorge's brothers were also in the crowded room—
but not crowded enough to stop a persistent intruder. Shortly after I
entered the stall, I heard:

OFFICER: Ah I got you this time, huh, white boy?
TIM: I don't know what you're talking about.
OFFICER: I'm talking about you waiting in that stall to fill your
    nose.

At this point, I lost my patience and decided, however unwit-
tingly, to be confrontational. "Look, I told you once and I'm not
telling you again, I'm not in here to use, I'm in here to empty a few
beers. And besides, I'm tired of your shit, I don't know who the fuck
you think you are."

The officer cut me off, "One more, I said one more fucking word
from you and I'll take your ass downtown and book you. You hear
me, motherfucker?"

I refused to cower, "I don't give a fuck what—"

He screamed, "Did you not hear what I just said, you stupid
motherfucker, you want to go downtown, do you?"

At this point, Jorge's brother Alexander intervened: "I'm gonna
tell you, you going after the wrong guy. He don't do drugs. I known
this guy a long time, and I'm telling you, he ain't your man, you got it
wrong, my brother."

Saving face, the officer made his parting comment to me, "You lucky I didn't haul your ass downtown, and if I did we'd take the long way. Don't forget one thing tonight, I will be watching your ass!"

If I had not already established good relationships with the crew I was with, my study may have come to an abrupt end that night. I naïvely thought that my confrontational behavior would earn me respect. I was wrong. Defying the authority of the cop emphasized my white privilege; but even more important, I realized that my whiteness could be a liability. Bringing me along to the bar—or for that matter to after-hours parties or anywhere on the streets—drew potentially unwanted attention to Jorge and his crew. Not only was I work for them (they felt a responsibility to protect me), I was also a potential liability (it was harder for them to blend into the rhythms of the night without notice).

My whiteness was an impediment in other ways as well. Although I audited several Spanish classes in the course of my fieldwork, I still lacked the competence necessary to understand a street Puerto Rican slang. Consequently, I made frequent demands on Julio and others to translate conversations, which no doubt was a drain on them—even Julio would impatiently say at times, "You got to learn Spanish, bro. What happened to those classes you were taking?"

There were many other cultural differences that had to be bridged as well, or at least tolerated. One of the ways that I could find common ground with these men was through our shared gender and heterosexual culture—we could just "be guys," talk guy things (e.g., sports and sexual conquest), but in doing so, I had to contend with blatant sexist and homophobic language, like the persistent use of the terms "bitch" and "faggot." Our masculinity was also shaped by our different social class locations, in very apparent ways (their value on toughness and fighting) and sometimes in small ways. For instance, where I grew up, most men don't dance. For these guys, dancing was part of their culture, central to their manhood. My efforts to learn the merengue and the salsa were at times amusing and, at other times, embarrassing to a crew of young men who had an investment in looking good. And on the issue of looking good, when we went out, these men were usually on the prowl, "rapping" to young women and exploring sexual opportunities. Bringing along a middle-age gringo didn't advance their cause. On one occasion, I was even given a shirt to wear and cologne to put on before we left for the night, as if to make me minimally presentable in the clubs. These differences had to be tolerated for our relationships to endure. My interest in making this work was clear—I wanted to understand their life worlds better and write a book. But what were their motives? These young men put up with my persistent questions, and often answered them even when they were not in the mood to. Why? Certainly, many of them tolerated me, at least in the beginning, because of their loyalty to Julio and his family. But over time, their participation in my work seemed to depend on a variety of reasons.

I suspect that as much as my race and profession created problems for me, it also worked in my behalf at times. The mere fact that a white college professor displayed interest in the lives of these young men was enough for some of them to engage me. When Fausto introduced me to others, he would invariably describe me as a college professor, as someone who had helped him and his family out, and, as time passed, as someone who had known him for many years. In some cases, he would also indicate that I was writing a book. The maxim that "people like to talk about themselves" is probably true, but when a member of the dominant group demonstrates an interest in the lives of a subordinate group, their need to be validated can be powerful due to internalized status hierarchies defined by race, ethnicity, and social class. Simply put, being a friend or hanging out with the white professor was valued by some of these young men because of our socially ascribed identities. Consequently, with the exception of Jorge and to some extent Fausto, most of the men likely to value my friendship and attention were men less attached to the streets. And when men moved in and out of the street economy, their interest in me would vary accordingly—usually seeking affirmation from me when they were working or going to school, indicating that they saw me as emblematic of that world. Interestingly, even when I attempted to connect with them outside of this identity, by talking about my teen years as a small-time drug dealer in a white rural community, for instance, they showed little or no interest. I was the white college professor, plain and simple, and for some of them this elicited positive interactions; for others it did not.

My social status, symbolized by my race and profession, also produced ambivalence, suspicion, caution, and sometimes opposition. One man in his mid-twenties told Fausto that my intentions to write a book shouldn't be trusted, because no matter how I presented the men in the book, it would be used against them by powerful white people. The most confrontational relationship I had in the course of my fieldwork was with one of Jorge's older brothers, Alexander Rodríguez—the one who came to my defense in the bathroom bar. One year into the street ethnography, Alexander was released from a short prison sentence for a minor drug charge. At this point, I learned that the drug business did not belong to Jorge—Alexander was the man with the connections and, of all the men I would encounter on the streets, was the highest-ranking drug dealer. As such, he had the most to lose by my betrayal. Years later, I would learn that Alexander had opposed my presence on the block in the beginning, reminding others of another man who had hung out with them for years under the pretense of being a friend, who turned out to be an undercover narcotics officer. But there was more to our mutual unease than Alexander's fear of my intentions. Growing up in Springfield in the 1970s fighting Italians in the South End had hardened Alexander's attitudes toward white people, and he made sure that I was aware of it.

> I watched these motherfuckers beat the shit out of this Puerto Rican guy and I asked them, "You gonna kill him or what?" And these niggas turned on me and next thing I'm waking up in the hospital. From that day, brother, I hate all white people, every one of you motherfuckers. No offense, Tim, but that's the way it is, brother. There ain't no white people we can trust.

In 1998, my work again pivoted when Jorge went to prison. Jorge anchored many relationships on the street and his absence forced men to reconfigure their lives—it jolted them out of their regular routines and created a juncture for change. For Alexander, his brother Jorge was his closest associate and his loss left a difficult void to fill in Alexander's business. Further, because of growing job opportunities in the late 1990s, Jorge's absence prompted many of the men to leave the streets and take jobs in the legal economy.

I also left the streets. I continued to make trips to Springfield to keep up with the men who both left and remained in the street economy, but I spent much less time hanging out on the block, going to clubs and after-hours parties. Instead, my focus shifted more to Julio and his partner, Clara. I spent more time at their apartment, discussing the difficulties of raising a child, observing Clara's struggle with balancing home and work responsibilities, and learning about Julio's involvement in the trucking industry. I tape-recorded and transcribed hours of conversations. Julio and Clara were formally married in 2002—a rare occurrence among this group of men—and my partner and I were honored to be the godfather and godmother at the ceremony.[33] My more intimate involvement with Julio and Clara resulted in spending more time at family gatherings, holiday and birthday celebrations, and community pig roasts. I even began taking notes on the children—the next generation.

In 2000, Fausto was released from prison and my study again intensified. About six months after his release, Fausto moved in with his mother in Hartford. I spent several evenings each week tape-recording his prison experiences, tutoring him to improve his literacy, and helping him to reintegrate into the community. During this time, my relationship with Fausto allowed me to see the difficulty that former prisoners face in their efforts to reintegrate. Fausto's life provided a window on to under-the-table jobs, a new group of men straddling the legal and illegal economies, and illicit drug use.

I took a sabbatical leave from my university in 2001 to begin writing my book. I was living in central Massachusetts then, making frequent trips to the Springfield Library's "local history" room to learn more about Puerto Rican history in Springfield, when Fausto's life once again began to spiral out of control with drug use and crime. At this time, Fausto was living in a nearby town in central Massachusetts. I was in regular contact with him, as much as I could be given the circumstances of his life. In the fall of 2001, with my help, Fausto moved into a Salvation Army alcohol and drug rehabilitation residential program, which was located just down the street from where I lived. As had happened before, just when I thought I was ready to turn my full attention to the book, a new twist occurred in my fieldwork that pulled me back in. I saw Fausto regularly—nightly during some stretches of time—until he left the facility in the late summer of 2002. In that fall, I moved back to Hartford and kept in touch with Fausto mostly by telephone and the occasional trip to central Massachusetts.

After returning to Hartford, my relationship with Fausto's younger brother, Sammy, deepened. In Hartford, Sammy had moved in with his girlfriend, fathered a child, and was working at mostly temp jobs. I saw Sammy regularly and tape-recorded about ten hours of his life history during this time. Sammy was then arrested on a drug charge that again extended my study. I walked through the court process with Sammy, kept in close contact with his partner and children, and visited him during his three years in prison. These experiences advanced my scrutiny of the War on Drugs.

Unexpected events and relationships drive this study—they have led the way to what I have learned and to the unforeseen directions that my scholarly interests have taken. The daunting task of the ethnographer is to be as honest and reflective as possible about his or her relationships in order to make observations and draw interpretations. As my research ends, it is clear that my relationships with the Puerto Rican men and women I have studied have changed. I have traveled through much of their lives with them since January 1990. By 2008, I had become very close to the three Rivera brothers. Some may argue that I have become too close and that I will err on the side of presenting them in a more positive light than may be warranted. Perhaps. But I believe it is vitally important that we see how social forces generally, and poverty and racism particularly, affect lives, and it is my closeness to the men and women in this book that has allowed me to gain an intimate understanding of their lives and to see the world that they encounter on a regular basis from their locations within it.

I have not attempted to hide the less flattering and sometimes ugly sides of their lives—the violence, crime, and self-destructive practices that Fausto and others participate in. It would be unwise to do so, for these behaviors and routines are an integral part of their lives and inseparable from the structural violence associated with life on the economic and social margins. Still, my analysis will no doubt reveal the passion and anger that I have empathetically acquired from the deep friendships I have developed and from the suffering these men and women endure because of social inequality and social injustice.

A NOTE ON THE EXPLOITIVE NATURE OF ETHNOGRAPHY

Over the course of my study, I have continually returned to the question of why I am writing this book. In fact, the most biting criticism directed toward me occurred late one night during a discussion about my book. Fausto was defending my intentions for writing the book, when Alexander Rodríguez turned on me: "You just using us to write a book and make a name for yourself, that's all." The comment stung because it was true. All ethnographies are exploitive in nature, because they do exactly what Alexander suggested, they advance professional careers and status on the backs of others, often the powerless. Researchers are notorious for going into poor communities and taking but rarely giving back—or, as local activists sometimes say, for "cutting and running."

I have attempted to redress the exploitive nature of my craft in a few ways, but the final judgment I suppose will rest with those from whom I have taken. First, long before Alexander made this criticism, I had decided to use whatever royalties I made from this book to set up an educational trust fund for the children of the Rivera brothers. This is but a small token; nonetheless, it does convey some effort, however modest, to "give back." Second, I have always approached my fieldwork as an exchange. As indicated above, I have attempted to use my status and privileges in helpful ways, whenever possible. This is nowhere more evident than in Chapter 11, when I describe an intervention I organized to confront Fausto's self-destructive drug use. In legal matters, I have consulted with several attorneys on behalf of all three of the Rivera brothers, and in one case arranged counsel to get Julio and his father out of jail. Further, I have written letters to and testified in court and even posted a hefty bail in one case. In job and educational matters, I have hired some of the men and their girlfriends as research assistants, written letters of recommendation, provided basic educational tutoring to Fausto, and helped him get into

GED programs. I have also assisted Julio and his wife, Clara, with home ownership, by looking at houses with them and trying to steer them clear of predatory lenders.

With a few exceptions, my efforts have been in behalf of the Rivera family—they are at the center of my work and have been the ones most responsible for making my research possible. In short, to use the more academic language to explain this exchange, I have used the cultural and social capital stemming from my racial and class status whenever possible to help, primarily, the Rivera family negotiate the social institutions that govern our lives. In return, they have used their cultural and social capital also stemming from their racial and class status to help me gain access to and understand a part of the world that should have been off-limits to me.

Finally, I am inclined to use the most common justification given for the intrusive and exploitive nature of research. As scholars, we participate in the competition and politics of ideas, which take place in an arena worthy of our most disciplined and rigorous attention, because ideas do matter. As such, I hope that my book enlightens the general public and policymakers, counteracts urban minority stereotypes popularized by the mass media, and leads to more just public policies.

But even as I write this, I am reminded of a session at the American Sociological Association meetings in Chicago in 2002 when William Julius Wilson, reporting on the preliminary findings of a multimillion-dollar three-city study, exclaimed in dismay that he had only wished the results of the study had come out before a recent vote in the Senate on welfare policy. He was certain that senators like Hillary Clinton (the example he used) would have voted differently if she had only known about the study. I'm afraid that my adherence to the common justifications of our profession goes only so far. I do not believe that research drives political agendas, even though research is certainly *used* to advance them. Further, I think that social scientists' knowledge about public policy does not always extend to a solid understanding of politics. To be frank, I do not believe that this book or other similar books are likely to persuade policymakers or to contribute toward shaping a policy agenda—this is a social science illusion that makes us feel good.

I hope my book will advance an understanding of how lives are located within a structure of opportunities and disadvantages and that it will shine light on the disparaging nature of racial and class injustice experienced by urban minority youth. I even hope that the book will make some people angry or sad to see the personal pain of social inequality, the limits to social mobility, and the futility of wasted lives. Still, no matter how much I would like to, I cannot look these young men in the eyes and tell them that this book and others like it will improve the conditions of their lives, and I certainly cannot tell them that Hillary Clinton or other elected officials will come to their rescue if they read about them. That will depend upon the hard work of organizing social movements and engaging in independent political action, something toward which scholars might devote a little more time.

PEOPLE IN THE BOOK

RIVERA FAMILY

Juan Rivera—father

Angela Rivera—mother

Julio Rivera—oldest Rivera brother

Fausto Rivera—one year younger than Julio; one year older than Sammy

Sammy Rivera—youngest Rivera brother

Clara—Julio's wife

Iris—Julio and Clara's daughter

Melinda—Fausto's daughter

Virginia—mother of Clara and Melinda

María—Sammy's domestic partner and mother of their son, Little Sammy

Cheryl—mother of Sammy's three daughters

Lynne—Fausto's domestic partner

MEN FROM THE BLOCK

Rodríguez brothers

    Jorge—prominent drug dealer, close friend of the Rivera brothers

    Alexander—prominent drug dealer

    Mundo—a regular on the block, leaves streets for job

    Benedicto—a regular on the block

    Carlito—oldest Rodríguez brother

Roberto—drug dealer, close friend of the Rivera and Rodríguez brothers

Elfredo—close friend of the Rivera brothers

Edgar—small-time drug dealer, works for Jorge, becomes truck driver

Paco—small-time drug dealer, works for Jorge, leaves streets

Jaime—small-time drug dealer, worked full-time job

Carmello—truck driver, introduces Julio to the trade

Freddy—small-time drug dealer, works for Jorge

Arturo—small-time drug dealer, works for Jorge

OTHERS

Alfredo Acosta—legendary 1980s drug dealer from Brightwood neighborhood

Manny Torres—takes over drug trade when Alfredo goes to prison

Little Acosta—Alfredo's nephew, prominent role in drug trade after 2000

Aurelio—worked for Manny in drug trade

Tito—friend of Fausto's from Hartford

Bolo—friend of Fausto's from Hartford

Gladys—girlfriend of Fausto's

Mario—gang leader, friend of Julio's

Linda—Mundo's domestic partner

Raúl—Crime partner of Fausto's

PART ONE

Social Marginalization

*This is what colonialism was and did: it distorted all
ordinary processes of the mind, made beggars of honest
men, sycophants of cynics, American haters of those
who ought to have been working beside us for world-
betterment—and would if we had encouraged them. . . .
And relief was something which the Congress made
Puerto Rico beg for, hard, and in the most revolting
ways, as a beggar does on a church step, filthy hat in
hand, exhibiting sores, calling and grimacing in exaggerated humility. And this last was the real crime of
America in the Caribbean, making of Puerto Ricans
something less than the men they were born to be.*

—Rexford G. Tugwell, 1941,
last appointed U.S. governor to Puerto Rico;
quoted from José Trías Monge, *Puerto Rico:
The Trials of the Oldest Colony in the World*

"I Am a *Jíbaro,* but I Get My Hair Cut in the City"

THE SOCIAL AND ECONOMIC conditions for Puerto Ricans today are rooted in their colonial history. The stories told by the Rivera family narrate their own lives and lay down the tracks of their biographical uniqueness, but, at the same time, reveal larger social and historical developments. This is particularly the case for Juan Rivera, the father of Julio, Fausto, and Sammy. Juan is a storyteller and his stories are personal, and yet his biography is like a prism through which the social drama of many Puerto Ricans living in the second half of the twentieth century can be seen.

Juan was born in Villalba, Puerto Rico, in 1948, the same year that Luis Muñoz Marín became the first elected governor of the island. Juan's birthday and Muñoz Marín's election marked fifty years since the United States had seized control of Puerto Rico and an important turning point in the historical relationship between the island and the mainland. As the first draft of this book was nearing its end in the summer of 2006, Julio and I visited his father in Villalba. Sandwiched between Juan and Julio in the cab of a small Dodge truck, we drove through the mountains while Juan told stories about his life—stories filled with personal triumph, anguish, humor, and poignancy.

I have known Juan Rivera for eighteen years. We have communicated across broken language—his broken English and my broken Spanish. When necessary, his sons have translated and filled in the gaps of his stories. Juan is a self-taught mechanic who left school in the third grade to work in the coffee fields in Villalba, but now draws disability income for a back injury that he suffered while making steel garbage Dumpsters in Springfield, Massachusetts. Juan's thick dark hair, droopy eyes, full mustache, boyish grin, and broad shoulders have left him a handsome man well into his fifties. He is gregarious, with an infectious laugh, and has refused to allow a heart attack to dampen his passions for drinking wine, smoking homegrown marijuana, and chasing women.

Juan has frequently moved back and forth from his home in Villalba to the U.S. mainland. Villalba is a short distance to the north of Ponce, the second largest city in Puerto Rico, named after Christopher Columbus's lieutenant, Juan Ponce de León, who was appointed the first governor of Puerto Rico in 1509 by the Spanish crown. With a particular interest in the Ponce massacre that occurred in 1937, a decade before Juan was born, I suggested early in our trip that we visit the Museum of the History of Ponce. Lingering in the room devoted to the island's political history, I described to Julio the events that had led up to the 1937 bloodbath. Puerto Rico has long been valued as a strategic military outpost, first by the Spanish, who used it as a fortress to protect the Mona Passage, a gateway to many of its Caribbean and Central and South American colonies, and then by the United States, which, two months after firing on the town of San Juan in October 1898, seized control of the island. Any hopes that the U.S. seizure of Puerto Rico would expand liberty and democracy on the island were quickly dispelled as American military interests in the island became apparent and as capitalist investments gobbled up much of the land for the production of raw sugar.[1]

For thirty-five years, the United States continued Spain's paternalistic domination of the island population. Schools were required to teach in English and to begin the day by reciting the Pledge of Allegiance and singing American patriotic songs. To dampen passions for independence, the U.S. government extended citizenship to Puerto Ricans through the Jones Act in 1917, but maintained that they were unprepared for self-government.[2] Meanwhile, local haciendas disappeared, independent farmers were forced off their lands and onto large plantations, and unemployment rates jumped from 17 percent in 1899 to 30 percent in 1926—three years *prior* to the stock market crash.[3] Political resistance to these horrid conditions became more organized in the 1930s. There were eighty-five labor strikes or actions across the island between July and December 1933 alone.[4] The Nationalist Party, operating in near obscurity in the 1920s, became more prominent under the leadership of revolutionary Pedro Albizu

Campos—whose photograph I pointed out to Julio in the museum. Inspired by the Sinn Fein Irish liberation movement, Albizu Campos and the Nationalists adopted a militant strategy, calling for independence by any means necessary.[5] Determined to eliminate the movement, the police adopted repressive measures that sparked a number of violent confrontations in the 1930s. Albizu Campos was arrested and sentenced to fifteen years in an Atlanta federal penitentiary. Marching on Palm Sunday without a permit in commemoration of the abolition of slavery, a peaceful Nationalist Party demonstration became the 1937 Ponce massacre when police opened fire on unarmed marchers. Nineteen people were killed, while more than a hundred were wounded in Ponce, the birthplace of Albizu Campos.[6]

As Julio and I were reliving the 1930s in Ponce, Juan drifted into memories of his own. With tears rolling down his cheeks, Juan pointed to a picture of one of his own political heroes, Roberto Sánchez Vilella, who succeeded Luis Muñoz Marín as governor in 1965. Muñoz Marín served as governor for seventeen years and shaped the political and economic legacy of Puerto Rico in the second half of the twentieth century by hitching Puerto Rico's wagon to Franklin Delano Roosevelt's reconstructed Democratic Party. Just as Roosevelt had navigated U.S. capitalism through its crisis in the 1930s and 1940s by establishing political reforms that regulated the economy and the labor force, his administration turned its attention to Puerto Rico in the 1930s in response to the political crisis that the Ponce massacre symbolized.

An earlier proponent of Puerto Rican independence, Muñoz Marín rose to power by embracing cultural rather than political nationalism, rallying Puerto Ricans around language and identity issues as he moderated his position on political independence. Thus, while English was dropped in 1948 as the primary language taught in the schools, Muñoz Marín's Popular Democratic Party (the PDP) sponsored Public Law 600—passed in 1950 in the United States and in 1951 by referendum in Puerto Rico—which defined Puerto Rico as a commonwealth of the United States or, more precisely, as the Free Associated State of Puerto Rico.[7] Commonwealth status preserved U.S. colonial rule in Puerto Rico and provided a new model for economic development on the island annexed to the expansion of U.S. industrialization.

Juan's hero, Roberto Sánchez Vilella, succeeded Muñoz Marín as governor in 1965. Sánchez Vilella embraced the youth movement on the island, which challenged the party's old guard and led to a split with Muñoz Marín. When the PDP ran a different candidate for governor in 1968, Sánchez Vilella started the People's Party and renewed populist efforts to reach out to people like Juan.[8] Juan revered Sánchez Vilella and emotionally recalled the time that Sánchez Vilella had sat with him and a group of men in a field in Villalba to have a sandwich and a beer and to talk about life in *el campo* (the country). Sánchez Vilella represented Juan's political and cultural values—not only had he acted with humility toward the men, but he understood life in *el campo* and the pride of the people who lived there.

LA HACIENDA EL LIMÓN

On my first day in Puerto Rico, Juan drove us from the airport in San Juan through the mountains and small barrios to his home in Villalba. Immediately, I could see the historical past in the present as we crossed major boulevards in San Juan named after Franklin and Eleanor Roosevelt and proceeded for miles of highway lined with every American chain restaurant, hotel, and retail store imaginable, to the point that I wondered if I had actually left my home in Connecticut. Eventually, however, the thoroughfares gave way to narrow roads, winding through the mountains, sporadically adorned with colorful small cement houses and shops. After a mid-trip gorging on rice and beans, roasted pork, fried *tostones*, and *cervezas*, we continued for another two hours, until the truck slowed as we approached a long, sweeping curve, the road narrowed to one lane, and Julio announced, "There's the house." In the middle of the curve sat a small blue wood house, in which only five cement blocks, draped with a thick rug, separated the road from the front porch. The porch provided a nightly arena of suspense, as car headlights poured onto the porch where we sipped rum and talked, while the rubber against the road momentarily silenced our conversations. In a spate of laughter, Juan pointed to trees a few feet away from the porch that had become markers where cars had not made the turn.

Juan built the house at the edge of la Hacienda el Limón, a five-hundred-acre coffee farm, just far enough off the property line to

6

avoid any legal reprisals from the property owners. Technically, the house was built on city land and, since it was erected before the city took notice, Juan explained that he was legally entitled to live in the home, as long as the city didn't decide to widen the road and bulldoze the house. The house has two bedrooms and a small bathroom in the back. Before Juan's last trip to the mainland, he failed to pay his electricity and water bills, so neither was operating during our visit, resulting in a cascade of shrieks emanating from the back room each morning where we washed ourselves with rainwater.

Juan was born on the hacienda. His father had been a year-round farmhand on the property, which was bought and developed by Boston native Walter McKown Jones in 1904. For years I had listened to Juan's stories about the hacienda and about "McK Jones" and his wife, Helen Buchanan, and the large ceiba tree where their ashes are enshrined. Both are held in high esteem by Juan's family, reflecting a period of colonial paternalism in which the survival of many people in the town was dependent on McK Jones and his wife. McK Jones, one of the founders of Villalba, was a close ally of Muñoz Marín's, and a member of Puerto Rico's House of Delegates from 1922 until 1928.[9] Furthermore, like some among the *hacendado* class of local landowners, he was an advocate of Puerto Rican independence. His wife was also politically active, serving as a Puerto Rican delegate to the Democratic National Convention in the 1940s.

Juan introduced me to his brother-in-law, Miguel, a tall, thin farmhand who is one of the few remaining workers on the hacienda, which today consists of a small sawmill, some rabbits, chickens, a few cows, and some remaining coffee fields. Miguel, suspicious of my intentions, refused to be photographed and by the end of my trip suspected that I would be just another rich, white American who would return, buy land in the area, and build a large house on it. Nonetheless, he respectfully showed me around the property and, along with Juan and Julio, reminisced about the past. They showed me the large, majestic ceiba tree and told me the fabled story that McK Jones would regularly ride his horse to this particular location and seek the wisdom inspired by the tree's magnificence. They pointed to the areas of the property where McK Jones had built a school, power station, store, theater, and police station, all of which were consumed by fire years earlier. Neither had ever met McK Jones—he died before they were born—but they do remember his wife, Helen Buchanan, who survived her husband by more than thirty years.[10] They remember her showing up at Christmas with presents for all of the children, caring for women during their pregnancies and for workers when they were sick, and providing workers with their first pairs of shoes. Juan reminisces about the time Buchanan brought the first motorized car up the mountain to the hacienda. Heavy rains turned the dirt roads into thick mud and Buchanan buried the tires. Two of the workers, according to Juan, hurried over to the car and carried Buchanan back to her house as if she were the queen of the hacienda. "She was loved by everyone," Juan insisted.

Fond memories notwithstanding, working conditions on the coffee haciendas were harsh. During the thirty years between the purchase of the land and McK Jones's death, the coffee industry collapsed in Puerto Rico. When the United States acquired Puerto Rico in 1898, coffee was the island's leading export, but declined relative to other primary agricultural and manufacturing exports from a high of 60 percent of total export value in 1897 to three-tenths of one percent in 1935.[11] Further, of the three main crops—coffee, sugar, and tobacco—coffee workers were paid the least. Work was seasonal, hours long, and living conditions abominable. The decline of the industry, however, made difficult conditions worse. After McK Jones died, the property was passed along to his godson, the son of his business partner. Juan still fumes about how the new owner refused to pay Social Security taxes for his father's pension and boasts about how anytime he needed his help—in building the sawmill for example—Juan wouldn't lift a finger until he was paid in advance. Juan's son Fausto captured this sentiment well when, exploring his early memories of the hacienda, I once asked him how the farmworkers viewed the property owner. "Hated and loved," he recalled. "Loved every Friday and hated Monday through Thursday. Remember," he continued, "they were the landowners and when it came time to pay, yeah, no one had an argument, but throughout the week they hated them. . . . They paid minimum, minimum wage . . . all right, for backbreaking work. . . . They were hated by the real poor ones."

Walking around the property, I searched for historical artifacts resisting the changes of time. I saw remnants of the sawmill that Juan had helped build and the old coffee dryers, both now replaced by modern machinery. I met the eighty-two-year-old grandmother of Julio's wife, who had cooked and cleaned in the "great house" and was still living in a bright pink cement home in the heart of the property. In the evenings, I sat on the front porch of Juan's home and listened to the stories of younger men, all sporadically employed and all of whom told stories about working in the New Jersey fruit orchards. Many years earlier, Juan had also made his first trip to the U.S. mainland as a migrant farmworker.

Born the fourth of sixteen children, Juan left school in the third grade to begin working on the farm. At the age of fourteen, he went to South Carolina to pick peaches under a farm labor contract, which he considered the worst abuse he ever encountered from an employer. Juan's trip to South Carolina was unusual at the time—few labor contracts were signed in the South in the 1950s and 1960s because of Jim Crow conditions.[12] Instead, most island labor was sent to Northeastern states. New Jersey received about one-half of all Puerto Rican migrant workers through the mid-1960s. Pennsylvania and New York were primary recipients in the 1950s, while Massachusetts, Connecticut, and Delaware increased their share of migrant workers in the 1960s.[13]

In the South Carolina peach orchards, Juan recalls long hours, unrelenting heat, dreadful food, and minimal pay. Tired and homesick, many of the boys pleaded to return home. Juan described a few boys who adopted extreme measures by climbing up in trees, dangling their legs in front of them at vulnerable angles, and then jumping twenty to thirty feet to the ground in an effort to break them so they would be sent home. Bosses enforced discipline and worker productivity by carrying a shotgun in one hand and a leashed dog in the other. When workers attempted to resist the grueling conditions, according to Juan, they were sent down the road into the South Carolina countryside. Juan stuck it out and, as the season changed, he worked his way up the Eastern Seaboard to New Jersey.

Why, I wondered, sitting on Juan's front porch listening to the stories of a younger generation, were these men still making their first trips to the mainland, forty-five years later, as migrant farmworkers? Certainly, the island's prosperity had increased considerably since Juan's birth in 1948 as evident from the suburbs of San Juan. The second half of the twentieth century in Puerto Rico, however, is a complex story that encapsulates both island prosperity as well as economic and social dislocation of large segments of the population, and making sense of it as well as understanding the lives of Juan and his family require a closer look.

OPERACIÓN MANOS A LA OBRA

Turning the clock back to the early 1930s, an examination of working conditions in Puerto Rico would not have been a pleasant sight—workweeks were brutal, averaging, for instance, eighty hours in the sugar mills and fifty hours in the cane fields.[14] In 1940, just eight years before Juan was born, the neglect of both Spain and the United States on the island was quite evident. Only about one-half of children attended school, most of the population lived and worked as sharecroppers (or *agregados*) in a still largely plantation economy, life expectancy was only forty-six, and infant mortality was extremely high, with only one physician for every 3,763 people on the island.[15]

Under FDR's New Deal in the 1930s, the United States began experimenting with economic reforms in Puerto Rico and implemented important labor policies, such as the eight-hour workday and worker's compensation.[16] In the 1940s, the Puerto Rican Development Company was created to manage a number of government-owned industries. However, by the late 1940s, this strategy gave way to "industrialization by invitation," more popularly known as Operación Manos a la Obra (or Operation Bootstrap), which rapidly industrialized the island by providing a package of incentives to labor-intensive U.S. manufacturers, especially in the apparel and food processing industries.

Tax incentives were extraordinary—most manufacturing industries operated on the island free of all taxes.[17] In addition, monetary stability, federal tax investment credits, duty-free access to U.S. markets, and U.S. regulatory exemptions from wage, labor, and environmental policies created a capitalist paradise where raw materials and semi-processed commodities were sent to the island for production, assembled by cheap wage labor, and then exported back to consumer markets in the United States. Under Operation Bootstrap, the economy grew rapidly in the 1950s and 1960s, per capita GNP more than doubled, and life expectancy and literacy dramatically improved.[18] In just twenty years, Puerto Rico ascended from what James Dietz described as the "poorhouse of the Caribbean" to the "showcase of democracy."[19]

What did this success, however, look like on the hillsides of Villalba and for people like Juan? Many workers left the farms and moved to the cities to work in the factories, and in the mid-1960s efforts were made to locate factories in the more remote areas of the island.[20] Certainly, increased prosperity resulted in more public investments in roads, schools, and medical clinics throughout the island. But industrial transformation failed to absorb displaced labor from the hillsides—in fact, between 1950 and 1970 the male labor force participation rate on the island actually *fell* from 71 to 55 percent.[21] Consequently, the U.S. mainland became a migratory safety valve for displaced labor, where more than one-fourth of the island's residents (27 percent) migrated during this time period, often described as the Great Migration.[22] Mass migration and declining numbers of workingmen was the story left untold as many heralded Puerto Rico as an "industrial miracle."

The economy cooled off in the 1970s and 1980s, and the types of jobs created under Operation Bootstrap failed to lift most workers above the poverty line—in 1980, 60 percent of the population still lived in poverty.[23] A second phase of Operation Bootstrap was launched to more aggressively recruit capital-intensive industries to the island as a response to increasing competition for labor-intensive industries in developing countries and as an effort to raise wages. These initiatives won the favor of pharmaceutical companies and electronic and scientific instrument firms. The number of semiskilled and skilled jobs increased as a result, which demanded a more educated labor force. These industries also proved more resilient to the boom-and-bust cycles of the U.S. economy. But because labor needs for these firms assumed a much smaller proportion of a firm's cost, less money remained on the island—in fact, the repatriation of profits to the parent companies on the mainland reached obscene proportions.[24] Revised tax laws, adopted in 1976, provided Puerto Rico with a mechanism for capturing a small proportion of these profits, which created a finance industry on the island that increased domestic investments as well as investments throughout the Caribbean.[25]

These developments, however, did little to ease the burdens of the majority of poor households, such as Juan's. Poverty decreased only modestly between 1980 and 1990,[26] another 430,000 people left the island, and the unemployment rate, reaching a low of 10 percent in 1970, climbed to over 20 percent in 1990.[27] Economic development increased inequality on the island and created a distinct class structure. While the island became a financial center for investment in the Caribbean, a haven for pharmaceutical companies, and a destination for tourists attracted to its pristine beaches, a large economically displaced segment of the population lived off U.S. government transfers (or public welfare), which increased from $500 million to $6 billion between 1970 and 1990, accounting for 21 percent of total personal income on the island.[28]

Class differences, characterized by urban and rural life on the island, were evident on the last day of my trip to Puerto Rico. Juan, Julio, and I had left for San Juan with plenty of time to walk around the city. For several days, I had witnessed Juan's world in Villalba—Juan yelling out the window of the truck to people as we wound our way down the mountain each day; Juan sitting with his friends at the breakfast truck in the mornings; and Juan dropping in on family and friends in the afternoon. Wherever we went, we left a trail of people laughing at Juan's wit, his jokes, his stories. As we lingered in San Juan until our departure time, Juan looked chagrined, out of place, uncomfortable. English was spoken in the restaurants, the food and beer were overpriced, and no one wore baseball caps or seemed to have the easy laugh so forthcoming in Villalba. On the hillside, Juan negotiated his world with the confidence of a king; in San Juan, he was reduced to a pauper.

EL JÍBARO

Survival in harsh conditions has been a historical reality on the hillsides of Puerto Rico, and the resilience and tenacity to do so is symbolized by the character of the *jíbaro*, whose origin can be traced back to the refusal of interior peasants to work on Spanish plantations.

Jíbaros were displaced, independent farmers whose self-sufficiency and irreverence became emblematic of a nation struggling for independence from Spain and the United States. Desperately poor, the *jíbaro* fomented a national identity that has remained symbolic of the irrepressibility of the Puerto Rican character. As always, domination produces the need for survival, and survival is found, partly, in culture—in the networks and practices that emerge through which people create and reproduce an identity in reaction to dominant social forces. In Puerto Rico, colonial domination helped to create the cultural boundaries within which a national identity solidified, and the *jíbaro* is often invoked to symbolize that anti-colonial identity.

The *jíbaro* is associated with living off the land and with rural community, emphasizing that survival is both a material and a spiritual endeavor. One must eat, but one must also preserve one's dignity amidst colonial oppression. In Puerto Rico, poetry and political oration reach deep into the cultural history, and playing music on homemade instruments such as the tiple, the cuatro, and the bordonúa, and singing, dancing, and feasting are practices that define the *jíbaro* and a history of cultural survival in Puerto Rico. *Jíbaro* poetry, music, political oration, wit, and values that respect land and build community provide a cultural framework that not only informs a national identity, but also shapes a national character that is resilient, defiant, and adaptive to harsh social conditions.[29]

For Juan, community is derived through an ethic of sharing. The first conversation I ever had with Juan in Springfield, he lamented the self-centeredness and greed of American culture. He wanted me to know that "people are poor in Puerto Rico, but no one goes hungry." Or as he would say on numerous occasions, "When someone makes rice and beans, everyone eats."[30] As a member of that self-centered culture Juan detests, I have continually been surprised and humbled by the generosity of impoverished Puerto Ricans wherever I have gone, from the front patios and airy living rooms of Villalba to the small, roach-infested apartments and the streets of Springfield.

When I asked Juan what a *jíbaro* was, he told me a story about a city man asking a *jíbaro* to change a $20 bill. The man expects to take advantage of the *jíbaro*'s poor education, but instead the *jíbaro* outsmarts the city man, demonstrating the cunning wit of the man educated in the *campo* rather than the classroom. Spending time in Villalba with Juan provided a more personal window on to *jíbaro* identity. He is a self-made man—the self-taught mechanic living by his wits alone, fixing cars for others, working in a local mechanic's shop when he needs money, or using his skills to rebuild a car engine so his niece can find work in the town.

Juan values his ability to make others laugh. His sister-in-law and her daughters in Puerto Rico laughed for hours when we visited, all-out belly laughs with tears rolling down their cheeks. I recall the time that Juan was being arraigned in court in Hartford for a charge that was eventually dropped: when the bailiff brought Juan into the courtroom, even the bailiff was laughing. Wherever Juan goes people laugh. Juan has refused to allow poverty to dampen his spirits. He can't read or write, but he can rebuild engines and repair industrial machinery—and he can make people laugh.

The *jíbaro* identity was appropriated by Muñoz Marín to symbolize his populist politics in the 1940s and 1950s, and the *pava*, the straw hat typically worn by the *jíbaro*, became the party symbol of the Popular Democratic Party. Moreover, the appropriation of the *jíbaro* by the government was part of the strategy to promote the industrialization of the island—the cultural counterpart to Operation Bootstrap referred to as Operation Serenity. In this respect, the *jíbaro* was advanced as the "spiritual anchor of the rural population" through which personal resilience and hard work became the backbone of urban adaptation on the island and on the mainland—it promoted what Gina Pérez refers to as the "new man." But as Pérez insightfully demonstrates, industrial work in the cities and on the mainland was often assumed by women, while the *jíbaro*, always a male symbol, preserved a continuity with an idealized past—one that attempted to preserve patriarchy in the face of emasculating economic change. She writes, "Puerto Rico's 'new man' was actually the emerging female factory worker, but *el jíbaro*'s soul—and the soul of the nation—was thoroughly masculine, embodying all of the pre-industrial moral virtues of an idealized past."[31]

This cultural bridge between an idealized past and the modern world is expressed by Juan when, with a wry grin, he says, "I am a *jíbaro*, but I get my hair cut in the city." Over the course of Juan's life, the irrepressible character of the *jíbaro* is evident in his ability to reinvent himself in response to changing economic conditions, from the young farmhand in Villalba, to the contract farm laborer, to the street mechanic, to the apartment building super, to the factory worker, and at times to the drug dealer.[32]

Juan's stories mostly articulate the personal dramas through which life is rendered—building the sawmill and a house at the hacienda, living in a rat-infested apartment in Philadelphia, meeting his wife, Angela, in Villalba, fishing for food to feed his family in New Jersey, pursuing his vendetta with the police chief in Villalba, gambling in Yonkers, and courting his girlfriends in Puerto Rico and on the mainland. They are personal stories, and sometimes the basis of family folklore, through which history and social life can be viewed. Take, for instance, the story about how Juan, at age twenty-one, met fifteen-year-old Angela. The same story is told by all three of Juan and Angela's sons, but the tale teaches us more about patriarchal *jíbaro* culture than it does about Juan or Angela. Fausto tells this version of the story:

> Pops was walking with this cane. I guess it made him look good, you know, like he was somebody. And you know Pops, he had lots of women, bro, lots of women. So Pops sends his sister to pick up my mother [laughter]. Can you believe it, sent his sister to get her [more laughter]? You know, he was going to have his way with her, you know, and then send her back where she came. But I guess they spent the night together and then she cooked him some food. Moms tells me that once he tasted her cooking, that was it. She never left. The next thing, she says, they were married. And Pops says it's true. He says the same thing, that he had her soup, and bam, he knew this was the woman that was going to cook for him.

Juan's *jíbaro* identity emphasizes his masculinity through the development of a trade skill that maintains his autonomy apart from the exploitive, unskilled corporate labor market, through sexual conquest that affirms his virility, through robust storytelling that places him in high esteem in his community, and through his efforts to protect or "patrol the borders" of his family.[33]

While we were sitting on his front porch late one night in Villalba, neighborhood dogs started barking along the roadside close to his house. Juan grabbed a baseball bat and walked up the road to confront a young man whose car had broken down. Recognizing the man and sensing trouble, Juan refused to help him and instead "sent his ass down the road" to get help from somebody else. Juan was protecting his son and his property (and on this night, myself), something I have seen Juan do on numerous occasions over the past eighteen years.

Historical dynamics that chiseled the male *jíbaro* character have been unforgiving in the latter part of the twentieth century. Despite his mechanical ingenuity, Juan has struggled to find work to provide for his family. The late-twentieth-century erosion of working-class wages and opportunities as well as his illiteracy have pushed him to the brink of economic obsolescence. Further, his efforts to protect his family proved inadequate on the lawless streets of Yonkers, Springfield, and Hartford. Perhaps these persistent challenges to his masculinity, or the erosion of his patriarchal role in the family, have rededicated Juan to his more hedonistic pursuits—women, cheap wine, pot, and a good laugh.

El Vaivén

Juan was one of 430,000 people to leave the island for the U.S. mainland in the 1980s and, during that same decade, one of 300,000 people to return.[34] Economic displacement under Operation Bootstrap (along with improved airline travel) generated mass migrations to the U.S. mainland beginning in the 1950s as Puerto Ricans sought better job opportunities, schools, neighborhoods, and health care. They returned when these hopes failed to materialize, or when family members on the island were in need of care, or simply to reclaim the cultural familiarity they had regretfully left behind. By 1990, 3.5 million Puerto Ricans lived on the island, while more than 2.5 million lived on the mainland. Circular migration, or *el vaivén*, became a lifestyle for thousands like Juan.[35]

After his first trip to the mainland as a migrant farmworker, Juan made two more journeys to the mainland before his twenty-first birthday, one to Buffalo, New York, and the other to Florida. In Juan and Angela's first few years of their marriage, they circled through Boston, Philadelphia, and Yonkers, New York. Their first two sons, Julio and Fausto, were born in Villalba, while their third son, Sammy, was, in Juan's words, "born in Boston, but made in Puerto Rico." Mostly, Juan worked in factories, typical of most Puerto Rican migrants in the 1950s through the 1980s.[36] Juan and Angela's circular migration remained in full throttle through the early years of their children's lives. They moved less after their children started school, as slowly, Yonkers became the Riveras' "other home." Yonkers provided a Puerto Rican community where members of Angela's family had settled. Julio started the first grade in Yonkers, but finished in Puerto Rico. Partway through second grade, the family moved back to Yonkers. There Julio completed second and third grade before returning to Puerto Rico. They then remained in Puerto Rico for four years, from 1981 to 1985, which was the longest Juan and Angela had lived anywhere since their marriage. In 1985, however, they returned to Yonkers, this time remaining on the mainland until long after their three sons were grown.

The pathways of circular migration are well worn between Puerto Rico and the U.S. mainland, producing what some call a transnational identity.[37] When the majority of Puerto Ricans, following the leadership of Luis Muñoz Marín, abandoned political nationalism for cultural nationalism, they intensified the boundaries of culture as a form of self-preservation. Citizenship identities may have remained contentious and confusing, but a national cultural identity was seemingly clearer. Language is the primary marker of this identity, just as the appropriation of the *jíbaro* as a symbol of national character and the reverence for his home in the highlands as "the heart of Puerto Ricanness" create cultural moorings.[38]

Circular migration, however, threatens the purity of this cultural identity. Julio recalls that returning to the island for his fourth grade year after living in Yonkers for two years was a difficult transition for all three of them. Julio, Fausto, and Sammy were nine, eight, and seven years of age. Julio explains that they were ridiculed and teased by students because of their American accents and referred to as gringos. Julio even felt the scorn of teachers who "didn't like the way we talked and didn't think we knew how to speak Spanish the right way anymore." Marvette Pérez explains that Puerto Ricans who were born or lived on the mainland for an extensive time are viewed "as dangerous, hybrid, and contaminated beings, and in danger of, upon returning to Puerto Rico, contaminating Puerto Ricans."[39]

The Riveras also encountered problems in their Yonkers neighborhood. While the block the Riveras lived on was Puerto Rican and African American, Puerto Rican identities were divided along the lines of island Puerto Ricans and Puerto Ricans born in New York, or Nuyoricans. Here they confronted similar tensions as they had in Puerto Rico, only the dominant group was reversed. As newcomers, and branded by mainland Puerto Ricans as *jíbaros* in the pejorative sense of the term (similar to "hillbilly"), they spoke with an accent that signified their difference and defined their inferior status in the neighborhood. All three of the Rivera brothers tell stories about their involvement in street fights to earn respect in the neighborhood. Many of these fights were with Nuyoricans, or as Fausto described, "Some of those guys didn't even know Spanish, they had lost their heritage and they hated us. You know, they made fun of us because we didn't know English very good."

The Riveras were experiencing the two worlds embedded in the cultural sphere of circular migration in the 1980s. As Duany describes, "Most island residents do not imagine Puerto Ricans living abroad as part of their community, while Nuyoricans continue to claim inclusion in a broader view of the nation." These differences are continually being negotiated as part of an evolving transnational identity, in which Puerto Ricans straddling "two linguistic and geopolitical frontiers" are forced to "live on either side of a divided border that they transgress and remap continually."[40] In both places, the Riveras were betwixt and between, and in both places they faced economic hardship and struggled to establish identities, social networks, and community life.

PLACES AND SPACES MAKE RACES

When the Riveras made their last trip from Puerto Rico to Yonkers in 1985, Juan and Angela had decided that growing up on the mainland would provide their children with more opportunities than the hills of Villalba. Their desire to settle was, however, at odds with a city that was on the verge of coming apart. In 1980, the federal government sued the city of Yonkers, their board of education, and their Community Development Agency for violations to federal civil rights statutes and the Equal Protection Clause of the Fourteenth Amendment. The following year, the NAACP joined the suit against the city. The plaintiffs argued that the city had intentionally discriminated against racial minorities in both housing and its schools for more than forty years. Even though blacks and Hispanics made up less than 20 percent of the population of Yonkers in 1980, 80 percent lived in the southwest quarter of the city, bordering the Bronx. Moreover, 97 percent of the city's public housing was located in this area, while 85 percent of minority elementary school children were sent to nine schools also located there.[41] In 1985, the year that the Riveras returned to Yonkers, Judge Leonard Sand ruled in favor of the plaintiffs, and insisted that every public school in Yonkers be desegregated by the 1987–88 school year.[42] Magnet schools and school busing were the principal strategies employed.

The Riveras took up residence along the city's southwest border with the Bronx, the area characterized by the lawsuit as poor and racially and ethnically segregated. In the 1970s, the South Bronx had become home to the largest Puerto Rican community in the United States, but the loss of nearly 10 percent of its housing stock in the late 1970s pushed Puerto Ricans into adjoining neighborhoods, including those across the Yonkers border, a predominantly black area.[43] The year after they returned to Yonkers, the Rivera boys found themselves on a school bus as part of the desegregation order. Julio recalled that on the first day of school angry whites lined up in front of the building and greeted his bus by shouting insults and "throwing eggs at us."

Establishing "enrollment desegregation" in Yonkers schools occurred rapidly, but ensuring that racial minority students would receive a quality education in the desegregated schools turned out to be another issue. "Those who escaped to white schools by bus found themselves in places where three-quarters of minority students were labeled 'retarded' or shunted into classes for the 'mentally disturbed,'" according to Brent Staples. Moreover, "one trial witness who attended an all-white school testified that every black student at the school had been confined to special education for 'poor, bad behavior.' "[44] In 1989 and again in 1992, Judge Sand dismissed the city's efforts to close the case by arguing that "vestiges of segregation" continued to undermine the educational achievements of racial minority students through low teacher expectations and inadequate multicultural curricula and teacher preparation.[45] In fact, as late as 1997, the court was still belaboring the point that numerical integration had failed to reduce educational disparities and subsequently endorsed another set of measures in the schools to accomplish this goal.

The educational experiences of the Rivera boys reflected Judge Sand's findings. They had retained little of their English language skills during their four-year hiatus in Puerto Rico and were enrolled in English as a Second Language (ESL) classes—Julio in the eighth grade, Fausto the sixth, and Sammy the fifth (both Fausto and Sammy had already been held back a grade). According to Julio, the junior high ESL class was particularly poor and representative of the negligence by teachers in the Yonkers schools that kept the courts involved for more than twenty years.

> That lady really fucked us up. She was really a counselor, not a teacher. But they, like, had her teaching all the ESL classes. She was an old white woman, you know, who didn't speak Spanish very good. She would have us do work—like homework you know—and then sit up there looking out the window. I was doing all right because of my other classes. I learned more about English in those classes than I did in her class. . . . But she really fucked up Fausto. The elementary school was bad for him and then he gets her in junior high. She just didn't give a fuck about him or any of the kids, you know.

The combination of racial tensions, forced busing, school reorganization, and inadequate bilingual programs disrupted the Rivera boys' education. Moreover, this disruption occurred at a crucial time in their lives as they were attempting to make the transition back into mainland schools, where they would remain for the rest of their school careers.

Neighborhoods were also sites of racial and ethnic conflict. Neighborhood conditions in Yonkers in the mid-1980s were reminiscent of an old saying that originated among Southern blacks: whites in the South don't care how close blacks get as long as they don't get too high; while whites in the North don't care how high blacks get as long as they don't get too close. Whites have historically maintained their privileges in the North through residential segregation, reminding us that it is places and spaces that make races.[46] White claims to a colorblind world where race doesn't matter are much easier to make when they can minimize overt conflict by keeping racial minorities at a distance, or geographically separate from the institutional and social networks through which power and advantages are derived. It is only when those boundaries—geographical, social, and cultural—are crossed that "race matters" and the seemingly "natural state" of the world is disturbed. Desegregation orders disturbed that world and forced whites to defend their privileges, usually through stereotypes that viewed racial minority families and communities as disorderly, dysfunctional, and pathological.

In poor segregated neighborhoods, racial and ethnic conflict is less hidden, particularly on the edges where white working-class and black communities, black and immigrant communities, or differing immigrant communities collide. Competition for limited resources among varying social networks seeking power through city hall, local commerce, or the streets is more apparent in these overcrowded spaces. Moreover, the struggle against invisibility in these areas produces exaggerated desires for recognition, which intensifies racial and ethnic differences. Sammy described the neighborhood they lived in as "rough . . . no matter what time you was around you saw some kind of action. There was always something happening. Either a crackhead getting smacked or two guys fighting over a girl." According to Sammy:

> All the fights that I saw it was blacks and Puerto Ricans from the islands. Every time I heard 'em talking and stuff, it was like

21

"these motherfucking spics, come from the island thinking that they're going to take over this block," and then I hear the Puerto Ricans talking, "ah these *molletos*, the *cocolos* [blacks], that's what they called them back then, the *cocolos* think that they going to come over here and we ain't going to put up a fight."

Sammy describes these fights in his own terms. "Well there was, like, two badasses, you know. And just like you put two mother crabs in a tool case, they gonna start fighting. . . . I mean everybody you talked to was like . . . trying to prove, like, who's the baddest."

All three of the Rivera boys were doing poorly in school and indulging themselves in neighborhood drama, but Sammy, the youngest, was far ahead of his brothers in street activity. Sneaking out of a window at night, Sammy was joining his friends on the rooftops of high-rise apartment buildings in Yonkers, which led to a smattering of delinquent activities like "fighting the kids from the Bronx," smoking marijuana, and, on a few occasions, stealing cars for a joyride through the city.

In response to poor neighborhood conditions, Juan and Angela guided their children into disciplined activities, like the martial arts and boxing, and weekend jobs. Fausto, for instance, worked at a local bodega, delivering groceries to older customers, and attended kung fu classes. Sammy, however, was less amenable to his parents' interventions and one night, after sneaking out of the house, was caught by Juan and given what Sammy would refer to over the years as "the lecture."

One time they found the window open . . . and Dad . . . found me on top of a roof, smoking weed with, like, four girls and two other guys. . . . He's lecturing me on the way home, telling me he didn't want me to go through the stuff that he went through, and that's why he came to the United States, was to get a better education and get a life and blah, blah, blah. So, you know, I used to always think of that lecture that he always [gave], 'cause it was like the same lecture that he used to tell us . . . and probably like two days later I was out doing the same thing again, you know.

Sammy's rejection of school (as well as the school's rejection of him) and his delinquent activities were occurring at the same time that street violence was on the rise in U.S. cities, attributable to a precipitous decrease in entry-level jobs for a less-educated labor force, market forces that enhanced the quality and decreased the price of street drugs, the hierarchical organization of street gangs, and the proliferation of guns on the streets. Sammy's street involvement in Yonkers exposed him to violence at a very young age, including being witness to two murders. In one case he watched a fight that ended in a shooting—"I just focused on the guy that he shot. His whole face like swelled up and that was the most ugliest thing I saw." In another incident, he was on the street when a man was tossed out of a fourth-floor window—"And all you heard was like a big like plop, like an echo sound. . . . There was blood all over, like for the splatter, 'cause I guess his head popped." Sammy's family believes that these were significant events that shaped Sammy's life, or as Julio stated, the type of experiences that "stay in your mind."

By the time the Rivera brothers were in junior high, their lives, like many stateside Puerto Ricans, were being driven by the historical vestiges of colonialism, the search for place along the routes of circular migration, and racial and ethnic struggles located in urban schools and segregated neighborhoods. Fearing the worst for their children, Juan and Angela consulted with one of the families they had grown up with on la Hacienda el Limón in Villalba—the Cruz family—who were living in Springfield, Massachusetts. The Cruz family was adamant that Springfield did not have the problems that Juan and Angela were describing in Yonkers, so in an effort to end their sons' street activities, the Riveras packed up and moved. The three Rivera boys enrolled in the Springfield schools during the middle of the school year—Julio in the ninth grade, Fausto the seventh, and Sammy the sixth. Whether or not the problems in Springfield were as severe as the problems in Yonkers is debatable, but Springfield did not provide the haven from street life that Juan and Angela were seeking. As Sammy put it, "Yeah, Springfield. We moved to Orchard Street, the biggest fucking drug-dealing place there was."

TWO

The Lost Generation

IN 1986, I moved to Springfield, Massachusetts, and settled in the Forest Park neighborhood. The apartment I rented was owned by the nephew of Springfield's former mayor Ted Dimauro, who in 1978 was the first Italian to be elected to that office.[1] The Riveras also moved to Springfield the same year, settling in the Brightwood neighborhood, on the *other* side of the city. My neighborhood had the fourth highest income of the seventeen neighborhoods in Springfield, was 96 percent white, with a family poverty rate of 10 percent and an unemployment rate of 6 percent. The Riveras' neighborhood, on the other hand, was the second poorest in the city, 63 percent Latino, with 54 percent of families living in poverty and a 20 percent unemployment rate.[2] When I moved out of Forest Park a few years later, the racial minority population remained small and many of the homeowners intended to keep it that way, including my landlord. When he called to tell me he was showing the apartment I was vacating, I asked if he had received many calls for the apartment. "Not many," the nephew of the former mayor replied, "unless you count all them Puerto Rican calls."

Puerto Ricans began migrating to Springfield in the 1950s and roughly two-thirds of them came from the rural areas of the island.[3] In the 1980s, the Puerto Rican population nearly doubled, increasing from 8 to 15 percent of the city's population. However, newer migrants included displaced manufacturing workers from New York City, and most, like the first wave, were poor. In 1989, per capita household income among Puerto Ricans in the Springfield metropolitan area was $4,658, only 37 percent of the average in the area and lower than any other Puerto Rican population in the country with the

24

exception of Lawrence, Massachusetts.[4] Over one-half of the city's Latino population (52 percent) lived in poverty.[5]

The Riveras and I moved into Springfield amidst the city's fifty-year skid from regional industrial prosperity to state receivership in 2004. The people I rubbed elbows with in Springfield in the late 1980s sang the virtues of the city's new economic makeover, as towering office buildings went up with the hopes of transforming an old industrial city into a new center for banking, insurance, and finance. Meanwhile, in the North End of Springfield, the Rivera boys lived in the shadows of these large buildings and amongst labyrinths of abandoned industrial buildings, where their elbow rubbing was with men left behind in the economic shuffle who were positioning themselves within the burgeoning 1980s drug trade. In fact, just a few months before the Riveras moved into the Brightwood neighborhood, American Bosch, a large metalworking plant, which spilled across the northern border into the town of Chicopee, closed its doors, marking an end of an era in Springfield. In its heyday, the plant had provided mostly highly skilled labor jobs for 7,300 workers. When it closed in 1986, it increased the number of Springfield's jobless by 1,500, tearing the heart out of the city's industrial North End, which had at one time been the lifeblood of New England industrialization.[6]

THE INDUSTRIAL BEEHIVE

Springfield has been known as the "Industrial Beehive,"[7] the hub of the "Precision Valley," and the "City of Homes." The first two nicknames symbolize the city's vibrant industrial past and its reputation for precision metalworking crafts, while the third refers to the ornate Victorian homes that decorated the city in the 1890s when the nickname originated. The shuffling of nicknames in the second half of the twentieth century, however, illustrates the city's demise. At the time of the federal armory closing in 1968, the Chamber of Commerce officially renamed the "Industrial Beehive" the "City of Homes," which signified not only the end of an industrial era in Springfield, but also a city desperately trying to hold on to the vestiges of its grand past.[8]

Springfield is located in the Connecticut River Valley near the center of a once vibrant two-hundred-mile industrial corridor reaching from Windsor, Vermont, to Bridgeport, Connecticut. Established as a federal armory in 1794, Springfield produced a metalworking industry that became the center of industrial development in New England for nearly two centuries.[9] As historian Robert Forrant explains, "Hundreds of skilled mechanics and machine designers took a stint at the Armory before traveling to other clusters of machine tool and metalworking companies throughout New England."[10] Bridges and canals expanded its commerce in the early part of the nineteenth century, and when the Western Railroad connected it to Boston in the late 1830s and a north–south line was extended through Springfield in the 1840s, it became "the crossroads of New England."

With the proliferation of industrial development, European immigrants flocked to the city in the nineteenth and early twentieth centuries. The Irish were among the early wave of immigrants to enter the city in the 1840s, joined shortly thereafter by French Canadians and Germans, including a significant population of German Jews.[11] Between 1880 and 1900, the population of Springfield doubled as large numbers of Polish and Italian immigrants joined Russian Jews in their search for new communities, and then doubled again from 1900 to 1920, reaching 149,900 residents in 1930. Despite dramatic population growth in Springfield, employment in the city was actually growing faster—at twice the state average between 1937 and 1947—creating a worker shortage in the city. While employment peaks were reached in 1919 in other thriving industrial Massachusetts cities—like Holyoke, Worcester, and Lowell—Springfield's robust economic growth continued, increasing its production workforce 62 percent between 1939 and 1947.[12]

As in Boston, Irish Catholics were the first ethnic group to wrestle control of municipal politics in Springfield away from New England Yankees and, by the 1950s, had a near lock on the city.[13] In the forty years following the end of the Second World War, only one Republican would be elected mayor and only two of the city's mayors would be non-Irish.[14] Political power was further concentrated in 1960, when Springfield changed its city charter to a strong mayoral system with a City Council elected at-large.[15] Ostensibly, the new charter was an attempt to overcome political inefficiency that had been attributed to a ward-based system foundering on patronage, ethnic squabbling, and fiscal improprieties. But the new charter served the interest of the political machine. Entrenched tensions between suburban Yankee Protestants, who had largely maintained control of city business, and the Irish pols were ironed out. A new generation of well-educated, often legally trained, Irish political leaders took the reins of city hall and directed the city toward new business initiatives, downtown development, and business-friendly tax policies.[16]

In addition, the new charter ended any prospects that racial and ethnic minority communities might gain political power. The at-large system stifled neighborhood representation, and all but assured a business-friendly council controlled by party gatekeepers.[17] Black representation in City Council was minimal, with never more than one representative on the council for the thirty years following the passage of the new charter. The black community was divided in the city across social class lines, or perhaps more specifically, by the political interests of a small middle-class black community, some of whom could trace their heritage to early New England settlements, and post–World War II Southern newcomers, many of whom remained mired in poverty.[18] Black elected officials navigated between the interests of this divided black community and the city's white elites, which effectively muted any confrontational edges that the candidate might have harbored and certainly eliminated any candidates who might rock the boat. Business-friendly black candidates provided city political elites with needed token representation— never more, never less.[19]

Puerto Ricans began to enter the ethnic drama of Springfield in the 1950s, at the time that Irish Catholics solidified political control of the city, and just when Springfield's Industrial Beehive would begin its unraveling. Moving into a small city totally dominated by white political and economic elites, and where a precision craft, industrial legacy was coming to a sour end, was not a recipe for acceptance and integration for the newly arrived migrants.

WRONG TIME, WRONG PLACE

Migrant farmworkers were the first Puerto Ricans to move into Springfield. Seasonal farmwork usually resulted in workers returning to Puerto Rico in the off-season, but those who remained sought year-round work in the city's factories. Population estimates ranged from two thousand to four thousand Puerto Rican residents in 1958, hit the ten thousand mark by 1970, increased consistently through the 1970s, and then accelerated in the 1980s to more than 26,000.[20] Puerto Ricans made their homes in the North End of Springfield, which looked much different in the first half of the twentieth century when Europeans arrived than it did by the middle of the century when manufacturing plants were closing.

The Brightwood neighborhood, where the Riveras moved, stretches for a mile along the Connecticut River to its west, and is separated from the city to the south by an industrial park (Pynchon Park) and a bridge. To the north, it is bounded by another knot of industries and the Chicopee town line. Along its east side is a set of railroad tracks. However, in the 1960s the North End became an island unto its own, when the completion of Interstate 91 sealed off the neighborhood from the city, forming a northern, eastern, and southern border (see map page 29). Geographical isolation and plant closures deepened the neighborhood's economic and social isolation and almost assured that it would become a magnet for criminal activity.

Housing conditions in the North End were particularly poor. The large two- and three-family houses that had once provided homes for an industrial labor force fell rapidly into disrepair, while landlords in other areas of the city refused to rent to the new migrants, pushing rents for Puerto Rican families above market value in dilapidated North End apartments. According to one survey conducted in 1969, Puerto Ricans paid, on average, 50 percent more for rent than other families residing in the same area.[21]

Newspaper stories documented the multitude of problems faced by Puerto Ricans in the 1960s and 1970s. A 1977 Springfield *Daily News* article noted that North End Puerto Rican barrios suffered from extraordinarily high unemployment rates, burned-out buildings, vacant lots and open garbage dumps, rat-infested buildings, lead paint, and broken windows and plumbing. The article quoted a health official, who said, "While absentee landlords collect the monthly rent, dozens of Hispanic children die from lead poisoning or rat bites each year."[22]

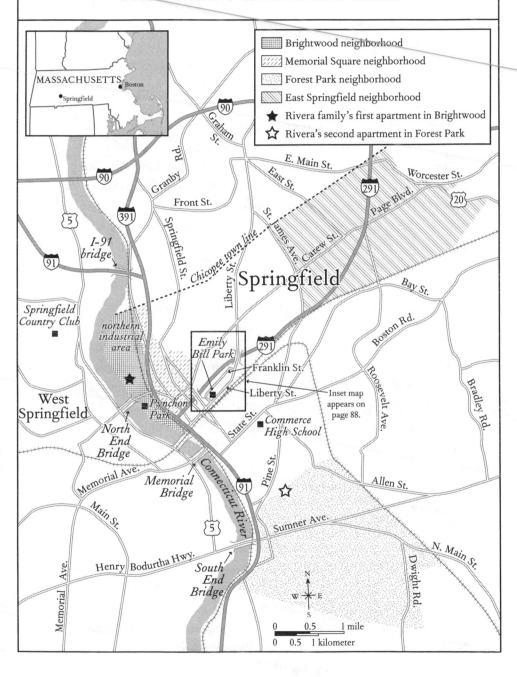

BRIGHTWOOD NEIGHBORHOOD AND SURROUNDING SPRINGFIELD AREA

MASSACHUSETTS
• Boston
• Springfield

Legend
- Brightwood neighborhood
- Memorial Square neighborhood
- Forest Park neighborhood
- East Springfield neighborhood
- ★ Rivera family's first apartment in Brightwood
- ☆ Rivera's second apartment in Forest Park

90

Graham St.

E. Main St.

Worcester St.

291

20

90

Granby Rd.

Front St.

East St.

Page Blvd.

5

391

Springfield St.

St. James Ave.

Carew St.

I-91 bridge

Chicopee town line

Liberty St.

Springfield

91

Bay St.

Springfield Country Club

northern industrial area

Boston Rd.

Emily Bill Park

291

Franklin St.

Roosevelt Ave.

Bradley Rd.

West Springfield

Pynchon Park

Liberty St.

Inset map appears on page 88.

North End Bridge

State St.

Commerce High School

Memorial Ave.

Memorial Bridge

Connecticut River

91

Pine St.

Allen St.

N. Main St.

Main St.

☆

Sumner Ave.

Dwight Rd.

Memorial Ave.

Henry Bodurtha Hwy.

South End Bridge

5

N
W — E
S

0   0.5   1 mile
0   0.5   1 kilometer

Puerto Ricans in the city organized against housing discrimination and other harsh conditions. The first Puerto Rican social club was established in 1956, while the Puerto Rican Affairs Committee, Spanish American Union, Casa Hispanoamericana, Boricuas en Acción, North End Area Ministry, and Memorial Square Neighborhood Program followed in the 1960s. These groups challenged stereotypes, especially those related to welfare myths; organized language courses in their community; fought housing discrimination and poor housing conditions; and addressed police brutality.

Nevertheless, earning potential for Puerto Ricans remained low. Few of the new migrants had completed high school, and few were bilingual. Further, neighborhood isolation persisted as white families refused to accept them as neighbors. As the Puerto Rican community eventually spilled out into the adjacent neighborhood on the east side of the interstate in the 1970s, whites moved out rapidly. As one Springfield reporter noted, "Community workers in Memorial Square said a section of Main Street near the Chicopee line went all-white to all–Spanish speaking in six months."[23]

There was nothing new about racial segregation in Springfield in the 1960s and 1970s. A school desegregation plan had been court-ordered in 1974 to address school segregation between whites and blacks. Latinos had been excluded in the initial order, something the court remedied in 1976. In the early 1960s, however, the issue of Puerto Rican segregation had centered on the construction of a new junior high school in the North End Brightwood neighborhood. In an effort to maintain neighborhood racial boundaries, School Committee member Vincent DiMonaco led the charge to build the school in Brightwood, arguing that the school was necessary for developing programs in the North End that would target "culturally disadvantaged children."[24] An NAACP official countered, "Using the School Department's own figures of projected school enrollment, this school will in its inception be a segregated school in which more than half of the student body will be nonwhite, and within the years, the likelihood is that the school will be 90 percent nonwhite."[25] Despite protests, the school opened in 1969 in Brightwood, and, indeed, the NAACP's projection was close. In 1984, when the School Committee got around to addressing the 1976 Supreme Court order to reduce

Latino isolation in the schools, the new North End middle school was
75 percent Latino.[26]

Discrimination against Puerto Ricans was fought by neighborhood groups throughout the 1950s, 1960s, and 1970s, but tensions
reached the boiling point in 1975. On March 29, a police officer shot a
Puerto Rican youth in a high-speed car chase. The community
protested the unnecessary use of violence. Springfield's police chief
fanned the flames of protest by suggesting that the problems in the
North End were due to socialist and communist agitators and by pro-
claiming to newspaper reporters that "Puerto Ricans should work to
help themselves and not accept handouts."[27] Refusing to accept that
police brutality was a problem or that law enforcement reflected ethnic prejudices, the police chief attempted to deflate the charges of
ethnic discrimination by claiming that Puerto Ricans had no special
claim to being ethnic minorities. He was quoted by the *Union News,*
"The Mayor comes from a minority, I come from a minority. That's
right, we're Irish."[28] The police chief expounded on the desperation
of Irish immigrants who had escaped famine and starvation in Ireland, but worked "18 hours a day, six days a week" to make a life for
themselves in Springfield, a story that the city's Puerto Ricans would
hear repeatedly.

Just as the dust was settling from the March shooting, five months
later another young Puerto Rican man was shot and killed by police
in the act of robbing an auto parts store. An inquest found the shooting unjustified, but the grand jury refused to indict the officer. Six
nights of violent protests ensued until city officials intervened with
promises to address the hostility between the Puerto Rican community and the police. Nevertheless, sixteen months later, a city requirement that Springfield cops take thirty hours of elementary Spanish
had been scrapped and the police force had yet to hire a single Latino
police officer. A Springfield reporter quoted one Puerto Rican leader
in the winter of 1977: "No question about it, the police are prejudiced. If the cops can break a couple of heads, they do." Speaking
more generally about discrimination in Springfield, a Puerto Rican
labor leader stated, "We feel discrimination every day, from the
police all the way to the white grocery store clerk."[29]

As the 1970s ended, conditions for Puerto Ricans in Springfield were poor and tensions high. The economic recession of the mid-1970s turned up the heat on ethnic tensions, as Springfield lost, on average, 12 percent of its manufacturing jobs each year between 1969 and 1976, only a taste of what was to come in the 1980s.[30] Many whites resented the presence of Puerto Ricans in the city, as illustrated by Springfield's public welfare director, who in the early 1970s complained about Puerto Ricans who "write home and tell them how liberal the welfare laws are."[31] A study released in 1978 demonstrated the toll that social, political, and economic isolation was taking on the Puerto Rican community. Less than 20 percent of Puerto Rican adults held high school diplomas, with the median educational level below eighth grade. Only six out of ten adults were employed, average family income had not increased during the 1970s at all, remaining less than $5,000, while over one-half of households were headed by females.[32]

Puerto Rican citizens groups continued their fight. In 1979, a coalition of North End groups filed a lawsuit against the School Department alleging discrimination in the placement of racial minority students in special education classes. Community groups kept the pressure on the city to desegregate schools with high concentrations of Puerto Rican students and to enforce fair housing laws. And the first Puerto Rican School Committee member was elected in 1981. But Puerto Ricans remained locked out of city hall, and the tide of industrial plant closings economically subdued their communities and undermined their political efforts.

As the Springfield Puerto Rican population was doubling in size in the 1980s, the city's blue-collar workforce was collapsing—and 86 percent of employed Puerto Ricans in Springfield in the late 1970s were working in Springfield's dying Industrial Beehive.[33] Between 1981 and 1984, 23,000 non-high-tech blue-collar manufacturing jobs were lost, mostly in large unionized plants, and then between 1988 and 1994 another 25 percent of Springfield's manufacturing jobs disappeared.[34] Springfield's heralded metalworking industry was collapsing as well. As illustrated in Table 1, in the latter half of the 1980s, fifteen metalworking plants closed, eliminating more than three thousand mostly unionized jobs. Almost all of these firms had been in Springfield for more than fifty years, but fifteen of the eighteen had been purchased by owners outside Springfield, and thirteen of them after 1979. Plant relocations to the nonunion South and overseas had rippling effects throughout the neighborhoods in Springfield, especially in the Puerto Rican North End where many of these plants were located.

The loss of these skilled manufacturing jobs eliminated an important rung in the ladder to middle-class social mobility. For white European immigrant groups who had lived in the North End before Puerto Ricans, these entry-level industrial jobs provided essential

TABLE I. PERMANENT CLOSINGS AND LAYOFFS OF SPRINGFIELD, MASSACHUSETTS, AREA METALWORKING COMPANIES FROM THE MID-1980S TO 1990

COMPANY*	STATUS	NUMBER OF JOBS ELIMINATED	CLOSURE DATE	YEARS IN CITY	PEAK EMPLOYMENT SINCE 1960
American Bosch	Closed	1,500	2/86	80	1,800
Chapman Valve	Closed	250	6/86	100+	2,700
Columbia Bicycle	Closed	250	6/88	80+	1,000
Kidder Stacy	Closed	90	9/89	100+	325
Northeast Wire	Closed	35	1990	22	125
Oxford Precision	Closed	60	9/86	40	120
Package Machinery	Closed	400	9/88	100+	950
Plainville Casting	Closed	65	4/87	65	75
Portage Casting	Closed	60	8/86	36	100
Rafferty Steel	Closed	50	11/85	40	—
Rexnord Roller Chain	Closed	200	6/89	100+	675
Springfield Foundry	Closed	75	4/86	100+	285
Van Norman	Closed	275	10/83	90	1,200
Van Valkenberg Plating	Closed	40	7/86	100+	135
Wico Prestolite	Closed	250	3/82	80	675
Atlas Copco	Layoffs	565	1980s	70+	1,000
Easco Hand Tool	Layoffs	2,000	1980s	75+	2,200
Storms Drop Forge	Layoffs	125	1980s	60+	250

*With the exception of Oxford Precision, Plainville Casting, and Rafferty Steel, all plants were unionized.
Source: R. Forrant, "Plant Closings and Major Layoffs in Springfield, MA," Springfield: Machine Action Project, 1998.

resources for community stability, but also provided a tax base that enhanced educational opportunities and services for children, creating the conditions for intergenerational class mobility. With resources declining, maintaining good educational and service investments would be more difficult and would certainly require bold, creative political leadership. But racial and ethnic segregation and white political leadership did not create the conditions necessary to address the decaying Puerto Rican neighborhoods.

At a special meeting convened by the state Commission on Hispanic Affairs in May 1984, Barbara Rivera, then a member of a North End citizens commission and later the director of a North End community center, delivered a blistering critique of the political leadership of Springfield and issued an important warning that echoes through the streets of Springfield today and through the lives of the young Puerto Rican men and women in this book. Citing the young median age of the Puerto Rican population, the lack of recreation facilities for Puerto Rican youths, high delinquency and substance abuse rates, occasions of neighborhood gang activity, the extraordinarily high rate of school dropouts, and the failure of teachers to inspire confidence in Puerto Rican youngsters, Rivera warned Springfield of a "lost generation" of Puerto Rican youth.[35] The commission heard her testimony in 1984, three years before Juan and Angela Rivera moved their family into the Brightwood area. This was the city that Juan and Angela had hoped would provide a better life for their three sons.

THE "LOST GENERATION"

The Riveras lived in the Brightwood neighborhood for only a short time before moving to Forest Park—the same Forest Park where I lived, but not really. Forest Park is the largest neighborhood in Springfield, with a population in 1990 of more than 25,000. At the end of the 1980s, only 5 percent of residents were black and 8 percent Latino. During that decade, Forest Park had lost 10 percent of its white population, while the Latino population, though still small, had nonetheless increased by more than 300 percent. Housing options throughout the city were opening up in the 1980s for Puerto Ricans as their population grew and as white flight accelerated.

The Riveras found housing in a set of row houses on the north-ernmost edge of the neighborhood, but other sections of the neigh-borhood remained off-limits (see map page 29).[36] Ten years later, University of Massachusetts sociologist Michael Lewis hired the old-est Rivera brother, Julio, to help with a door-to-door survey about Springfield residents' use of the public library. Julio had no problems with the survey until he reached my old neighborhood in Forest Park. The resident in the first house on the block questioned his motives behind a locked door before refusing the interview. The sec-ond resident opened and closed the blinds, leaving Julio standing at the door and, by the time he reached the third house, the police had arrived.

The brief time the Riveras lived in Brightwood introduced them to a street network of men who would continue to play a prominent role in their lives, even after they moved to Forest Park. Many of these men would be part of my street ethnography ten years later, a group Sammy refers to as the "old school." The twelve-year-old Sammy, already disposed to street life from his Yonkers experiences, was the first to ingratiate himself with street hustlers in Springfield. Referring to Orchard Street where his family first moved, Sammy recalled, "There was always blood on that street. That street there, that's when I got really mature when it came down to being in with people, and hanging out with much older people." Street life thrived in the dying industrial neighborhood of Brightwood in the 1980s and the local schools struggled with increasing numbers of alienated youth. Barbara Rivera's warning of a "lost generation" of Puerto Rican youth had come true and many in this generation were concen-trated in North End neighborhoods and schools.

The Riveras moved to Springfield after the school year had begun. Sammy was assigned to Brookings Elementary School, Fausto and Julio to Chestnut Middle School. In a city in which the Puerto Rican population would reach just 15 percent in 1989, nearly one-half of students at Brookings Elementary were Puerto Rican.

SCHOOL'S OUT

By the time Sammy reached Springfield, his school career had al-ready been gravely disrupted. He was in the sixth grade and had not learned the fundamental skills of reading, writing, or math. Sammy internalized the failure.

> I used to go to school and I was like slow, not slow, but hard for me to learn the stuff and figure out the stuff that they were talking about, you know . . . like writing and stuff like that, it was like wicked hard . . . so I really didn't want to pay too much attention to it, like, so I just started hanging out more.

"School was hard" is all that Sammy can squeeze from the memory vault of school failure; instead, these memories are papered over with stories that are more apparent to his street identity. He talks about his friends in the sixth grade.

> There was two guys there that their fathers was big coke dealers and stuff. . . . So, they started bringing coke to the school and, remember those desks that used to pop up and put books inside, well we used to put that up and do lines and stuff while we was in class. And around lunchtime we was gone.

School was no longer a consideration for the young Sammy, who had quickly found his place among Springfield's lost generation. Or, as Sammy put it, he had found a "new route. We used to go down to Orchard Street to sell coke and stuff."

Despite Sammy's truancy, the school promoted him to middle school the next year. "How did you pass if you guys were leaving at noon every day?" I asked. "I have no idea," Sammy replied, "but I passed it [laughs] or they passed me, I guess, to get me out of that school." After Brookings Elementary, Sammy joined his brother Fausto at Van Sickle Middle School. In the 1987–88 school year, two-thirds of the students at Van Sickle were nonwhite, with a little more than one-third identified as Latino. In middle school, Sammy's patterns continued.

> When I went to Van Sickle, there I didn't use to go to school period. I mean I used to act like I was going to school, and go to

breakfast, pick up all the muffins and everybody used to rack up and we used to take off with a whole bunch of other people that wanted to skip school and go to lakes and rivers and stuff like that you know.

By the time the Riveras moved to Forest Park, Sammy's network of street friends had been well established. Each day they would pick him up at the bus stop and Fausto would watch as he left with a carload of guys. Fausto was having problems of his own in school, but when I met him in January 1990, Sammy was the family's preoccupation. "My mother cries about him," a fifteen-year-old Fausto would tell me.

They're all worried about his street friends. He's good on the streets, man. He gets more pussy than Julio or me. He's got pussy calling him all the time. My mother yells at him about it. She's just worried. He says he's not selling or nothing, but the dealers all like him. . . . Me and Julio, we try to talk to him. We set him down at the table, you know, but it don't do no good. He didn't do nothing in school and he don't listen to us. I guess he likes the streets. But he's killing my mother. She cries a lot at night because of Sammy. I hate to see her cry, more than anything else in the world, I hate to see her cry.

As in Yonkers, Juan and Angela attempted to intervene. But, as Sammy describes, feelings of helplessness created tensions in their relationship.

TIM: Did your father and mother know you were not going to school?

SAMMY: Yeah, they're trying to ground me, I always used to sneak out. Mom was still saying it was Dad's fault for me coming out like I did.

TIM: Why was she blaming him?

SAMMY: 'Cause he used to go to gambling and I guess he used to smoke weed and stuff and she used to blame him, "that's why he came out like that, because of you."

Juan tried to disrupt Sammy's street activities, but there were limits to what he could offer. Juan's third-grade education prohibited him from helping Sammy improve his school performance. As he had done in Yonkers, Juan encouraged him to attend a local boxing gym to get involved in disciplined activity that would focus his mind and develop his body. For a short time this strategy worked. "I like stopped a little, when I was boxing, of hanging out and stuff," Sammy recalls. "When I was boxing . . . like for two months I was doing pretty good in school and everything else." These "pretty good" periods were only short interludes in Sammy's street career.

Juan and Angela did not give up on trying to keep Sammy in school, even though after a while, school staff stopped calling. Juan continued to give Sammy "the lecture" about how hard his own life had been without an education and to stress his desire for his sons to do better. Still, Sammy's best efforts to "straighten up" could never be sustained.

> My parents was really pissed off about it and every day was a lecture about it, you know, so it was like "You got to go to school" and blah, blah, and "If not, we going to put you in a home." . . . So what I used to do was, yeah, I'll go and then show up like once or twice and then just don't go again, you know. . . . After a while it was like, I never went back . . . and I started hanging out more on Franklin [Street].

Once it was clear that Sammy was not returning to Van Sickle, school staff assigned him to Forest Park Middle School in an attempt to thwart his street connections and to foster new beginnings—but the strategy was too little, too late. The Forest Park principal was a former football player who adopted a "tough guy" approach toward Sammy. He would pull him out of the cafeteria in the morning and, according to Sammy, "take me on the stairs when nobody was around and started swearing at me. Like 'You think you're a fucking badass' . . . this is like a kick to him, every morning he will do this shit." Whatever the principal's intentions were, Sammy stopped attending school, but again, not without his father's extraordinary efforts to keep him off the streets.

Dad used to hide out in the car and wait until I walk out and
bring me back in. He would go in late for work just to keep
[on me], and I used to walk out and cross the street and I'
this horn a   e was Dad, and I'm like, shit, I got caught. And
he'd bring me   I'd wait a little while to make sure he left and
I'd walk right out ag n.

Sammy (and Juan) finally gave up on school—he had fallen so far
behind that the schoolwork was beyond his comprehension and ability. But he was not alone. One of every   Puerto Rican students
who began high school in the mid-1980s in Springfield left before
they graduated.[37] Despite the fact that Sammy's life recapitulated this
larger trend, he blames himself. He described himself as "slow" and
unable to do the work, and years later expressed his school failure as
his life's biggest regret: "Yeah, I felt sometimes like, if I could be
born again or anything else, choose a whole different path, instead of
going out and everything else, I think I would choose school, college, and everything else, and become more than what I am now,
that's for sure."

Schools are one of the first arenas where individuals get sorted
and labeled, where future expectations are articulated, and where cultural dispositions and practices are rewarded or penalized. Because
schools embrace a meritocratic understanding of success and failure,
the experiences of Puerto Ricans in the schools were not given an
institutional hearing. Michelle Fine, in her study of a New York City
high school, describes this process as "silencing," whereby "those
aspects of social life or of schooling that activate social anxieties" are
silenced by an individualistic achievement-oriented culture. This
silencing, she argues, "precludes official conversation about contro-
versy, inequity and critique."[38]

With a 50 percent dropout rate, the education of Puerto Ricans
begged for serious conversation. But having such a conversation was
difficult as long as the Puerto Rican population was seen through
race-tinted lenses as undisciplined and unruly intruders threatening
the quality of education in the public schools. And students like
Sammy reinforced these fears and stereotypes. He and his friends,
disruptive and unrepentant, lived up to their reputations.

Self-blame within an institution that does not provide an alternative way of understanding school failure often gets expressed outwardly—toward school authorities and school routines. Sammy, like many from his neighborhood in Brightwood, responded to the meritocractic version of school failure by adopting an identity that was repugnant to school authorities. His oppositional identity provided him with a sense of self-respect and alleviated the humiliation of his "place" within the school. Sammy's rejection of school authority—eating breakfast before "racking up" and "skipping school," doing lines of coke at his desk, and arguing with the principal—became part of his daily routine that provided him and his co-conspirators with what Richard Sennett and Jonathan Cobb call alternative "badges of dignity."[39] Clearly, Sammy was on a well-trod path toward school dropout, but school and city leaders' failure to understand and intervene in the social circumstances in Springfield that gave rise to a lost generation made them complicit in this process. Sammy and his friends were on their way out, but clearly they were going on their own terms.

A DIFFERENT PATH

Sammy's oldest brother, Julio, found a different path through the schools in Springfield.

In the ninth grade when his family moved to Springfield, Julio enrolled in Chestnut Middle School, the depository for Puerto Rican youths.[40] In 1986, Chestnut had the highest rate of Puerto Rican students (69 percent), nonwhite students (89 percent), and low-income students (76 percent) in the Springfield schools.[41] Julio finished ninth grade and enrolled in Putnam High, the city's vocational alternative. Looking back on Putnam years later, Julio described the school as academically deficient: "It seemed like they wanted us just to do good in the shops and that's what we were there for. It's a vocational high school. So they didn't care if we were just like mediocre in classes." After one year at Putnam, Julio transferred to Commerce High School, where he spent his final two years of school before graduation.

I met Julio in his senior year at Commerce High. There are three important differences in Julio's and Sammy's lives that help explain their divergent school trajectories. First, Julio became a school athlete. His size drew the attention of the athletic department at Putnam High, where he was encouraged to play football, made the team, but quit before the first game because of an after-school job. At Commerce, however, he became a starter on the football team and a wrestler. When I started my study in the winter of 1990, the Riveras' living room was decorated with plaques, pictures, and varsity letters that commemorated Julio's eleventh-grade achievements. Julio's identity as a student-athlete was also reinforced by his personal relationship with his coach, who kept tabs on Julio's academic progress, hired him to work on the weekends at a shoe store he owned, and encouraged him to go to college. He even gave Julio money so that he could attend his senior prom.

Second, Julio is the oldest of the Rivera brothers, and during the eighteen years I have known him, he has assumed the big brother role frequently, providing guidance to and, in some instances, attempting to rescue his younger brothers from street-related problems and drug dependency. As the oldest, Julio internalized his father's expectations. Julio left the Yonkers schools with barely passing grades, but said that he did a little better academically in Yonkers than his brothers and hung out less on the streets with friends. Moreover, despite Julio's street involvement later in his life, he was never the operator on the streets that his younger brothers were. He was not a graceful storyteller, did not have the easy laugh, the charm, or the savvy that his brothers exercised in their daily lives and on the streets. In part, these were all qualities that their father, Juan, possessed. Adept on the streets, quick to turn an opportunity into a hustle, and deeply committed to his Puerto Rican identity, Juan nonetheless communicated his hopes and dreams to his children—that they would not suffer the humiliations of poverty and illiteracy that he had. Fausto and Sammy acquired their father's savvy and charm; Julio internalized Juan's strong desire for his sons to succeed.

Third, Julio completed high school in the bilingual program. Like his brothers, he had difficulties with the English language, especially learning the rules of grammar. He tested out of the bilingual program when he enrolled at Putnam High, but was placed in the program after failing to make progress in the regular English class. When he started Commerce in the eleventh grade, school authorities were reluctant to place him in the bilingual track, and were even suspicious about his placement in the program at Putnam.

> When they transferred me into Commerce, the teacher said, "Do you comprehend English?" And I was like, "Yeah, I comprehend what you're saying." And she said, "Well why, if you comprehend English, do you want . . . us to put you in bilingual?" . . . I was like, "I don't know, that's up to you guys. I wasn't the one that put myself in bilingual, you guys did."

I would witness similar comments made by white school staff in Springfield who believed that Latino students wanted to stay in the bilingual program because it was the easy way out, an issue I take up in the next chapter. Nonetheless, Julio was placed in the bilingual program with the understanding that the teachers in the program would determine when he was ready for regular classes. This never occurred and Julio graduated high school in the program, which he identified as one of the reasons for his school success. He was an ardent defender of the program at the time.

> What got me into school is that all the time I would see people talking about homework, and it was like people were into the school. Those people who were in the bilingual classes, it was like they wanted to be somebody. . . . It was competition, you know.

Julio found academic success in the bilingual program as well as encouragement and support from classmates and teachers. Julio argued that he received the same education as students in regular classes, only his instruction was in Spanish. Because of his athletic and academic accomplishments, and his relationship with his coach, Julio developed a student identity at Commerce High. According to sociologist Nilda Flores-González, these processes are key to student success. In her book *School Kids/Street Kids,* Flores-González explains that students become engaged in school when they feel competence; that is, when they acquire the intellectual and social skills that lead to adequate performance in school. To achieve competence, they must develop a sense of membership or belonging to school through meaningful interactions with teachers and peers. They must also find academic work to be meaningful, connected to the real world, engaging, fun, and rewarding.[42]

Flores-González argues that "school kids" develop niches within the school that reinforce these identities. Julio developed a niche as a school athlete and as a serious student within the bilingual program. His niche provided an institutional space that reinforced a student identity through daily interaction with students, teachers, and his coach, and also created some physical and cultural distance from street life manifested in the schools. These two years were transformative for Julio. By the time he graduated, he had adopted middle-class dreams and aspirations and intended to continue his education—in fact, in 1990, Julio dreamed of becoming a doctor.

Of course, Julio was not impervious to the streets. He lived in neighborhoods where street activities were common, managed relationships with "street kids" in the schools, and his brother Sammy was already well integrated into street life. Nonetheless, Julio found his own path within the schools and, as the first to graduate from high school in the family, was the pride of Juan and Angela—he was their dream come true. Their son had not only graduated high school, but Julio enrolled in Holyoke Community College en route to becoming a doctor. The dream ended, however, within a year—he left college with failing grades.

On the surface, Julio flunked out of college because he couldn't do the work in English. Even though he graduated from high school, Julio's English language skills were only marginally better than his brothers, and his Spanish grammatical skills were mediocre at best. His grades in language classes at Commerce High always lagged behind his performance in other classes. After one semester of community college, Julio's views on bilingual education changed—he became critical of the program for not educating him better in English. I suspect, however, that more was going on—after all, many students arrive at college with poor reading and writing skills, but most are able to negotiate classes and remedial programs that move them through a college curriculum.

One explanation is that Julio lost the support he had received at Commerce High that had reinforced his student identity. The community college was a commuter school located in another town and Julio never developed a network of support—an academic community—within the school. Community colleges often cater to students from low-income backgrounds like Julio, but just as Julio's high school success required that he develop a student identity, reinforced within social networks, his success in college required the same. This can be more difficult to accomplish at commuter schools, where social interaction is more limited, and can also be more problematic for students from poor and working-class neighborhoods, where daily routines, conversational styles, valued identities, and forms of comportment may feel incompatible with college academic expectations and routines. Articulating images of middle-class success, like wanting to be a doctor, is one thing, but developing the cultural dispositions and routines that get rewarded within an academic environment is quite another.

When Julio left for school each day, he walked out the front door of a home located in a community that did not easily support college academic achievement; he drove a car that was kept on the road by his father's mechanical ingenuity; after he left school he went to work before returning home late at night. The house was crowded, with mattresses stacked along the living room wall to compensate for the limited number of bedrooms, and there were no spaces in the house that provided a comfortable, well-lit place to study. Without the institutional support that can help students like Julio negotiate the cultural disjunction they often experience when entering college, the likelihood they will remain open to new identities and routines is diminished—anxieties quickly become voices of self-doubt, academic performance gives way to insidious procrastination, and aspirations become leveled and internalized as personal failure. As Julio's dream of a college education withered, he pursued more familiar routines—he began to work more, to spend more time repairing cars with his father, and to participate more readily in the daily activities of those around him.

College was already falling away when his girlfriend, Clara, became pregnant. Clara is the daughter of Virginia Cruz, the friend who had encouraged the Riveras to move to Springfield. Virginia's family had lived in the same barrio in Villalba, Puerto Rico, and she and Clara were living in the Riveras' apartment when the pregnancy occurred. Clara was only thirteen. An overcrowded apartment may have contributed to their occasional trysts, but Julio and Clara, despite their age difference, considered themselves young lovers.

The pregnancy disrupted both Julio's and Clara's fragile life trajectories. Clara's mother was angry. Clara was a shy student who earned As and Bs in her classes, and was in the "I Have a Dream" Program, which guaranteed her college tuition if she graduated from high school in good standing. Julio was shamed by Virginia's and his family's responses. He reacted by demonstrating to Virginia that he would take responsibility for the situation he had created. He and Clara found an apartment and started their life together. When Clara miscarried a few months later, she and Julio remained together in the apartment anyway and she became pregnant the following year at age fourteen. Soon after, Clara dropped out of school.

Years later, both Julio and Clara would confess that they had wanted to get pregnant and start a family. During this conversation, Clara abruptly turned toward Julio and stated, "He didn't want to use condoms because he wanted to have a child." Julio looked sheepish, but didn't deny Clara's assertion. I suspect that his failure in school and aborted dream of a college education strengthened his desire to start a family and become a provider. And even though Clara likes to take the victim role by claiming she was too young to know better and by placing the blame on Julio for the early pregnancy, she too would later confess that she wanted to start a family with Julio, even at the early age of fourteen.

Of course, it is not uncommon for teenagers to begin imagining their lives as adults, and these fantasies are shaped by both their cultural expectations and by opportunities. While Clara was a good student, she had never felt comfortable in school. The pregnancy gave her an opportunity to leave school and to assume domestic duties, which she had been culturally prepared to do. Taking care of a home, a child, and a man was typical of young women in Villalba where she was born and consistent with the model provided by her mother. Even though Clara's mother, Virginia, had stressed the importance of school and wanted her daughter to complete her education, the promises of a college education and the accolades of good academic standing were not culturally reinforced in her daily routines—not in her community, her home, or even at school—in a way that could integrate this opportunity into her emerging adolescent identity. As Clara would say years later, "I liked school, but I wanted to be a housewife." When the opportunity arose, Clara was happy to leave school, attend to her pregnancy, and prepare for a domestic life with Julio, with the vague promise that someday she would study for her GED.

Although Julio felt responsible for her early school departure, and even though he insisted that "every morning, I used to kick her out of bed and tell her to go to school," Julio was embarking on a life of working-class respectability that also made sense within the social parameters of his life. Julio left college and adopted a language of responsibility. "Pops said now you got to take responsibility for what you done," he said. Julio took a job at a local factory and assumed male working-class routines. College had been a sobering experience, leveling his aspirations. In lieu of his disappointment, a different direction opened up to Julio and he seized it, embracing the more familiar—"I've always worked, worked ever since I can remember." Julio may have disappointed his mother and father by not remaining in college to become a doctor, but he assumed responsibility as a provider and father, which carries with it a large premium toward male working-class respectability. The family rallied around his decision, and Iris was born in the fall of 1991.

In Between

Ask either of Fausto's brothers what they remember about Fausto's first year in the Springfield schools and both will immediately recall multiple fights and school suspensions. School fights reflected racial conflict in the city. Racial and ethnic segregation defined geographical boundaries in Springfield that were vigorously protected—in the adult world by real estate agents, lenders, and homeowners; in the adolescent world by verbal and physical aggression. Not long after the Riveras settled into Brightwood, Fausto learned this lesson when he and a few friends rode their bicycles across the bridge separating his neighborhood from white West Springfield. "We almost got thrown off the bridge! We had to run! We had to run from them white kids over there. . . . We jetted, man, 'cause they wanted to hit us. These guys were big." The same, he pointed out with a sense of pride, happened to the white boys when they came into Brightwood.

Conflict in the schools, however, rarely involved white students, but was usually between African Americans and Puerto Ricans. In Springfield in the 1980s, the Latino newcomers were moving into black neighborhoods, competing for neighborhood resources and jobs, and contending with racial identity in a racially polarized nation. Fausto had already internalized racist attitudes in Yonkers, where he learned that "black people are dirty or be careful with them. They'll jump you, they'll steal, they'll rob you." When Fausto attended Van Sickle Middle School in 1987, the student body was 37 percent Latino, 28 percent black, and 33 percent white, with 60 percent of students defined as low-income. Fights between blacks and Puerto Ricans were common and Fausto adopted a New York tough guy identity.

> Van Sickle with a black principal and black kids all over the place, right, and, you know, like any other kid we had to earn our respect there. . . . You know, came from New York . . . I was like kind of a big guy to stand out and didn't take it. You know what I mean? I would fight anybody anywhere. I became very rebellious—very angry . . . I started getting tossed out . . . the most smallest thing a black person would say to me and that was all it took—there goes Fausto fighting again. I was goin' more to that principal's office than anybody else in that school.

The bilingual program was on the third floor of the building and was considered safe space for Puerto Ricans. According to Fausto, these boundaries were violently protected, something that teachers themselves understood, and, in patrolling the borders, Fausto began to highly value friendship and ethnic loyalty.

> But the teachers, the bilingual teachers there protected me a lot. . . . They liked me as a student but they saw that the black kids, they had no business upstairs in the third floor and that was all bilingual classes . . . so they came up there messin' around with us, lookin' for fights. 'Cause one of 'em got it bad for me. . . . And then they came to try to jump me. . . . And sometimes they'll wait for me down in the breakfast room. Some days I came ready to fight. I came with no books or nothin' to school because that's—I knew that's what was gonna happen. . . . One thing I gotta say, that the guys that I had in Van Sickle, like RayRay and Hiram and a couple of those guys, every time that I told him, "Hey, yo, tomorrow we might be fighting these guys," they never let me down. They were always there the next day. They were some hard-core Puerto Ricans.

At the young age of fourteen, Fausto's five-foot-seven-inch frame supported 225 pounds of well-distributed weight. He had learned to fight in Yonkers—on the streets and in the gym. While Fausto was not yet as street-savvy as his younger brother, Sammy, he was acquiring skills that would later be respected on the streets.

Fausto remembers himself as an angry, rebellious boy in his first few years in Springfield. Not only was he fighting for a sense of respect within a community organized around racial and ethnic status, but he had also prematurely crossed a threshold into adulthood when, at the early age of thirteen, he became a father. The mother of his child was Virginia, Clara's mother, who in her late thirties decided to introduce the young Fausto into the passages of adulthood, resulting in the birth of Melinda. Shortly thereafter, the police arrived at Fausto's classroom door. Taking him into the hallway, the officer informed Fausto that he was the victim of statutory rape and that he could press charges. Fausto tells the story a few years later in a spate of laughter, "I told 'em don't arrest her for that, she didn't hurt me. I told 'em, I liked it."

Juan and Angela were angry at Virginia, but abortion was out

48

of the question. Instead, Virginia became an integral part of the extended family, sometimes living with the Riveras, sometimes living in adjacent apartments, and often making her own apartment available to family members over the ensuing years. Meanwhile, Juan sat Fausto down and told him that his life would change and that he would need to learn the responsibility of fatherhood. Indeed, responsibility was thrust on Fausto the moment his daughter was born with a severe degenerative heart and lung condition. Melinda would spend most of her first few years of life in the hospital. "They have tubes going from her heart to her lungs," Fausto explained. "The doctors, they own my little girl, they the ones that have kept her alive." Neither Juan nor Angela spoke English well, nor did Virginia, so Fausto communicated with doctors, nurses, intake workers, and social workers at the hospital. He spent a lot of time traveling back and forth to the hospital in New Haven, which required his absence from school. Looking back on this time many years later, Fausto attributes some of his anger and rebellion to early fatherhood.

> I became rebellious because [my daughter] was born sick. . . . I was just a kid . . . I had to go to New Haven to see Melinda. . . . I know that I felt love for her 'cause it was my daughter, but I didn't know how to be a father . . . too much responsibility given to me at once . . . 'cause that's when all the problems started to burn. . . . I just got mad all of a sudden.

In addition to the stress of being a young father of a very sick child, Fausto was also suffering the indignities of school failure. He may have been passed along to tenth grade, but he couldn't read or write in English or in Spanish. No doubt, the fights in middle school that disrupted the boredom and the order of the school day also provided students like Fausto an avenue to overcome their feelings of inadequacy in the classroom. Nonetheless, when Fausto began high school, he was not nearly as integrated on the streets as Sammy. His younger brother had introduced him to some of his street friends, but Fausto had not yet given up on school.

His brothers were offering him different alternatives. Fausto started high school in the fall of 1989. Bereft of academic skills and increasingly aware of his street potential, Fausto nevertheless desired to follow in his older brother's footsteps. He wanted to play football and to wrestle—in fact, Julio's wrestling coach had allowed Fausto to attend a few practices when he was still in middle school, and Fausto had apparently impressed him. Julio loomed large in Fausto's life as an exemplar of success. Both were going to the gym, where they spent hours lifting weights and carefully sculpting their bodies through rigorous workouts recommended by the gym's veterans. As Fausto entered the tenth grade at Commerce High, he recalled Julio's influence.

> Julio sat me down and he said, "Hey this is it. You're in high school now, you've got to straighten out your shit. It's 'bout time you get serious and get your life together." You know, I was no longer a kid. I had to get into myself, to take care of me. I had to let the other shit go—the fighting and shit—especially, if I was going to wrestle, to be heavyweight champion [laughs]. Julio straightened my shit out.

I met Fausto in January 1990 at Commerce High—he was fifteen years old and in the tenth grade. He was ineligible for sports that year, but was intent on raising his grades so he could play the following year. He had already transitioned out of bilingual classes, but wanted to reenroll in the program so he could succeed academically like his older brother. But Fausto was terribly unprepared for tenth-grade academic work. As his two brothers symbolized, Fausto's future hung in the balance between the respect he could earn on the streets and the school promises of conventional respectability.

THREE

Bilingual Education and the School Dropout

WHEN I MET FAUSTO, he was in a precarious position. He was in the tenth grade and had not been taught to read or write either in English or in Spanish, and yet he wanted to follow in his older brother's footsteps and become a school athlete. How could it be, I wondered, in 1990, that no one—not his parents, teachers, friends, social workers—had taught this fifteen-year-old how to read and write? Moreover, Fausto's illiteracy stood in stark contrast to his intellect. He was a storyteller, and he appeared eager to learn. He asked questions and listened; he thought about things we talked about between my visits; he applied ideas we discussed to understand his social world and others around him. I found him more engaging than many of the undergraduates I was teaching at the time and certainly more interesting. Fausto's situation was tragic and his illiteracy would become the bane of his life in so many ways—which would take time for me to see. The question kept ringing in my head—how did this happen?

It didn't take a genius to figure out that the problem was systemic. At first, I saw the particular circumstances of his life—his father was illiterate, his mother didn't speak English, he had frequently changed schools migrating back and forth to Puerto Rico, had attended schools in Yonkers amidst white hostility to court-ordered school desegregation, and was placed in poorly developed bilingual classes in Yonkers and Springfield. But quickly I began to see the unique, personal elements fade into familiar, larger social patterns. Looking through newspaper archives I found a quote from Springfield's former bilingual education director Yolana Ulloa, who only one decade before the Riveras moved to Springfield observed, "We get children who have lived in New York for two years and have not had bilingual education. They do not have basic reading skills in either language."[1]

It was clear that Fausto's circumstances were not peculiar to him—many students had parents who could not read or write and many had moved back and forth between Puerto Rico and the mainland, had lived in impoverished school districts with poorly developed bilingual programs, and many, as Ulloa had observed, could not read or write in English or Spanish. With school dropout rates for Puerto Ricans in Springfield reaching 50 percent in the late 1980s, it was hard to ignore the systemic causes of the problem.

In the tenth grade, Fausto thought the only answer was to reenroll in the school's bilingual program. The program was a Transitional Bilingual Education, TBE, program—in fact, Massachusetts had been the first state to implement TBE programs in 1971. These programs emphasized that instruction in the student's first language should be used in classrooms, but only as a means of transitioning students into the mainstream English-speaking curriculum within three years. Fausto's brother had graduated in the bilingual program, so the option held out some hope for him. Fausto claimed he had been tricked into leaving the bilingual program by a middle school principal. "In the middle of the year," he explained, "he told me to try regular classes for a few weeks and if I didn't like it, he said he'd move me back." Fausto consented, but recalled, "Those classes were way over my head." When he attempted to reenroll in the bilingual program, he was told that he was no longer eligible due to a provision in the policy that prevented students who had moved into the English-speaking curriculum from returning. The program emphasized its transitional objective—it moved students in one direction, but not in the other.

Since Julio had been placed back in the bilingual program at Putnam High, however, Fausto knew that exceptions were possible, and failing in most of his classes, he was planning to take his case to the school principal at around the time that I met him. The principal granted the meeting and Fausto took his mother, Angela, with him; the principal, however, was unsympathetic and refused Fausto's request. I spoke to Fausto shortly after the meeting. He accused the principal of racism because he had not provided an interpreter for Angela, precluding her from defending her son. The principal was unwilling to make an exception to the school policy and justified his decision by emphasizing the imperative of learning English to acquire a job after Fausto graduated. Fausto was enraged by the principal's inflexibility. "How can that motherfucker tell me he knows what is best for me? How can he possibly know? . . . [He] tells my mother he knows what's best for me and she doesn't. That's fucking rude."

Afterward, we drove to my apartment and I suggested that Fausto compose a letter to the principal on my computer. I explained that we wouldn't send the letter, but would just treat the exercise as an opportunity to vent his anger and have a laugh at the principal's expense. Still in the early stages of my relationship with Fausto, my agenda was to assess his writing skills. The first draft of the letter read:

> Der MR _____,
> yu are a twelve sadwes eting mether foker. Yu wer the same sut
> to school every day. Yur mother her is so napi that sy hat to take
> payn kealers to koun her har. And yor father is so bor that he
> wen to mak Danalo und but a milk sake on layoway. Yo are a buk
> yu don't now what yu tok abut othe time not som time. Way yu
> have yuar waef workeng in leamon st.
>
> fuk yu,
yuare wayf bib

The revised draft read:

> Dear Mr. _____,
> You are a twelve sandwich eating mother fucker. You wear the
> same suit to school every day. Your mother's hair is so nappy
> that she had to take pain killers to comb her hair. And your
> father is so poor that he went to McDonalds and put a milk shake
> on layaway. You are a punk. You don't know what you are
> talking about all the time, not some time. Why you have your
> wife working in Limen Street [a prostitute hangout]?
>
> Fuck you,
your wife's pimp

The letter expressed Fausto's fury with the principal and, through a litany of insults, exposed some of the humiliations that poor minority youths live with. It also illustrated Fausto's illiteracy in the English language. Examining the letter more closely, I realized that Fausto was spelling many of the English words by their phonic pronunciations, more consistent with the Spanish language. With focused instruction and tutoring, I thought this could be corrected, but later discovered that Fausto couldn't spell in the Spanish language either. I wondered why he had been transitioned out of the bilingual program if he couldn't spell basic words in English—like "you," "had," "make," "were." Moreover, I questioned how he was expected to do tenth-grade work or how he ever ended up in the tenth grade in the first place.

Under these circumstances, Fausto's efforts to return to the bilingual program made sense to me, but I was also rapidly learning that he would not find much support among school administrators. Like the principal, the head counselor, Ms. O'Connor, emphasized the transitional nature of the program and bristled at the suggestion that Fausto and others would remain in, let alone return to, the bilingual program.

> It's because they baby them over there [in the bilingual program]. They don't expect as much work. It's easier. Students come in here looking for the easy way out. They don't realize that it's not in their best interest. The bilingual program is not very good. There aren't enough qualified teachers to begin with and because of shortages we have teachers who are teaching classes they shouldn't be. You know, math teachers teaching chemistry and things like that. . . . They stay there because it's easier and because they are sheltered over there. If they're going to do anything worthwhile after they leave here, they have to be in regular classes.

Ms. O'Connor had taught Spanish before becoming a guidance counselor and there was no doubt some truth to her assertions. Recruiting enough qualified teachers to fill positions in bilingual programs has historically been a challenge. It also came as no surprise that students might prefer to be educated in programs that reaffirmed their culture rather than in white-dominated classrooms. Further it occurred to me that since both teachers and students in the bilingual program were outside the school mainstream, protecting their turf and defending their culture and curriculum might easily be viewed by white school authorities as being overprotective of students, or in Ms. O'Connor's pejorative terms, as "babying" or sheltering them.

The sting of cultural politics, according to Fausto's seventeen-year-old brother, Julio, was felt by both Latino teachers and students in the school.

> White teachers, they think they got it all, they think they are the best teachers, you know. . . . What the bilingual teachers say doesn't count . . . because there are so many white teachers there, they like rule over them. It's like it's a real big issue there, it's like, they're always arguing about things, you know. . . . American teachers, they think we're stupid. . . . They think about us as inferior.

The cultural politics surrounding bilingual education I was witnessing, however, were not (and are not) unique to Commerce High. These issues are part of a larger debate on bilingual education that reaches back to the early twentieth century—a debate that has gone through several permutations as it has woven its way through varying waves of immigrant groups, significant historical events, and political-cultural epochs.[2]

Critics of bilingual education argue that students languish in TBE programs for six or seven years, despite the three-year objective; that the teachers are often underqualified and materials poor; that the programs segregate students and deepen ethnic differences; that the cultural and material interests of minority middle-class teachers and administrators are served by creating bureaucratic enclaves at the expense of the practical needs of poor children; and that despite several decades of program practice, Latino school dropout rates remain high.[3] Several of these criticisms are consistent with the research. Most school districts adopted either TBE programs or ESL, English as a Second Language, classes,[4] which emphasized rapid integration of students into mainstream classes, and both have been found to be minimally effective in advancing educational literacy.[5] Further, the success of bilingual programs is limited by family poverty and by a scarcity of qualified teachers. And as the experiences of the Rivera brothers illustrate, TBE programs do segregate and isolate cadres of ethnic minority students in designated areas of the school building, which deepens the stigma of bilingual education.

These criticisms notwithstanding, there are many examples of successful bilingual programs. Some scholars trace the 1960s revival of bilingual education back to Miami, where Cuban exiles, expecting to return to Cuba, instituted effective bilingual programs.[6] With a strong interest in preserving their language and culture, these exiles established successful "two-way" bilingual programs in an elementary school in Dade County.[7] Two-way programs overcome the stigmatization and isolation of language minority students by teaching both English-speaking and non-English-speaking students together in the same classrooms in all subjects in two languages. Both groups of students develop language competency in two languages and neither language nor group is privileged in the classroom.

The success of the Cuban dual-language programs in Dade County is attributable to several factors. The program received abundant federal resources (stemming from anti-Castro politics), was taught by highly trained Cuban teachers, and was supported by parents. Further, the curriculum was nonstigmatizing and there was minimal racism directed toward a light-skinned, professional Cuban class.[8] The political history of Cubans in the United States made governmental support generous and two-way bilingual programs defensible, while their social class and control over their own curriculum made the program effective. This suggested that if implemented properly, two-way bilingual programs could be effective, which the preponderance of the research supports.

Virginia Collier and Wayne Thomas provide the most comprehensive empirical studies on the topic. Their research shows that no other programs besides dual-language enrichment programs have closed much of the gap in secondary school test scores between English Language Learners, known as ELLs, and English-speaking students, but argue that success requires *six to eight years* of varying dual-language instruction, with larger doses of students' first languages provided in the early years and more exposure to their second languages in the latter years.[9] Their research builds on what most research studies for the past twenty-five years have demonstrated, that acquiring educational literacy in a first language expedites learning in a second language.[10]

Two-way programs are nonetheless rare, and the recent trend in the United States has been to replace TBE and ESL classes with English immersion programs.[11] Even during the 1960s and 1970s, when the English-only language hegemony was preempted by civil rights legislation and successful court challenges, ensuing remedies still tended to define English Language Learners' first languages as deficits, and to emphasize rapid transition into the English-speaking curriculum, which violates the central principle of two-way language programs.[12] The limited success of TBE and ESL programs is therefore not surprising, but understanding how bilingual education practices have subverted Puerto Rican communities requires that we consider these policies in relation to Puerto Ricans' unique history.

When the United States acquired Puerto Rico in 1898, Spain's educational neglect of Puerto Rico was apparent. There were no universities on the island and a secondary school system had not existed until 1882. At the time, Puerto Rico had the highest illiteracy rate in the West Indies, estimated at 83 percent.[13] Initially, the United States did little to change this—by 1940, less than one-half of children attended school on the island. As discussed in Chapter 1, literacy rates improved with Operation Bootstrap and the rise in living standards, but economically displaced Puerto Ricans, mostly from the rural areas, who migrated back and forth to the mainland remained uneducated. Consider for instance that when the first major study of Puerto Ricans in Springfield was released in October 1978, it found that *less than 20 percent of Puerto Rican adults held high school diplomas and that the median education level was below eighth grade.*[14] In 1990, the high school completion rate for all Latinos twenty-five years and older in Springfield was still just 39 percent.[15] Remedying this would require major investments in the schools and well-designed bilingual educational programs, neither of which was forthcoming.

Puerto Rican history is also different from the history of Cubans in Miami in an important respect. The United States was sympathetic to the Cuban exiles, who were viewed as victims of revolutionary war. Ironically, Puerto Ricans were also victims of war. When the United States took Puerto Rico from Spain, it did what most colonial powers do—imposed its culture to broaden and legitimate its power. As we saw earlier, Puerto Ricans survived this onslaught through cultural nationalism, and central to their cultural survival was and is their language. Preserving language preserves cultural dignity, and as former attorney general and chief justice of Puerto Rico José Trías Monge put it, "Puerto Rico spent decades in the melting pot, at high heat, and never melted."[16]

This historical uniqueness of Puerto Ricans is important when we consider the debates on bilingual education in the United States. Because of this history, bilingual programs that treat Spanish as a deficit and encourage rapid transition into English-speaking classes are not likely to be culturally embraced by Puerto Ricans. Moreover, when white school authorities express their indignation at students and teachers who embrace bilingual education in the schools, as did the head guidance counselor and the principal at Commerce High, they are pushing at exactly the place where Puerto Ricans are likely to push back. As Sonia Nieto explains, Puerto Ricans expect accommodation, not assimilation: "For most Puerto Ricans, getting a good education and remaining who they are have always been equally important goals."[17]

The racial and ethnic politics of the schools in Springfield reflected the organization of power more generally in the city. As a local Puerto Rican educator in Springfield explained to me:

> It sets up kind of an us versus them, which they [Puerto Ricans] can't win. . . . You know, their [bilingual students'] experiences aren't affirmed, their language that they choose to use, their style of dress, whatever it may be just isn't appreciated in the least. . . . I heard that constantly from students that were like, you know, "Why do I even bother coming? No one's personally vested in this except me, you know."

Without a forum to express their own indignation in the Springfield schools or to carve out their own spaces to create effective bilingual programs that meet the needs of their communities like the Cubans were encouraged to do in Miami years ago, Puerto Ricans in the late 1980s were speaking with their feet and dropping out of Springfield schools in droves.

Looking back, Fausto's fury after his meeting with his principal might have been a crucial turning point in his life—there was nothing offered from the meeting that was encouraging and Fausto didn't return to school for a week. Further, as I would later learn, it was during this time that Fausto's involvement in the drug trade in Springfield began. Still, when he did return, he met with his counselor, the only Latino in an administrative position at Commerce High, and with Ms. O'Connor, who in addition to being the head of the Guidance Department was the director of the school's dropout prevention program.

When students entered Ms. O'Connor's small office, created by cheaply constructed partitions, they were greeted by an empathetic but no-nonsense face, which communicated her frenzied work schedule, and a shiny plaque, carefully displayed at the edge of her desk, which read:

NO ONE EVER FAILS, THEY ONLY QUIT TRYING

Ms. O'Connor and Fausto's counselor both tried to encourage Fausto and recommended that he enroll in the school's dropout prevention program. Fausto returned to school because he wanted to play football and wrestle for the school team—he wanted the accolades that his brother Julio had received. He decided to stay in school and said he was going to apply himself to his studies like he had never done before. And, as must have pleased Ms. O'Connor, his determination reflected the American individualist creed: "Once I set my mind to something, I can do it." In the winter of his tenth-grade year, Fausto enrolled in the school's dropout prevention program, Project ACCES.

PROJECT ACCES

School dropout prevention programs serve two purposes: one, they provide students on the margins with one more chance to develop some academic skills before they part ways with the school and, two, they are intended to enhance the community's educational profile by lowering the school's dropout rate. In the spring of 1985, sociologist Michael Lewis and I began studying Springfield's school dropout prevention program, Project ACCES (Achievement Through Coordinated Community Educational Services).[18] The program was initially located in Springfield Technical High School, which was slated to be closed down at the end of the 1985–86 school year and consolidated with Classical High School to form the new Central High School. The consolidation was a bold move to stem the tide of white flight from the city, or as Mayor Ted Dimauro publicly stated, to keep Springfield from becoming a "minority city."[19] Furthermore, the move also was an attempt to racially balance the city's high schools. The year prior to the consolidation, Technical High's student population was 82 percent nonwhite compared to 28 percent at Classical. Similarly, 47 percent of Tech students met the low-income criteria, while only 10 percent of Classical students did so.[20]

Project ACCES was moved to the new high school along with the Tech students, but neither the program nor many of the students were welcomed by the principal. Central was created to be a high-achieving school that would maintain a significant white student body, but also a racially mixed one. Disciplinary measures were strict during the first few years. There was little support for the dropout prevention program, which maintained the "wrong type" of student in the school. Students and staff felt the scrutiny, but so did we as evaluators. When we released our two-year report in 1989, we found little to praise about the program and recommended significant reforms.[21] The principal took advantage of our critical conclusions to remove the program from his school. The program was moved to Commerce High, but became very different. At Technical, and then at Central, the program provided students not likely to graduate with an exit strategy. Students enrolled in a separate remedial curriculum intended to teach basic academic skills and, after completing a course on the "World of Work," were assigned part-time jobs in the community. The program allowed mostly truant tenth graders who had been held back several years with an opportunity to graduate in a year—truly an exit strategy.

At Commerce the program dropped the remedial curriculum, but maintained the World of Work course and the after-school work program. The underlying theory of the program at Commerce was that part-time work would increase students' self-esteem, teach work values and discipline, and change students' attitudes toward school—or at the very least provide an incentive to attend school. Unlike at Central, the program was referred to as an after-school work program rather than a dropout prevention program.

Through Project ACCES, Fausto was placed at the Boys Club. The atmosphere at the club was important to Fausto's wavering self-esteem. His excitement toward the job indicated that he desperately wanted to please his co-workers and convince them of his competency, which was sorely lacking in the classroom. He took the position seriously and quickly won the respect of his co-workers by demonstrating his abilities to work with African American and Puerto Rican youngsters. Even the club's executive director took notice. Fausto volunteered to help the club's wrestling coach prepare youths for local competitions. At the end of the year, he won a trophy for the most outstanding employee at the Boys Club. The executive director called him into his office to talk about his future—was he planning to go to college? Was he aware of permanent work opportunities with the Boys Club? Did he have a summer job?

Despite Fausto's disappointment with the principal at the beginning of the school year, Project ACCES had achieved its main objective—it increased Fausto's self-confidence and reinforced his desire to perform better in his classes. Moreover, with the support of the executive director at the Boys Club, even college seemed like more than just a remote possibility. On the academic front, Fausto continued to struggle his sophomore year, but was applying himself nonetheless. During the year, he set up a meeting with his counselor to discuss strategies for doing better in his courses. He began to drop in on his counselor more often and, occasionally, stopped by to see Ms. O'Connor as well. He explained to both of them that he was struggling in his classes and needed additional help. The program, however, did not provide tutoring—in fact, due to budget constraints, tutors were not available in the school at all. They suggested that he arrange to meet with his teachers for additional help, but Fausto didn't believe that the teachers could help. "I can't understand them in class and I can't understand them when they tutor me," he insisted. Fausto did, however, find a Puerto Rican classmate willing to tutor him. A Jehovah's Witness who tutored some and proselytized some, he nonetheless devoted an evening or two a week to Fausto. The tutoring appeared helpful and Fausto's determination in his courses was rewarded at the end of the year when he received passing grades: one B, two Cs, and four Ds. His reading and writing liabilities notwithstanding, Fausto was promoted to the eleventh grade and looked forward to football practice in August. Fausto's counselor was impressed, and he commented to me toward the end of the school year:

> I have to hand it to Fausto, he's busting his ass, trying harder than I've ever seen him. Taking books home and everything. He wants to pass all of his classes. He comes in to see me quite a bit. His teachers I've spoken to say he's doing better. He may just do it. I hope he does, I really hope it all pays off.

At the end of the school year, the students in Project ACCES were honored at a banquet attended by the school's superintendent, the mayor, and representatives from the private industry council. A student had been asked to give a short speech at the banquet about her experiences in the program, but overcome by the fear of speaking in front of a large and distinguished audience decided not to attend, nor did she inform anyone of her decision. Her absence was discovered ten minutes before she was scheduled to give the speech. Ms. O'Connor asked if anyone would volunteer to replace her—no one raised their hand. Finally, Fausto agreed to fill the void. Standing before his audience, he praised the program and provided a few anecdotes of his experiences at the Boys Club, all to Ms. O'Connor's delight. "He was unbelievably poised and confident," she would later say to me, "just did a brilliant job!"

For Fausto, the summer months reinforced his resolve. While other Commerce High students were terminating their employment at the Boys Club at the end of the school year, Fausto was accepting the club's offer to work in both their day and overnight camps through the summer. In the day camp, his co-workers were all college students. At the overnight camp, they were not only college students but also students from countries around the world. Fausto's initial fears of not fitting in gave way as he made friends and became central to the camp's activities. The staff responded very positively to Fausto—his supervisor even referred to him as a "godsend."

At the end of working hours in the day camp, Fausto started a weight-lifting program for staff members. In the early evenings, he could be found hustling from station to station in the weight room, yelling instructions to each of his co-workers and counting out repetitions as he pushed them through rigorous individual routines he had devised for them. His supervisor, with sweat pouring from her forehead as she pressed leg weights one evening, turned to me:

> Can you believe we are sitting here taking this shit from a sixteen-year-old kid? He has convinced us that he knows what he is doing in here and we don't have the slightest idea if he is bullshitting us or not. And yet we obey while he screams orders at us—something seems to be wrong here.

"No pain, no gain, Jody," Fausto retorted like a drill sergeant. "With all that jabbering over there we're going to be here all night, huh [laughter]?"

Fausto was a Project ACCES success, but what the audience at the school banquet, the staff at the Boys Club, and the host of college students he had befriended didn't know was Fausto's deep and dark secret—he was still virtually illiterate. He could speak both Spanish and English with accomplished ease, but he couldn't write or read either at the most fundamental level. He managed to deliver a speech spontaneously and eloquently at the banquet. At the summer camp, he would converse competently about current events and about problems in the inner city with his co-workers because of his own experiences and because he began watching television news to appear informed. The executive director of the club recognized Fausto's talent and assumed that with some encouragement and advice he would pursue college. Fausto told him he was extremely interested but was careful not to reveal his secret. No one knew! At the end of the summer, Fausto was evaluated and given a letter of recommendation by the assistant executive director of the club. In each of the evaluation categories, he received the highest mark, a 10, as testimony to his summer accomplishments, while the letter used phrases like "a hard-working, conscientious individual" and "a definite asset" to describe Fausto, and emphasized the "very good rapport" he had established with "both campers and staff."

No one at the Boys Club seemed to know that Fausto couldn't read the letter. He gave the letter to others to read and carefully noted their reactions. Since whoever read the letter complimented his success, Fausto assumed that "it's pretty good, huh?" No one understood the significance of his reply. It was sometime later, at a party at his grandmother's house in Hartford, that Fausto pulled me into a room and sheepishly asked me if I would read the letter aloud. As I did, Fausto could finally relish the words that others had read before and that he had only known by carefully observing their reactions— by studying their faces and their gestures and listening carefully to their words of praise. It was indeed a deep, dark secret.

In the middle of July, Fausto received a letter from the football coach inviting him to practice, which was scheduled to begin two weeks before school started. Fausto had been lifting weights all summer in anticipation, but now he really bore down. He started lifting every day and running sprints in the evening, while maintaining perfect attendance at the Boys Club. Furthermore, he was playing street football in a summer league. This was a rugged league largely made up of older jocks as well as younger street kids. The players didn't wear pads, so injuries were common. Fausto understood the risk but he wanted to be ready in the fall.

On opening day of practice, Fausto was the first to show up, even before the coach. When the coach arrived Fausto recalled shaking his hand but then standing in utter disbelief as the coach told him that he wasn't eligible to try out this season. Fausto had assumed that if he passed all his classes that he would be eligible; however, a school policy instituted in 1985 required all athletes to maintain a C average with no failed courses to participate in school athletics.[22] The coach had sent Fausto the letter by mistake; he was surely sorry. During Fausto's many conversations with his counselor, the ACCES coordinator, his teachers, and his student tutor, no one had mentioned this to him. He ran all the way home sobbing, withdrew into his bedroom, and fell into a deep depression. I saw him three days later.

Fausto was bitterly angry and his fantasies of getting revenge were raging. He was going to change schools and help his new school's football team beat Commerce High. And as a member of his new school's wrestling team, he was going to pin the "pussy" from Commerce High. He felt betrayed. He said things like "Fuck 'em, it's their loss anyhow" and "Someday they'll be sorry they fucked with me." He exclaimed, "That's it, I'm taking care of myself and fuck the rest of them. If they want to play the hard way then let's get down." In more sober moments, he just couldn't believe that he had worked so hard and still turned up on the short end of the stick. Bruised, his determination was strengthened. He was going to show them once and for all. Fausto decided he would withdraw into the books again. Besides, he was eager about a few electives he had selected for the next school year—a course in psychology and one in sociology. If they wanted to play with his head, he reasoned, then he would learn psychology so well that he could retaliate by playing with their heads. Most of all, he would bring his grades up so that he would be eligible for wrestling in the spring. But when they eagerly expected him to join the team, he would refuse. He would make them beg and then he would still refuse. This was his fantasy—he would not only have the last word but also the last laugh.

"He Was One of My Best Ones"

Unfortunately for Fausto, his plan would never materialize. In fact, the football fiasco turned out to be a portent of things to come his eleventh-grade year. If his tenth-grade year had consisted of changes in his life that were inspiring and hopeful, his eleventh-grade year resulted in a series of disappointments that sank his hopes. After the first month of classes, Fausto saw the handwriting on the wall. He was failing English, biology, and math. Fausto's sports career at Commerce hung in the balance and he was losing his resolve. I wrote in my field notes at the time, "Fausto wants desperately to avoid the internal voices of failure that are growing louder, but he can't put off the inevitable for much longer—he is losing the battle." He began to study less and to sleep more. He began missing school. He was slowly sinking into a depressed state; furthermore, he was spending more of his evenings on the streets, becoming more involved in the drug trade. Finally he quit attending school.

After Fausto had been absent for several weeks, his Puerto Rican counselor called him. They met and Fausto again requested to be transferred into the bilingual program. This time his counselor was supportive. He sent Fausto to the Springfield School Department to speak to the bilingual program coordinator. When I saw Ms. O'Connor later that week, she was furious that "someone had gone over our heads," and demanded to know who had sent him. I professed ignorance, but as it turned out, Ms. O'Connor had nothing to worry about. Fausto met with the coordinator, but she refused to pursue the matter with the school principal.

Next he took his case to one of the vice principals who he thought might be sympathetic. She was an African American woman and a friend of his counselor's (the only two racial minorities in the administration at Commerce High at the time). Fausto brought his mother to the meeting. After threatening to leave school if he wasn't transferred into the bilingual program, they worked out a plan and a new schedule for Fausto. When he returned to school, he found that the three administrators (the vice principal, his counselor, and the head of the bilingual program) had indeed rearranged his schedule. As requested, they left him in his history and psychology classes—both teachers agreed to allow him to make up the work he had missed. They changed Fausto's English class to an ESL class, taught by a teacher who was fluent in both English and Spanish. However, the agreement, as it had been understood by Fausto, ended there. He had expected that part of his new course schedule would include Spanish-speaking classes—his case, he believed, would set a precedent for similar cases to follow. Instead, the remainder of his class schedule was changed to special education classes. Fausto was insulted and found the classes worthless. He didn't like being associated with people "who aren't all there up here" (pointing to his head), students he considered to be "real badasses."

Again, Fausto's attendance dropped off until finally in early November he quit going to school altogether. As Fausto's prolonged struggle in the school neared its end, I approached Ms. O'Connor to discuss his case. She was irate. From her perspective, they had done so much for him and he had given up. Making her case, she spun hastily in her chair, clicked on her computer, typed in Fausto's name, and professed, "He's missed over half of the school year already!" Counting for a minute under her breath, she went on:

Thirty-three! He's missed thirty-three days of school already. What are you gonna do? I was going to give him a real good job this year in ACCES. They really liked him down at the Boys Club. But what are you going to do? Now, do you see what I'm up against? And he was one of my best ones in the program. You should see some of the others.

Fausto searched for a rationale to quit school altogether and he found it—his family was suffering financially. They had moved in order to reduce their rent burden but were still waiting for their name to turn up on a waiting list for subsidized housing in Springfield. Fausto decided he would look for work to help take care of his family and his daughter and assumed his family would be supportive of his decision—he assumed wrong.

Fausto's family had pulled up roots before to seek a better life for their children and they would do it again. The entire family moved to Hartford, Connecticut. Their intentions were twofold: to find Fausto a school that offered a bilingual curriculum and to get Sammy away from the streets in Springfield. After settling into their new community, Fausto and his mother visited a public high school to enroll Fausto. They were pleased to find that many of the school's administrators, teachers, staff, and students were Puerto Rican. The new surroundings felt good to Fausto and, again, he began to imagine the possibilities of playing sports. Fausto was doing adequately in his classes by midterm; but shortly thereafter, his family received notice from the Housing Department in Springfield that, after four years, their names had finally turned up on the waiting list. This meant returning to Springfield and Fausto's family couldn't afford to do otherwise. Fausto's mother was sorry for him, but he had to understand the relief the subsidy would provide for the whole family. They just couldn't afford to continue paying 75 percent of their income to rent. Fausto understood but he took a stand. He told his mother she would have to go without him. He had found what he was looking for in his new environment and was going to find a way to stay.

After long discussions with Virginia, the mother of his daughter, he persuaded her to stay at least until the school year was out. He could live with her until then and perhaps figure out another plan (over the summer) for his senior year. But first, he needed to find a job to help provide for them and, second, he had to call a social worker to find out what benefits he would be eligible for if his mother moved back to Springfield. And then there was the onerous task of transferring his daughter's fragile health care over to a new set of doctors. At sixteen years of age, he was consumed with worry. He wasn't sleeping at night and was nodding off in his classes. He missed several days of school in order to carve out a stable set of circumstances amidst the chaos that currently characterized his life. His search for a job proved futile, but his exchange with the social worker sank the ship.

The social worker was anything but sympathetic. She scolded him for not living with his mother. She informed him that he would not be eligible for any benefits until he was eighteen unless he was living with an immediate relative. Lastly, the social worker told him that as soon as his mother returned to Springfield, he would be illegally enrolled in the city's public high school. He couldn't go to school here, she told him, if his mother lived elsewhere—not unless he was residing with a court-appointed legal guardian. Forced to return to Springfield with his family, he again felt the futility of his situation. Riding in my car, his eyes welled up with tears and he lamented:

It's fucked up. I'm trying and just keep getting beat. Sometimes I feel like giving up, you know. I'm gonna keep trying, but it's hard. . . . I move here to get educated, to do something for myself, and welfare fucks me up. In Springfield, the school fucked me up. I'm down right now, but I'm going to keep trying, to keep fighting, you know.

Back in Springfield and out of school, Fausto turned to the streets. At the same time, we considered his options. We talked about GED programs and about visiting the Boys Club to see if there were any opportunities. He didn't know what to do. Ideas raced through his mind with manic rapidity. In the meantime, he was spending more and more time on the streets. Finally, he decided to drop in on his co-workers at the Boys Club—he had heard that people over there were asking about him. We went together.

At the Boys Club, he was greeted with hugs and handshakes. Where had he been? Couldn't he drop in once in a while? The summer is coming up and they were getting worried he wouldn't show up. How were things going? How was school? How did the football season go? Boy, it sure is good to see you. It's going to be a good summer. And guess who's getting a promotion to administrative assistant at the overnight camp? The reception was warm, but he couldn't face telling them the miles of life he had traveled since he had seen them last. He lied. School's fine. I decided not to go out for the football team, there are more important things to do, you know. Sorry, I would've dropped in but I've been busy with school and all.

As Fausto sat at an empty table in the corner of the room to fill out his application, it was obvious that there was a whole side of Fausto he couldn't bear to let them in on. "How do you spell counselor?" he whispered. "How about street?" "Does this look right?" His anxiety was mounting. I glanced at the half-completed application—there were no spaces between the words, capital letters appeared in the wrong places, punctuation was incorrect. Fausto whispered, "Why do they want me to write a paragraph anyways. They already know me." His eyes darted around the room searching for an answer, for an escape. Perhaps he could tell them he was in a hurry and would have to finish the application later. What was he to do? He couldn't let them know. They think so highly of him.

At a table in the corner of the Boys Club sat a boy with an exceptionally mature mind, but with the education of an eight-year-old. He didn't know what he was going to do when the summer was over. But right now he was among people who appreciated his abilities and his personal drive. For Fausto, he was willing to let "right now" last forever; after all, September seemed a long way off.

FOUR

The Tail of the Drug Trade

CITIES ARE THE TAIL of the global drug trade. Production, preparation, and transportation of illicit drugs occur long before they reach U.S. cities. The United Nations Office on Drugs and Crime estimated in the late 1990s that the global drug trade accounted for 8 percent of international trade. In 2003, they estimated that the total value of illicit drugs produced was $13 billion, which jumped to $94 billion at the wholesale level, and $322 billion at the retail level.[1] Judging from the retail markup, it might seem that the tail does wag the beast, but those at each end of the trade—the farmer and the corner drug dealer—see very little of this money. Instead, those who coordinate and control the processes from the poppy, coca, and cannabis fields to the primary markets in the United States and Europe rake in profits from the multibillion-dollar market. The huge economic value of the illicit drug market creates competition among criminal syndicates; makes the illicit drug economy an increasingly common alternative to poverty in developing countries; is relied upon by political resistance groups to fund militant operations and by state governments to fund paramilitary groups to suppress resistance; and has been used by governmental intelligence agencies, including the CIA, to funnel money into mercenary military operations. The young men profiled in this chapter—Sammy, Fausto, Manny, Alexander, Roberto, Jorge—and millions like them in urban areas throughout the United States are minor players on a very large playing field.

Beginning in the 1960s, the illicit drug trade in the United States grew dramatically, driven largely by the greater demand for a variety of recreational drugs. The power of consumer markets in the United States often drives the world economy, and illicit drug production is no exception. The increase in drug use in the United States in the 1960s, as well as in Europe, turned the drug trade into the multibillion-dollar business that we know today. International interdiction efforts have done little, if anything, to stem the tide. The breakup of one organized drug route simply results in an alternative route—for instance, the breakup of the infamous French Connection in Marseilles that channeled most of the heroin into the United States in the 1960s and early 1970s created a market void that was first filled by Chinese syndicates in Southeast Asia, and later by heroin production in Mexico.[2]

The popularity of cocaine began in the United States in the late 1960s, but it did not become widely marketed and available until after 1973, when it was organized by the Medellín Cartel in Colombia.[3] The demand for cocaine, particularly on college campuses and among the professional classes, flourished in the early 1980s. In 1985, when "base" or "crack" cocaine hit the market, an inexpensive, smokable variant of the drug produced by removing the hydrochloride from powder cocaine, the availability of the drug reached beyond the middle class to include lower-income groups, becoming one of America's favorite illicit drugs.[4]

The increased demand for marijuana, cocaine, and heroin in the United States, along with more technologically sophisticated drug cartels, transformed the global drug trade in the United States in the second half of the twentieth century. At the same time, manufacturing industries were closing their doors in U.S. cities throughout the Northeast and Midwest, destabilizing communities and depleting job opportunities for the working classes. In short, as U.S. cities became important nodes for drug distribution networks extending from Colombia, Mexico, Jamaica, Afghanistan, Pakistan, and other places, economic opportunities were crumbling in U.S. cities and thousands of young men were seizing new opportunities that emerged as local drug organizations competed for control of these growing markets. Springfield, Massachusetts, was no exception.

The Riveras' relocation to Springfield in the mid-1980s occurred just as the drug trade was blossoming there. By the early 1990s, the local district attorney's office recognized Springfield as the major distribution center for drugs throughout the western part of Massachusetts. The county DA's office estimated that 75 percent of all crack cocaine, 51 percent of cocaine, and 59 percent of heroin in western Massachusetts came from Springfield. Police responded. From 1988 through June 1991, 13,748 drug-related arrests were made in Springfield, where the total population was not quite 157,000. Sixty-eight percent of individuals arrested were ten to twenty-nine years of age.[5] Accordingly, drug arrests and convictions greatly expanded the prison population in the state, increasing 236 percent from 1980 to 1990.[6] Cities like Springfield were being whipsawed by the forces of economic capitalism in the 1980s—by the evisceration of U.S. manufacturing on one side and by the emergence of a lawless drug economy on the other.

ENTRÉE INTO THE DRUG TRADE

Sammy was the first among the Rivera brothers to find his way into the drug trade in Springfield. His street experiences in Yonkers, his dislocation within the schools, his neighborhood and school friends who shared his alienation in Springfield paved the way. Soon after arriving in the Brightwood neighborhood, Sammy ingratiated himself among a network of young men who would play a large role in shaping his and his brothers' lives in the years to come. Key among them was Alfredo Acosta.

> So we used to go down to Orchard Street to sell coke and stuff, you know, and there I met Alfredo Acosta and he . . . had a lot of respect anywhere he went and . . . the respect for him was real, real respect, you know. I mean everybody and anybody that used to come and, "Oh that Alfredo Acosta" and "Oh for real?" And, you know, go shake his hand like he was a god or something, you know.

Alfredo and his brothers controlled much of the drug distribution in Springfield's North End in the 1980s, and being close to Alfredo provided the thirteen-year-old Sammy with a taste of power and respect. School was no contest.

> So I started hanging out and instead of going to school in the morning I used to go to his house first and he used to give me the

keys to his car and said, "Go get the newspaper and go get two soups for me and you" . . . and I used to help count a whole bunch of money . . . there was so much for me to do and driving the cars and dealin' with the money and stuff at this point, you know, that I didn't really want to be in school.

Sammy's street trajectory, however, required more than deteriorating neighborhood conditions: he had to negotiate street networks in order to compete with other young men facing similar circumstances, which was no easy task. Sammy worked hard to impress Alfredo by demonstrating his loyalty, his fighting skills, his willingness to take risks, and his daily labor. In turn, Alfredo moved Sammy into his inner circle, mentored him, and used him to maintain his drug fiefdom. They clicked, and being a central part of Alfredo's operation enhanced Sammy's reputation on the streets.

Now, from there on it was like anybody who saw me and—"Hey, how ya doing, Sammy? You need a couple bucks?" . . . It was like way different than, than anything before, you know. . . . I used to go to down Orchard Street and everybody used to say, "Hey, Sammy, c'mere a minute. Want a couple beers?" I was really young, you know. I never liked to drink or anything and they always used to give me stuff, you know. Like, "Hey, look. I just bought this watch from this guy. Here, have it." You know, a lot of respect from these people and the kids that I used to go to school with, you know, like Aurelio and Elfredo and stuff like that, they started, um, like, "Damn," you know, "What's up?"

There were many rumors that circulated about Alfredo. He projected an image of ruthlessness. He was reputed to have shot a man and disposed of his body in the Connecticut River. Another story told is that he showed up at a police drug bust on the street and, backed by fifteen men, took the confiscated bags from the police officer, ripped them open, and poured the cocaine into the city sewer. Another story was that when the police raided Alfredo's house and found drugs and guns, Alfredo beat the case. True or not, these stories illustrate the legendary status of Alfredo Acosta and explain

Sammy's idolatry. The invisibility that Sammy felt in school was compensated for by the exaggerated visibility he felt on the streets with Alfredo.

Fausto's entrée onto the streets came later, but he knew Alfredo and his brothers and, like Sammy, found their power intoxicating.

FAUSTO: Yeah, I looked up to them.

TIM: What was it about them?

FAUSTO: The fear that everybody had on 'em. You know, they
could go up into a bar and everybody would be like,
"Whatcha need, whatcha want?" You know, "You need a
drink?" . . . Everybody owes them money and they had all
the nice cars and shit like that. You know, the Acostas had a
lot of power back then, you know what I'm saying? And the
devils would fight—they had fifty million back 'em up, you
know? That power, you know, kinda answers the
question . . . the adrenaline that you get from that.

Sammy introduced Fausto to Alfredo during his tenth-grade year while Fausto was bearing down in school. Fausto sold small amounts of marijuana at school that year for Alfredo, but his involvement in the drug trade would not escalate until his eleventh-grade year, after the police finally prevailed in sending the Acosta brothers to prison. The Acosta brothers did not leave behind a tightly developed organization, but a drug distribution network that was largely organized around Alfredo's street charisma. Consequently, their absence left a vacuum in the drug trade that was quickly filled by two characters, loosely related to the Acosta brothers, whose lives would become intertwined with the three Rivera brothers.

Manny Torres was a New Yorker whose involvement in the drug trade reached deep into his family. The rumor was that Manny had thrown a kilo of cocaine off the George Washington Bridge while being chased by police officers and had then decided to leave New York for greener pastures. Small-town Springfield apparently fit the bill, where Manny easily stepped into the drug business because he was a nephew of Alfredo Acosta. Manny smoked a lot of crack cocaine when he first arrived in Springfield, but he gave it up to organize drug dealing in the North End.

Alexander Rodríguez is Manny's cousin. A heavy cocaine user in his twenties, Alexander established a connection with a Dominican man married to Manny's sister. The Dominican dealt large quantities of cocaine (in kilos) and had just finished a ten-year prison term when Alexander met him. Alexander transformed himself into a successful businessman. He gave up cocaine and alcohol, a decision that was prompted by both a heart attack and the demands of his business. His place in Springfield's drug networks was further secured when he married Alfredo Acosta's sister. His marriage not only deepened his ties to the Acosta brothers, but to Manny as well.

Manny stepped quickly into the void left by the Acosta brothers. He went to work establishing a clientele and organizing dealers out of an auto repair garage in the Brightwood neighborhood, while Alexander drifted into the background, out of view from the street level. Fausto would eventually work for Manny; however, Fausto's involvement in the drug trade would be gradual. Manny, along with two young men working for him, would introduce Fausto to street opportunities, and, certainly, Fausto was prepared to take advantage of these opportunities—he was failing in school, was a skilled fighter, smart, and willing to take risks. But unlike Sammy, Fausto also found the prospects of school, sports, and "legit" work appealing, and there were important influences that supported this alternative trajectory as well, particularly his older brother, Julio, his supervisor at the Boys Club, and me.

When I started my ethnography in January 1990, I entered the schools as a potential mentor for youth identified as "at risk" of dropping out of school. I developed relationships with several young men, but none as close as my relationship to Fausto.

THE WAYWARD MENTOR AND HIS PUPIL

The night that Fausto told me he was leaving school, we were sitting in his living room, and he was holding a copy of Arthur Miller's *Death of a Salesman*. He explained that he was keeping his schoolbooks because he wanted to educate himself, that he was not giving up on the prospects of going to college someday. He was deeply hurt by the school's refusal to place him in the bilingual program and talk about street life was becoming more common. I encouraged Fausto to enroll in a GED program and framed it as an opportunity to show school authorities that he could get a degree. He consented, but his nights were getting longer, his street associations more pervasive.

At this crucial juncture in Fausto's life, he was attempting to weave an identity from the web of influences that surrounded him— his parents, brothers, school authorities, Boys Club supervisors, friends, street acquaintances, and me. I was an influence in Fausto's life, in part, because I recognized his intelligence and knew his potential. We spent hours talking about our lives and I was genuinely impressed by his insights into the social world. He had a capacity for reflection that was impressive, that was rooted in personal angst, and his wounds were raw enough that they had not yet become hidden by layers of denial or clouded by years of drug use. His adolescent turmoil was very accessible; mostly, he wanted approval and validation. My age, race, and education gave me influence; after all, not many educated white guys were praising Fausto for his intellect. Of course, my white skin and my education were overvalued by Fausto. He held me in high esteem for reasons that had less to do with me and more to do with his internalized frames of reference, stemming from being a person of color in a white-dominated world. Getting beyond the socially scripted nature of our relationship would take time; it would be years before my vulnerabilities could be seen and before Fausto would reveal other parts of his life.

Fausto and I spent hours playing hoops on outdoor courts, taking long walks in the woods outside Springfield, driving around the area, and always talking. We talked about the streets, about inequality, racism, girls, drugs, politics, school, sports, our families, and about his future. At the age of only fifteen, Fausto was keenly observant, had an unusual capacity for empathetic understanding, was articulate and extremely inquisitive. I directed our conversations toward nurturing a sociological imagination, a concept developed by C. Wright Mills in the 1950s. A sociological imagination refers to the ability to see how larger social forces influence the lives of individuals. Fausto's inquisitiveness lent itself easily to this project, and in a short time Fausto was developing a language that reflected a deeper, more critical understanding of the social world around him. Drawing on his experience, a young Fausto described racial inequality:

> There are three types of backgrounds. There are those kids who grow up and see violence every day, who don't have no money, whose families don't have money, who go to bed sometimes hungry. They don't have a chance. . . . Pretty soon they start selling, getting them some action, making some money. . . . Then there are kids who live in neighborhoods and families a little above that—like me. You see some violence, you hungry sometimes but not all the time. You know these kids have more chances, but there's still the money thing. It's hard to move up there . . . the people usually up there are white. There are some blacks and some Puerto Ricans moving up now, but when you look up you see white.

Commenting on Puerto Ricans who are upwardly mobile, Fausto continued:

> What happens to the guy—the fuckin' Puerto Rican who makes it up there. He gets up there, he starts mingling, uh, what you call it, socializing with the big people and he forgets where he came from, he forgets his own. He doesn't want to think about his past. He says, "Fuck you, I've made it." He never looks back, he forgets his people.

At sixteen, Fausto expressed a desire for "activist judges," who would make more of an effort to intervene in the lives of young delinquents:

> What pisses me off is you get a judge in court who doesn't know where these kids came from, you know, their background. I've seen it, I've seen my friends get in trouble and get time, big time because they were hanging out on Franklin [Street] and they had some stuff on 'em, just a little bit of shit. The judge sits up there and sees these kids and he's just like disgusted—"Five years!" he says. "Get the scum out of here, next case!" You know, then they

get a record, they get out of jail and they're fucked. No jobs with a record, so they back out there dealing again. But the fucking judge sits there, "Five years!" Why don't he get down and go out and talk to these kids, find out a little about their backgrounds? Why he's doing these things? Help 'em out if you can. I mean the law's the law, but you can talk to 'em and try to learn about their background. Judges don't do that.

My early interest in Fausto was driven by the conundrum that someone so intelligent could find himself in the tenth grade unable to read and write above an elementary school level. He had not learned academic routines, but had instead adopted folk routines—he learned from everyone around him by studying them, asking them questions, taking from them whatever they had to offer. This was his father's strategy for survival, a strategy born from illiteracy, from leaving school in the third grade to work on the farm.

After Fausto dropped out of school, it was clear that his street contacts were growing and that he would soon find a place in Manny's crew. I wanted to keep another pathway open by helping him to get into a GED program as soon as possible. In the winter of 1993, I heard that a human services agency in Springfield was starting a GED program and was eagerly recruiting students. Fausto and I contacted them and were told that to qualify for the program, he would need to score at the seventh-grade level on an eligibility exam. Fausto scored a 6.8 and the program declared him ineligible. I was incensed and was unable to hide my feelings on the phone. There had been too many recent disappointments in Fausto's life and he certainly didn't need another one, especially when he was only two-tenths of a point away from qualifying. Rules are rules, I was told, but Fausto could take the exam again in a few weeks. Fausto and I developed a nightly study routine.

In tutoring Fausto, I observed how the subtleties of inequality affected educational achievement. Far away from the privileges of middle-class neighborhoods, the Riveras lived in a small two-bedroom apartment on a noisy street in Springfield. Eight people lived in the apartment and there were no spaces in the home that were set up for studying. Each evening, we rearranged the living room, moving mattresses, a coffee table, a dining room table, a lamp, chairs, toys, ceramic knickknacks, and whatever else might be in the way. Lighting was particularly poor.

Fausto and I studied a minimum of three hours each night. When Fausto retook the exam, he scored at the ninth-grade level, a 9.6, on the exam, strengthening my contention that with appropriate remedial help, he could overcome his educational deficiencies so that his education was more commensurate with his intellect.[7] However, instead of being immediately placed into the program, he received a call from Mr. González, the director of the program, who wanted to meet with him right away.

Fausto was nervous about the meeting, stemming from tensions he had felt with Mr. González during a prior meeting, which I had attended.[8] Mr. González was a large man with a thin mustache who wore a toupee, prompting Fausto to nickname him "the wig dude." He was very opinionated about school dropouts and adopted a tough-love approach toward Fausto during the initial meeting. First he lectured Fausto about the importance of a high school degree by pointing to a work crew outside his window: "Do you want to be the person holding the shovel or the person telling people what to do?" Next he launched into a tirade about bilingual education, dismissing Fausto's claims that the reason he had left school was because authorities had refused to place him in the program. "When my daughter was in the second grade," Mr. González explained,

we lived in New York. One day she comes home with a note explaining that they were going to put her in an ESL program. I went crazy. I got on the phone and I told the principal of that school, in no uncertain terms, that they were not going to move my daughter out of English-speaking classes, period! That would've been the kiss of death. Many bilingual parents would not have known to call. They would not have known any better; they would've assumed that the school authorities knew what was best for their kid. No way, I said, if my daughter is going to live in this country, she's going to learn English. So they put her back in the regular track and it's the best thing that ever happened to her.

79

Fausto was cautious in his response. He agreed that learning English was important but stressed that ESL classes are needed in some cases.

Mr. González then asked how far Fausto's parents had gone in school. When he replied that neither had graduated and that his father had left school after third grade, Mr. González nodded his head knowingly and explained that most high school dropouts he sees are from similar situations. He asserted that these families do not value high school education because the parents did not complete high school. Fausto viewed the comment as an insult to his family. He was noticeably angry, but kept his composure. Later he would remark to me:

> Yo, does that motherfucker know my family? Huh? What is that shit? You know what I'm saying? The reason I'm trying to get my GED is because of my family. They always telling me to get my education. They want this more than anything for me and my brothers. My father quit school in the third grade because he had to work, he had to help his father on the farm in Puerto Rico and shit. He didn't get good promotions because he can't read and write. Does that motherfucker know what it's like to be my father, to suffer like he has because he can't read and write? Does he, you know, does he know what my father has been through? I should've tripped that motherfucker, 'cause my father, my father would do anything, anything to make sure we don't have to suffer like he has. Anything, yo!

At the end of the first meeting, Mr. González made one last observation. He told Fausto he would need to learn to put himself before his family, that he could be helpful to his family only if he took care of himself first. He described family as "a noose around your neck." Mr. González was articulating the middle-class value on individualism that contradicts the norms in impoverished communities where scarce resources are more likely to be shared and where a strong value is placed upon reciprocity.[9] This is particularly true in low-income Puerto Rican communities where traditional rural values of communal responsibility are reproduced in poor urban neighborhoods. Mr. González recognized the problems that this creates for individuals who are trying to improve their economic and social status. But describing family as a "noose around your neck" violated the family-centered orientation of the culture and the importance of taking care of one another. Fausto again felt insulted. He was particularly incensed by the liberties Mr. González was taking in discussing his family. Mr. González and Fausto may have shared ethnicity, but their class differences fostered ill will between them—and their second meeting would not resolve the rift.

I phoned Fausto shortly after he returned from the second meeting. He sounded triumphant and explained that he "had gone eye-to-eye, face-to-face with the wig dude." According to Fausto, Mr. González opened both of his exams and expressed doubt about the improvement in his scores. Fausto defended himself by describing his hours of preparation, but felt as if Mr. González was accusing him of cheating. Then Mr. González explained that the program was reserved for people who were sponsored by other organizations and that since he wasn't sponsored he wouldn't be able to attend. Fausto had applied when the program was in its beginning stages and had therefore been encouraged. Since then, they had received a large number of applications and most of the participants were either state- or company-sponsored. Fausto was not receiving state funds, which meant the program would not be reimbursed for his participation. Fausto said that, at this point, he let the wig dude have it. He asked why he was asked to take the test a second time if he wouldn't be eligible. Mr. González acquiesced and admitted him, but not without emphasizing that he would be allowed only three absences in the program before he was shown the door.

Fausto didn't last long in the program. Shortly after he began attending classes, he moved into a housing project with his family that was farther away from the agency. At the same time, his street involvement was deepening. Less than halfway through the program, he missed his third class and was dismissed. I was angry at the agency, mostly because I could see the direction Fausto's life was taking. Moreover, I was beginning to recognize that my mentoring efforts were like shoveling sand at the tide—Fausto was following a well-trod pathway. He could hardly read or write, was a high school dropout, a racial minority, smart, and desperately seeking a place for himself in the world. The forces shaping his life were pushing him into social spaces where he would be valued, and one of those spaces was organized by Manny.

STREET STATUS

Fausto was hanging out regularly with Aurelio, which gave Fausto only one degree of separation from Manny Torres. Aurelio, a skinny young man who had been part of Sammy's earlier school adventures, was Manny's right-hand man. From the same town in Puerto Rico as Alfredo Acosta and Alexander Rodríguez, Aurelio provided Fausto with a glimpse into the world of a successful drug dealer—he had a nice car, money, drugs, and women. Moreover, Aurelio liked having Fausto around because of his size and his fighting skills. Fausto began making "a few dollars" from Aurelio by collecting debts—he became Aurelio's muscle. In turn, Fausto was also spending more time with Manny.

One night, Manny asked Fausto to help him count some money. Their hands buried in $100,000 in different-denomination bills, Manny then asked Fausto to go to New York the following day to drop off the money and "bring something back." This was Fausto's eleventh-grade year, when things were not working out in school. The trip was Fausto's first exposure to big-time drug dealing. He remembers sitting in the car in the middle of New York City when Manny returned with several kilos of cocaine in a grocery bag, which he tossed in Fausto's lap. "You can smell it from a distance," Fausto recalled. "It smelled like medicine." They drove to a safe place and deposited the cocaine in a custom-made compartment in the car before heading back to Springfield.

Fausto's admiration for Manny grew during this period—he considered Manny a mastermind and felt fortunate that Manny had chosen to teach him the drug business. According to Fausto, Manny was one of the first dealers in Springfield to learn how to convert large amounts of powder cocaine into base, or crack cocaine. Fausto recalls going to the grocery store with Manny to buy large jars to use in the preparation. They brought twenty-five jars of pickles to the cash register and Manny apparently told the cashier that "my wife is having a baby." Fausto quipped, "He should've said at least I'm openin' up a restaurant or something." Fausto described the conversion process as well as his admiration for Manny.

> That shit stinks, man, oooh! That shit gets in your blood and you'll get high. . . . 'Cause, you have to use baking soda, water, then bottle placed in the middle and just cookin' all them ounces of coke. . . . Believe me, it's some potent shit. He is like a fuckin' chemist, yo. He knew everything about coke, how to deal with it. He was a good accountant type of guy, you know. He was really fuckin' smart. And counting money—ha, you couldn't beat him. Very good with numbers.

Manny had completed some college and had followed his father into the drug trade. "Smart, educated, and personable," as Julio described him, Manny created a drug enterprise that reached up to the University of Massachusetts in Amherst in the early 1990s and then eventually as far north as Vermont and Maine. He expanded his inner circle of dealers during this time and hired Fausto. He believed Fausto was not using drugs—or that at least his use was controlled—and that he was reliable, and certainly Fausto had proven himself to have "heart"—be willing to do whatever was necessary to get a job done. Fausto was paid $700 cash a week to make deliveries.

At around the time that Manny hired Fausto, Aurelio's status within the organization was in jeopardy. Aurelio had developed a heroin addiction, which made him untrustworthy. Manny began to rely more on Jorge Rodríguez, Alexander's younger brother, as his closest confidant. Jorge looms large in my ethnography. Smart and handsome, with a calm demeanor, Jorge is not a drug user. I've known Jorge for more than ten years and he has never used cocaine, heroin, marijuana, or any other illegal drug. He does, however, like to drink, but only Budweiser and lots of it. Manny began turning to Jorge and Fausto more often to take care of business demands, while he was trying to break Aurelio's drug habit by sending him to Puerto Rico to be nursed back to health by his family.

Fausto enjoyed his increasing status in the drug trade as well as the money in his pocket. He referred to Manny as "a millionaire" and admired his business acuity. The organization had a large supply of beepers and cars registered in other people's names. Manny also had protection within the city, because some of his customers worked for the city in places where they could warn Manny if any busts were imminent. Fausto was moving up in a lucrative organization and was no longer dealing on Franklin Street. As he described it, he was dealing "to people with titles. You wouldn't believe it, people who don't even want music played in their driveways."

Fausto would frequently comment, almost as if to console me, that he was not a dime-bag dealer standing on some corner, that he had "a position" and was part of something big. Fausto felt relatively safe because his work was not in high-profile places. He would get a call on his beeper and make deliveries rather than stand on a corner where police surveillance was likely. He worked around the clock, by himself, recording transactions in a notebook. Still, Fausto never entirely embraced a street identity, at least not to me—his friend "the professor"—who remained interested in his education and his chances of finding some way off the streets. Fausto still harbored fantasies about "going legit." He enrolled in a second GED program, completed it, and took the test in the summer of 1993. Sitting outside on a hot July day at the housing complex where he lived with his family, he described his ambivalence:

> Recently, I don't know, bro, I feel lost, you know, like things are moving too fast. I'm waiting for my test scores [from his GED test]. I need a goal to live by day to day. I want that goal to be education. Now it's just money. The goal behind what I do now is money, girls, cars, that sort of thing. I don't want to do this forever, but the money is good and my family needs it. But there are too many problems that go along with it. Too many headaches. . . . It's just my work. But I know what I want and this ain't it.

It was true that Fausto's parents had fallen on hard times. Juan had suffered a back injury on the job and was in severe pain. He was self-medicating frequently with marijuana and was facing the prospect that he would be out of work for a long time. In the meantime, he was drawing unemployment, which was well beneath his pay, and had initiated a worker's compensation claim, which would take years to settle. The family was struggling financially, even more than usual.

Juan and Angela were aware of Fausto's street activities, long before he showed up at the house with a safe full of money and drugs. Juan put his foot down and told Fausto he had a month to either get rid of the safe or else he had to go. Responding to children's involvement in the drug trade, however, can be difficult for parents in poor neighborhoods. While these activities are often forbidden by parents, they also provide badly needed resources in the home. Parents may maintain a façade of disapproval while turning a blind eye toward the source of their food, clothing, rent, furniture, and so on.

Juan is street-smart, enjoys smoking marijuana, snorting cocaine, and gambling. His responsibilities as a father have included both teaching his children how to be street-smart as well as insisting that they stay in school, work, and become responsible fathers. Juan issued the ultimatum to Fausto because he was placing his family in jeopardy, and yet a safe full of drugs and money was hard to resist. Access to such an abundance of resources is unusual and it provides for the satisfaction of fantasies, especially among a population that could never afford such luxuries as vacations. Years later, looking back on those days, Fausto recalled:

[My father] robbed me, man. He robbed me big time! . . . He took $2,000 and a whole bunch of coke and left to Florida to have a good time [laughter]. And I had just got the shit, yo! They had just given me the job. . . . I had a kilo and a half of cocaine in my house, all right, a kilo and a half and I had some money in there— like two or four Gs or somethin' like that. And I said, Dad, watch this shit, all right? 'Cause he told me . . . I'm gonna give you a month to get that shit out of the house. . . . I had it in the safe and everything. . . . The next thing you know . . . when I came back, Mom is like, your father, I haven't seen him the whole day. And then the next day . . . your father hasn't come back. Now, I'm worried. Can we call the cops or something? Then he fuckin' calls—he's in fuckin' Florida! [laughter] Runnin' with the money, my mother's all upset and . . . I just laughed. I just said, yo, we got robbed. . . . What can I say? He said we owed him that [laughter] for three hours of work probably sittin' down in the chair in the livin' room?

Fausto did move out of his parents' apartment shortly after his father issued the ultimatum. He moved in with Gladys, a woman a few doors down in the housing project. Fausto's mother had encouraged the relationship. A tall, beautiful Puerto Rican, Gladys was the mother of two children. Angela would invite her over when Fausto was around, but Fausto showed little interest and insisted that he could never be with a woman who didn't shave her legs. The day after this admission, Gladys dropped by the Riveras' apartment with smoothly shaven legs and took Fausto back to her apartment to consummate the relationship. Fausto moved in, bringing his safe with him.

During this period of time, Fausto sat at the crossroads. I helped to keep alive his fantasy of one day sitting in a college classroom—perhaps this was my fantasy as much as his. I envisioned Fausto as a future leader of a social movement to change the social conditions that had victimized him. However, Fausto had not been formally educated and his work with Manny as well as his lifestyle was intoxicating—it provided him with an opportunity to be part of a successful enterprise and to indulge himself in more creative and pleasurable forms of living compared to monotonous, low-wage jobs that awaited people like himself.[10] Fausto's quick wit, intelligence, and willingness to take risks were compatible with street life. He set up two households. He bought new furniture for Gladys's apartment and gave her expensive gifts, while at the same time he also lived with a woman he met in his GED class, providing for her needs and showering her with gifts as well. His drug use also increased during this time and, unbeknownst to Manny, he began exploring heroin euphoria.

Still, there was a downside to Fausto's lifestyle that rarely gets portrayed in media accounts of the drug trade. Much of his work was solitary. He spent much time alone, waiting for his beeper to signal the next delivery, and had to be prepared to make a run anytime around the clock. He often looked tired and haggard. His drug use was also largely solitary, and began to take on a more personal, rather than social, connotation. There were also limits placed on his lavish spending. Even though Fausto bought furniture and gifts for his girl-friends, Manny insisted that his workers limit their public displays of wealth. Fausto dressed modestly and drove an older car.

Fausto's life trajectory was moving forward with reservations, doubts, and contradictory feelings, but it was moving forward nonetheless, and a set of routines and dispositions associated with a street identity was taking shape. Clearly, Fausto took his position within Manny's organization seriously, and he derived important status on the streets by being a step removed from the street corner. Meanwhile, his brother Sammy's own street career was ascending, but in a different manner from Fausto's.

SELLING AN IMAGE TO SELL A PRODUCT

Before Alfredo and his brothers went to prison, they established Franklin Street as their drug depot. Franklin Street was geographically ideal for their business purposes. The street was located outside the Brightwood neighborhood, which was teeming with police by the early 1990s. It provided a park, and, most important, there was easy access in and out of the area from Interstate 291, making the location less threatening to white drug users (see map page 88). Franklin Street was Sammy's spot; it was also his playground.

As much money as Sammy made selling drugs on Franklin Street, he discovered that selling in a white town was much more lucrative. Sammy found out about Greenfield, an old mill town about forty miles north of Springfield, from one of his dealers, Tee. Sammy had never heard of Greenfield, and when told it was "in the boondocks up there past Northampton," he recalls that he was dismissive, even though Tee insisted that "whatever you sell here for $10, you'll sell it for $40 over there." Sammy said he didn't think much about it at the time, but noticed that Tee kept showing up on Franklin with a "knot of money" in his pocket, asking him for larger amounts of their product. Sammy decided to test Tee's new venture.

> So I gave him a little something, to make himself something and make myself something, you know. So he goes up there and he comes back, the same night, and I had gave him like $300 worth. And so he comes back and gives me $400. I'm like "Yo man, you

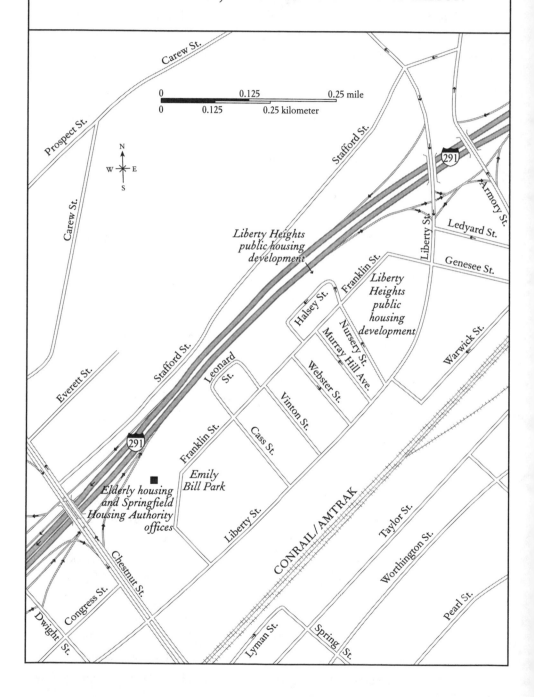

FRANKLIN STREET, FORMER DRUG SPOT LOCATION

Carew St.

Prospect St.

Carew St.

Stafford St.

291

Armory St.

Ledyard St.

Liberty St.

Genesee St.

Liberty Heights
public housing
development

Franklin St.

Liberty
Heights
public
housing
development

Halsey St.

Nursery St.

Warwick St.

Everett St.

Stafford St.

Leonard
St.

Murray Hill Ave.

Webster St.

Vinton St.

291

Franklin St.

Cass St.

Emily
Bill Park

Elderly housing
and Springfield
Housing Authority
offices

Liberty St.

CONRAIL / AMTRAK

Taylor St.

Worthington St.

Chestnut St.

Dwight St.

Congress St.

Lyman St.

Spring St.

Pearl St.

0 ___ 0.125 ___ 0.25 mile
0 ___ 0.125 ___ 0.25 kilometer

N
W — E
S

already got rid of it." "Yeah, and I need more," and blah, blah, so now I'm thinking, damn, this guy's serious about what's going on up there.

Despite some trepidation about going to a white "hick town," Sammy loaded up a 1970s Buick he had purchased for $30 and he and "his boys" headed north.

Over the next year, before the police pushed Sammy's crew out of Greenfield, he would make a lot of money, develop a heroin addiction, and meet a woman who would become the mother of three of his children. What Sammy's story in Greenfield would illuminate, however, is how racial stereotypes shaped his relationships. Prior to this, Sammy's interactions with whites were restricted mostly to drug users and institutional authorities, such as police officers, teachers, school counselors, and social workers. In Greenfield, Sammy entered a very white town—of the 14,016 town residents in 1989, 98 percent were white.[11] What Sammy learned about race and ethnicity during this year, he would often describe to me using phrases like, "What was amazing to me" or "You wouldn't believe it."

Sammy and his crew's point of entry in Greenfield was the generational divide between parents and adolescents. Sammy claims his worst fears about white people were reinforced, especially in the beginning, when they would walk along the main strip in downtown Greenfield to a teenage juice bar. He recalls that "everybody's looking at us real crazy, you know, I'd never been in that situation before." From some passing cars, he said people would lean out the window "calling us spics, niggers, and shit like that, and I'm like [to Tee], 'Yo, bro, we need to get the fuck out of here.' And he's like, 'Nah, man, don't worry about them punks.' " Their reception at the club, though, was a different story.

When we go to the club, you know, they play rock 'n' roll and I'm like, "Yo, man, this ain't me, man, we need to go." And Tee's like, "Come on, man, don't mind none of this. We here for one thing, right?" . . . So he starts, you know, introducing me to people. He's like, "Yo, you all want to meet some girls?" . . . So he brings over like six girls, and he's like, "Yo, man, they love Puerto Ricans up here."

Sammy realized in this first encounter that the girls were attracted to an image they had of him and his friends.

> Now they start asking us questions, "Oh, where you all from? Are you in a gang?" . . . Real, you know, real suburban, they don't know nothing about Puerto Ricans . . . probably by TV or something, you know. But they want to be like hip, you know, they want to be into this hip-hop stuff, you know . . . and there's a whole bunch of girls, country girls and boondock girls . . . and it was amazing the way shit was going on, you know. So that night, he goes um, "Well, these girls want us to go over to their house" and . . . when we get to this house, it's a mansion. . . . Now [this girl], her father owns oil companies and owns a whole bunch of gas stations. This house was amazing. It was like three houses put in one, you know what I mean?

The social class of the youths that Sammy met in Greenfield is unclear. Were the white girls truly from rich families or from the white working class, or both, since mixed-class friendships are more likely to occur in small white towns? Was the house a mansion or just a large house, and did the girl's father own oil companies or a gas station? And what did Sammy mean that the girls were "country" or "boondock" girls? Just as the white youths were looking at Sammy and his friends through lenses developed in segregated white communities, Sammy was looking at them through his own lens acquired from living in segregated racial minority communities. The white woman Sammy would eventually develop a relationship with lived in a trailer and her father was a heroin addict, suggesting that at least some of the youths he hung out with were, to use Joseph Howell's concept, hard-living working-class.[12] But Sammy's stories also indicate that many of the teenagers were bringing hundreds of dollars with them to buy cocaine at parties. While this is hardly a marker of social class, it was not something that Sammy was accustomed to at parties in Springfield.

Irrespective of social class, Sammy's adventures in Greenfield provided a glimpse into white privilege. For instance, Sammy tells several stories about police harassment, such as being videotaped by the police as an intimidation strategy and being told by police that since there weren't any Puerto Ricans in Greenfield, any white friends they had there must be "wiggers," a term Sammy explains as "a nigger lover." These experiences with police were in sharp contrast to what Sammy would witness one evening at a party at one of the white teens' homes, when her parents were vacationing in Hawaii.

> [The police] did come [to the house] once, saying that they heard a whole bunch of noise when nobody was making any noise. . . . Now everybody's geeked up [high on coke] . . . so the [kids say to the police] "What are you talking about making noise?" and blah, blah. "Oh no, we just had a call and we just wanted," and they trying to look around. But Samantha ain't trying to let 'em in, you know. . . . So they talking to Samantha and they're like, "Oh you know you ain't supposed to have these people in your home" and blah, blah. And Samantha's like whatever and just slams the door in their face, you know. And I'm like, "Yo, man, they going to come and bust that door." She says, "Ah, they can't touch my property."

To Sammy's astonishment, the police left and no arrests were made. He had no personal experience with property rights and had never seen anyone talk to police like that before, or at least not without consequences.

Sammy's stories suggest that white adolescent girls saw Sammy and his friends as exotic and hip. Their interest in them marked the contours of adolescent rebellion—a desire to explore the forbidden and invert white racist attitudes and beliefs. After all, Sammy and his Franklin Street friends were Greenfield parents' worst nightmare— Puerto Ricans coming to town to sell their kids drugs. But the scenario Sammy describes is not unusual. White teenagers from working-class and professional homes do copious amounts of drugs in high school—these white kids did not need Puerto Ricans to be deviant.[13] Being hip or street is an identity that appeals to adolescents struggling to develop identities that are separate from and often in opposition to those of their parents. Sammy's street disposition, his access to potent drugs, and his sexualized, pleasure-seeking identity were seductive to these youngsters, the very type of influence that their parents fear and that galvanizes police scrutiny.

But it wasn't only the girls. Sammy described other incidents with white boys, for whom the exoticism of Puerto Ricans from the "big city" was also evident:

> So I had a little bit of weed and I told 'em, "Yo, try this." And they're like, "Oh shit, man, where you get this from?" and "Ya'all guys are from New York, right?" . . . and "No, I'm from Springfield." "Oh, ya'll from the city, ya'all from the city" [laughter]. And then they are talking about Springfield like it was, you know, a big ghetto looking like, you know, and I'm like, oh, I was just amazed at the whole thing, about how these people was acting when we was around them and everything.

Learning a lesson that could have come from a marketing textbook, Sammy realized that selling a product is about selling an image. He and his friends seduced these white youngsters through claims to "street authenticity," even taking them on a "field trip" to Springfield.

> So me trying to keep the customers and stuff, I was real cool with these guys, you know, I told 'em, "Yo, tomorrow I'm going to pick you up and bring you down to Springfield and I'm going to show you around." . . . And when I go up there, I see this big old crowd, right? I'm like what the heck is going on? . . . So we drive up and two hockey players, they come over, "Hey, what up?" blah, blah, acting real bad. He like, "Yo, you going to take us down to Springfield, right?" I like, "Yeah, man, I told you that's what I came up here for, to pick you up." He turns around and goes, "See, I told you, I told you [laughter], I told you, I told you. So we leaving?" Like, "Yeah, come on." So we drive off, now I'm thinking, look at this shit, you know, he must have tried to pull a little points with these kids or something.

When they reached Springfield, Sammy was unsure what to do with them.

> Now I'm just driving around and now I didn't really want to introduce them to anybody 'cause they like really hick-like, you know. So I brung them to Mom's house. And he's like, "Yo, man, when we walk out there, they're not going to jump us or anything" . . . this is when we used to live [in] the projects, there's a whole bunch of black people. So they walking all scared and I'm like, "Yo, man, relax." . . . Now Mom's got a big old feast, you know how Mom cooks. . . . You know Mom can't talk English and shit, right. So I'm like, yeah, that's my mom. . . . It's amazing the way they acting and everything, you know.

Wide-eyed white youth, eager to explore the forbidden as it had been fed to them through Hollywood and in their white communities, embraced the images that Sammy and his friends were spinning. In one conversation I asked Sammy if he and his friends were playing it up in the presence of the white youths in Greenfield.

> Oh yeah, we played the whole thing, I mean we was acting more ghetto than what we was. We was talking slangs and giving dabs every time we said so. It was crazy, yo, it was crazy. Then we used to talk about it, you know, when we used to drive back, we like, "Yo, did you see the way that girl was acting when, when I was talking?" You know, we used to talk about it and stuff, that's why I say it was amazing every time I went up there, it was like a big school for them. It was a school of hip for them.

While Sammy may have enjoyed the company of white youths, as a shrewd businessman he also kept his eye out for older, heavier drug users, to enhance his profits. For a short time, Sammy made very good profits, enough that even his older brother Julio, working at a factory in Springfield, began investing in Sam's business to supplement his own wages—giving Sammy money to buy larger quantities of cocaine and marijuana. Sammy found some hard-core drug users in Greenfield who traded merchandise for drugs, including guns. Sammy acquired a Tech 9, two .45 caliber pistols, and a sawed-off shotgun from some of these customers. Again, drawing on cultural stereotypes to advance his interests, when a few of his customers refused to pay their debts, Sammy and Tee showed up at their houses with guns to scare them into compliance.

> Now I was in the car and he went and knocked, and the guys go . . . "Nah, we ain't got your money, we told you, we ain't got no money to pay you." So he goes uh, "Yo, the owner of the shit is right there and he want his money." Yo, these guys when they saw me [with the guns], they ran in the house, and they was like, "No, tell 'em not to kill us, tell 'em not to kill us." They screaming the shit out, you know, and I'm like, "Yo, man, tell 'em to shut the fuck up, I'm not going to do shit to them." I'm panicking myself right now, you know, thinking they going to call the cops and shit. . . . I'm like "Yo, man, you better talk to these people, man." They come out with VCR, TV in their hands, they like, "Yo, take anything you want, don't kill us, don't kill us." I'm like, "Yo, man, I ain't going to do shit to you-all, man, I just want my money." . . . These guys are going by movie shit, you know, everything that they see in the movie they thought that I was going to do and shit.

While Sammy's primary interest in Greenfield was to make money—or as Tee kept saying to him, "We here for one thing, right?"—the recognition that Sammy received was also important, especially when we consider his social status as a Puerto Rican school dropout. Sammy developed friendships as well as customers, and a sense of power that stemmed from inverting the social and racial hierarchy. However, within a year, Sammy's trips to Greenfield ceased for two reasons—the local police were targeting him and his heroin use increased considerably. Besides, the youngsters' attempts to "act ghetto" were wearing on Sammy. Exasperated with the whole scene, he described how he eventually busted the ruse he had spent months creating.

I used to lecture 'em about what they was doing wrong. It was like . . . "You want to be cool but not be a fool and fuck up everything that's around you." They were like, "Oh, I thought we was hanging out and being rough, rugged, and raw" and talking all this shit, you know. Like "No, it ain't about that, man, you know what I'm saying, you want to be hip and you want to be a little ghetto, but yet you acting, you breaking shit and acting like you can't control yourself. So now you changing all this, you want this to be a ghetto, believe me, you want to live in a ghetto, you go live in my house and I'll live up here."

The status Sammy acquired in Greenfield faded quickly as the police pushed his friends and him out of the community. His moment of adolescent idolatry rooted in the inversion of the social and racial hierarchy was short-lived. He did take something from Greenfield with him: Cheryl, a white girlfriend, who gave birth to twin girls shortly after she and Sammy moved into a working-class community outside Springfield. But Sammy's drug habit was blossoming and his life was increasingly organized around heroin use on the streets in Springfield. This juncture in Sammy's life was perhaps best captured by Julio a few years later when he confronted his youngest brother. "You know, bro," Julio lectured, "one time you looked hip using those drugs and hanging out and shit, but now you starting to look just like another old junkie."

URBAN COWBOY CAPITALISM

In Elijah Anderson's book *Code of the Street*, he explains that the code is "a set of informal rules governing interpersonal public behavior, particularly violence," in areas of concentrated urban poverty, and that "at the heart of the code is the issue of respect—loosely defined as being treated 'right' or being granted one's 'props' (or proper due) or the deference one deserves." He continues by explaining the code as "a cultural adaptation to the profound lack of faith in the police and judicial system—and in others who would champion one's personal security."[14] Anderson's description is similar to what I observed as a form of street justice, where one claims and preserves one's personal interests, social status, and respect through violence. Attributing patterns of street violence to a breakdown in law enforcement and a general mistrust in the police, however, seems to miss a more salient explanation. Interpersonal and cultural codes of violence are shaped by the unregulated drug market, what I refer to as urban cowboy capitalism.

Behavioral patterns surrounding competitive drug markets in urban areas are what social life looks like when lucrative free markets take hold without any legal and institutional regulation of the market.[15] In urban drug markets, power and control are acquired largely through violence, or the threat of violence, and the "might is right" philosophy shapes a street culture in which interpersonal relationships are defined. Still, militant control of markets is moderated through formal and informal negotiations among varying social groups and through a normative set of neighborhood routines. For instance, in *Off the Books,* Sudhir Venkatesh shows how licit and illicit economies coexist in poor urban communities and how, in lieu of legal and governmental market regulations, social and economic life is informally regulated through a variety of stakeholders, including gang leaders who organize the drug trade.[16]

Maintaining organizational discipline, however, is difficult in an unregulated market environment, where violence is valued and opportunities for acquiring status and respect are limited. In this context, the rugged individualist of the past becomes the defiant individualist, whose lawless behavior is paramount in the pursuit of status and respect.[17] Groups form around mutual self-interest—sometimes as street gangs—and the depth of group loyalty is intensified by the risks that accompany lawlessness and drug market competition; yet, at the same time, the defiant individualist character erected from the culture of urban cowboy capitalism poses a threat to group loyalties. The challenges Manny Torres faced in managing his drug operation illustrate these individualist-organizational tensions.

Manny's rules were constantly broken within his organization—even among his inner circle. Maintaining a disciplined and obedient workforce was difficult, if not impossible. Despite a demotion and temporary exile to Puerto Rico, Aurelio, Manny's closest associate, continued to violate two of Manny's central business principles: he used heroin frequently and drew attention to himself on the street by throwing money around. Similarly, Fausto's heroin use also increased while he was working for Manny. As his heroin habit grew and as he began to see how much money Manny was rolling in, Fausto became bitter, felt exploited, and designed ways to skim profits. Once when Manny was out of town, Fausto robbed him. Seeking validation of his defiant individualism, Fausto even offered to cut me in.

The fragile loyalty to Manny's business and the organizational undercurrent of lawless violence became clear in a series of events that occurred after federal narcotics agents attempted to arrest Manny. It is commonly believed on the streets that Aurelio colluded with federal authorities in setting Manny up for the bust. Aurelio had been arrested a short time previously and Manny had refused to post bond in an effort to break his drug habit in prison. According to Sammy, "That's when [Aurelio] wrote all the statements and everything else. Now, he wrote a map how the stuff came in . . . from New York . . . and up to Mass." In any event, Manny pulled up next to a car at an arranged location in Springfield. He was passed $5,500 in marked bills and was in the process of handing over a large quantity of cocaine when he became suspicious of the peculiar manner by which the narcotics officer in the car lit his cigarette. Manny apparently heard car engines and, with the money and the coke, hit his accelerator in a getaway attempt. Police came from all directions and Manny rammed several cars, resulting in the injury of two officers, one critically. In the last collision, Manny's car turned over and both he and an associate attempted to escape on foot. His associate was apprehended and later given an eighteen- to twenty-year sentence. Manny escaped and managed to avoid detection by staying at his brother's house, which was ironically a stone's throw away from the police station in Springfield. Shortly thereafter, Manny left town and assumed another identity.[18]

The arrest threw the group into chaos as the structure of the organization dissolved and as Manny's ability to enforce discipline was attenuated. Manny tried to maintain control of the organization from a distance, but there was a lot of money at stake: money in safes, money to be collected on the books, drugs to be cashed in, and even the marked $5,500, which Manny had stashed in a pipe in an abandoned house. Manny called a member of his group and told him where he had hidden the money. On the evening that Julio, Sammy, and a few others rented a moving truck to remove Manny's belongings from his home, they slid through a basement window of the abandoned house and took the $5,500 from the pipe. The police, however, pulled the truck over shortly thereafter and took all of the men to the police station to acquire information about Manny. Despite some rough treatment, no information was obtained, while Sammy walked out of the station with the $5,500 carefully hidden in his underwear. Manny, however, would never see a penny of it.

Meanwhile, Fausto and Jorge were busy collecting whatever money they could on the streets and selling the remainder of their inventory. Fausto justified his actions by accusing Manny of being a "greedy motherfucker." He correctly suspected that Manny would not return to Springfield and claimed that Manny wanted them to collect the remaining money on the books, sell the remainder of their stash—somewhere in the neighborhood of a kilo—without any reward or agreement to share the profits with them. Manny, in the view of Fausto and Jorge, was going to tie up loose ends in Springfield and leave them high and dry.

Fausto attempted to outsmart Manny. He reported that he had been in a high-speed car chase with the police and had thrown his supply of cocaine out the window. To verify the story, he and Sammy smashed up their car with a pipe and took it to a remote park and drove it into some trees. But Manny wasn't buying the story; his father and another man showed up in Springfield carrying guns to collect the money. Jorge contacted Fausto to warn him and tell him he had escaped by jumping out of their car at forty miles an hour. Jorge disappeared shortly thereafter to Florida to stay with family until things cooled off. Fausto consulted with his father and they decided to arm themselves and confront Manny's debt collectors. The showdown happened at Juan and Angela's apartment as the older generation worked out the details. Fausto denied taking any money, produced the records he had kept, and stuck to his story about the police chase. Apparently, they all piled into a car and retraced the route of the alleged chase. In the end, Manny and Juan avoided family war and dropped the issue. The prospects for violence, however, stemmed from claims to street justice. After all, when legitimate businesses dissolve, or the head of a family business dies, internal disputes often follow, but, if necessary, are resolved in a court of law. Drug markets are not mediated by legal institutions and, as such, interests are often violently protected. Success in street drug markets may accrue from charismatic leadership, but it also requires ruthlessness.

Alexander Rodríguez, the other dealer besides Manny who stepped into the void created by the arrests of the Acosta brothers, provides another example of urban cowboy capitalism. Alexander's business benefited from Manny's departure and, many years after the attempted bust, the main competition to Alexander's business was ironically Alfredo Acosta's nephew, "Little Acosta." Alexander's control of the market rested on having a good supplier and hired hands to enforce his authority—it did not rest on charisma. Alexander was neither trusted, nor particularly liked, on the street, but he was respected for his business success and his street smarts. Roberto, a street hustler whose stature in the drug business would later grow, talked about robbing one of Alexander's big customers. He planned out the operation and even told some of the guys, including Julio, about his plan. But Roberto was in recovery for drug addiction and eventually decided against it. He didn't want to mess up his recovery, risk losing his domestic life with his common-law wife and kids, and endure the burden of "going to war" with Alexander if he found out.

Alexander's luck, however, did not hold out. Competitive pressures with Little Acosta mounted and Alexander was accused of stealing $125,000 from a safe that belonged to him. In retaliation, Little Acosta drove by the house where Alexander lived with his wife and kids and fired some shots. He also vowed publicly to hunt Alexander down and kill him. Several months later, he found Alexander alone on a back street in the early hours of the morning and stuck a knife in his chest, just missing his heart.

There are countless examples of violent street justice organized around urban cowboy capitalism—in fact, we read and hear about them regularly in the popular press. Participating successfully in this world requires the development of a defiant individualist character and the willingness to participate in a violent culture. But the patterns, routines, dispositions, and skills that characterize street culture are shaped by struggles to capture markets, lawlessly protect them, and compete within the related status hierarchy. Ironically, the use of prisons to battle the urban drug economy has strengthened the violent culture of the streets as well, a topic I take up later.

No one within this drama is more vulnerable to violence than drug dealers themselves, especially smaller drug entrepreneurs (compared to larger corporate drug operations).[19] Throughout my study I heard references to robbing drug dealers. Drug dealers, of course, are convenient targets because they can't turn to the authorities. Roberto, the young recovering heroin addict mentioned above who had plotted to rob Alexander, later established a successful drug business by robbing a drug dealer in New York. Ironically, Alexander set up the robbery for him. Roberto was eager to establish his own drug business and was tired of laboring as a nickel-and-dime man, selling for others. The robbery yielded nearly a kilo of cocaine and provided the initial investment he needed to develop his business. Once he sold the kilo he was awash in cash, which he then reinvested in a wholesale purchase of his product. On the streets, robbery is not simply a practice engaged in by desperate drug addicts, but also a coerced form of venture capital.

DOWNWARD MOBILITY, DRUG ADDICTION, AND CRIME

Just before the attempt to arrest Manny, I noted that Fausto's health seemed to be declining. Dropping in on Fausto at Gladys's house, I wrote in my field notes that Fausto rarely looked happy—his street status seemed to be compromised by anxiety, fatigue, and isolation. As I suspected, his heroin use had escalated, but this wasn't the first time. A few months earlier, he confided his addiction to his father, who relied on a folk remedy. Fausto told Manny that he would be away for a little while, and Juan locked him in a bedroom for three days. Juan went into the room regularly and boxed with Fausto so he could "sweat it out," while his mother provided plenty of chicken soup. Fausto emerged after three days feeling better and returned to work with Manny, but his heroin use continued.

Fausto and Jorge made off with a lot of money after Manny was gone, but the money didn't last long. Fausto's drug habit escalated and his street status fell—a deadly combination. He found himself back on Franklin Street selling dime bags and surrounded by junkies. Fausto's world shifted. During this time he found out he had passed his GED exam, but he was unable to enjoy his accomplishment. He and I met with a counselor at the community college in Springfield to talk about enrollment in the fall, but the dark circles around Fausto's eyes told another story. Unlike before, Fausto was throwing money around. His loss of status resulted in a desperate need to show everyone he was still a player. One afternoon around this time, he and Gladys came to Hartford to collect his last payment for work he had done for me on a research study in Springfield. Over lunch, I noted that Fausto was struggling to maintain his charm, his face was ashen, his eyes receded behind dark circles, and one eye drooped badly. I hated handing over the money. I tried to get Gladys to divulge information when we had a free moment, but he was leaving her in the dark, too.

I saw Fausto only once in the next two and a half months. I tried to find him on several other occasions and was told that he was running, sleeping in various places, robbing jewelry stores. When I saw him, he talked about one of the robberies, expressed concern that he had been videotaped by a security camera, denied that he was drug-addicted, and claimed, instead, that he was only helping out his dope-sick friends. One other time I spoke to him on the phone at a hideout in Westfield, Massachusetts. He was distant and explained that he was "doing what he had to do." Surrounded by people who woke up each day dope-sick, Fausto was the man with the brains and the "heart" to get them through the day. He cooked up the plans and led the way into the stores—check-cashing places and jewelry stores. His status on the streets had changed from drug runner with one of Springfield's most prominent dealers to fearless street maniac willing to do whatever it took to get what he needed.

Sammy was also addicted to heroin at the time and for a few months their lives converged on the streets. Sammy recalled:

Now, Fausto is hooked and, I guess, after a couple months he ran out of money. Now, I'm gettin' in more into the dopes and, hangin' out more, you know, and I'm usin' more and Fausto shows up one day and he's talkin' to [the guys] but he didn't want me to know about it. . . . Next day I go to the bar and I'm like, where the fuck is everybody at, you know. Called Fausto up, Fausto's like, "What's up? What's the matter?" He's all hyper and I'm like, "Yo, man, I'm about to go to your crib, gonna check you out." I go over there, I see all this money and like, "What the fuck, Fausto! What's goin' on?" . . . [One of the other guys] told me, "Oh, we did a robbery last night" and blah, blah. "What you mean, you did what!" "Yeah. We stuck this place up" and I'm like, "What the fuck, Fausto? What you doin'?" So they started showin' me all this money and shit like that and I'm like, "Oh, man! Why you didn't tell me y'all was goin'?" you know, "I would've went down witcha."

Robbing showed "heart"—the willingness to do whatever needed to be done to achieve the goal. Sticking up stores is not an easy hustle to develop; it requires rationalizing or neutralizing one's conscience, managing anxiety, and mustering the courage to act. But like any hustle, the more you do it the easier it gets; in fact, the more you do it, the more the hustle becomes an art that has its own parameters for reflective action in which strategies get refined.

Several robberies followed. Donning ski masks and carrying fake guns, Fausto's crew targeted pawn shops and jewelry stores in the Springfield area. Street drug dealers were not spared Fausto's frenzy. Sammy described:

[Fausto] calls me and he goes, "Yo, let's go do some shit" and we go down Main Street. We got two dealers in the car and Fausto jumps in the backseat and goes, how much you got? He goes, well, I got five bundles and this guy, Fausto starts grabbin' him and fuckin' throwin' him out the window. These guys are like, "No, no! What the fuck! Stop the car! Stop the car!" Fausto's throwin' him out the window, wrestlin', punchin' him. It was crazy. It was crazy and one time we was over at . . . the other side of Jefferson . . . and there was this dude there. He asked him for two bundles and the guy brings the two bundles. Fausto stepped on the car [accelerator] and almost ran the guy over. I'm like, "Yo, Fausto, man, he wasn't even gonna do nothing."

The frequency of the criminal acts increased. Springfield is a small city and Fausto had not only been captured on a few security cameras, he was burning his bridges on the streets as well. His ten-week road to self-destruction ended in the failed bank robbery, which prompted the phone call that introduced this book.

Both drug addiction and the loss of status that Manny's organization provided led to Fausto's decline. I don't want to make light of the former in my rush to illustrate a more sociological explanation. Heroin addiction is a powerful determinant of behavior. As Sammy said about Fausto, "I didn't even believe that he was able to do the things that he was doin', you know. 'Cause it was a whole different Fausto . . . when he was hooked." I agree with Sammy—this was not the Fausto I knew either, which is one of the primary reasons that I continued with my study after the arrest and wrote this book. Fausto's disregard for others around him—his family, friends, Gladys, me—was indicative of the obsessive quality of his life organized around addiction. But prior to Manny leaving town, Fausto's drug use had been bounded by the structure that Manny's organization provided. It was only in the chaos that followed the arrest and the loss of a reliable income that Fausto's behavior changed. Moreover, I recall many conversations with Fausto about his involvement in the drug trade at this time, usually as part of an effort to explore strategies for convincing Fausto to consider an educational alternative. The words that continue to play in my head are, "I'm not on the street corner selling dime bags, Tim, I'm part of an organization."

The breakdown of the group landed Fausto where he feared being the most—back on Franklin Street selling dime bags and rubbing elbows with street junkies. Fausto's street status had fallen and he was faced with the unbearable truth that the road he had traveled since he left high school had led him back to Franklin Street, where gazing at street junkies was like looking into a mirror. When the conditions that had both bounded Fausto's drug use and provided him with an identity as a successful drug dealer dissipated, Fausto refused his place on Franklin Street and developed a new identity as a fearless stickup artist.

During the period leading up to the court date, I met several times with Fausto's assigned public defender to discuss his case. I pointed out that this two-and-a-half-month period was an anomaly in Fausto's life, that he was bingeing on heroin at the time, that he had just finished his GED, that they had used fake guns during the robberies, and that I was sure with drug treatment and opportunities he could turn his life around. I questioned the logic of sending him to prison for a long time at this juncture in his life. I tried to explain the circumstances that led up to the robbery in sociological terms, expounding on the processes of social marginalization and reactions to it. The sociological paradigm obviously had no place in the court of law. His attorney said there was little he could do. There was no doubt about his guilt and, with a large caseload, he had to choose the cases he invested his time in and this one was an "open-shut case."

I contacted character witnesses to speak at the trial in Fausto's behalf. On the morning of the trial, I watched empathetically as the bank tellers filed in, trying to imagine their terror on the day of the robbery. I saw the resentment in their eyes as well as their determination in seeing that Fausto got what he deserved. Noting the contradictions that swelled inside of me, I went forward with my plan to speak in Fausto's behalf. Fausto's brother Julio, his former supervisor from the Boys Club, University of Massachusetts sociologist Michael Lewis, and I spoke at the trial, asking the judge for leniency and elaborating on Fausto's potential. Fausto never looked at any of us that morning; he bowed his head and sobbed quietly through each of our statements. The judge was less than sympathetic, dismissed our statements impatiently, and sentenced Fausto to ten to twelve years. As Fausto parted with his lawyer at the courthouse to board the police van, his lawyer smiled, assured him he would do fine on the inside, but told him to call if anything did come up while he was incarcerated. "And," his attorney added as Fausto was being taken away, "if it makes you feel any better, you should know that all my clients do time."

PART TWO

Jobs

Work spares us from three evils: boredom, vice, and need.

—Voltaire

But if a man doesn't have a job or an income, he has nei-
ther life nor liberty nor the possibility for the pursuit of
happiness. He merely exists.

—Martin Luther King Jr.

Without work, all life goes rotten. But when work is
soulless, life stifles and dies.

—Albert Camus

FIVE

The Block

JULIO PROVIDED me access to the block. After his brother Fausto went to prison, Julio and I spent countless hours driving to prison facilities throughout the state to visit him. My relationship with Julio deepened at just the time his life was falling apart. But it wasn't just Julio who was suffering—the recession of 1991 was a breaking point for many in Springfield and beyond. Preexisting problems became crises, while youth gangs organized in cities across the United States. The conditions that created the ascendancy of youth gangs in Springfield were obvious to anyone paying attention, or certainly if they were paying attention to Barbara Rivera's warning about a "lost generation."[1] The precipitous loss of industrial jobs between 1988 and 1994, the extraordinarily high rate of Puerto Rican youths dropping out of Springfield schools, the growth and organization of the international drug trade, and deeply embedded racism in Springfield converged to create conditions that were ripe for gang proliferation in the mid-1990s. What was perhaps less predictable was that Julio Rivera— the pride of Juan and Angela, the starting lineman for Commerce High, the high school graduate who dreamed of being a doctor— would find himself in the backseat of a car, cruising rival gang territory in the city, with a shotgun perched on a tinted glass window.

There had been no signs of organized youth gangs in Springfield since the mid-1980s when the Latin Kings moved north to Springfield from Connecticut in the early 1990s.[2] Shortly thereafter, intra-gang violence left a member of the Springfield Latin Kings dead. Friends of the victim avenged his death by starting a chapter of Los Sólidos, a gang that already had joined forces with an African American gang in Hartford to push the Latin Kings out of that city. According to Julio, when a Springfield chapter of La Familia was started in prison, they asked "for the blessing" of the Latin Kings to show their respect to the more powerful prison gang. This made La Familia a cousin of the Kings, and by extension, an enemy of Los Sólidos.[3] When Sammy was in prison for driving-related charges in 1993, he joined La Familia and, upon release, found himself in the middle of the 1994–95 Springfield gang wars.

In the meantime, Julio had lost his job as a forklift driver for a reputable Springfield company. After leaving community college and moving in with Clara, Julio worked in a nursery in Connecticut, but also enrolled in a tractor-trailer driving school. Julio had taken out a federal student loan to attend the school but, after completing the courses, lacked the money to take the driver's test and acquire his commercial license (which costs several hundred dollars). While saving money for the test, Julio began working in a warehouse, where he was quickly promoted to forklift driver and earned $13 an hour, a good salary in the early 1990s.[4] Further, Julio supplemented his wage in the drug business—not only did he invest in Sammy's Greenfield drug operation, as discussed earlier, but he also established a connection with one of the Acosta brothers and sold drugs to co-workers. Julio's partner, Clara, supplemented the family wage by receiving welfare benefits and taking care of the home and their daughter, Iris, with the daily assistance of her mother and sisters. Between Julio's working wage, drug money, and welfare assistance, Julio and his family were financially secure. This came to an end in 1993 when Julio lost his job.

Julio was fired because of a fight. A co-worker owed him $78 and refused to pay him the money. According to Julio, "The guy was taking me for a sucker. . . . If I let him take me for a sucker, then others think they can too." Julio, who was training as a boxer at the time, gave the guy an ultimatum and, when his co-worker failed to come up with the money, left him unconscious on the break room floor. The official unemployment rate in the Springfield metropolitan area was approaching double digits at the time and Julio was unable to find another job. He returned to the driving school to take his test, but was told that the one-year period allowed for taking the exam had expired and that he would have to start the course over. Shortly thereafter he joined La Familia.

At six feet one inch, 250 pounds, a former athlete and trained boxer, Julio was not one to tangle with, and besides, his brothers had already established the family name on the streets. Julio was recruited into the gang by his friend Mario, who was older and envisioned that he and Julio would lead the newly formed organization in Springfield. Julio recalled:

> Sammy was already in the gang. . . . I just got in because, you know, I didn't want Sammy fucking up, doing shit. So me and Mario, we checked these guys out. And Mario, he wanted to do it. He said, "Come on, man, we could be the heads." . . . So we went to a meeting with Sammy and, you know, some guys saw me and next thing I know I'm godfather of the Warlords. I had my own special crew and we were the ones who did special missions and shit. My guys were the baddest of the bunch, you know. I had the best fighters and shit.

Julio was doing more than simply fulfilling his big brother role; he was embracing a street identity as a warrior.

To understand the changes in Julio's life, we need to examine the particular interaction between the social conditions changing around him and the personal decisions he was making. Julio had lost his job at a time in which unemployment was on the rise. There were few if any comparable jobs, which threatened his identity as a breadwinner. Julio's identity had been organized around working-class male respectability and the family wage ideology while he was working at the factory—he was the provider for his extended family, the head of the household, the man his father had wanted him to become. However, as the opportunities changed around him, he spent more time on the street, at first to simply make money to take care of his family, but then later as someone to be feared because of his fighting skills. "One-Punch Julio" began to compete with "working provider Julio" as a dominant part of his identity. Of course, one part of one's identity doesn't disappear as the other appears, but changing social conditions—both opportunities and social networks—can nurture different parts of one's identity, or of one's self-potential. Like most of us, Julio struggled to fuse these different parts of himself together within the context of changing social conditions. He strived to be a provider for his family by working and also maintaining a drug connection—and the latter particularly paid off when he lost his job. Joining La Familia, ostensibly to keep an eye on Sammy, and assuming a leadership role in the gang, Julio validated his toughness, his discipline, and his valor. Julio's life was in transition—as social conditions change, individual identities and personal routines often get reorganized.

Julio's gang involvement came to an end after he fired a round of bullets one evening at Los Sólidos members, but not before he had lost a few good friends to the gang wars in 1994–95. In May 1994, a friend of Sammy's and Julio's was shot and killed on the streets by members of Los Sólidos. The friend, a twenty-two-year-old woman, was considered the "godmother" of La Familia and Sammy was at the site when the shooting occurred. In February 1995, a rash of shootings left two more members of La Familia dead, one eighteen, the other nineteen. As godfather of the Warlords, Julio was in the middle of the gang's retaliatory actions.

One afternoon, Julio and Mario were walking along Main Street in the North End when they were confronted by members of Los Sólidos. Main Street turf had been divided up between the Latin Kings, La Familia, and the Ñeta, a newer gang in Springfield, and together they had pushed Los Sólidos out of the North End to the "hilltop" in Springfield's black neighborhoods. Just being on Main Street, especially in the context of the gang war, spelled trouble for Los Sólidos members. Squaring off, Julio thought that one of the guys was reaching for a gun, so he grabbed Mario's gun from his pants and began firing. Julio described what happened:

> I was there with Mario and these guys . . . were talking shit. And I thought we were going to rumble, you see. And this one guy reached in his pants like he had a gun, so I look over at Mario like, what you going to do. Mario had the gun in his pants, but he didn't do nothing. I don't know if this guy was just fronting me or what and I still don't know to this day if he was carrying a piece. But at that time, I thought, well, it's either him or me. So I

grabbed the gun [from Mario] and pointed it at this guy's heart and I pulled the trigger. But, I'm telling you, God must've been looking down right at that moment, bro, I'm telling you. The gun jammed and so I pulled it back like this [demonstrating motion of cocking a gun], the bullet popped out of there, and I just started shooting. These guys were running and I just started shooting, you know.

Julio hit three guys—in the butt, the stomach, and the arm.

After the shooting incident, Julio disappeared to the hills of Villalba, where he stayed for a few months.

That's when I decided to go to PR. I needed some time to think, you know. I needed to get my head together. My father told me to go. So I did, and when I came back I decided to start doing some things differently. You know, I had to take care of my daughter, and well, I was in too deep, bro. I had to change things before I got real fucked up. It was good to get away and start using my head better, you know what I mean?

This would be another turning point in Julio's life.

When Julio returned, he left the gang. Normally, this would require a "beat-down" in which gang members surround the departing member and deliver a barrage of punches for his betrayal. When I asked if this would apply to him, Julio replied, "Ssshhit, who's going to do that shit, bro? Huh? They know that I'd run into them on the street." Julio also got Sammy out. But Julio had established a street reputation and would draw on his street resources at times during the next several years. For instance, a few months after Julio returned from Puerto Rico, he was broke with few places to turn. His drug connection had left for Puerto Rico without notice, Sammy's business had collapsed in Greenfield, and he could no longer rely on gang resources. Christmas was approaching, which is one of the hardest times of the year for unemployed fathers. Jobless, Julio recalls, "I was desperate, bro. I had hit rock-bottom. I felt like I had failed my family, like I had let down my daughter." Without money to buy his daughter gifts, he turned to his childhood friend Elfredo, who was a member of La Familia.

Elfredo had met a Dominican man in jail, a novice who wanted into the drug trade. After both were released, the man contacted Elfredo to purchase $5,000 worth of marijuana. Elfredo subsequently presented Julio with two options—to sell the pot together; take the $5,000 and "re-up," or reinvest it in more marijuana or cocaine as part of a long-term profit venture; or to rob the man of his money. "I told 'em I can't wait," Julio replied. They set the Dominican man up by arranging a time and place to make the exchange. The place was an apartment that was rented by La Familia and, when the man arrived with the money, Julio shoved the barrel of a gun against the man's temple and took the $5,000. The event further solidified Julio's street reputation, so that even when his drug connection did finally return from Puerto Rico, Julio, still angry at his abrupt departure, refused to pay $500 that he owed them. "I looked them in the eye and told 'em, you ain't getting your money. You left me here empty. So you do what you got to do." His connection let it slide, which Julio attributed to the reputation he had earned on the street. "I got known out there, and people didn't fuck with me after that."

Julio's life hung in the balance at the time he and I were making our trips to state prisons to visit his brother Fausto—more so, per-haps, than either of us realized. Looking back, it is clear that one of the defining aspects of Julio's life trajectory is luck. In July 1996, less than a year after Julio had left La Familia, ten of its members were indicted on drug and firearm charges, including Mario. Fed-eral agents had threatened one member of the gang with arrest and thereby solicited his participation in attending meetings wired. Once they had collected enough evidence, they used the federal racke-teering statute, RICO, to prosecute the gang members.[5] Sentences varied, but as one of the gang's leaders, Mario received a twenty-years-to-life sentence. In an eighteen-month span, Julio had been lucky on two occasions—he had shot but not killed three men on Main Street and he had left the gang before the federal investigation. Had the gun not jammed when it was pointed at the heart of his gang rival or had he remained godfather of the Warlords in 1996, Julio too might be spending his life behind bars.

HANGING OUT ON THE BLOCK

After the "holiday robbery" of the Dominican man, Julio turned to his friend Jorge Rodríguez to sell cocaine, while he looked for work. Like Jorge, Julio didn't use drugs. Together, they could rapidly empty a thirty-pack of Budweiser, but neither of them indulged in "the product." For Julio, marijuana made him feel silly and cocaine made him anxious and want to fight. He avoided both, and maintained some moralistic distance from others who indulged. He was simply taking care of business to support his family and still attempting to retain some semblance of working-class respectability.

> I'll do whatever to take care of my family, you know what I'm saying? I don't care what I got to do, my family comes first. I've always worked, bro, but if I'm not working I still got to take care of them, you know. I'm not going to do this forever, but it'll hold me over, you know, and my family will eat.

It was at this time that Julio agreed to introduce me to some of the guys he was hanging out with on the block.

The block was a small enclave set apart in one of Springfield's wealthier neighborhoods. We might think of the block as a post-1980s phenomenon. As the reach of metropolitan areas continued to grow with urban sprawl at the end of the twentieth century, housing opportunities for racial minorities opened up in more city neighborhoods and in the inner ring of suburbs as white flight occurred. In Springfield, the number of census tracts with at least 40 percent of residents living below the poverty line remained the same between 1990 and 2000, but the population residing in these high-poverty areas declined by 20 percent. Sixteen percent fewer Hispanics lived in these areas in 2000 than in 1990.[6] As Puerto Ricans moved out of high-poverty neighborhoods, pockets of poverty emerged within wealthier neighborhoods in the city and within the inner ring of suburbs, which of course facilitated even more white flight.

Interestingly, just as the Franklin Street drug spot had been located where there was easy access off the interstate highway, another quarter of a mile along the same highway, an exit led into a labyrinth of streets that surrounded the block. It was as if a piece of the Latino drug trade was on the march, migrating east along the interstate, almost equal distance from the Brightwood neighborhood to Franklin Street to the block. According to information accumulated by the Springfield Planning Department, the block was located in the fourth wealthiest neighborhood in Springfield, even though it had the largest percent increase in the Puerto Rican population in the 1980s.[7] Still, as the 1990s began, only 19 percent of the neighborhood was Latino and only 13 percent lived below the poverty line. But in the corner of the neighborhood where the block was located, 40 percent of the population was Latino, nearly one-quarter lived below the poverty line, and median household income was one-half ($20,250) of the larger neighborhood.[8] Driving into the heart of this enclave to the block, one would never have believed they were in the fourth wealthiest neighborhood in Springfield.

In a city that had largely turned its back on them, Puerto Rican men utilized public spaces in Springfield to create their own identities, often in opposition to school authorities and police, and to white-dominant culture in general. The block was one of these places. Warm weather brought a group of men to the block each evening for Budweiser, laughs, and camaraderie. Occasionally, there were police and DTs, narcotics detectives, who drove through the neighborhood, but for the most part the block felt like claimed space that the authorities had ceded, at least temporarily, to this group of young men. It was an open-air market for drinking beer, smoking blunts, and snorting cocaine, a place where salsa and merengue music blared from large stereo speakers, where people spoke Spanish, and it was a place to have laughs—and lots of them.

In Paul Willis's book *Learning to Labour,* he explains how having a "laff" is central to the oppositional identity of a group of working-class youth in a school in Manchester, England:

> The space won from the school and its rules by the informal group is used for the shaping and development of particular cultural skills principally devoted to "having a laff." The "laff" is a multi-faceted implement of extraordinary importance in the counter-

school culture. . . . In many respects the "laff" is the privileged instrument of the informal, as the command is of the formal.[9]

Similarly, the men on the block gathered to party and laugh—to laugh at one another, at police and DTs, at drug addicts, at white and black people, at women, at gays and lesbians. The "privileged instrument of the informal" was a means of acquiring respect. It allowed for social jockeying within the group and created roving targets for being the butt of the joke. And yet sharing a laugh promoted community and solidarity—it was their space, Puerto Rican space, defiantly marked off from the white-dominated city. The only white people I ever saw on the block were there to buy drugs, excluding of course the police.

The police were the guardians of the larger city—the protectors of the status quo reflecting a history of white, largely Irish, leadership. While their interventions were sparing—most likely because the block was newly emerging territory for defiant Puerto Rican behavior—they did interact with the men on the block, and many of the laughs in the evening were directed at them, reinforcing the men's oppositional identities. When the drug trade had been located on Franklin Street, I heard similar stories about the police. Sammy and Fausto referred to the police by nicknames, like El Bigote (the mustache) and Clark Kent, and they laughed hysterically when telling a story about a friend who drove by them three times on Franklin Street pumping his fist in the air as if he were taking victory laps, while one, two, and then three police cars chased him.

On the block, stories and laughs about the police were common, and they reflected the conflict that existed between this minority population and white power. The following conversation between Jaime, Benedicto, Omar, and myself illustrates this conflict, as well as how shared oppositional identity is derived from the laugh.

> JAIME: I went to the courthouse yesterday for that warrant I got and they said they didn't have anything on it. You know, they checked their computer and said it ain't here. So I said, "Okay, excuse me, I'll see you later." [laughter]

TIM: What was that case about?

JAIME: Oh, what a fucking day that was. Alexandria [Jaime's girlfriend] wanted to buy a car from this guy. So I go over there to test-drive it, I get a few blocks down the road and here comes a cruiser. The car's not registered. . . . So these motherfuckers pull me over, check me out, and give me a warrant for driving an unregistered car. Then they call a tow truck and take the car away and tell me to get lost. So I start walking back and I get a few blocks down the road and all of a sudden here come three cruisers, whoop, whoop, whoop. I'm like, what the fuck? And then these motherfuckers are yelling, "Down on the ground, down on the ground!" One guy grabs me and throws me down and pushed his knee in the back of my head. And I'm laying there like what the fuck is going on now, you know? And they grab my arms, here come the fucking cuffs. Now I got my hands behind my back, this motherfucker's knee on my head, and then they want my ID and they're pissed because it's not in my back pocket. So I'm like, it's in my shirt pocket with a warrant because some other motherfuckers just pulled me over. You know what I'm saying? Motherfucker's knee's bearing down on my head, hands behind my back, and my fucking ID's in my shirt pocket! [laughter] So this motherfucker takes his knee off me, rolls me over, looks at my ID, and says, "Oops, wrong guy. Sorry, he looked just like you." Then they're like brushing me off, apologizing and shit. One of 'em says, "Sorry man, if I had a dollar I'd buy you a beer." I'm like, "I don't want your motherfucking beer, I want to go home, sit down in my fucking living room, and get as far away from you motherfuckers as I can." [raucous laughter]

OMAR: That's like what happened to Bene and me.

Looking uncomfortable, Omar turns to Benedicto to continue the story.

BENEDICTO: Yeah, just the other day, we're walking right down here [points down the road]. And here comes the cruisers.

TIM: Why?

BENEDICTO: Because they know us. So Omar throws his beer. And they're like, "I saw that, I saw that." But I put mine under my shirt like this.

Because of Bene's girth, he can set the can of beer on top of his belly under his shirt without it being visibly detected.

BENEDICTO: And I say, "What seems to be the problem, Officer?" [laughter] But they're worried about Omar. They know Omar's a runner.

Omar starts shaking his wrist and jumping up and down with apparent joy and discomfort at being in the spotlight.

BENEDICTO: They know he be jumping over fences and running under clotheslines and through the alleys and shit. So this cop is pointing his club at Omar and he's like, "Hey, don't you move, you stay right there, don't you move." [raucous laughter] And then they like, "Well, we're going to let you go this time, but we be watching you."

TIM: So they were just fucking with you?

BENEDICTO: Shit, that's their job to fuck with us. [laughter]

Defiant identities come through in the stories—Jaime refused the officer's apology, Bene hid his beer under his shirt, and Omar could outrun any cop on the force—and their opposition to city authorities was shared in laughter.

While all of the men who gathered on the block shared an ethnic identity, their motives and even their employment status varied somewhat. The block was a place to party, to have fun, and, although it was also a staging ground for Jorge's inner group to go to the bars to conduct business later that night, most of the men who hung out there were not part of the Jorge's late-night drug operation. Several indulged in cocaine on the block and some left with small quantities in their pockets to deal to friends and co-workers, but they didn't pile into cars later that night to go to the bars. Instead, the men on the block represented the gamut of employment opportunities available to young Puerto Rican men in Springfield. Only a couple worked in good-paying unionized jobs in the construction, trucking, and metal-working industries. A few worked on the books in warehouses, assembly plants, fast-food restaurants, and in the tobacco fields; others worked off the books, mostly in roofing, construction, warehouses, and household-moving jobs, while the remainder worked in the illicit underground economy dominated by the drug trade.

The men's different locations within the tiered employment structure provided important sources of information about job opportunities, which several of the men took advantage of. Still, Jorge's drug business was at the center of the activities. Jorge always had a small group of men working for him, even though his cast was constantly changing. Some of the men were less attached to the labor force, some were between jobs, and some were even working day jobs, although this was rare since the nights ran long and, at times, ended when the morning sun appeared—"breaking night." A few of Jorge's brothers were part of his network—Benedicto, who was mentally challenged and lived with his mother, and Mundo, whose storytelling kept us in stitches throughout the night. Bene's large-bellied laugh could always be heard above the noise of the block, and when I drove up, he was always the first to yell some variation of "Ahhhh, it's Timbo, we're going to party tonight!" Bene loved to party—to snort, smoke, and drink—to the point of annoying many of the men, especially his brothers, and losing an eye in a bar fight a few years later.

Mundo, skinny as a rail—or, as he used to say, "I'm 135 pounds wet"—also loved to party, often snorting cocaine until the early morning hours. But Jorge was the maestro of the evening. The youngest of five brothers and two sisters, Jorge had assumed his brother Alexander's drug business when I first arrived on the block, while Alexander was locked up for a small drug possession charge. Jorge was a smooth operator, whose carefree life integrated the demands of his business with loyalty to "his boys." At the core of his identity was an "I don't give a fuck" attitude that was manifested in a laid-back character who enjoyed a perpetual Budweiser buzz, the companionship of his changing networks of friends, nightly games of 8-ball, merengue and salsa on the dance floor, and women. Jorge decided who went to the bar and in what cars, who carried the cocaine, where we went, and even when the night ended. Moreover, Jorge paid for everything throughout the night. He paid cover charges to get into clubs or after-hours parties, bought everyone's beers (even though he usually sent someone else to actually purchase them), and paid for food in between the bars' closing and the after-hours' opening. Jorge enjoyed being in control, throwing around money, and taking care of everyone.

Jorge particularly took care of anyone who was working for him at the time. When they weren't on the block or at the bars, they were often shopping at the mall, riding motorcycles, or finding numerous other ways to have fun that were always bankrolled by Jorge. In the earlier stage of my street ethnography, life on the block and at the bars looked like one big party—drinking; getting high; laughing; "cracking" on one another; shopping; playing dominoes; fighting; dancing; listening to music; fucking; swimming; playing volleyball, basketball, or handball; and cruising for *chicas*. Jorge took pleasure in organizing these activities, in acquiring and sharing resources with others, and in the power and status that his central role in these activities gave him. Moreover, he provided an alternative to the toil of low-wage work and a place for men who were laid off, like Julio, to make money. Jorge took seriously his attitude about not being serious about anything—and he projected this as an image that challenged the identities of men working in dead-end, low-wage jobs. "I'm not going to be anybody's slave," he was fond of saying.

About six months after my street ethnography began, Alexander was released from prison and he resumed his place at the head of the drug organization. But Jorge remained his partner and any changes that occurred due to Alexander's release were imperceptible. Jorge continued in his role at the front of the organization, managing personnel and nightly activities. Alexander took care of bigger customers, but remained largely in the background, sometimes surfacing on the block for a few laughs, sometimes at a bar for a game of 8-ball, and almost always later in the night for some soup at an after-hours.

The period I spent on the block provided an opportunity to see how the drug business intersected with other jobs, and how in the social spaces between the streets and work, these men negotiated status and respect with one another.

SOCIALLY BOUNDED RESPECT

Jorge was the embodiment of the streets. He articulated the cultural boundary between work and drug dealing, lived by his wits, and commanded respect for outsmarting the system. Even in the face of aggressive police and judicial enforcement, Jorge refused to show any cracks in his demeanor or his strategy. This was evident one afternoon when, sitting in a crowded living room, I asked Jorge about his court cases. He was facing two charges, a state charge for gun possession and a more serious federal charge for transporting drugs across state lines, stemming from his earlier involvement with Manny. The rumor was that Manny had signed a statement against Jorge and a few others in an effort to reduce his long prison sentence.

Jorge's state case had been postponed until his federal case was heard and Jorge took the opportunity to be sure that everyone present understood the conditions of the $10,000 bail he had posted. He had seen his lawyer earlier that day and pulled out a document and asked me to read it aloud. Raucous laughter filled the room when I reached the line about refraining from excessive use of alcohol. In addition to submitting to random urine tests for illicit drug use, Jorge was also expected to be working for a local cleaning service. I had known Jorge for a year, during which time both cases had been pending and Jorge had yet to work one day. Anticipating my response, Jorge produced a check from the cleaning service identified on the form. With a triumphant grin, Jorge explained that he had worked out an arrangement with the manager of the business. He paid the manager the amount of the check in cash, along with a small fee, in return for a handwritten check. Jorge enjoyed the laughter and the respect that his wits earned him among the men in the room.

As the afternoon gave way to evening, more young men came into the apartment, and with each new arrival, Jorge again presented the check and repeated the story. When Jaime, Jorge's sister's boyfriend, showed up for an after-work Budweiser, Jorge did the same. Jaime was exhibiting the residue of a long, hot day of furniture delivery—soiled pants, sweat-stained shirt, scraggly hair.

JORGE: Yo, I get off [work] in thirty minutes. It's been a long
    day.

JAIME: What's this?

JORGE: My paycheck. I'll be off in thirty minutes—this is just
    my break time. [laughter]

JAIME: What? He wrote this out for you?

Jaime, with obvious strain in his face, forced himself to laugh along with the others, but the interaction emphasized the cultural boundary between paid employment and the streets. Jaime was playing by the rules, deriving a moral identity from the cultural expectations of work, but he couldn't make enough money to pay his bills. Instead, he relied on Jorge to supply him with small amounts of cocaine to sell in order to supplement his income. Jaime derived his identity in contrast to Jorge and other drug dealers: he rejected the streets in an effort to derive working-class respectability—to be a workingman taking care of his family—and yet ironically, he was dependent on Jorge to make ends meet.

The humiliation that Jorge foisted upon Jaime that afternoon, by parading his success in beating the system while Jaime wore the exhaustion of a long, hot day of labor, went deeper than met the eye. The frustration of Jaime's work life extended beyond the monotonous routines of manual labor and inadequate pay to finding work that treated him with respect. In fact, Jaime had traded better pay for more humane working conditions. In his prior job, he was making $9 an hour, posting and tracking deliveries on a computer. When the company was sold, the new management increased labor discipline intended to boost productivity, which Jaime's labor union did little to resist.

You know, they took the food machine out of there and then cut our breaks so we wouldn't have time to go get food. They wouldn't let us drink anything—you know, like a soda . . . it got bad. If we were one minute late we got a point. They had this policy, if you get nine points, you get canned. . . . I mean they treated us like children. When we went out to take a cigarette break, when we came back in we had to draw these pins from this container and the pins had a color on the bottom—yellow or red—and if you drew the red pin, they would frisk you. This guy was fucking with us; I mean, I really liked my job before he came. I had it made, but he fucked things up.

Jaime left this job for a lower-paying, nonunionized job with no health insurance and just one week of vacation, which started only in his second year of employment, but to him the trade-off was worthwhile simply because management didn't subject him to the same scrutiny and humiliation as his previous employer. Experiences like these gave more currency to Jorge's rejection of work and his refusal "to be anybody's slave."

Jorge also inadvertently provided a safety net for many of the men on the block. If they lost a job or quit, they could always fall back on Jorge in the interim before finding another job. Moreover, they could lower their thresholds of tolerance in the workplace by refusing to put up with what they considered to be unreasonable working conditions. Many of the men cycled in and out of Jorge's drug operation during the first few years I was on the street.

Julio had utilized Jorge's safety net on a few occasions, once after he had left a job for a national trucking company because of what he considered to be unbearable working conditions. He had returned to Springfield and was dealing drugs in the evening and looking for work during the day. A temporary agency assigned him to an assembly plant, as he described to Edgar, a man in his late twenties working for Jorge while on disability leave from his job, and me.

> JULIO: I was working seven to five-thirty putting basketballs and shit in boxes.
> TIM: How much were they paying you?
> JULIO: Five bucks an hour.
> EDGAR: Ah, fuck that shit.
> JULIO: Yeah, bro, they had me standing there all fucking day putting these fucking balls in boxes. I said, what did I spend all my time in [driving] school, to do this? This is not what I went to school for. I said fuck this.
> EDGAR: You quit?

JULIO: What you expect? I told 'em I can drive trucks but they send me down there to do that shit. Yeah, I quit. What you think?

Julio invoked his ethnic identity to describe his threshold of tolerance.

You know why us Puerto Ricans have so much trouble getting jobs? It's because we don't take no shit. I'm not going to stand there from seven to five-thirty for five bucks an hour and put up with somebody yelling at me and shit. If someone gets in our faces, we don't back down, we don't put up with that shit. But the Vietnamese and the Russians, they put up with everything. The bosses get in their faces and scream at them, and they don't say nothing. They take it. We're not like that. We don't back down. The people up there [at the packaging plant], they are all shoving those balls in those cartons as fast as they can to get a bonus. If you put so many balls in the boxes you get a little more pay. Nah, man, I didn't go to school all that time to do this.

Julio's ethnic advantage in this situation was obviously tied to the privileges of citizenship, but Julio also defined what he was willing to tolerate in the workplace, and he, Edgar, and others did so by relying on Jorge when they walked away from jobs. Jorge became their safety net and provided them with leverage to reject poor pay and inadequate working conditions, and to confront exploitive bosses. In another situation, Sammy was working under the table for a contractor who lashed out at him for not working fast enough and made racial slurs about "fucking spics." Sammy walked off the job and rejoined Jorge on the streets. Other men on the block also followed this pattern.

Jorge had achieved status and respect on the streets and derived satisfaction from his accomplishments . . . or so I thought. One evening, Jorge, Julio, and I were shooting pool, having a few beers, getting an early start on the night. At this stage of my work, I was enamored by how well Jorge had made a life for himself on the streets and in the drug trade, and as we moved around the table in a light-hearted game of 8-ball, I decided to explore Jorge's success with him.

TIM: Jorge, man, you got it made, you're a smooth operator who
  seems to have life figured out.

JORGE: What you mean?

TIM: I mean, look at you, you got money, you got nice clothes,
  you got a lot of respect, you party every night. I mean, it
  looks to me like you got it made.

Jorge looked distressed and annoyed by my observation. The light-
hearted nature of the moment quickly changed.

You think I like living like this? I live like this because I'm a
fuck-up. I fucked my life up. I dropped out of school, I got no
education, I do this shit because I can't do anything else. I fucked
up and I'm not proud of it. I ain't got shit. I'd give this up in a second to have what you got.

I was caught off-guard by Jorge's remarks. How could someone who
had seemingly taken the conditions of his life and woven them into
patterns of hedonistic play and economic prosperity, for which he
was admired and respected, harbor such self-contempt? Charisma
emanated from Jorge's laughter, his steps on the dance floor, his
double-bank shots on the pool table, his large wad of dollar bills, and
his childlike playfulness. But beneath this lurked self-repudiation for
making bad choices that my presence elicited. I was white, privileged, educated, and confident in most situations, and despite Jorge's
success in establishing himself within the social constraints of his life,
my presence reminded him of his "failures." Moreover, in my
socially secure location in the world, I could indulge and admire
Jorge's achievements, but to Jorge, this was his world—it was not
exotic, it was often monotonous, and it did not seem as hedonistic to
him, I suspect, as it did to me.

Jorge reminded me that the social world is more complex than my
oversimplified observation suggested. Jorge was still a ninth-grade
dropout who could barely read and write; he lived his life in defiance
of the law, and his freedoms had been taken away from him by incarceration before, and would be again. In my eyes Jorge had crafted a
place for himself that was self-validating and accomplished; in

Jorge's eyes, he was a "fuck-up" and my presence and the presence of the broader white world evoked his feelings of self-contempt.

Jorge maintained both views of himself simultaneously. In his social world, he had achieved respect as a successful drug dealer and hedonist, who indulged himself in masculine pleasures (beer drinking, sexual conquest, accomplished pool playing, dancing). As his brother Mundo would say years later, Jorge loved being "a big shot." And for the time being, Jorge had managed to avoid self-defeating, dead-end, poorly paid jobs. Still, Jorge had internalized the racial and class hierarchy and blamed himself for his location within it. Respect, Jorge reminded me, is socially bounded. Within all social locations, there are cultural practices that confer respect, and often they are valued in contrast, or even in opposition, to cultural practices in other social locations. Nonetheless, the ubiquitous influences of the dominant culture are powerful and difficult to defy or escape, and these practices and ideology, central to the organization of our social institutions, affirm and privilege the identities of whites, particularly white professionals, and particularly white professional men. My presence reminded Jorge more of who he was not than of who he was.

A similar dynamic, illustrating socially and culturally bounded respect, played out in a late-night conversation that occurred years later between Jorge, Alexander, Julio, Fausto, and myself. In this case, however, Fausto adopted a more sociological perspective in challenging the others' perceptions about their lives and their freedoms. At the time, Julio was driving a truck and earning a union wage, Jorge was recently released from prison and had resumed his place dealing drugs with Alexander, and Fausto was working an off-the-books construction job. Fausto combined the style of an evangelical preacher and a prizefighter as he stood toe-to-toe with each and lectured them about social inequality in an intense exchange that began at three-thirty in the morning and lasted until the sun came up.

Fausto challenged them to see racism in their lives, to understand how opportunities are limited, and to examine the self-hate that he argued they carried within themselves. The argument ensued with the others dismissing Fausto's claims and insisting that he was a "fuck-up" like the rest of them. Throughout the argument, Fausto would check in with me. "How am I doing, pops? Do I sound okay?"

Receiving affirmation, he would bound back into the ring and resume his verbal jabs and hooks. In many ways he saved his most vicious confrontation for his brother Julio, who had achieved the most success.

> You think because you drive a truck and you making some money, you all that, bro? And let me tell you, bro, I'm proud of you, as my brother, I'm proud of you! You taking care of your daughter. But why you living in this rat-hole, huh, answer me that? Why you only making enough to get by? You been driving what, seven years, why you still living like this? What you got, fucking bills and more fucking bills, that's all you got. How come? Because you a fucking slave and you don't know it, man. You no better than the rest of us, you a fucking Puerto Rican who's going to struggle your whole life. And you look at the rest of us and you think you all that, man, I know. But you should have more, bro, you deserve to have more. But when it comes down to it, when the day is over, bro, you the same as the rest of us, because this is a racist fucking world, bro!

And on Fausto went through the night, to the taunts of Alexander ("What you becoming, some uppity nigga?") and Julio ("You just need to get off yo ass, bro").

The reactions to Fausto that night were largely shaped by varying experiences and different understandings of what constituted respect and freedom. Julio felt under attack, because he had achieved working-class respect, was employed at one of the few blue-ribbon working-class jobs available to this group of men, and, as such, had done better than most of the men around him. He fought back, insisting that Fausto was making excuses and needed to stop using drugs and get off his ass. Jorge was self-effacing. He, like Alexander, thought that Fausto needed to accept who he was—a high school dropout who had messed up. Jorge insisted that his ethnicity had nothing to do with the outcomes of his own life, and even said that some of the people who grew up in his neighborhood had gone on to become doctors and lawyers (even though he was unable to name any of them). Alexander took it further, and accused Fausto of trying to be somebody he wasn't—an intellectual who was throwing around fancy words, trying to be an "uppity nigga." Indeed Fausto was seeking respect from his intellectual understanding of the world and had fused this with a street delivery intended to crush his foes. I remained largely on the sidelines during the exchange, adding some support to Fausto's exposé on structural inequality. The tensions that already existed between Alexander and me were certainly not going to be overcome that night—quite the contrary.

Alexander's and Jorge's reactions to Fausto were complex, in a similar way that Jorge's response to me at the pool table was. When I saw Alexander next, I was in the back of a camper parked at the block and had just settled into a game of dominoes and was catching up on news. When I asked about his brother Mundo, Alexander, who had just lit a blunt, exhaled smoke and stated sarcastically, "Mundo? Oh he's just strrruuggling like the rest of us." I realized at that moment that Alexander was responding to Fausto and me, based on our last conversation. Alexander did not like the fact that I saw them as people struggling on the social margins—he didn't like the fact that I viewed him as struggling at all. He was, after all, a very successful drug dealer, a businessman who had become successful within the social conditions that bounded his world. He and Jorge may not have commanded respect in the social world I inhabited, but they did in theirs. Alexander and Jorge insisted that not only was Fausto no better than they were —he too was a fuck-up—but that they were in fact more accomplished than Fausto and the rest of the fuck-ups around them. The conditions for acquiring respect differ as one moves across social locations and the accompanying cultural terrain that gives meaning to those social spaces. Alexander and Jorge had figured out how to beat the system and develop success, status, and respect within their social world, but they were still battling voices of self-loathing, and those voices were part of the larger dominant culture that I symbolized.

MASCULINITY AND RESPECT

The challenge of understanding marginalized populations is in seeing both their differences from as well as their similarities to mainstream groups. Masculine identities are valued across all social locations, though they may take different forms. On the block, masculinity was often expressed through fighting skills, sexual conquest, and verbal aggression. On the face of it, this may appear unique to the cultural spaces associated with the streets, and yet masculinity is often expressed through the exercise of power and control in varying social arenas, including the academic gamesmanship of one-upping through wit and argument, the use of legal means to bankrupt one's enemy, the workplace games of sexual seduction, and the backroom mutual back rubbing of wealth accumulation. Moreover, masculine power and honor are commonly associated with violence and aggression, whether it is milder forms of aggression organized through institutionalized sports or more explicit forms of violence organized through war. The public appeal of President George W. Bush's swagger and his tough talk as he unleashed "shock and awe" on the much smaller country of Iraq testifies to the public's respect and affirmation for male aggression—especially during a time of widespread public fear. Bush's rallying cry to "Bring it on!" at the start of the war and his public statement that Osama bin Laden was "wanted dead or alive" were public celebrations of masculinity—and the appeal cut across most, if not all, social groups.[10]

Still, similarities notwithstanding, social location does matter. When ways of achieving respect are limited, the need for it is exaggerated, if not dramatized. Sammy described how just being recognized on the street is experienced as a form of respect. If jobs don't pay living wages and the failure to be a provider for one's children places excessive strain on relationships and families, or if minimum-wage jobs foster the monotonous routines of "the living dead," the relief provided by a simple "What up, dawg," as Sammy said, or "getting the respect from others, being seen . . . feels good." Personal recognition can transcend personal demoralization. Wherever I went with these men—to a bar, a party, an after-hours, to the block, to the basketball or handball courts—we would always circulate and greet everyone there; in other words, we would "pay our respects."

Feeling disrespected by someone on the streets can result in a violent encounter. Because of these men's subordinate status within the racial and class hierarchy, respect is at a high premium, and demonstrating self-respect is considered a prerequisite to getting respect.

On the streets, there is perhaps no more important form of self-respect than physically defending oneself, which is actually more important than winning a fight—it is showing that you "have heart," that you will not back down, even if the odds are against you. This always concerned me because I knew that if I was ever violently confronted by someone on the street, that I would lose respect if I failed to physically defend myself, and yet I, like most of the men who occupy my social and cultural spaces, am no fighter. Fortunately I was never placed in that situation. There were a few close calls, but Julio was vigilant and quick to intervene—he was my protector. Paco wasn't as fortunate.

Paco is a thin, good-looking man whose father is Sicilian and mother Puerto Rican. Paco had been in the Marines and was stationed in Japan, where he met his wife and had two daughters. Not long after Paco was sent back to the United States, he received a Dear John letter and has not seen his wife or his children since. The separation from his daughters has caused him great anguish: "They are growing up and I don't know a fucking thing about them. Nothing! I think about them all the time." Paco appeared more sensitive than most of the men and always seemed to have an ambivalent attachment to the group. He kept a distance from many, but was close to Jorge, who nurtured Paco's potential as a drug dealer. Paco liked snorting coke and was popular among the women, and in a short time became part of Jorge's inner circle.

One evening in the winter of 1996, Jorge, Julio, and I were shooting pool when a guy approached the table to pay his respects. After he left, Julio turned to me and said, "See that guy. He slapped Paco." The conversation between the three of us continued, underscoring the importance of self-respect, masculinity, and fighting.

JULIO: Yeah, but you know what he did? Get this. This guy walks up to Paco and slaps him, and he just hangs his head down like this and doesn't do nothing about it. Can you believe that? I mean, he didn't show no self-respect. I mean, we were all here and we would watch his back, but we are not going to do nothing if he doesn't even have enough respect to defend himself. You know what I'm saying?

TIM: That guy's pretty big. Maybe Paco didn't want to get his
ass kicked?

JORGE: It doesn't matter.

JULIO: No, bro, we were here. We would've done something;
he hangs with us. But we're not going to back up anybody
who doesn't have no respect for himself. I mean, he could've
picked up a pool ball or a [pool] stick. You got to do
something, you can't just take it.

TIM: Isn't Paco just out of the Marines?

JORGE: Yeah, and the nigga is supposed to know kung fu and
shit. But he just hangs his head [imitating him and laughing].

Paco's failure to defend himself was viewed as a betrayal of his manhood and was an embarrassment to Julio, Jorge, and the others. For
several months after this, he was constantly badgered on the block for
his failure to be a man. About six months later, he redeemed himself.
Julio describes:

JULIO: Paco finally showed some heart last night.

TIM: Yeah, what happened?

JULIO: We were at [this club] and Paco was supposed to meet
this woman there. So when he gets there, she's talking to
some other guy.

TIM: Uh-oh. What did Paco do?

JULIO: He didn't do nothing, but wait. You see, this guy—and
he's young too—he walks by Paco and he bumps into him
like this and looks at Paco like this [to show him up]. Paco
says, "Hey, what's your fucking problem?" Right, and so I'm
thinking hey, he's finally going to show some heart. But he
doesn't do nothing.

TIM: Do you think he should have?

JULIO: Well, he would've got kicked out, but if it had've been
me, I would have done it . . .

TIM: What did Paco say?

JULIO: He's always saying things like I've got values and shit like
that. But Eugenio and Freddy are pissed 'cause this guy showed
Paco up and so they want to do something. So when the night's

over, this guy walks out and they're giving him the stare-down, you know. And then Paco comes out and this dumb fuck starts making out with his woman while Paco is standing there. So Paco hits him and then the security guard is right there and they take hold of Paco and put a choke hold on him and I'm like, "Hey, what you doing? Stop choking the guy." So the security guard knows me and he says, "I'll let go but you tell your boy to let go of me." And I look back and Jorge's got the security guard's arm behind his back. [laughter]

TIM: Jorge? Jorge jumped in!

JULIO: Yeah, he's got the motherfucker's arm bent back. But while this is going on, Freddy grabbed the guy and held him up and Eugenio knocked him out.

TIM: One punch?

JULIO: Yeah, one punch. He don't look big, but he can fight. But anyway, Paco finally showed some heart.

TIM: Was he hanging with you guys last night?

JULIO: Yeah, he drank a few beers with us last night.

TIM: What did he say about why he didn't hit him in the club?

JULIO: Oh, he came out with all that shit about "I've got values."

Paco's reluctance to fight and "show self-respect" was problematic for most of the men on the block; it emphasized his difference and threatened his status in the group. Jorge was not a big guy and neither was he a good fighter but, as the above story suggests, he would still throw himself into the melee when bar fights broke out (even though Jorge was careful to choose his moments and points of entrée, something I would witness on a few other occasions). Both Paco and the others would stake contradictory claims on "having values"—Paco by walking away from a fight, the others by standing up for themselves and defending their masculinity. Of course, Paco's behavior also threatened the value the group placed on loyalty—he could not be trusted to assist in a bar fight or to "watch their backs." Paco and I shared a perspective on street violence, which culturally distinguished us from the group. A few months after the above incident, I witnessed Paco's dilemma. He had been dating a stripper at one of Springfield's many strip clubs, a place that Alexander frequented and maintained a clientele, including many of the dancers. While sitting at the block one evening, the dancer showed up with another man, and the ribbing from the men began immediately. As it escalated, Paco's embarrassment and discomfort were evident. At one point, Paco leaned over and asked, "Should I go slap her around?" "I don't think that's what you really want to do," I replied. Paco was looking for reassurance and turned to perhaps the only guy in the group who would give it to him. He grinned uneasily and stayed seated. He and I would remain the two "pussies" in the group, even though it was much easier for me to define myself as culturally different and not lose as much respect as Paco. I was obviously different—white, older, non-Spanish-speaking, educated. Paco was one of them . . . and yet he wasn't.

HAVING ONE'S BACK

Because Paco refused to adhere to masculine street expectations, his loyalty was suspect, and despite the defiant individualist character that is prevalent and respected on the streets—or perhaps because of it—there is a high premium placed on loyalty. One night just before closing time at a bar, one of Jorge's brothers approached me. With heavy-lidded red eyes, Carlito grabbed my hand in a familiar manner, but with a serious demeanor that interrupted the usual late-night lighthearted embrace of mutual recognition. "I want you to know," he stated firmly but affectionately, "I consider you my brother and I will give my life for you." My first impulse was to make light of the situation, but the firmness of his grasp and the intensity of his voice forced me to recognize the gravity of the moment. Perhaps inspired by too many beers and high-grade cocaine, Carlito was nonetheless articulating an unspoken feeling that was often present in the interactions between many of the men, the feeling of loyalty and affection.

Beyond the public demand of mutual respect, loyalty reached deep into the relationships of these young men. Friendship rested on unmitigated, unconditional loyalty. Perhaps the result of personal vulnerability of being on the streets, or the *personalismo* of Puerto Rican rural culture less encumbered by the forces of modernity, or even the fragility of internalized racism within a society that buried them in the status hierarchy, loyalty was their lifeblood, the bond that sustained and provided them with some semblance of connectedness and integrity in an unforgiving world.

The importance of loyalty was made clear to me on the block in 1996 when Elfredo was released from prison—a respite from incarceration that was always short-lived for Elfredo. Of all the guys I have known on the streets, Elfredo is the most violent, the most overtly self-destructive, character of the group. He hung out on the block but also in the more violent parts of Springfield as a gang member. Elfredo's relationships with Jorge and the Rivera brothers extended back to childhood—in fact, Elfredo was one of the boys who regularly piled into cars with Sammy and left the school grounds in the middle school years. He was also the friend and gang member who set up the $5,000 robbery for Julio described earlier. There are numerous stories about Elfredo expressing his friendship through extreme measures of loyalty, and there is perhaps no better test of loyalty than violently defending one's friends, or putting oneself in danger on behalf of others. The unregulated drug trade and lawlessness of the streets increase the ante on loyalty. For Elfredo, this was his life. Deprived of other avenues of respect, he earned respect by sacrificing his body on behalf of friends. To illustrate the intensity of his loyalty, however, he needed an enemy that defined "them and us," that allowed his loyalty to be seen and appreciated. As a gang member, he was particularly violent and loyal. The fact that Elfredo was around for me to meet in 1996 is nothing less than miraculous—he had been stabbed seventeen times by rival gang members and had been left for dead. His survival meant that, as Julio put it, "he slept with one eye open."

Hanging out at the block soon after his release, Elfredo noticed that a Dominican guy living in an apartment across the street from Jorge was dealing drugs, something Elfredo considered an affront to Jorge's business and a sign of disrespect. Elfredo became obsessed with the situation, talked about it frequently, asked others repeatedly what they were going to do about it. No one else seemed to care except Elfredo, who had found an enemy that would serve as his foil in reaffirming his loyalty to "his boys." One evening, high on cocaine, Elfredo borrowed a gun from one of the guys on the block, and along with a partner, waited for the Dominican guy to leave his house. When he did, they robbed him at gunpoint and told him to find another place to run his business. When the young man resisted, Elfredo shot him in the butt.

When I heard the story, my response was to blame Elfredo for senseless violence, for drawing unnecessary attention to the block, and for making the location of my ethnography unsafe. I was the only one who felt this way. No one else blamed Elfredo; instead, they blamed Arturo, who had given Elfredo the gun, and banned him from hanging out on the block. Arturo had also been recently released from prison. Soft-spoken with a passive demeanor, he had served a short sentence and was working for Jorge at the time. I was amazed to be the only one angry at Elfredo. Julio exclaimed:

> That's just Elfredo, bro. He's crazy, that's all. We all know he going to do shit like that, that's all. But, what's his name, Arturo should never have given him that gun. He gave it to him loaded. If he was going to give him the gun, he should've taken out the bullets, yo. He's a stupid motherfucker. You don't give Elfredo a gun with bullets in it.

Everyone agreed with Julio's assessment: Arturo was the "stupid motherfucker" for not taking the bullets out of the gun before he turned it over to Elfredo, especially when he knew that Elfredo was "geeked up" on coke. I was incensed and confronted Jorge and Julio.

> TIM: How are you going to blame Arturo for something Elfredo did?
>
> JULIO: Yo, Tim, Elfredo, he's crazy but he's our boy, you know what I'm saying? He goes way back with us, you know, to when we were kids. That's just the way he is. But everybody knew he was geeked up and everybody knows that when he's that way, that he's crazy, he'll do anything. It was stupid to give him a gun. I mean, look it, you can give him the gun, but take the fucking bullets out of it first.
>
> TIM: No, man, you guys are the fucking crazy ones. Arturo didn't do shit to you all. What's Elfredo going to do now? They'll throw his ass back in prison just like that.

JORGE: Well, they got to catch him first. Besides, he don't care,
my boy don't give a fuck.
JULIO: He's going to PR. He'll lay low down there, but he'll be
back.

Loyalty cut both ways here. On one hand, Elfredo expressed his loyalty to Jorge by attempting to scare off his competition from the block. The extreme measures demonstrated his loyalty to Jorge—nobody dealt in his friend's territory without answering to him. But Jorge's and Julio's defense of Elfredo also demonstrated their loyalty. Friendship is rooted in shared history—in being "out there" together—and both Julio and Jorge felt indebted to Elfredo for the many times he had come through for them in the past. They extended him both understanding and tolerance. Elfredo is known to be violent, this is his character, and to be his friend, one must simply accept it and deal with him accordingly (for instance, you don't give him a loaded gun). Besides, he exercised his "craziness" on behalf of his friends, and it's even more difficult to be angry and intolerant when violence is an expression of loyalty. And violence on the street is often an expression of loyalty.

Still, while the bonds of loyalty are deep and abiding, they are also often transitory. Loyalty is rarely unconditional and is always threatened by conflicting self-interest. Family rifts, divorce, broken friendships, damaged business relationships remind us of the transitory nature of loyalty and trust. This is also true on the street. While it is easy to find deep loyalty, at the same time most everyone on the street will insist that they don't trust anyone. Acts of loyalty are also expressions of self-interest—they assume that loyalty will be returned by others. But in an arena in which men are continually maneuvering and positioning themselves to control resources, loyalties shift and betrayal can evoke rage and violence. Years later, during one of Elfredo's reprieves from prison, he became enraged with Jorge and others because he felt that they were excluding him from the drug trade—that they were not giving him what he was entitled to as a loyal member of the network. The man who staked his reputation on loyalty to others walked into an apartment and, feeling betrayed and desperate, confronted Jorge and others with a gun.

The complementary tension between loyalty and self-interest is something we all live with. Betrayal certainly has consequences, but on the streets, it has its own particular dynamic—a dynamic that has been largely shaped by economic and social marginalization, the lawlessness of the drug trade, defiant individualism, and by aggressive drug policies with mandatory and lengthy prison sentences (an issue I will return to later in Chapter 8).

In a poignant moment of reflection, Fausto articulated the strains placed on loyalty by the lawless drug trade, or urban cowboy capitalism:

> You see, it's the money. Money fucks people up. It fucked us all up. Before we started getting involved in this shit, we were all good friends. We hung together. If I had a dollar in my pocket, I threw it in to buy a 40 and we all drank it. We all reached in our pocket and gave whatever we had and that was never much. But we were tight. We hung together, had some laughs, never worried about somebody stabbing you in the back. That's the way it was—we were all brothers. But then the kis [kilos] started coming and there's big money to be made, and that fucks us all up. There starts being jealousy and everybody starts robbing one another, fucking over one another. We even got contracts out on one another.

Life on the block was complex and diverse. Differing identities, social networks, and social locations created permeable cultural boundaries and a changing matrix of status and respect that was bounded by larger structural conditions, reflecting the loss of living-wage jobs, the growth of the urban drug trade, and the war on drugs and its burgeoning prison industrial complex. By the end of the 1990s, many of the men were leaving the streets—some voluntarily, some not. Those who left the streets to find jobs in the formal economy were seeking a different type of status and respect from Jorge, Alexander, Roberto, and Fausto—they were seeking personal validation derived from working-class respectability.

SIX

Leaving the Streets

IN THE SUMMER OF 1999, I was standing in front of Julio's apartment when Paco drove up and hopped out of a shiny new red car he had just bought on credit. Working for a machine shop in Springfield, making $10 an hour, Paco announced that he had put street life behind him.

> I just made my first deposit in a bank. It's like this money is real, you know. All that money I had on the streets, it was like play money, you know. . . . I can't explain it, this money, it's like really mine, I earned it, I take it to the bank and shit. Come here, you gotta see this stereo I got in here.

Sitting in the car, pushing buttons on the stereo, Paco claimed he was no longer hanging out.

> It gets old, bro. That's what nobody sees, that shit gets boring, the same ole every night. What it looks like on the outside, the money, the girls—you know, hanging with the guys—it's not what it seems. . . . I'm done with that shit.

Paco's newly formed identity was not all that surprising—his street identity never seemed to fit quite right anyway. He always seemed on the margins of street life and often distinguished himself from the others by insisting that he lived by values different from those embraced on the street, especially when it came to fighting.

But it wasn't only Paco. I would have similar conversations with others as well, and with men whose street identities had been much more entrenched. For instance, when I first started hanging out at the

137

block, Mundo was the life of the party—a storyteller who kept us laughing through the night—and a street guy who regularly expressed antipathy toward work. In those days, Mundo often "broke night" because of his insatiable desire for cocaine—something else he had a reputation for, as Fausto once described:

> That motherfucker could never walk away from cocaine. When he used to do that shit, he would do so much no one could believe it. He was fucking crazy. And it was good stuff, man, back in the day when that shit was pure, when we was getting it from Manny, you know. The amount he would do at one time—one sniff, you know—woulda killed anybody else. But that motherfucker could not get enough.

In the summer of 2003, however, Mundo had just completed his fifth year at a small machine shop in West Springfield. With some distance from the streets, he talked about his own transition:

> One day, I don't know what it was, a wake-up call, I guess, but I just asked myself the question, What am I doing? Is this what I was put here on earth to do with my life, wake up every fucking day with nothing to look forward to except getting fucked up? I was feeling terrible about myself, I was being a real fuck-up. You know, Tim, it always comes back to my dad. I didn't want to be like him, I guess. You know, hanging out ain't what it seems. You can't see what's inside. You hate yourself when you're out there day after day. You can't help asking yourself, what the fuck am I doing? Is this it? Is this what life is about? It may look good, the clothes, the money, the girls, but inside it don't feel that way. Trust me, everybody has to look themselves in the mirror, buddy, everybody out there.

I had similar conversations with others. Julio, the most successful of the men on the block, looked back, at times, in disbelief that he had "been so stupid" and attributed his survival, let alone his success, to either providence or pure luck.

Even Sammy, whose street identity was nurtured at a young age on the streets of Yonkers and whose heroin addiction had become his albatross, offered a critical perspective of the street. Prepared to enter a detox facility in the winter of 2002, Sammy was working at a temp agency, embarking on a similar transition to that the others were making.

> Tim, man, I really want it this time. I'm tired, you know. I'm tired of looking at myself in the mirror. I'm really down, man. I don't like what I see. I'm not doing good. I see a guy who's a fuck-up. These drugs bring you down. I look at myself and they, the drugs, you know, they be like, look at yourself, you're nothing, you ain't shit. Look at what you are, you're a fucking loser.

What accounted for these changing identities among these young men?

Identities change for a variety of reasons, especially among older adolescents and young men and women in their twenties, but the particular topography through which these changes occur depends on social location. For these men, street and job networks shaped their income opportunities, while overlapping cultural orbits attributed value and meaning to the different places and choices within this constricted range of opportunities. As they embraced identities, they often emphasized a rejected identity—identities became inversions or negations, grounded in who they *were not* as much, if not more, than who they *were*. In each of the discussions above, Paco, Mundo, Julio, and Sammy emphasize a rejection of street life—their emerging identities are articulated largely in terms of what they are moving away from, or who they are not, rather than what they are embracing, or who they are becoming.

Drug dealing, as we saw in the last chapter, can be explained in similar terms. For many men on the streets, drug dealing is just a means to put a few dollars in their pockets or to supplement other sources of income. For others, drug dealing is also articulated as a negation—a rejection of work, especially dead-end, exploitive work. A cultural boundary between drug dealing and work gets erected—even though this boundary is frequently transgressed. Identities get articulated on each side of the boundary—and yet identities change.

As men's lives shifted from the streets to the workplace, their identities changed. They viewed their decisions to take paid work as maturing, getting older, and as a rejection of the streets. They became critical of the drug trade and the street lifestyle, and even critical of Jorge and what he represented. Many began to talk about Jorge as a guy who was drinking himself to death, who was lazy, and who didn't want to grow up. His brothers (even Alexander) lectured him, Julio and Fausto humored him, and his mother berated him. As they left the streets, men adopted more conventional views of their lives and derived moral status from being a family provider. Further, they were "coming clean" or exposing the truth about the monotony and boredom of the streets, and about the self-loathing that lies beneath the surface. Of course, operating in the background of their lives were the changes taking place in the economy that made it possible for *some* of these men to leave the streets and adopt new identities.

MUNDO'S CONVERSION

Despite Mundo's professed rejection of the streets, seven years earlier when I first met him at age thirty-two, he and his brother Jorge cultivated a street identity that was in opposition to paid work. This did not mean that Mundo had never worked. Quite the contrary, he had a checkered work history that included working seasonally in the tobacco fields; helping to rebuild storm-battered Jackson, Mississippi, in the late 1980s; working under-the-table jobs in construction and roofing; and working in a metal machine shop, where he was a union steward. The job in Mississippi is part of his repertoire of stories: "There were no Puerto Ricans there, bro, none! I had all kinds of girls . . . they had never seen a Spanish guy before."

The machine shop job securely located him in the working class, but triggered memories of anguish and was rarely spoken about. His position as a union steward was stressful, in part, because he felt loyalty to the manager, who was a family friend. When two members of the union filed a complaint against the manager, Mundo recalled:

[The complaint] was serious and if I had pushed it, it would have gotten the supervisor fired. But he knew my father for over twenty years. I couldn't do that. My guys were right, though. He fucked up. But I couldn't push the issue. Man, the pressure, I'm telling you, the pressure was too much. I couldn't take it any longer. That job sucked. I was always in these kind of things. I hated it, bro, just hated it. So I quit.

It was during this time that Mundo also separated from his common-law wife. His partying had escalated while he was working at the metal shop, which had placed a strain on the relationship. Quitting his job, moving in with his mother, and immersing himself in the masculine pleasures of the block was his solution to the circumstances of his life. Not long after Mundo had quit his job, he was arrested for drunk driving, spent six months in jail, and received an additional two years of probation. I met Mundo while he was serving probation in the summer of 1996, and his antipathy toward work was just as evident as his nightly indulgences in cocaine and Budweiser.

For two years, Mundo made money dealing small quantities of coke, mostly in a local bar, and partied nightly (except for the weekends when his daughter stayed with him). He worked in the tobacco fields in the summer, which appeared to be more a requirement of living with his mother than self-initiative. However, after two years, his mother was threatening to kick him out if he didn't find a job and the guys loved razzing him about "his mama" and about being a "lazy motherfucker." Moreover, Mundo had violated his probation and there was a warrant out for his arrest. Rather than finding a job, Mundo decided to turn himself in to the court and spend a few months in jail during the winter to clear the charge from his record. Mundo objected to the state controlling his life, but this became secondary to the banter about Mundo refusing to work. As Julio and I drove Mundo to the courthouse on the snowy morning he had decided to turn himself in, we discussed his circumstances and motives.

> TIM: So you'd rather go into jail and finish off your sentence than accept the conditions of probation.
>
> MUNDO: Yeah, I wasn't keeping appointments. So they kept sending me stuff, so one day I go in there and they say, "Are

you ready to take a urine test?" I say, "Sure, come on," knowing that the night before I had snorted almost an entire 8-ball [laughter].

TIM: So your test showed dirty urine and they're sending you back to jail.

MUNDO: That, and I wasn't keeping my appointments. I'm not going to check in with them. I don't want those people telling me what to do, fuck that. You know what I mean, you want people telling you, watching you? I told them I'm not going to do it. I told 'em I would only accept unsupervised probation. You know, if I get caught again, then I have to do the time. I was supposed to go in on the thirtieth, but I wanted to wait to see what happened to Jorge [his federal case], so we could go in at the same time, you know.

JULIO: No, what happened is that his mother told him last night that he was going to get up at six A.M. and that he was going out the door at seven to find a job. So then he says to Jorge, isn't your case tomorrow. So he decides he's going to turn himself in so he doesn't have to get a job [laughter].

When we dropped Mundo off, he said his goodbyes, stepped out on the curb to Julio's taunts about his mother and about working, turned, put his hands together, lifted them to the sky, fell to his knees, and yelled, "Please take me, put me in today, keep away from my mother, please take me." We drove off in laughter.

Several hours later, standing in Alexandria's kitchen, we heard the door open and a voice yell, "I've got to find a job." Raucous laughter followed as Mundo appeared. Despite his pleas to the contrary, the court had ordered his case back to conference. One-liners followed, none better than his sister Alexandria's: "Well, Mundo, if the courts don't want you, I guess we all now know you are a *total* society reject" [laughter].

Mundo was eventually given electronically traced probation, during which time he took a dishwashing position at a chain restaurant. The job required long weekend hours—Friday (eight hours), Saturday (twelve hours), and Sunday (twelve hours), and finding transportation was particularly problematic, since he had to arrange for someone to pick him up at two-thirty in the morning, often his estranged ex-wife. Further, Mundo claimed he wasn't permitted a break, not even a lunch break, and described how he would eat while he was working: "I be doing this [gesturing with hands] taking a bite, shoving food off the plate, taking another bite, my hands all dirty. I think that's against the law, you know, them not giving us a break." The wage ($7.50 an hour) sufficed as an interim measure to complete his probation, but for Mundo, "the only good thing about the job is all the college women there. Ooh-eeh, I'm telling you, bro, they look nice."

When his probation ended, Mundo's brother Jorge was in federal prison. Mundo moved back in with his ex-wife and never looked back to the streets. He began working temporary jobs until he landed the position at the machine shop. Mundo's rejection of work shifted on its axis and became a rejection of the streets. Five years later, after Jorge's release from prison, the same brother he had spent two years on the block with would become a foil for Mundo's working-class identity.

> Jorge's a show-off . . . drug money, it ain't shit. Sometimes you got it, other times it's dry out there. The other night, Jorge and I went out to eat, and the nigga didn't have a dime. I had to buy dinner. You know, you may look good out there, you got the clothes and shit, but it don't mean shit, Tim. Who cares about some fucking clothes? For what? I don't even like it now when my wife buys me clothes. I'm like, don't spend money on that shit. Who cares? Now that I have a job and a paycheck, I know what's important, and it ain't clothes. But when you out on the streets that's all you care about, looking good and shit. The money comes and it goes. You look good, but inside you feel like shit.

THE ROLLING 1990S

The decade of the 1990s did not begin the way it ended. The beginning was cast within a larger set of political and economic forces that could be traced back to the 1970s and 1980s when a domestic-based manufacturing economy was rapidly restructured. This marked what

Robert Pollin and Stephanie Luce call a transition from a post–World War II golden age to a leaden age.[1] The golden age had generated improved living standards, especially for the white working class, which secured housing equity, retirement pensions, health insurance, and educational opportunities for children. When declining profit rates appeared to be systemic in the 1970s, corporate and political elites lined up behind Paul Volcker, the chairman of the Federal Reserve Board, in 1979 and Ronald Reagan in 1980 to attack the forces that had created workers' rising living standards. "Free trade" and "free market" initiatives increased competition by deregulating markets and removing controls on finance and industrial capital. The mobility of capital (and the threat to move) weakened the negotiating power of labor unions and extracted tax concessions from state, local, and foreign governments. Manufacturing industries moved around the United States and the globe in search of lower-wage nonunionized workforces, fewer environmental and workplace safety regulations, and minimal tariffs. Meanwhile, corporate leaders moved quickly to take advantage of labor's weakened position by pressing for wage concessions, implementing two-tier contracts, and outsourcing jobs.

Rising living standards for the working classes were reversed, and indeed by 1997 corporate profit rates were again approaching 1970s levels. Economic restructuring, however, did not eliminate the cyclical nature of economic markets and if these changing conditions resulted in a blow to the working class, the 1991 recession made it a one-two punch. By 1993, the increase in income inequality had deepened class divisions. From 1979 to 1993, the bottom one-fifth suffered a 15 percent decline in income while income for the top one-fifth increased 22 percent and, for the top 5 percent, 39 percent.[2] Consequently, as median income was rising, so was the poverty rate, increasing from 11.6 percent in 1979 to 15.1 percent in 1993, prompting Richard Freeman and Peter Gottschalk to observe that the labor force had reached "levels of inequality not seen since the Great Depression."[3]

Conditions in Springfield were particularly harsh. In June 1992, while the formal unemployment rate for the nation was 7.8 percent, in the Springfield region it was 9 percent and in the city itself well over 10 percent, which didn't even include the men from the block and others like them who were not formally "looking for work."[4] Manufacturing jobs that had been the backbone of the Springfield economy through most of the century and had provided living-wage opportunities for working-class men and women were still declining. Accounting for 33.9 percent of all jobs in 1960, manufacturing jobs had decreased to 18.5 percent in 1990. The slide continued through the 1990s despite economic growth, as manufacturing jobs declined in the Springfield metropolitan area from 44,100 in 1990 to 35,700 in 2000, and then to 28,800 in 2002, totaling a 35 percent loss in a twelve-year period.[5] This decline removed money from the local economy, particularly from working-class communities. In 1990, manufacturing accounted for 27.2 percent of total private earnings in the Springfield metropolitan area; by 1997, that figure had dropped to 24.4 percent, and then in 2002 to 19.8 percent.[6]

These changes may have pushed up profit rates and greatly rewarded surviving corporate leaders and stockholders, but they pushed members of the working class to the edges of the labor force, where a world of off-the-book jobs and an illicit drug economy operated to funnel resources into cash-starved communities. The Rivera brothers and their networks of friends were becoming young adults at a time in which the labor force was not likely to absorb them. In 1992, nationally, 41 percent of male Hispanic high school graduates between the ages of twenty-five and thirty-four earned less than $15,000 a year. For school dropouts, the rate was 69 percent.[7] The Springfield gang wars and an exploding prison population reflected these social and economic conditions. But 1993 was a significant marker in another respect as well—after two years of a tepid recovery, 1993 marked a turning point in which the economy gained momentum that would be sustained through the end of the decade.

The economic recovery was initiated largely by expansions in information technology. Profit increases peaked in 1996, after which the period of sustained growth was shouldered by foreign investment and debt—corporate debt as well as consumer mortgage and credit card debt.[8] In the early part of the recovery, living standards for low-wage groups remained stagnant, while profit margins grew and the stock market flourished. It wasn't until 1997 that wages began to rise at the bottom, when three increases in the minimum wage in the

1990s and the benefits of a tight labor market finally reached more marginalized populations.[9] In the Springfield area, the formal unemployment rate dipped to 3.8 percent in 1998 and to below 3 percent in the last quarter of 2000. For the men on the block, job opportunities became more enticing as wages began to push upward—$5- to $7-an-hour jobs became $8- to $10-an-hour jobs, and in some cases pushed beyond $10. It is in this context that identities began to change and understandings of the streets became reconstructed.

The other event that resulted in men exiting the streets was Jorge's incarceration. Jorge was given a five-year federal sentence, which he began serving in 1998. Jorge may have evoked ambivalence among many of the men like Paco, Mundo, and Julio, who were finding pathways off the streets in the 1990s, but his charisma and lifestyle remained attractive to a nucleus of young men, Sammy included. Jorge's absence meant that men would have to work directly with his brother Alexander, which many refused to do. Jorge and Alexander engaged their work, their employees, and their friends very differently. Alexander was a strict capitalist—he didn't spend money on anyone and shrewdly exploited weaknesses to make money. There was no pretense—he was making money on the backs of others. Alexander's stature in the drug trade was based on his connections to suppliers. His profits went into building a house in Puerto Rico, to providing for his wife and daughters, and to various investments. Fearful of opening a bank account that might leave a trail of his drug business, Alexander bought and sold cars, owned an unlicensed auto body shop, and even bought a large fishing boat. Anyone working for Alexander understood he was about making money, or as Fausto would say, "Everybody knows he's a greedy motherfucker."

In contrast, Jorge nurtured relationships with young men who worked for him and offered them a means for acquiring status as well as a source of income. He made money, but was more likely to invest his money in "his boys." He still made a profit and provided for the household needs of his longtime common-law wife and himself, but most of his profits were spent on developing relationships with the men who worked for him. He took care of them and enjoyed the status derived from being in control. As his brother Mundo would say years later, "Jorge likes being a big shot."

Alexander adopted the individualistic creed of American capitalism, extracting surplus labor from his employees in pursuit of material success and personal status. Jorge utilized the market to benefit himself as well—to make money and acquire status—but by sharing his profits with the network of young men working for him, he nurtured a more loyal workforce and earned the affection of many around him. Jorge was well aware of the differences between his older brother and himself. When Jorge was leaving to begin his five-year bid, one young man was grousing that he would now have to work directly with Alexander. The comment pleased Jorge; he smiled and responded, "Well, he's not me."

GAINING TRACTION IN THE 1990S LABOR FORCE

The searing August sun was Julio's worst enemy in 1991 as he knelt in the fields of a Connecticut nursery waiting for the clock to reach 3:30. Depleted, Julio still managed a grin when I showed up in the evening cradling a twelve-pack of Budweiser. A recent graduate of Commerce High School (and still a few years before he and I would begin making our trips to state prisons to visit Fausto), the eighteen-year-old Julio did not sound like a man who expected a great deal from the world. "I may join the Marines. But it's hard, you know, when you come from a [neighborhood] like this." Pointing to the bullet holes marking the front porch, Julio said, "You could get shot tomorrow by somebody just driving by." Whether it was the long, hot day or the daily grind of life during the first year since Julio had graduated high school, his vision of himself at thirty was resigned.

> There aren't a lot of opportunities when you come from a place like this and you're Puerto Rican. I work out in the hot sun every day for $5.25 an hour. Most employers don't want to hire you when they see you're Puerto Rican and you live in this type of neighborhood. I don't know, I guess I see myself living in a place like this and being a father, you know, taking good care of my family.

Taking care of his family has been Julio's primary objective since he graduated—the family that he and Clara extended when Iris was born a few months after our conversation. As the oldest, Julio has also been the steadiest wage earner, whom his parents and even brothers, at times, have depended on for a hearty meal of rice and beans and fried meat.

Like Mundo and many of the young men from the block, Julio's work history caromed through a late-twentieth-century storehouse of working-class jobs with many beginnings and just as many disruptions. Already before the sun-parched Julio talked about his future at age eighteen, he had worked in a bodega located beneath a crack house, a shoe store owned by his football coach, and a chicken processing plant. As described earlier, after a short stint in community college, Julio completed a tractor-trailer driving program, but didn't have the money to take his driving test. Six months at a plant nursery earned him an opportunity through the New England Farm Workers' Council to drive a forklift at a local manufacturing plant. After he left a co-worker unconscious on the break room floor, and returned to take his driving test only to be told that a year had expired and he would need to start the course over, he then turned to the Acosta brothers to make money dealing drugs, while, with unnoted irony, enrolling in a law enforcement program at a local community college.

With his family's needs pressing, Julio didn't remain long in college, but continued dealing cocaine while he spun through a series of jobs working for two security companies and for temp agencies. After his abruptly interrupted tenure as a leader of La Familia and a three-month stay in Puerto Rico, Julio and his family moved to Hartford, where he began a rigorous training program to become a diesel engine mechanic. Julio had completed the first of four modules, when he and his father were arrested for discharging firearms in a family brawl. After spending two months in jail, they were released when a witness stepped forward to challenge the statement that the Hartford police had taken on the night of the event. My then wife represented him in court.[10] Julio tried to resume his diesel mechanic training program, but his long absence and transportation problems led him to drop out and default on another federal loan.

Settling into Hartford for a brief time, Julio drove a van for $8.50 an hour, transporting the physically disabled throughout the metropolitan area. In the five years after graduating from high school, Julio had worked nine on-the-books jobs, attended three training programs, and enrolled in community college twice. Throughout, Clara supplemented the family wage with cash welfare and food stamps she received for their daughter, Iris, as well as formal child support from Julio—as peculiar as that may sound. To maximize their income sources, Julio claimed residence with his mother so his income would not be counted against Clara's monthly state check. He was therefore considered a noncustodial father and, since Clara was receiving welfare benefits, was required to submit monthly child support payments to the state. Fifty dollars of Julio's payment was passed along to Clara, while the state kept the rest as compensation for the money they were providing for Iris.[11] Julio and Clara utilized whatever resources they could to make ends meet—even if it meant submitting a check that circulated through the state welfare bureaucracy and returned to the same address where it originated, minus a few dollars for the state.

Driving the van in Hartford kindled in Julio a long-standing desire to drive tractor-trailers for a living. This time Julio answered an ad from a national trucking company that promised to pay for his training in return for one year of dedicated employment to the company. Julio left his family for Ohio, where he enrolled in their training program. He completed the program and was sent on the road to train with an embittered driver who hated the company and found it difficult to make a living wage. To make matters worse, he wouldn't talk to Julio on their trips cross-country, which Julio attributed to the white driver's racism. To save money, the driver refused to leave the truck idling at night, prohibiting Julio from resting in a heated sleeper. By the time they reached Texas, Julio was fed up; he called Jorge to send him money for the bus ride home. Julio left the company, but not without obtaining his CDL, Commercial Driver's License. However, since he had failed to live up to his end of the agreement by working for a year, he was presented with a hefty bill from the company for the training. Out of work and back on the streets in Springfield, Julio's debt continued to pile up.

Julio and Clara moved back to Springfield from Hartford. Clara wanted to be closer to her mother and Julio to Jorge, whom he turned to as a resource while he searched for a living-wage job. Julio worked a series of short-term jobs for a security company, an assembly plant, and in an office building cleaning bathrooms. The most bizarre income option involved an old passion. While in high school, Julio had boxed in the Golden Gloves competition in Holyoke. He had only one fight and lost, but apparently was remembered by his opponent's coach. Several years later while working out in a local gym, he saw the coach, who asked him if he was interested in entering some statewide fights. Julio was not a trained fighter, but he was promised $300 a fight, and told to "go down" in the first few rounds. His presence in the ring had only one objective: to build the records of new prospects climbing their way up the ladder toward the big time. For Julio, it was fast money for taking a few punches. Because he was not legally allowed to box for sixty days after a fight, he registered at different locations in New England under different names. On one occasion in the Boston area, Julio landed a good punch in the first round, knocking down his opponent. Reminding Julio of their purpose, the coach whispered in his ear between rounds, "You do that again, we may not get out of here alive."

I seemed to be the only one concerned about Julio's revived boxing "career." When I saw one of Julio's names listed in the local paper to fight at a nearby venue, I made some inquiries about his opponent and, when told that he was undefeated and well on his way to earning a reputation in the ring, I expressed my concern to Julio.

> TIM: Julio, man, there's a big difference between being a good
>   street fighter and climbing into the ring with guys who are
>   trained boxers. You make a wrong move and they may
>   disconnect your head from your shoulders.
> JULIO: Sheeiiit, I got no pride out there. They hit me once and
>   I'm not getting back up. I'm staying down there. Everybody
>   can boo all they want, I'm hugging the fuckin' mat till the
>   guy does his count, then I'm picking up my check and getting
>   the fuck out of there [laughter].

Fortunately for Julio, his boxing career ended without serious injury. He boxed in a half-dozen fights, but as truck-driving opportunities began to materialize, he lost interest in the ring.

Julio's driving career finally gained traction because of the tight labor market in the late 1990s, changes in the trucking industry, Julio's persistence, and an important contact on the block. Carmello was an experienced truck driver who liked to spend his days off hanging out on the block in the early evening drinking beer and telling stories. The joke on the block was that even though Carmello was well employed, he had not found work that suited him. He had been suspended on a number of occasions for reckless driving related to his penchant for falling asleep behind the wheel, and in fact tended to show up on the block more often during his suspensions, becoming the target of many jokes. His driving record had cost him better jobs in the industry, as he had fallen to the bottom rung of companies willing to hire anyone in the latter half of the 1990s who, according to Julio, "had a license and wasn't blind." Still, he understood the industry and could inform others about obtaining a Commercial Driver's License, job openings, and pay structures—information that a couple of the men benefited from, including Julio.

Carmello was suspended in the summer of 1996 for reckless driving and was hanging out on the block in the early evenings. Julio now had his CDL, but needed to log hours on the road to build his résumé. After about six months of promises, jokes, and lots of Budweiser, Carmello helped Julio get hired by a Springfield trucking company that carried loads cross-country, with the arrangement that he would train Julio. On the second trip, Carmello lived up to his reputation and Julio returned to the block with a story:

> So I'm catching some Zs, you know? I'm out, man, I been driving all night and I'm out, you know what I'm saying? And the next thing I know, I'm being thrown all over the fucking place, and I hear this cht, cht, cht sound. I climb back into the cab and I'm like, what the fuck's going on? And this motherfucker fell asleep and we were driving through the fucking ditch, I'm telling you. I'm like, get the fuck out of that seat before you kill us! [laughter]

After the second coast-to-coast trip, Julio's beefed-up résumé enabled him to secure a job with a local carrier that made regional runs, mostly to New York and New Jersey.

Julio's life after high school was representative of many from the block who lived on the margins of the restructured, post-1970s economy. While there may be men who fit more widely publicized images of the "underclass"—raised in concentrated urban poverty moving directly into the drug trade as boys and remaining there, while circling in and out of prison until they are in their twenties with little or no formal job experience—most of the men I encountered on the block did not fit this profile. The "twilight zone" between work and the streets fosters another well-traversed path, where men like Julio and Mundo enter into a whirlwind of unstable jobs and street opportunities. By the time Julio began his driving career, he had worked more than a dozen formal paying jobs and had relied on the streets and Clara's welfare benefits to support his family. Gaining traction in the labor force required perseverance, opportunities, and good fortune. Julio's career as a truck driver was finally launched during the late 1990s economic recovery, but it would take many years for him to find stability in the trade. In his first eight years of driving he would change jobs nine more times, reaching a tally of more than twenty jobs in the fourteen years after he graduated from high school. He and Clara would also change residences fourteen times during this period. The difficulty of finding stability in the trucking trade stemmed from economic restructuring, or, more specifically, from the deregulation of the trucking industry that began in the late 1970s.

The Deregulated Trucking Industry

America's mythological infatuation with the automobile and the open road infuse trucking with the symbolism of freedom and self-determination. Truck drivers might be the twenty-first-century's version of the cowboy, driving their large, powerful machines off into the sunset while preserving the American way of life by carrying the economy on their backs. Moreover, drivers have a degree of independence that is rare in a service-dominated economy—a sense of autonomy that comes from being "on the road" that affirms masculine identities in ways that ringing up cash registers, selling tires or mufflers, sweeping and mopping floors, or even unloading trucks in warehouses do not. Edgar, an ex-Marine and former machinist, who spent a few years on the streets snorting coke, chasing women, and working for Jorge, followed Julio into the trucking trade. He articulated the image of the twenty-first-century rugged individualist: "I love driving. I'm my own boss. I don't have no one looking over my shoulder. I drive when I want to, stop when I want to. Nobody's there to give me shit, just me and my truck."

Edgar's indulgences in masculine illusions and American mythologies of freedom and independence notwithstanding, the trucking trade has always been mired in political-economic dynamics and collective struggle. It is a huge, central part of the economy, whose services accounted for nearly 5 percent of the total gross domestic product in 1997.[12] Wages and benefits for drivers vastly improved in the 1950s and 1960s as trucking expanded with the growth of interstate highways and as the Teamsters Union centralized bargaining, ironed out regional differences in wages across the country, and organized much of the transportation industry, including warehouse workers. By 1980, interstate trucking had grown into a $67 billion industry and hourly wages for truckers and warehouse workers had reached levels paid to auto and steel workers.[13] However, in response to rising inflation and general economic malaise in the late 1970s, the Carter administration began exploring deregulation policies and the trucking trade was among the first industries targeted.

The political culture in Washington that navigated the economy at the end of the twentieth century was different from the earlier part of the century. Mistrust of corporate monopolies at the turn of the century had fueled an antitrust populist movement, while the collapse of the stock market in 1929 exposed the need for more governmental intervention. In 1935, Franklin Delano Roosevelt placed the trucking industry under the regulatory control of the Interstate Commerce Commission, which had been established in 1887 to regulate the railroads. Concerns that competition would destabilize the industry made price and wage controls widely acceptable, especially among carriers themselves whose livelihood was threatened by fly-by-night operators attempting to drive the industry into the ground, so to speak.[14]

To avoid destructive competition, the ICC limited entry into the industry and set tariffs that ensured pricing reflecting the value of service.[15] Routes and terminals were closely monitored through public postings of tariffs and scheduled services. By the end of the 1970s, however, the political climate was changing. Falling corporate profits and rising consumer prices provided common political ground for corporate elites and consumers, while "big" government's regulations, "rich and powerful" labor unions, and thousands of women of color "living on the dole" became public scapegoats popularized by neoconservative academics and pundits, paving the way for Ronald Reagan's presidential campaign in 1980. But the era of economic deregulation had begun before Reagan, when in the 1970s the ICC had started loosening controls over prices and markets, foreshadowing the Motor Carrier Act of 1980. The new act reduced ICC enforcement and distanced government from the industry, relying instead on heated market competition to determine prices and wages.[16]

As Michael Belzer explains in his book *Sweatshops on Wheels*, the industry that Julio would enter in 1995, the year before the ICC was eliminated altogether, was divided into two types of carriers—Less than Truckload (LTL) and Truckload (TL) carriers. LTL carriers utilized an elaborate labyrinth of terminals, where trucks pick up and deliver merchandise.[17] The LTL network requires capital investment in terminals, efficient routing management, and coordination among trucking companies, shippers, distributors, vendors, dockworkers, and handlers. The 1980 statute greatly increased competition and resulted in a shakedown in the LTL industry—many carriers went bankrupt, while ownership of the industry became more concentrated in the hands of four companies. However, because of the intricate network of LTL operations, workers in this part of the industry were still likely to be unionized. So while the rapidly growing TL sector was siphoning off jobs from LTL lines, wages in the LTL sector remained relatively high.

TL operations circumvent the terminal system altogether, contract directly with vendors, and deliver large loads across country. With satellite technology, all that is needed is a radio, a truck, and a dispatcher to place drivers on the road. All of the new TL carriers entering the business after 1980 were nonunion and most were smaller, specialized carriers—some were solely dependent on one large contract.[18] The shakeup in the industry that ensued from the 1980 legislation fostered a period of chaos. Bankruptcies increased dramatically, with more than 1,400 companies failing in 1984 and over 1,500 in 1985 compared to only 167 in 1978.[19] Meanwhile, new carriers swamped the market, increasing from 16,606 in 1977 to 47,890 in 1991. Employment increased an average of nearly 4 percent a year in the early 1980s, while average wages declined 24 percent between 1977 and 1990.[20]

Deregulation created a two-tiered wage structure in the industry—LTL carriers continue to get decent wages procured largely through collective bargaining, while wages and working conditions for TL drivers collapsed, prompting Belzer to describe driving in this sector as sweat labor. As Belzer documents, drivers, freight handlers, and other nonsupervisory workers in the trucking industry lost 29.5 percent in average earnings between 1977 and 1996, compared to an 8.2 percent loss among other manufacturing and service production workers.[21]

Deregulation opened up opportunities for new drivers, as the downward pull on wages resulted in extraordinary turnover among drivers and as economic growth increased demand for them. In 1977, large freight trucks rolled over 47 billion miles of road, but by 1997, more than 112 billion miles, a 139 percent increase.[22] Opening up the floodgates to entry-level drivers resolved this dilemma, and a growing Latino population seized upon these new opportunities. Between 1983 and 2001, the number of Latino truck drivers increased from 125,500 to 400,000, or from 6 to 13 percent of all drivers.[23]

Deregulation also injected chaos into the industry as Julio's experiences in his first five years of driving illustrate. Large companies attempted to stay afloat by squeezing wages and keeping drivers on the road for as long as possible.[24] A 1997 University of Michigan survey found that nonunion, long-haul drivers were on the road an average of sixty-five hours per week (five over the legal limit) at wages that averaged around $10.75 per hour if drivers were not paid overtime rates. Turnover in these jobs was 100 percent, and carriers often scrambled to hire two or three drivers a year to keep a truck on the road.[25]

Smaller single-contract companies sprang up all over the place, while dispatchers seemingly hung their signs on "satellite shingles," where, literally, having a radio "will travel." Others cobbled together down payments to buy trucks that they subsequently leased for exorbitant fees to novices trying to figure out the trade—and in some cases with unwritten promises that the driver would own the truck after making payments for a set amount of time. Julio meandered through this minefield. He took his first job in 1995 at $10 an hour, with minimal medical and vacation benefits. He stayed for three years to gain experience, and was making $12.80 an hour when he decided to test the market. For the next two years, he changed jobs seven times, working for five different companies.

During these two years, Julio learned the variables that determined the quality of the job: regional compared to cross-country driving; rules regarding who unloaded the trucks; how driving and warehouse time were paid; and how tolls were compensated. Wages did not vary much for entry-level drivers—hourly wages hovered around $12 an hour, while long-haul jobs tended to pay 32 cents per mile. Julio worked for single-contract companies that went bankrupt when they lost their contract and closed shop without paying owed wages. He leased a truck for two months in an attempt to establish more autonomy in the trade, but unfavorable and unwritten terms resulted in no income for the two months, after which he walked away from the deal. Julio left a job after one day, when he found out that he was required to unload the truck himself and that the job paid paltry wages while he was in the warehouse. He left another job that required daily routes to New York City, but paid by the mile and not while he was sitting for hours in traffic jams.

Fed up with small seat-of-your-pants companies, Julio finally landed a job with a larger TL carrier. After a week of orientation and training in Indiana, Julio returned to Springfield with a truck. He drove throughout the East, largely in Pennsylvania, New Jersey, and New York, and was away from home for long stretches of time. After about a month on the job, he realized that his checks were turning up short. The company apparently withheld the amount of the tolls on his check until they could verify that he had actually paid them. Julio objected to this practice, claiming that they had failed to explain this in orientation and that the verification process was so slow that it often took more than one pay period to reconcile the paperwork with his logbook and receipts—and even then Julio still found discrepancies in the company's favor. He felt the company was cheating him, and after complaining several times decided to quit. He was on the road, near a terminal in Pennsylvania, when he made the decision, and suggested to the dispatcher that he return the truck to the terminal. The dispatcher begged him to drive to New Jersey and do a few more pickups before he returned the truck. He complied, but when he completed the pickups and delivery, the dispatcher again attempted to keep him on the road. Julio drew the line. The dispatcher then angrily explained that he could drop the truck off at the terminal in Pennsylvania.

A few weeks later, Julio received his last check from the company. Expecting $1,200, he received $300. When he called the company, they explained that an employee had driven the truck from the Pennsylvania terminal to the company's headquarters in Indiana and that they had charged Julio for the employee's time and transportation costs, which totaled $900. Julio was livid, but felt he had little legal recourse—paying an attorney and filing a claim in Pennsylvania was not financially feasible.

Returning home out of work, Julio called the company where his driving career had begun. They explained that they didn't have any openings at the time, but that they would contact him if circumstances changed. Desperate for work, Julio then called a temporary employment agency. Not only did they tell him that they could place him right away in a driving job, they placed him with the same company that had just told Julio they didn't have any openings—the company where he had worked his first three years. The arrangement was a classic outsourcing case—the hourly wage was $13 an hour, 20 cents more than when Julio left the company two years prior, but it came without any benefits. Julio swallowed his pride and accepted.

And so it went. Deregulation was a two-way street—on the one side, it opened up the labor market to more groups; on the other, it unleashed a set of forces that stood as a reminder of why industrial regulation had been valued in the earlier part of the century. However, in 2000, Julio's perseverance, accumulated hours logged on the road, and flawless driving record, topped with perhaps a sprinkle of good luck, resulted in a job offer that would lead to a unionized position. Six months later he was admitted into the union, earning $14.75 an hour for a regional LTL carrier. In 2004, his hourly wage increased to $16.88 and then to $18.88 in February 2005, after two years of contract negotiations between the management and union were finally completed.

Julio was the most successful of the men on the block to find gainful employment and leave the streets. His rejection of street life occurred as he forged a new identity. He made reference to his friend Jorge, who after his release from prison was "still out there doing his thing" dealing drugs and "just being stupid. I guess he ain't learned yet." Julio's movement away from an old identity coincided with his language of growing up, taking care of his family, of not being "stupid anymore." As Julio would remind me, "I always worked, bro." And yet, as we will see in the next chapter, his old street identity would continue to surface at times, putting his achievements at risk. Still, Julio's identity was solidified by the rewards and status that went along with it—he had achieved working-class respectability, was providing for his extended family, and had fully entered into the world of the American consumer.

Fatherhood

Unlike the manufacturing era, the dearth of entry-level, living-wage jobs in the deregulated, postindustrial period meant that many of the men who left the streets for jobs at the end of the 1990s would spend time working for temporary job agencies. At thirty-eight, Mundo described this:

> It sucked, but it [the temp agency] was somewhere to go, you know. They send you out and I'm a good worker. So you wait ninety days to see if the company is going to hire you. But what would happen is they don't pay you shit when you working for

the agency. The agency makes all the money. Then when they want to hire me, they want to pay 10 cents more. I'm like, fuck that, you know. They paying the agency all this money, but they want to pay me 10 cents more.

Temporary job agencies played an important role in the restructured economy, but not a role that was primarily intended to benefit workers.

Prior to the 1990s, employers routinely laid workers off during economic recessions with the expectation they would rehire them once the next recovery was under way. After the 1990–91 recession, however, many temporary layoffs became permanent layoffs, as employers augmented their outsourcing strategies by sending more jobs overseas and by utilizing temporary staffing agencies in the United States.[26] The strategic use of temporary agencies to rehire during the recovery periods allowed employers to create more "flexible" workforces or, in other words, to place surplus labor more effectively at employers' disposal. So even during the 1993–2001 period of uninterrupted economic growth, the use of temporary workers increased 92 percent, from 1.32 million to 2.54 million jobs nationwide.[27]

Mundo utilized temporary agencies, until he landed his job at a machine shop in West Springfield. He started at the shop making $9 an hour and, having survived an economic downturn that reduced the workforce from thirty-five to thirteen employees, was making $13 an hour in 2003 and was the second longest working employee at the shop. In turn, Mundo rarely hung out on the block any longer, even after Jorge was released from prison. Occasionally he would have an evening out, usually with his brothers, and spend a night at the bar, but it was rare. His attitudes about the street changed as he settled into a more domestic lifestyle.

As described earlier, a snapshot of Mundo in 1996 would have identified him as a thirty-two-year-old man whose life had been shaped by a culture of the street. But with the benefit of a longitudinal profile, we see that Mundo, like others, is much more complex than that —to reduce him to a street character would be misleading. The change in his life trajectory included past experiences that he drew on to engage the current circumstances of his life. He was neither "street" nor "decent," the categories used by Elijah Anderson to describe inner-city blacks. Instead, Mundo's life was made up of an accumulation of experiences that shaped his view of life and his expectations, as well as changing opportunities from which he made decisions, developed strategies, and created an identity.

Unlike Julio, however, Mundo's job did not provide much status, nor did his wages allow for much consumer joy. Instead, Mundo described his trajectory off the streets in terms of fatherhood. When Mundo rejected the streets as a lifestyle that masked feelings of self-loathing, he saw his own father in the life of his brother Jorge: "He [Jorge] wants to look like he's got what he ain't got. He's just like my father. That's how he lived too." Mundo described his father's desperation to be somebody at a cost to his family:

> He wanted to be a big guy . . . my father was a gambler, you know. So one time I saw him win $11,000. Really! Eleven thousand fucking dollars. He liked to take chances and he was lucky. The family didn't see a penny of it, though. He didn't give my mother a dime.

Mundo's father was a broken man, an alcoholic who was extremely abusive toward Mundo's mother and who damaged people around him in his quest to be somebody in a world that had cast a dark social-economic shadow over him and his generation of Puerto Rican migrants and had left him largely invisible and obsolete.

Mundo was sitting in his aging Ford Bronco with his daughter in the driveway in the summer of 2003 when Julio and I rolled up. "What the hell are you crazy bastards doing here?" he bellowed. We jumped into the backseat and rode along as Mundo took his daughter, then fourteen, to softball practice. Mundo proudly exclaimed that her team had "won the championship for the past three years." On the ride to the field, Mundo talked mostly to his daughter. When we returned to the house, we met his three-year-old son. The house was small, but Mundo and his wife had created a bedroom for their daughter by finishing the basement. Their son had his own room, covered with stuffed animals, "but he never sleeps here, he's always in our bed," Mundo added. Reflecting on the last several years of his life, Mundo commented, "It's great, man, my kids are everything. I mean, that's what we're here for, right, Julio?" A few weeks later, during a lengthy conversation with Mundo on a range of topics, including fatherhood, he described his devotion to his children as an attempt "to be the father that my father wasn't." Pointing to a picture on the wall of his father and brothers, Mundo explained, "He was a fuck-up, a drunk you know, and it took me a long time to forgive him."

For Mundo, the transition from the streets to the home provided him with a position of power and status within the patriarchal family. Mundo adopted authoritative forms of parenting, what might be popularly referred to as "tough love" strategies, as he threatened to spank his son for misbehaving on numerous occasions during my visits. Although Mundo never followed through on his threats, the "spare the rod, spoil the child" philosophy was evident and Mundo was the primary disciplinarian. He described his parenting struggles with his daughter. "She's a good kid. She went through a rough patch when she was thirteen, she didn't want to listen to nobody. But she grew out of it. She's a good kid, but it took a few spankings to get that, you know what I mean?"

When Mundo left the streets in 1998, he adopted a father identity, but reviewing my field notes I noticed that this identity was not entirely new. During the two years I had known Mundo on the block, I noted his absence from the block every other weekend when his daughter visited him. Mundo stayed in his mother's house on these nights, cooking, talking, and watching television with his daughter. On these weekends, he refrained from his substances of pleasure and devoted himself to his daughter. At the time, I noted with surprise the two sides of Mundo: the gregarious, funny, drug-indulging, center-of-the-party side of Mundo and yet the tender, attentive, devoted father side. There was more than one current running through Mundo and my eagerness to document street life almost prevented me from seeing it. When Mundo left the streets and fathering became his dominant identity, I "rediscovered" this side of Mundo that had of course been there all along, reminding me that individuals are a complex swirl of tendencies, dispositions, and sensibilities, and that identities change as the conditions in which we live give validity to different parts of our selves.

Managing Drug Addiction

Fatherhood did not only pave Mundo's way off of the streets, it was also central to Sammy's transition as well, although it would take several years before this would occur. As described earlier, Sammy's drug business in Greenfield resulted in a relationship with Cheryl, a white woman who had grown up poor with a heroin-addicted father. Cheryl and Sammy had three girls together—the first two twins— and lived in Chicopee. After three years, Sammy left Cheryl and moved to Springfield. Sammy and his family continued their involvement with his three daughters—Sammy provided money, albeit irregularly, and made frequent visits, while the rest of the family celebrated birthdays and holidays and regularly took the children for weekend visits.

In many ways, Sammy had been lucky up to this point. During the early 1990s, he had survived police surveillance in Greenfield and gang wars in Springfield. In 1996, Sammy was in the thick of the drug trade in Springfield, working closely with Jorge to organize the distribution circuits and "breaking night" regularly. Sammy had sweated through the withdrawal symptoms of his heroin dependency and with the support of Jorge had stopped using—business came before pleasure and Jorge was adamant that heroin and business didn't mix. Sammy drank beer, smoked weed, and snorted lines of cocaine nightly, but had managed to stay away from heroin for a little more than a year. In 1998, when Jorge went to prison, Sammy was still standing.

When I arrived on the block in 1996, Sammy and Jorge were making and spending lots of money. Sammy was receptive but cautious around me—he had a lot to lose. His brother Julio had given me clearance to hang out with the group and Sammy had seen me around with Fausto in prior years, but developing trust would take some time with Sammy. Sammy's experience on the streets was obvious. He worked the bars with apparent ease and experience, demanded respect on the streets, was both charming and unforgiving, and could read situations on the street better than anyone I knew. As Fausto would comment years later, "Sammy is an encyclopedia of the streets."

In 1997, unbeknownst to Jorge, Sammy ran into an old friend and started using heroin again. He used the drug sparingly over the next year, mostly because of Jorge's vigilance. But when Jorge went to prison in 1998, Sammy's heroin use escalated. Jorge's absence also meant that Sammy would have to deal more directly with Alexander, a partnership that was a recipe for disaster. Sammy didn't like, or trust, Alexander. At this time, Sammy also met a Puerto Rican woman who would help decrease his street involvement.

María was street-savvy, smart, independent, and assertive. Raised in a predominantly white community and educated in white schools, María had acquired some educational skills—certainly more than Sammy—but had been on her own since she was fourteen. The mother of three at the time, María had survived a nine-year violent relationship with the father of her children, but left him when he went to prison. She was then involved with a successful Dominican drug dealer for four years. ("He wasn't out there dealing on the streets. All of his customers were white.") He treated her well and was a good provider for her children, but his frequent absences to the Dominican Republic and the stress of his trade had diminished María's interest in the relationship when she met Sammy.

Standing on the dance floor with María in his arms, Sammy introduced me to "his girl." He had talked about her for weeks prior to the introduction and was eager for me to meet her. After a brief exchange, I asked Sammy if he had seen Alexander. He answered abruptly: "I don't know where he is and I don't care." María didn't like Alexander and was determined to get Sammy away from him. But Sammy was playing both sides of the fence. When I saw him a few days later by himself, I teased him: "Hey, what's up, Sam? Looks like you in love, bro." "Nah, man," he quickly retorted, "that's the way I treat all my women." But his relationship with María was different.

The tension with Alexander had increased because Sammy told him he was going to sell independently, which meant using his own source, most likely one of Alexander's competitors. And María was intent on monopolizing as much of Sammy's time as possible. Pushed in one direction by his disdain for Alexander and pulled in the other by his new relationship with María, a realignment occurred when Sammy and María moved to Hartford together. Sammy distanced himself from the streets—he didn't know any of the players in Hartford and, besides, the streets were carved up by Hartford gangs in 1998. But his heroin addiction escalated and he continued to make occasional trips to Springfield, usually to get high with his childhood friend Roberto. Finally he broke the news to María—he had a problem and was checking himself into detox. María's street savvy had failed her on this one: "I was so naïve. I didn't know. I'm living with this guy and I didn't have a clue!"

After detox, Sammy began taking methadone every morning and working for a temporary job agency in Hartford. Despite Sammy's street involvement, he was no stranger to work. Even while he was living in the apartment in Springfield and dealing with Jorge, he was working under-the-table jobs. He worked for a demolition crew three days a week and could usually find construction or roofing work in the warmer months. Even when he was breaking night with the guys, he would put in ten-hour days pounding cement basement floors into rubble and carrying the pieces away in buckets. The work kept him in shape and, even though it was under the table, provided an alibi to his drug income, or as he said, "Cover-up-like. They [the detectives] will see you coming from work . . . if you're working, you have an answer for them."

María took a full-time job in Hartford entering data for a research center, while the temp agency assigned Sammy to cafeteria work for an insurance company in a Hartford suburb. Not long after, María became pregnant. When Sammy Jr. was born, he became the third child in the home (María's oldest child was living with her father). Together, Sammy and María worked each day and took care of the children. Sammy shared the child-rearing responsibilities for all three children in the home, and he and Sammy Jr. were inseparable. He had also reached out to his three daughters in Massachusetts. Every other weekend, I watched in utter amazement as he and María took care of six children in their tiny two-bedroom apartment.

The father identity was central to Sammy's drug recovery and to keeping him away from the streets of Springfield. Like Mundo,

Sammy devoted his life to his children—it provided him with a sense of purpose. Work, fatherhood, a supportive relationship, and methadone maintenance created a viable foundation for Sammy. The methadone made him drowsy, especially in the morning, but it seemed to take away the immediacy of his daily heroin craving. On occasion, Sammy would still slip away and get high. He was most vulnerable to these urges when "three things happen: whenever I got money in my pocket, when I'm stressed, or when it's free." To manage the first, he gave his paycheck to María, and the latter, he stayed away from Springfield.

Poorly educated and lacking work experience in the service sector, Sammy's prospects in the "new economy" were not promising. Economic expansion did, however, open up new possibilities that inspired him. While working in the cafeteria at the insurance company, Sammy was trained as a grill cook in a far different work environment than prior construction and demolition jobs had provided. The food subcontractor for the insurance company hired Sammy full-time, transferring his work status from the temporary job agency. His supervisor was supportive of Sammy and encouraged him to enroll in a program at the culinary institute to become a professional chef. The supervisor's validation of Sammy's budding professional identity was central to his confidence and motivation, but to enroll in the institute he had to face one major obstacle—he could barely read or write. María agreed to help him read the book and prepare his written lessons, and they took out a governmental loan to meet the hefty enrollment fee.

Sammy's experiences at the culinary institute were transformative. At enrollment, Sammy received a textbook, a chef's hat, and a set of knives. During a summer birthday party in his mother's backyard, Sammy briefly disappeared in the house and returned wearing the hat and wielding a twelve-inch chef's knife. He skillfully sharpened the knife, stuck it in the picnic table, and entertained us: "Welcome to Chef Sammy's, where today you will be cooking with Chef Sammy in the 'hood." He and María talked about their dream of opening their own restaurant and even described some of their planned nightly menu specials. Sammy would cook, María would take care of the rest. At one point in the evening, Sammy turned to me. "Tim, I know how you must feel about your teaching, because now I'm feeling passionate about something like you."

Sammy brought out a large textbook to show us what he was learning. He talked about food-borne illnesses. He had just taken a test and was awaiting the results, but his fears of failing were evident. Attempting to recall lessons about food bacteria, he would forget a concept, close his eyes, stamp his foot on the ground. "Oh, why can't I remember this? Wait, wait, I know what it is! Ah, what is it, damn it!" His brother Fausto was less than supportive and taunted him: "Can you read this book?" Sammy replied defensively, "What are you talking about, of course I can read the book." Fausto was unrelenting. "All these words?" he asked as he thumbed through the pages. "Most of 'em," Sammy replied, "and the ones I can't, well, I leave that to my tutor," pointing to María. Angry, María snatched the book from Fausto and snapped, "Don't you worry about it, we'll get through it."

Unfortunately, Fausto's provocation revealed a deep truth that both he and his brother suffered—they were virtually illiterate. Despite María's assistance, Sammy failed the test by one point. Because he was so close to passing it, he was allowed to take it again. But while preparing for the exam, conditions changed at work. His supervisor left and he didn't get along with his new supervisor, whom he described as prejudiced. A few of Sammy's friends were fired and Sammy no longer received the approval and support he needed. Moreover, after working a full day, he was attending the institute every evening and was wearing out—falling asleep at school and further behind in his course work, and missing work more often. These were circumstances that threatened Sammy's sobriety.

Sammy asked for a transfer to a different cafeteria in the Hartford area. He was transferred, but his hours were reduced. Amidst these changes, Sammy began slipping away to get high, which caused problems between him and María, who was no longer so naïve about his drug use. He was fired at work for absences. He knew his recovery was in jeopardy and thought the best remedy was work—or something that would preoccupy him. He had fallen hopelessly behind at the institute, so he formally discontinued his training with the dream of returning someday. He went back to the temp agency.

For the next several months, Sammy worked a flurry of jobs. He accepted whatever work was available, often working fifty to sixty hours a week at several locations. The pay was usually between $7 and $8 an hour. The agency sent him to light-assembly plants and warehouses in the region. For a brief time, they assigned him to a desk job, working on a computer. Sammy called one night in need of a ride to work the following morning and, just as his cafeteria job had piqued his imagination, the desk job triggered class fantasies. On the ride to work Sammy kept repeating, "I can't tell you what it means to me." He emphasized that he was "sitting at a desk all day" and "working on a computer," and that "it makes me feel good, like I really am somebody." But the job was only temporary and two weeks later Sammy was moving on. He received a job tip from a friend and was hired full-time delivering furniture for a large retail outlet. He continued working part-time in the evenings whenever the temp agency had work for him.

The pillars of support that stabilized Sammy's life were methadone maintenance, fatherhood, his relationship with María, and a job in which he could make a significant contribution to the family wage and was valued by his employer. When these pieces of Sammy's life were working together, he felt strong and confident, and able to confront his addiction. It is difficult to document personal feelings of inadequacy that stem from social marginalization, because few people, irrespective of how close you are to them, are comfortable revealing the depth of their vulnerabilities, even to themselves. As Sammy's comments at the beginning of this chapter suggest, at times he would let me in—he saw himself as a "fuck-up," or a "fucking loser" who "ain't shit." He attributed these feelings to his drug addiction, but I suspect the reservoir of these feelings ran deeper. Drug use for Sammy was both the cause and consequence of these feelings.

Many of the men from the block left the streets at the end of the 1990s. As they did, their identities changed and their biographies were reconstructed. Many men will age off the streets at some point. The lower echelons of the drug trade often consist of young men (and increasingly women) who cycle in and out of the trade, but few stick around for long if they manage to avoid prison terms. But how they come off the streets varies. The particular permutations of aging off depend on social networks, institutional interventions, job opportunities, personal vitality, and no lack of good fortune. Sustained economic growth expanded job opportunities for men less attached to the labor force at the end of the 1990s. Certainly, post-1970s economic restructuring that advanced deregulation, deindustrialization, capital mobility, corporate mergers, and flexible labor force strategies placed important restrictions on 1990s job opportunities for working-class and low-income populations. Still, many men left the streets behind as a result of a tighter labor market. Sustaining these transitions, however, would not be an easy task.

SEVEN

Transitions

JULIO WAS AN EXCEPTION. He was among the small group of the urban poor that Katherine Newman refers to as the "high flyers," who found their way into middle-income jobs during the tight labor market of the late 1990s.[1] Most of the men from the block, however, meandered between two pathways—the school-to-prison pipeline or the path to unstable postindustrial jobs. Transitions involve both continuities and discontinuities, and permanent movement from the streets to the workplace required these men to manage racial and ethnic conflicts in the workplace, meet family needs and expectations, negotiate street loyalties and former street identities, cope with social isolation, and, for some, deal with drug addictions. There were gains to moving off the streets and into jobs—in social status, in the moral identity of being a father and family provider, and as consumers. There were also losses— in male camaraderie, street status, and the excitement of the streets that reinforced masculine identities.

Truck driving was an easier transition for men with masculine street identities to make than retail jobs characteristic of a service economy. Just as warehouse jobs, assembly work, cab driving, security and prison guard labor, or even military enlistment are more likely to reinforce masculine identities than the multitude of cashier, telemarketing, or floor-room sales jobs, truck driving provided a sense of control over one's own work life. It emphasized autonomy and independence, if not the defiant individualism observed on the block. At a party several months after Edgar, the ex-Marine who followed Julio into the trucking trade, had been driving for a nonunion company, he described conflicts he encountered at some of his stops:

I don't stay. I tell them they got one hour to get this load unloaded or to give me an empty trailer. If they don't get it done in one hour, I go home. People on the docks, they union, and they don't like us nonunion, you know. They got an attitude, but I don't take their shit. They be like, we don't have time to unload now. And I say okay, the load's going back. And they either unload it or I bring it back.

Edgar continued his male posturing:

In the yard, they know me. When the boss comes out, he be shaking. He walks up to me, he's shaking. "Yeah, Edgar, what is it?" I tell them the way it is. They know me there, they know I'm not going to take anybody's shit.

Conflicts with authority in the workplace are inevitable, especially in most working-class positions. Collective bargaining provides a process for addressing conflicts in an arena where the stockholders' primary interest is to increase the value of their holdings, the managers' is to increasing productivity, and the workers' is to acquire a good wage and be treated with dignity. In the work spaces provided within manufacturing industries, male workers develop a shop culture in which their identities as workers are grounded in masculine forms of resistance expressed through dress, language, jokes, after-work drinking, or, as Edgar aptly put it, in "not taking any shit from bosses." Philippe Bourgois points out that in a service economy, retail and office jobs are incompatible with a shop-floor culture and provide fewer spaces for masculine resistance and identity.[2] Truck driving is peculiar in that it does not provide shop-floor solidarity, but still reinforces masculine identities, and perhaps, as Edgar suggests, masculine forms of resistance.

Edgar's bravado, however, most likely exaggerates his confrontational behavior—individual resistance to authority has to be moderated in any job context, especially when managers have the option of replacing the individual and where collective resistance is less likely to occur. Julio was perhaps more honest about this. He knew that he must walk the line between deference to authority—keeping silent when it appeared strategically worthwhile to do so—and self-respect—maintaining the boundary between self-validation and legitimate supervisory behavior. Still, the male culture found on the block and on the street reinforced a masculine identity that served Julio well in the trucking trade and provided a relatively smooth transition to the workplace. Julio described some of the conflict he had to manage at the warehouses where he made his deliveries:

> People on the docks be fucking with you. You know, I have to make sure they count everything. Sometimes they don't want to do that; they want to keep things moving. There'll be trucks backed up at the dock and shit. Drivers want you to move your truck and the warehouse guys don't want to take the time to count. I tell 'em I'm not going to lose my job because you in a hurry. I make 'em count it. They be like, "Fuck you, man. Get that truck out of the way, we got work to do." I tell 'em, "I ain't moving. . . . You want another truck up here, you get your fucking pencils out and start counting, because I ain't moving." They be cussing me out and shit, but fuck that. You think I'm going to lose my job because of a bunch of motherfuckers I don't even know? . . . So they cuss me out, but they count the shit. The other drivers be like, "Get this truck out of the dock, we got a schedule." But I don't move it until it's all counted and the paperwork signed. I'm like, "Fuck you guys, you know that truck is going to sit there until my shit's done and I'm ready to move it."

Julio's familiarity with "in your face" male interaction allowed him to engage warehouse dynamics in a manner that provided continuity with the cultural dispositions he had already developed, but would be unacceptable in most service sector workplaces.

Masculine defiant behavior is more likely to be tolerated by managers when it is bounded by labor unions and collectively defined codes of conduct or when a tight labor market exists. But masculine identities can also result in conflicts between co-workers and can therefore threaten successful transitions from the streets to the workplace, especially when racial and ethnic tensions are added to the mix.

RACIAL AND ETHNIC CONFLICTS

All of the men who transitioned into the workplace encountered racial and ethnic conflict. Julio was one of three Puerto Rican and ten African American drivers in a white-dominated workforce of around sixty. Deeply embedded racial status hierarchies made interracial interaction uncomfortable, difficult, and awkward. Cultural stereotypes advanced suspicion and mistrust, which were infused with a male workplace culture that emphasized mutual respect. At Julio's terminal, racial and ethnic tensions were generally managed through humor, as he described.

> So this white guy says to me, "Who left the gate open?" I'm like, "What you talking about?" And then he says, "Well, someone left the gate open because all these Puerto Ricans are coming in." So I just tell him, "You right and you better get used to it, 'cause we are taking over and you gonna be eating rice and beans before you know it."

In another instance:

> There was some money sitting up on this table and this white guy comes along and says to me, "Hey, I should take that money." I say to him, "What you mean?" He says, "I should take that money, because they not going to blame me, they going to blame you Puerto Ricans." So like I told him, "That may be true, but what you going to do when you can't find your teeth?"

Julio recalled one incident in which tensions boiled over and a racial epithet was hurled at a racial minority driver, but Julio was not involved, and the company fired the white driver for using aggressive language. Most of the ethnically loaded comments directed at Julio stemmed from the white perennial fear that racial minorities are "taking over." Other comments focused on language differences:

> Some of the white guys, like my supervisor, he will say that when his family came over, they learned how to speak English. They

learned English in the schools unlike us Spanish people, who can't learn how to speak English properly. I tell 'em, yeah, how many languages you speak, one? Well I speak two, so who's superior to who? You know I try to get 'em that way. . . . And then I tell them, "Yeah, well, you got no pride, 'cause when the Americans told your family to give up their language and learn English, they did. But my people got pride they wouldn't give their language up. We said hell no, we'll learn English, but we ain't giving up our language or our ways for you all." [laughter]

Julio's response reflected the Puerto Rican historical struggle to maintain cultural identity and integrity in the face of U.S. colonial domination discussed in Chapter 1.

During the 2004 presidential election, Julio described another exchange with his supervisor that invoked stereotypes. When his supervisor learned that he was supporting John Kerry, he taunted Julio: "What, you don't like extra money in your paycheck?" referring to President Bush's tax cuts. Julio reasoned, "It depends on what you doing with that tax money. If it's going to help people out, help people eat, you know, then I don't mind." His supervisor retorted, "All your tax money is doing is buying drugs for crackheads." Julio shot back, "Hey, you calling my family crackheads? 'Cause my family received welfare, you calling us a bunch of crack addicts?" These interactions occurred with some levity, but they nonetheless produced a work environment where the dominant narratives of white culture pressed upon the Puerto Rican struggle for dignity in the workplace.

In 2006, Julio had worked in the same plant for six years, but had not established friendships outside work with any of his co-workers. Clara was present during one of our conversations about racial dynamics in the workplace, and she pointed out that Julio had changed, that he had learned to take the ribbing and to give it back. "In the beginning," she continued, "you would never have taken it, you would have lost your temper and punched someone out." Interestingly, Julio had a difficult time accepting her compliment and snapped at Clara, "What you trying to say?" He suspected Clara was criticizing him for "taking it." Clara assured him that she wasn't criticizing him, but his response revealed the difficulty of managing these situations, of protecting the boundaries of his masculine self-respect within a larger context of racial subordination.

Mundo encountered similar situations where he worked. Like Julio, most of Mundo's co-workers at the machine shop were white. After five years at the shop, Mundo remarked, "They love me there, I'm real cool with the boss, I even got high with him." But the predominantly white workforce kept Mundo on guard, in a state of hypervigilance. Although small and wiry in build, Mundo exudes the persona of a tough guy. His torso and neck are covered in tattoos, which he regularly displays with tank tops, and his self-presentation is aggressive and confrontational. At thirty-nine, he lets everyone know that he can still handle himself in a fight. He described a confrontation with a twenty-year-old white co-worker:

> This guy kept fucking with me, talking shit, you know. Saying he could break me in half and he was real muscular, you know. Big guy, big fucking muscles, but you know me, Tim. I don't give a fuck. So this guy kept saying shit to his *white* friends and so I got tired of it and I told him, in front of everybody, I told him, "Look-it, you want to take this somewhere else, we can settle this shit. . . . You're big and you may beat my ass, but we'll see." The guy didn't do nothing. So a few days go by and I'm walking through the place and he says something to his buddy about me and they start laughing. That was it, I beat his ass. His face was all fucked up. . . . This *black* guy went to the boss and he told him that I kept telling the guy to lay off. So he stood up for me. My boss said why didn't you take it somewhere else, and I told him I tried to but the guy wasn't having it. My boss, he didn't do nothing. Matter of fact, Tim, he told me, he said, "You know, Mundo, just between you and me, that guy needed to get his ass kicked." [laughter]

Mundo has managed racial tensions at his workplace, in part, by gaining his white boss's acceptance.

Mundo's transition from the block to work has meant leaving behind his ethnic community and integrating himself into a white world. His humor has helped him to negotiate ethnic differences, but he is constantly on guard, testing white prejudice, attempting to break through. In the following anecdote, he described the white neighborhood bar he hung out at until his brother Jorge "fucked it up for me":

> The guys came over, so we went to the bar. Now, I used to be the only Puerto Rican that went in that bar, the only one! I never had no problems in there, I got treated good in there. No problems, but the fucking guys come over, and they got some nice-looking bitches in there, you know, so Jorge tries to rap to one of them and she doesn't pay him no mind. She just walks on by. So Jorge is pissed off, you know. A little later this bitch walks by and she's with this dude and another couple. And Jorge, that motherfucker, says real loud, "Well, aren't they a nice-looking couple, two dykes and two faggots." Now this dude is pissed, so he starts following us around. And he's talking shit to me, to me! I'm like, I didn't say nothing . . . I'm just minding my own business. But this guy kept it up, talking shit, so I took a swing at him and all hell broke loose. One guy got hit by a bottle and was taken out of there in an ambulance. Chairs and bottles were flying and shit. That's it, I haven't been back since. You know, you bring the Puerto Ricans in there and the whole place goes to hell. Jorge and those guys, you can't take them anywhere.

As the discussion continued, Mundo, Julio, and I returned to the topic of Puerto Ricans "fucking shit up." While entertaining, Mundo was nevertheless self-loathing in his ethnic humor.

> MUNDO: And Puerto Ricans are thieves, bro. Isn't that right Julio, we're a bunch of fucking thieves [laughter]. I been watching in the paper, and you know the white kids are stealing too, but mostly it's kids with Spanish names. My fucking car got broken into the other night. They smashed the windshield, fucking glass all over the place, and I bet you it was fucking Puerto Ricans. You know what I'm saying, Julio? You can't trust them Puerto Ricans, let them in and it

all goes to hell. [laughter] . . . But you know what I notice? Back in the day, white people hated us, bro. There was lots of prejudices. But now, I got white friends, I've been to their houses. There are a lot of white people I work with and they'll tell you it's changed, that their attitudes have changed, it's different now than back in the day. They cool with us.

JULIO: I seen the same where I work. I mean, they keep to themselves and all, but they cool, they polite, you know, nice toward us. I think it's different than before.

TIM: So now it's just you guys that hate Puerto Ricans. [laughter]

MUNDO: It's true though, too many thieves, man, too many fucking thieves.

While this exchange occurred in a spate of laughter, humor revealed a world of struggle. Both Julio's and Mundo's class mobility hinged on being integrated into the white world—they both worked in predominantly white workplaces and lived on the borders of racially and ethnically changing neighborhoods. For each of them, this produced tension and a need to perceptively discern the motives of the whites they encountered regularly. Moreover, for Mundo, acceptance by whites produced a repudiation of his own ethnic group, where white prejudices became internalized as his own.

Mundo's internalized blame has surfaced in other ways as well. Sitting at his dining room table, I once asked him about his school experiences. Mundo shied away from the conversation, admitting in a quiet, defeated tone, "I regret that most of all." Mundo dropped out in the tenth grade—"the streets are a bad influence," he added, "a strong temptation, Tim." Missing in Mundo's reconstructions of his past are the societal influences that shaped his life—the residential segregation of Puerto Ricans in Springfield in the 1970s, the unaccommodating school system, the lack of decent-paying jobs for residents in his community, the cultural assault on Puerto Rican dignity. Mundo spent his childhood fighting for his dignity—both literally and figuratively. The streets were his life, his place of survival in a world that had marginalized him. Today, he turns the blame toward himself and those "damn Puerto Ricans," as he tries to hold on to his fragile newfound status.

Racial and ethnic dynamics have also interfered with Sammy's efforts to transition off the streets into the workplace. At a temp agency in Hartford where Sammy worked, he was often sent to jobs in the suburbs. One of his job assignments required him to work from sunup to sundown on a Sunday, taking down large tents from an antiques show in a wealthy suburban town. It rained throughout the day and when Sammy returned to his car, it wouldn't start. He dried the distributor wires, but the engine still wouldn't turn over. He called me to pick him up and we left his car there overnight. The next morning I drove him back and we worked on the car for a while, but found it needed a new rotor. After some searching, we located a rotor and I dropped Sammy at his car and went to the university. I agreed to check on him later that afternoon, but when I returned Sammy was nowhere to be found. I waited for an hour before calling María. She was incensed. She had given Sammy money to buy parts for the car and, knowing that Sammy was in a vulnerable period of his drug recovery, she feared he was out getting high. I had no reason to think otherwise and went home.

The next day I swung by Sammy's on my way to work and, to my relief, he was there and had not spent the prior afternoon getting high. While Sammy was working on his car, the town police drove up and asked for his identification, which he didn't have. Sammy described the incident:

> They were going through the car while they were asking me for my ID. When I told them I didn't have one and they could check my Social Security, they got smart with me. They said, "Hey, am I the President of the United States? Well, I could tell you I am and make up some numbers. Would you believe me?" You know, he comes with, "You can tell me anything."

The police handcuffed Sammy, drove him to the police station, locked him up until they could verify his identity. Sam continued:

> I was kicking that fucking door, man. They locked me up for nothing. So I was kicking it. Finally they came and, you know, asked what was my problem. I told 'em, "You got me locked up

and you don't got no charges on me. That ain't right." They said it was going to take some time to verify and that if I didn't calm down they were going to charge me. I told 'em go ahead and charge me, 'cause at least then I could make bail and get the fuck out of here.

The police later verified the ownership of the car. When they were releasing him, they mentioned that they knew he was out on bail, which Sammy felt was an attempt to justify holding him. Sammy said bitterly, "They unlocked the door and said I was free to go. That was it, man. Four fucking hours and they didn't even apologize!" Sammy had $8 on him, so he took a bus. But the bus left him around seven miles short of his home, which he walked, arriving at his apartment late in the night, fuming.

Racism was a formidable barrier for men attempting to make the transition from the street economy to the formal workplace. Racial dynamics are complex and have to be managed, and doing so within a context in which racial and class subordination exacerbates the needs for respect can be difficult and, at times, self-effacing. But there are other salient dynamics that threatened street-to-workplace transitions as well.

Family Loyalties and Expectations

Mr. González, the "wig dude," said to Fausto when he was trying to get into a GED program that family can be "a noose around your neck," referring to how the multiple needs of poor families can hold back individuals who are attempting to establish careers and acquire assets. The agency director's comments contrasted sharply with the lessons that Juan and Angela had taught their children about family. As Julio once described, "I was taught that no matter what, you always got family." As Julio's driving career developed, he experienced these colliding cultures—one represented by middle-class individualism, the other by a community culture derived from poor rural life in Puerto Rico and reproduced on the urban mainland.

Julio is devoted to his career and derives many rewards from it—working-class status, the esteemed identity of family breadwinner, and consumer pleasure. And yet Julio has always had to make considerably more money to make ends meet than the typical nuclear family household because he is the primary provider for his extended family. Julio doles out money to his family whenever they are in need—which is often. He sends $100 to his father in Puerto Rico every month and, more recently, an airline ticket from Puerto Rico to Springfield when his father needed to be hospitalized for a heart condition. When his brothers were incarcerated, they regularly sent him lists of clothing needs and expected him to deposit cash in their commissary. He sent Fausto rent money when he was short and has bought him clothes on more than a few occasions. He has sent his nephew money for school clothes each year and even paid for a lawyer when one of his nieces was in trouble. While family members try not to impose, Julio has the deepest pockets in the family.

Julio gives unreservedly. Work is necessary to provide for family, and sharing resources is an expectation of family members, but Julio's job is more than work, it is a career. Such opportunities were rare on the hillsides of Villalba, or in the tobacco fields, the fruit orchards, or the manufacturing plants where his father found work on the mainland. Julio derives identity and satisfaction from his career, from climbing into his cab and steering his eighteen-wheeler down I-90 toward Boston. His paycheck is a sign of success, but so are the driving skills he is valued for within a postindustrial economy. He is fiercely loyal to his family, but he is also loyal to his career, and sometimes these loyalties come into conflict.

One afternoon, Julio, Sammy, and I drove to northeastern Massachusetts to pick up Fausto. On the return trip to Springfield, Sammy and Fausto exploited Julio's conflict between career and family. Their mother was cooking dinner to celebrate their birthdays, all of which are within three weeks of one another. But Julio had to work that afternoon, so I was dropping him at the terminal.

SAMMY: Mom's cooking for us, man. This is for all our
    birthdays. How you gonna go to work, you know what that's
    going to do to Mom? How you gonna do that? This is family.
FAUSTO: How many times you called in?

JULIO: Once, that's all, when I had to get in between Clara and
Iris. I couldn't leave 'cause Clara had lost it. Iris was acting
up and Clara lost it!

FAUSTO: Once! What you doing, bro? [Turns to Sammy] Jules
is trying to get his picture on the wall there as one of those
employees of the month. You know, he be smiling like this
[big toothy smile, laughter]. Yeah, you know, Sam, he be
smiling: "Hey, I'm the employee of the month."

Julio deflected their entreaties, but his discomfort was evident as he
sat in the front seat next to me. At one point he turned to me, the only
person in the car who he knew would validate his career identity, and
asked softly, "What you think, Tim?" I replied in a low voice, beneath
the raucous banter coming from the backseat, "I think you know what
you got to do and your brothers will understand." He turned to
Sammy and Fausto, "I'm going into work, I told this guy I was coming in. I already seen Mom, she knows. So, I'm going in."

Refusing to concede, Fausto and Sammy took another tack.
Fausto told him that he needed Julio to put an alternator belt on a car
so that he could drive it back to his home; otherwise, he would be
stranded. This broke Julio's resolve. For a moment, he seriously considered calling in sick. But when it was revealed that Fausto didn't
have the part, Julio regained his composure. He told them where to
find the tools and where the auto parts store was located, but again
declared he was going to work. Sammy made one more attempt,
telling Julio that he "calls into work when things come up and it's no
big deal." Julio fended this one off easily; he knew the difference
between a career job and a temp job, even if Sammy was unwilling to
discern between the two. But the conversation exposed the value conflict that Julio struggles to manage. When I dropped him at work, the
brothers exchanged words of affection as they said goodbye. Julio
appeared relieved as he climbed out of the car—he had, for the
moment, navigated through the intersection of history, family, and
social mobility.

Negotiating the demands of family and career has been difficult
for Julio, and indeed as Mr. González suggested, it has slowed Julio's
class mobility. Getting ahead is much easier when one can disassoci-

ate himself from family needs and focus on his own achievements, pleasures, and asset acquisitions. Julio cannot. As we will see, he has spent many years spinning in place—paying accumulated debts and taking care of his extended family's needs— before gaining any traction toward working-class stability. In other words, it has taken Julio longer than most to convert middle-income status into personal and family stability. There are several reasons for this, which we will return to shortly. But first, it is not only family loyalty and expectations that threaten his transition from the streets to work, but also loyalty to friends.

STREET LOYALTY AND STREET REP

Sitting on his father's veranda in Villalba in the summer of 2006 sipping rum, Julio and I talked about the "old days" on the streets. Julio insisted, "I had me a reputation out there, you know what I'm saying? And if you got a rep, nobody's gonna fuck with you." During the prior six years while Julio was developing his driving career, I had noted on several occasions that he had nonetheless put his career at risk. He had continued hanging out with his street friends and had been involved in several fights and barroom brawls, while his wife, Clara, begged him to find new friends. "As a matter of fact," Julio slipped into our conversation on the veranda that night, "I still got me a reputation."

Having a reputation and demonstrating loyalty to friends are highly valued on the streets, and making a transition off the streets into the workplace means that both of these will have to be managed or relinquished. A reputation, however, is a form of status, and status a form of power, and no one gives up power easily. At the same time, loyalty, as we saw in Chapter 5, runs deep on the streets, especially when it reinforces one's reputation. Julio and Jorge are close friends and their friendship is embedded in their biographies, in being out there together, in "war stories," in late-night inebriation, in deep mutual affection. Moreover, on the streets, Julio and Jorge played central roles among a network of men who together produced valuable social and material resources that were rooted in mutual expectations of reciprocity. In 2003, however, they found themselves in different places—Julio driving a truck and earning a union wage, married and a committed father; Jorge a drug dealer and carouser, with reversed days and nights. But loyalty runs deep and one incident (among many) illustrates the point.

Shortly after his release from federal prison, Jorge was thrust into the street war between his brother Alexander and Little Acosta over stolen money and drug market competition. Little Acosta sent Jorge a warning by peppering his car with bullets while it was parked on the street. Not long after, Julio and Jorge were sitting on a curb next to a bar, having a beer and a hot dog, exhausted from a long day of working on a car, when Little Acosta suddenly appeared from behind Jorge and hit him in the head with the handle of a knife. Julio was incensed. He confronted Little Acosta, who, according to Julio, was hiding "behind his boys." Julio told him to "quit acting like a pussy and be a man." Some of the men protecting Little Acosta knew Julio and tried to defuse the situation by telling Julio their beef was not with him, but with Jorge. Sizing up the situation, Julio finally backed down but emphasized to Little Acosta that "this ain't right and you all know it. This ain't right!"

Julio and Jorge regrouped and showed up at Little Acosta's birthday party the following weekend, only this time with Fausto, Roberto, Benedicto, and Roberto's cousin. Julio and Roberto went with guns.

So we get there and we're standing outside and everybody is coming up to me, "Hey, Julio, what up, man? We know that what this guy did wasn't right, but we don't want no trouble, you know, let it go." . . . So while I'm standing out there some of his boys are starting to surround me, they be moving in. So I reached behind me and cocked the gun like this [makes sound], and they all be running [laughs], they scattered. So then I went upstairs and I said to Little Acosta, come down here, bro, and fight this guy [Jorge] like a man. Just you and him. But he be like, "I got nothing with you guys. I don't want nothing with you." So I told him that Jorge is Jorge and Alexander is Alexander and you can't be going after Jorge for what Alexander did to you. I told him, yeah, I'd be pissed too if some guy took me for my money, but I told this guy, Jorge didn't have nothing to do with that. He was locked up when that shit was going down. I told him that shit ain't right and that he knows it. So he apologized. And so we left.

Curious about why Julio continued to put himself in these situations, I asked him why it was so difficult to leave the streets behind.

JULIO: Man, I can't get away from the streets, they just follow me.

TIM: Look, Julio, I'm not saying what you should have done, but what if you were to say to Jorge, "Sorry, man, I can't get back out there, I got a wife and a kid and I got to think about them. Sorry."

JULIO: Then I take myself out of the game. I'm out. I got nobody to watch my back, I can't hang out, go to the bars or nothing. I mean, I can take care of myself, but it will be different. If I let this go, I don't do nothing. I mean this guy was hanging with me. Little Acosta disrespected me. He and I are supposed to be boys and he hits this guy when he's hanging with me. He disrespected me, and if I let that go, these guys will take me as a sucker.

Julio's reasons for going after Little Acosta with a gun are varied. First, he is demonstrating his loyalty to Jorge—they share a history, they are brothers on the streets, and, as we have seen, street loyalty is a matter of honor. Second, Julio is reestablishing his street reputation. He's respected on the streets and what Little Acosta did was disrespectful toward him. Speaking on behalf of his brothers, Sammy put it this way: "We got a reputation out there. When we show up, people know that shit is going to happen, that we mean shit, we do what we got to do." Julio was upholding his street rep, doing what he's got to do. Third and relatedly, the law of the street is that if you don't defend yourself, you become a mark, and others will take advantage of you, begin to "try you." Julio is constantly being drawn back to the street to avoid being seen as a sucker. Finally, as Julio suggests, the betrayal of loyalty violates mutual expectations or the ties of reciprocity and can result in abandonment. If he doesn't respond to Little Acosta, he may be taken for a sucker, but he may also find himself without anyone to watch his back.

The persistence of masculine street culture threatens Julio's career transition. His efforts to maintain a street reputation in order to protect himself and his family, and his unwillingness to relinquish his ties to the streets and the social and material resources these networks provide, place him in situations that could threaten his career due to incarceration, or could threaten his physical well-being. From 2005 to 2008, I watched these dynamics unfold further. Julio's routine of working during the week and then hanging out with Jorge and Alexander on the weekends almost came to an end after a bar fight in 2005. Julio had a beer bottle broken over his head during the fight. He later questioned why he was putting himself in situations that could jeopardize what he had accomplished and, for about a year, placed more distance between himself and Jorge. At one point in 2006, when I asked about Jorge, he replied, "I don't know, I don't see him no more."

Unable to develop friendships at work, however, and distancing himself from street networks, Julio had to manage something new in his life—isolation. He began spending more time at the gym lifting weights and taking kickboxing lessons. Some of his co-workers also went to the gym after work, but polite acknowledgments of one another never developed into friendships. Julio continued to go out on weekends, but usually by himself. He did eventually develop a friendship with a young Puerto Rican man who lived in the area and was not involved in street life.[3] Still, a few years later, he ran into Jorge at a bar and they renewed their friendship. Afterward, he went out a few times with Jorge and a mostly new cast of younger men to the coke bar where we had hung out regularly. Once again, a bar fight broke out and Julio found himself in the middle of it, only this time one of the young men he was with, Jorge's nephew, had his neck cut, slicing an artery, and nearly died before being rushed to the hospital. After this incident, in 2007, Julio insisted, "That's it, I'm done. I can't do this shit no more." When we discussed the incident, Julio expressed sadness that the young man nearly lost his life and, again, recognized that he was putting himself and his family at risk by going out to the bars with Jorge and the others. But Julio was also bothered by something else, something that conveyed the importance of reciprocity on the streets, the "give to get" mode that lies at the core of these networks.

JULIO: During the fight, I was fighting this guy and I got hit with a pool stick from behind. When I looked back, I saw this guy standing there and he knew the guy that hit me.

TIM: Who was standing there?

JULIO: Jorge.

TIM: You saying Jorge was standing there and knew the guy who hit you?

JULIO: Yeah. He was just standing there. He didn't do nothing. He should have had my back and he didn't. That's still in my mind. I won't forget that.

TIM: But why would Jorge just stand there? That doesn't sound like him.

JULIO: I don't know. I think he knew the guy and was cool with the guy and he didn't want to do nothing. So I don't know if I can trust him anymore, you know what I'm saying? I can't get that out of my mind.

For Julio, Jorge violated what is, in many ways, the most valued resource on the streets—loyalty, or reciprocity. Of course, this may have been a consequence of the distance that had developed between them during the prior two years, but for Julio this was the final straw. He insisted that he was done with Jorge, the guys, the block, and the bar scene—that he had to take care of his family, and to do so he needed to stay off the streets for good. And yet, in 2008, when his mother, Angela, died suddenly from a brain hemorrhage, a group of us gathered at the hospital for the night to give comfort and support to the family. Jorge was among them. And when Julio, the new patriarch of the family, was several thousand dollars short of funeral and burial expenses, he turned to the two deepest pockets he knew—me, who had just received my advance for this book, and his old friend Jorge.

Relinquishing old ties on the streets has its consequences and is not likely to happen without some reservations. Moreover, as we saw above, it can result in social isolation, which creates its own challenges. Transitions from the streets to the workplace may mean learning to cope with social isolation, especially when the workplace is predominantly white and it is difficult to establish new networks to support changing identities and routines. This was also evident in Mundo's life.

Mundo's rejection of the streets also removed him from his network of friends and, to some extent, even his brothers. He constructed a moral identity as a working father, providing for and nurturing his children, taking care of his lawn and flower garden, and living in a racially transitional neighborhood in an adjacent town. He is proud of his accomplishments, distinguishes himself from his brothers, and has become the father his father wasn't. But whenever I visited Mundo in the warmer months, I found him in his garage, smoking cigarettes and drinking a beer.

> Tim, this is where I spend most of my time, right here [in the garage]. My mother-in-law even bought me a T-shirt at the fair that says, "I Love Being in My Garage." It's true. She [his wife] don't like it. I sit out here and drink a few beers and smoke, she don't like it, but this is how I get by, you know.

Mundo's angst is his social isolation. He has traded in his days of partying and male camaraderie for fatherhood, life in a semiurban town, and a working-class job. He has reconstructed his past street life as self-negating or "empty," is angry at himself for dropping out of school, and holds on to a fragile social status that requires him to negotiate a white world—his wife, his job, and his neighborhood. Social isolation can make transitions from the streets difficult. Julio and Mundo have had to manage their isolation—Julio by going out alone at night and Mundo by keeping a regular stock of Budweiser on ice in his garage.

ADDICTION ROUTINES

Finally, nothing threatens the transition from the streets to the workplace as persistently as drug or alcohol dependency. Most men age off the streets while excessive drug and alcohol use diminishes, but there are casualties. Of course, the same is true of college students who enter the dens of dormitory pleasures in their late teens—most will move on after graduation, while others will struggle with alcohol and drug addiction for a lifetime. I've seen both—old college friends with gin and cocaine habits who are lassoed by concerned friends, spouses, and family members and sent to well-funded, medically sustained rehabilitation clinics, and men from the block, with crack cocaine and heroin addictions, who meander through methadone clinics, shelters, and prisons.

Both Sammy and Fausto have struggled for years with heroin addiction. Like any recreational drug, heroin use begins with modest intentions—it elicits a euphoria that is desirable when celebrating, combating boredom, managing stress or personal anguish, or sharing a life world with other users. But when heroin use slides into physical dependency, these routines also engender self-loathing, fears of self-annihilation, and the guilt of failing others. In turn, these feelings produce more drug use and so the wheel turns with increasing velocity. The euphoric moment of heroin converts the multiple streams of life experiences, memories, and emotions that preoccupy us at any given instance in our lives into a singularly focused presence on drug pleasure. Like orgasm, for a brief moment the world dissolves into euphoria, the heroin "rush." Sammy searched for words to describe the power of heroin:

> This is how I know Satan exists. There ain't nothing on this earth that is as powerful as that fucking powder, I'm telling you, nothing, bro. It's fucking gold, you know what I'm saying. Once you have it, you be wanting it more, it's always in your head with you. It's the most powerful thing on earth, I swear to God, it can make you do things you could not imagine.

Fausto lamented his addiction to the drug:

> When you have heroin, you have the most evilest drug I've ever seen in my life. Heroin is, to me, the most evilest and the most addictive and the one that would make anybody do anything . . . it brings a lot of destruction with it, you know.

The routines of drug addiction, and at least some of the destruction that both Sammy and Fausto alluded to, are not, however, only defined by physical dependency, but also by a lifestyle that develops in response to the criminalization of drug use. Because U.S. public policy has not approached heroin addiction as a public health issue— at least not among low-income populations—but rather as criminal behavior, addicts are at increased risk of using dirty needles and contracting HIV and hepatitis C, turning to crime to generate income, and going to prison, where substance abuse gets cursory treatment.[4] For this reason, I prefer to describe social and personal problems associated with drug addiction as a consequence of addiction routines rather than simply drug dependency.

Further, relapse is a reality of drug addiction and, as such, drug addiction is always a threat to transitions. Fausto began to transition from the streets to the workplace on several occasions, but drug addiction drove him back to the streets each time, to self-destructive routines that threatened his health and his life. Sammy was more cognizant of his addiction. When he found himself sliding, he tended to check himself into a detox facility and to seek whatever help was available. Relapse and drug treatment, however, require tolerance from workplace supervisors and managers, spouses, family, and friends in order to sustain jobs and relationships. And tolerance is not always available from low-wage workplaces where labor is expendable, from spouses or partners when meeting financial needs is stressful, or among family members and friends who get worn down by addiction routines.

Addiction routines, racial and ethnic conflicts, loyalties to extended family and friends, the social and economic benefits embedded in old street networks, and social isolation can all be impediments to permanent transitions from the streets to the workplace. Consequently, men may move back and forth between the streets and the workplace—especially if their only prospects are dead-end, low-wage jobs—or they may straddle the fence for some time, attempting to derive the most from both worlds, while at the same time slowly acknowledging that neither world offers them much. For the men who make this transition successfully, they often derive self-value from moral identities associated with working and fathering. For the few, like Julio, who acquire decent-paying jobs, they also derive pleasure from consumerism. Sustaining these transitions, however, can be difficult, not only because of the impediments described here, but also because working-class stability is so hard to establish in the post-1970s labor force.

DOMESTIC PARTNERS

The focus on men in my study overshadows the lives of women. While it was much harder for me to develop close relationships with women, Sammy's and Julio's domestic partners were exceptions. I was the godfather at Clara and Julio's wedding in 2000, and knew Clara even before her relationship began with Julio in 1991. María and Sammy began living together in 1998 and I have interacted weekly with María since 2000. I know much less about Mundo's domestic partner, Linda, even though their relationship extends back to the 1980s. All three of these women are central to acquiring and maintaining family stability—they contribute to the family wage, manage the household, and are the primary caretakers for the children. Their daily routines are harried, rigorous, and exhausting as they attempt to squeeze pleasure from relationships with their partners, children, and their own mothers.

Linda works for a small private company that provides substitute nurses to local hospitals and clinics. Her job pays more than Mundo's and is essential to the family wage—to paying the rent and making ends meet. They are trying to save enough money for a down payment on a home. The greatest threat to this dream may be Linda's health. She suffers from several problems and although receiving treatment, misses work on days in which she is curled up on the couch unable to meet life's demands.

María is also the primary breadwinner in her family. She has worked for a university research center for seven years, managing databases. Her salary in 2006 was around $35,000, lending financial stability to her household. She and Sammy dream about buying a home together, someplace "in the country where it's quiet." For now, her salary and Sammy's $11-an-hour job pay the rent and utilities, keep an older car on the road, and provide for the needs of two children still living in the home. María is finishing her bachelor's degree, which she has been working toward part-time since the late 1990s. She and Sammy are relatively stable in their jobs. The greatest threat to their stability and to their relationship is Sammy's addiction routines.

Clara was a stay-at-home mom in the early years of Iris's life. She nurtured her daughter, took care of the home, and managed the family's finances. Foremost, during the many years that Julio bounced around at low-wage jobs and worked the streets with Jorge, Clara became a sharp resource strategist who learned the rules governing welfare subsidies and used them to the maximum benefit of her family.[5] She was part of a larger network of women, mostly within her family, who cooked, cleaned, raised children, and took care of their men. The thrust of the 1996 welfare reform policy to decrease already meager governmental subsidies to poor families and require that mothers get jobs pushed Clara into the labor market. She went reluctantly, not because she disliked work or was lacking a work ethic, but because it removed her from what she saw as her primary responsibilities—taking care of Iris and the household. I am most familiar with Julio and Clara's struggles to achieve working-class stability. Clara's contribution to the family wage has been essential to their middle-income status, but her jobs have frequently conflicted with family routines and expectations.

A straight-A student in school, Clara is bright and has impressed all of her employers. Only a few months after assuming her first job at a plastics factory, she was asked to become foreman. Not only did she refuse, but to the dismay of her state caseworker and Julio, she quit the job a few months later because it was interfering with her family life. Julio and Clara worked different shifts, rarely saw each other, and argued when they did. Clara explained: "Me and Julio had problems. Little things, you know. We would argue over small things a lot. But that was because I was never home." The arrangement was unacceptable to Clara—it undermined her family, and keeping the family together was her responsibility, not sitting on some factory floor every afternoon inspecting plastic containers. Julio disagreed and wanted her added income, but Clara insisted, "Julio doesn't like it, but he'll get over it."

At Wal-Mart, Clara was immediately moved from the cash register to the service desk. She worked the first shift, and even though Julio was then driving nights, she saw more of him than before, and much more of her daughter. Julio returned from work about the time Clara was leaving, and would usually give her a ride to work. Clara was home in the late afternoons to cook dinner for Julio before he left for work and to spend evenings with Iris. This worked better. But the pay was low, $7 an hour, and the job demanding. She reported that working at the service desk, she was not given a break and often ate her lunch while sitting behind the counter waiting on customers. The woman working the next shift was frequently late and Clara couldn't leave until she arrived. Sometimes the woman wouldn't show up at all and Clara would be stuck until they could find someone to come in and relieve her. Further, the money simply didn't justify the grief she tolerated from unhappy customers. Clara worked there for about six months, left the job, and began working at McDonald's.

At McDonald's, Clara's managerial potential was instantly identified and she was promoted to assistant manager, a much more flattering title than wage, which started at $7.75 an hour. The store was located in a Puerto Rican area of Springfield, owned by a Jamaican, and managed by a Mexican who hired only Spanish-speaking staff. Clara began opening the store at 5 a.m. and managing the morning shift. Julio was leaving for work around 5:30 p.m. and returning in the morning about the same time Clara was leaving. They would have breakfast together when possible and then Julio would drive her to work and sleep during the day. Returning from work around two, Clara would spend a few hours in the late afternoon with Julio before he left for work. Their time together was sparing, but, as at Wal-Mart, at least Clara was home when Iris returned from school and could spend the evenings with her.

Together, Julio and Clara were making enough money to live comfortably, and, during this time, even began talking about buying a home. The job at McDonald's was not very satisfying, but it supplemented the family wage and did provide some important benefits. For one, Clara's increased decision-making responsibility at the store allowed her to make hiring decisions and members of her extended family benefited, including her sister, nephews, and nieces. In addition, paid training opportunities allowed her to spend a few nights in a luxury hotel in Boston, which she had never done before. But there were many drawbacks to the job as well. Foremost, claiming that the franchise fee and general store overhead were high, the store owner was very cost-conscious. He attempted to repair broken equipment himself, paid low salaries, and required managers to send staff home when business was slow.

Tensions mounted. Clara refused her manager's orders when she felt he was being unreasonable—she declined to send staff home and would tell him to "back off" when he "gets an attitude with staff." At times, the store owner could be quite Machiavellian. After the Mexican manager was reassigned to another store, the Jamaican owner was at the store regularly. He forbade the staff to speak Spanish, another policy that Clara refused to enforce. "He finally just told us," she explained, "we couldn't talk at all if we were going to speak Spanish. No talking on the floor at all! He's such an ass!" Around that same time, he put a moratorium on paid vacations, even for managerial staff, and required that all staff sign a statement recognizing his right to fire them for no cause—an intimidation strategy intended presumably to increase productivity.

After two years of working for the store, Clara's salary had increased 25 cents an hour to $8. Staff could not afford to purchase the health insurance policy the franchise offered, but fortunately for Clara, she and Iris were on Julio's policy. Integrating work and her family responsibilities, however, was difficult, and Julio did not make it any easier. Invoking patriarchal privileges, Julio was insensitive to Clara's exhaustive daily routines.

> CLARA: Well, what I don't like about it is, I work all day and then I have to clean and cook. That's not fair. He will come home and complain because the place is dirty, he'll say, "Clara, how come you don't clean this house up?" I'm like, why don't he clean it up?
>
> TIM: Do you do any of the cleaning?
>
> JULIO: Shiiittttt, no way, bro. That's what she's for.
>
> CLARA: See what I mean? He don't do nothing around here.

JULIO: Girl, you want to pay half of everything, huh, we go half and half, 'cause you know you don't do that. I take care of these bills, you know that, but hey, you want to go half and half and, yeah, I'll clean then.

CLARA: But that's not fair.

JULIO: Half and half, girl.

CLARA: Just because you make more money than me, that's not fair.

JULIO: Why I make more money, huh? 'Cause you working at McDonald's, 'cause you lazy, girl. You could've gone to school and made something of yourself, but you lazy, just admit it. I been working since I was thirteen, except for when I went to college.

Julio minimized Clara's contributions to the family wage and insisted on traditional gender roles in the home. Clara was herself ambivalent about this. While she wanted Julio to assume some of the household work, her preference would have been to resume the caretaking work in the home and avoid the workplace altogether. Clara ended this conversation, first, with a concession: "That's what I like about Julio, he has always worked," and then with a sly challenge to his manhood within the patriarchal structure that they had both internalized: "But a real man would let me stay at home."

I have witnessed the harried life that Clara and Julio live for many years. Since he began driving, Julio has often worked jobs that require sixty hours of driving a week. Clara on the other hand has usually worked forty to forty-five hours a week, done the work in the home, and the preponderance of the child rearing. For a while, she suffered from headaches and didn't have the patience to deal with daily nuisances in the home. She was getting up at 3 a.m. to pick up Julio from work and making breakfast for him, before leaving to open the store at 5 a.m. Returning home between one and two in the afternoon, she gave Iris the attention she needed when she returned from school, prepared dinner for the family before Julio left for work at five-thirty, and cleaned the house at night. But her efforts often went unnoticed by Julio. Sitting at the table on a Sunday morning, after a night in which Julio and I had been out with the boys, Julio looked at Clara through bloodshot eyes: "Are you going to do laundry today?" "Yeah," she responded. "Good, 'cause I need some clothes washed."

Even more demeaning was the frequently mentioned status difference between Julio's and Clara's jobs. Julio insisted that Clara work to supplement the family wage, but at the same time devalued her job at McDonald's. Recognizing this, twelve-year-old Iris would occasionally exploit the issue. Sitting at the dinner table, she would coyly suggest to Julio that she didn't have to apply herself in school because she was going to work at McDonald's when she graduated. Later Julio commented, "What can I say in that situation, that there is something wrong with working at McDonald's when half of Clara's family works there?" Pointing to Clara, "She will say, 'What's wrong with McDonald's?' and I can't say anything." Clara snapped back, "What is wrong with McDonald's?" Julio looked sheepish, "I'm not saying anything's wrong, but I tell Iris, you know, you should want to be a doctor or lawyer or something like that. But you see this is the problem, Tim. I want her to do better than work at McDonald's but then if I say so, Clara is going to get mad at me for saying that about her job in front of Iris."

In 2004, Clara was stolen away from McDonald's. Her frustrations at the store had mounted. The owner had recently hired a new store manager—a twenty-three-year-old white man—who undermined Clara's authority regularly. Not only did he forbid the workers to speak Spanish, but he would rehire staff that Clara had laid off for poor performance or absenteeism. Besides, Clara had worked at McDonald's for three years and was only clearing $300 a week and had only recently been granted one week of paid vacation. Clara was recruited for a bank teller position by an employee at the bank where she made deposits for her boss. The store owner was furious and threatened that if Clara took the job and it didn't work out, he would never hire her back. The twenty-three-year-old manager made a scene at the bank and offended the personnel there so much that the bank manager "told me that if I wanted to quit right then and come over to the bank that I could, because of the way he acted. I told them I just wanted to finish my two weeks there." However, when the reality of the situation sank in, the young white manager changed his tune and begged Clara to stay, or at least to help them out with the upcoming holiday season. "Are you crazy?" she retorted. "I'm not working for you no more. Get over it!"

Clara's starting wage at the small bank was $8.50 an hour. At the end of her second year in 2006, she was making $10 an hour and, for the first time, was working at a job she enjoyed. In the beginning the learning curve was steep, and she was still surprised by how comparatively little they did at the bank. At McDonald's she was "used to a mad rush coming through the door. Now I just sit there and maybe somebody comes in once in a while." The bank manager has encouraged Clara to train as a customer service representative and her success at the bank has emboldened her in conversations with Julio. One evening, she turned to Julio and said, with a twinkle in her eye, "Remember what you said, if I make more money than you someday, you gonna pick up that broom."

Clara, like María and Linda, has played a central role in establishing working-class stability by contributing to the family wage and assuming primary responsibility for the household and children. Achieving and sustaining stable transitions from the streets to the workplace depend on family dynamics such as these. Because of their income, Julio and Clara represented the best-case scenario of achieving and maintaining working-class stability, but transitioning into the middle class raises another set of issues.

GETTING AHEAD

In 2006, Julio and Clara had attained middle-income status with a combined income of around $80,000. Converting *middle-income* achievements into *middle-class* status, however, can be difficult—it requires asset building, or creating a foundation of wealth through which a family can acquire advantages and privileges. Access to good primary and secondary schools, college educations, down payments for first homes, quality child care, financial buffers for emergencies, and expedient social networks are all extensions of class privilege. The easiest way to access such privilege is to be born into social classes that already possess these assets—which is how social class is reproduced in the United States. Lower-income groups have only two ways of accessing these advantages. The first is through governmental policies and investments (for instance, scattered-site public housing, state and federal subsidies to poor school districts, college loan programs for low-income students, child care subsidies and tax breaks, family allowances and asset development accounts, and sub-sidized home ownership programs). Increasing economic inequality and cuts in social welfare spending over the past thirty years, how-ever, have diminished these opportunities.[6]

The second route is through increasing income and converting that income into assets that confer class privilege. For populations like the men from the block, however, the labor force simply does not provide many opportunities for acquiring living-wage jobs with prospects for asset accumulation. The post-1970s restructured job market has increased the volume of low-paying jobs—in 1999, nearly one-third (31.7 percent) of household heads worked at jobs that paid less than $10 an hour.[7] For this reason, a large segment of the working class consists of dual-earner families that scrape by with little oppor-tunity for asset accumulation.

For poor urban minority populations who represent the struc-turally unemployed and off-the-books employed, their routes to middle-income job opportunities are rare.[8] In this context, illegal markets may be more appealing for generating income with prospects for asset accumulation, but income from street drug deal-ing is difficult to convert. Legal finance structures established for income-to-asset conversion are difficult for street-level drug dealers to access—where they are successful, their ventures are illegal money-laundering operations. But this requires legal expertise (or cultural capital) that is often beyond the capacity of most street-level drug dealers.[9] More often, money comes and money goes, pouring instead into consumer pleasure instead of savings accounts or invest-ments. Bank accounts are rarely utilized, mostly because of the fear of being tracked by the state, but also because of unfamiliarity with banking processes.

There were a few exceptions on the block. Alexander invested some of his money into a home in Puerto Rico—which was being built in stages—and for a short period owned a boat. He also pur-chased an auto mechanic shop, which he ran illegally for a while, and bought and sold cars as an investment strategy, but without being licensed as a dealer. Certainly, these strategies generated additional income, but they never gained the legal traction that would result in substantial asset accumulation, especially given the extent of his drug profits. One other successful drug dealer attempted to pursue a more typical asset accumulation strategy by buying a home in a middle-income, working-class neighborhood. His lifestyle, however, was incompatible with his neighbors—the steady stream of traffic in and out of his home, the late-night parties and loud music—resulting in a drug bust, prison time, and state confiscation of the property.

Deposited at the bottom of the labor force, the urban minority poor also face another barrier to mobility and asset accumulation that is rarely acknowledged by the popular media—that it is expensive to be poor in the United States. Low-income families are more likely to live in areas where car insurance rates are higher, to buy furniture and appliances from rent-to-own stores that charge extraordinary interest rates, to use fee-based check cashing services instead of banks, to shop at more expensive, smaller grocery stores or bodegas, and to pay higher interest rates for first-time mortgages, when they can get them.[10]

Because of their comparatively higher legal income, Julio and Clara had the best prospects for transitioning into the middle class. Class mobility rested on their capacity to purchase a home. Toward the end of 2003, Julio and Clara were pushed out of their apartment by an investor eager to convert the two-family house into government-subsidized, or Section 8, apartments. After their rent was raised from $575 to $800, Julio and Clara moved in with Clara's mother, while the landlord went to work converting the dining room into a bedroom so that he could maximize on the government's rent subsidy.[11] Attempting to turn their misfortune into opportunity, Julio and Clara began searching for a suitable home to buy.

Neither Julio nor Clara had established the good credit needed to secure a mortgage. Julio had defaulted on $8,500 worth of college and career training loans, mostly acquired through the federal government, while the state was claiming that he owed money for past child support. Both the federal and state claims were slowly being paid through tax return withholdings each year. Still, despite their high income, neither Julio's credit union nor any reputable lending institution would issue a mortgage until he paid off his debts. Predatory lenders made offers—a 20 percent down payment was commonly required and interest rates were quoted as high as 15 percent at a time when middle-class homeowners were refinancing mortgages in the 5 to 6 percent range.

Clara's credit wasn't bad; she simply had none. No one in either of their families had ever been issued a credit card, or bought anything on credit, and Julio had only recently opened a bank account. Julio asked his credit union about his options. He was told that he could consolidate his debt and pay it off with a loan, but that he would need a mortgage first. In other words, once he had a mortgage, he could take out a supplemental loan to pay off his debts, and then write off the interest on his taxes—one of the many lessons Julio was beginning to learn about middle-class tax privileges. The logic, however, was stupefying to Julio: "So what they saying is I got this debt so I can't get a mortgage, but if I get a mortgage then I can get a loan to pay off my debt. Tim, man, that's crazy, that don't get me nowhere." The circular logic did, however, provide the basis for a plan.

Julio and Clara found that they could qualify for a first-time homeowner program for low-income families in Springfield and acquire a loan without a down payment; however, because of Julio's bad credit, the amount of the loan would be based solely on Clara's income at McDonald's. They figured they would buy a house, continue paying off Julio's debts, and sell the house once his credit was restored to buy a nicer home. They qualified for a loan up to $54,000 for a single-family and $92,000 for a two-family house. For several months they looked, but the price thresholds simply did not buy much in Springfield. As Julio said, "They all falling down or need lots of work." Still, the American dream of home ownership was beckoning. They narrowed their search to three houses and asked if I would take a look at them.

The first was a duplex located in an extremely poor neighborhood, with several boarded-up buildings and a vibrant street life. They liked the idea of a duplex and seemed unconcerned about the neighborhood. The second was a two-family home located in a marginal, but more stable, neighborhood; however, the house was already under contract, awaiting final sale approval. The third was in a relatively stable working-class neighborhood, but the single-family house, owned by a bank, was small and in need of work. None of the three houses fit into their plan. They needed a home that would at least maintain its value for the purposes of resale once Julio paid off his loans. The first two were in neighborhoods that were high-risk investments. The third house would have required significant investments to repair and remodel it, which contradicted their interest in paying off Julio's debts as soon as possible. In fact, what they learned was that the limits placed on their loan eligibility were incompatible with their plan—none of the housing options provided good resale opportunities. After looking for several more weeks and feeling the stress of living in crowded conditions with Clara's mother, Julio and Clara gave up and decided to rent while they paid off Julio's debt.

Julio and Clara found a place to rent for $650 and began aggressively working on their debt. By the end of 2004, they had paid off their state debt, had finished paying one federal loan, had reduced another by one-half, and had called the trucking company to arrange a payment plan for the final $2,500 they owed. In the meantime, however, neighborhood conditions were ratcheting up the stress in their lives—their apartment was robbed, a shooting occurred on the sidewalk ten feet from their front door, and the police made several drug busts at the park across the street. After the shooting, Clara insisted that they move and on the eve of the 2005 New Year, they moved into a three-bedroom apartment in a three-family house located on one of Springfield's early-twentieth-century prominent boulevards. The three bedrooms provided for Julio, Clara, and Iris, as well as their niece and Julio's father. Listed at $800, Julio promised to take care of the premises for a reduced rate.

The dining room and living room in their new apartment were larger than most apartments they had lived in. They had purchased a large dining room set from a rent-to-own store and squeezed it into the apartment they had rented before, but the table now looked elegant sitting in their large Victorian dining room with hardwood floors, built-in china cabinets, and large bay window. By comparison, however, the living room was bare. Clara relied on familiar and convenient forms of purchasing home furnishings—she returned to the local rent-to-own store. Clara haggled for the best deal she could get and they delivered a beautiful maroon sofa and love seat, with matching window dressings, but the costs were greatly inflated by a 50 percent interest rate. Increased debt, however, did not deter Julio and Clara from moving forward toward their goal—they lived in the apartment for a little more than a year until they paid off Julio's debt and, once again, returned to the housing market.

Home ownership is the cornerstone of the middle class, encouraged and protected by federal tax policies. Homeowners can deduct the interest paid on homeowner loans, can deduct state and local taxes paid on their homes, can take out home equity loans and roll other debts into it (credit card debt, for example) and deduct the interest on these loans, and do not have to pay taxes on the profits made from selling their homes up to $500,000 if they've lived in the residence for two years.[12] These incentives not only encourage home ownership, but often push families to buy and sell homes regularly, and to buy homes that, because of their investment potential, are beyond their immediate financial reach. Families cobble together down payments from family members or from supplemental loans, and live in circumstances commonly referred to as "house poor." But there are many benefits in doing so. If the house appreciates in value, there are obvious financial payoffs. Relatedly, the more expensive the home, the greater the likelihood that the town and neighborhood will provide better services, including the most prized of all, better schools, which will, in turn, foster the reproduction of middle-class advantages.

Clara and Julio's three-year journey to home ownership exposed some of the barriers that class-mobile racial and ethnic minorities confront in this process. First, because Julio's and Clara's families are poor and were not part of U.S. postwar prosperity, they could not rely upon their parents to assist them in securing a loan. No one in their families had a savings account to help with a down payment, nor did they have a credit history that would enable them to co-sign for the loan or to make Julio and Clara better risks. Second, and relatedly, their families were unable to help them take care of their debt. Julio's total debt was quite manageable for most stable working-class families—only $8,500. But there was nowhere Julio and Clara could turn to resolve his debt—not to family or to creditors. Their families' poverty continued to hold them back. He had to first pay off his debt with his income before he could proceed with home ownership. This forestalled their plans to buy a house and set them back financially, especially when we consider the appreciation of houses in the late 1990s and early 2000s that they missed out on.

Third, Julio and Clara's social location, defined by their families' poverty and their ethnicity, provided them with limited experience and information concerning house buying, information needed to maximize on their options. Their families could not be helpful because they did not have the experience of buying a home and, therefore, were not schooled in the dynamics of housing markets— in securing loans, getting the best interest rates, and determining the best investments. Julio and Clara were not raised within an environment in which these issues were discussed; instead, they acquired this information from co-workers, the city's first-time homeowner program, from lending agents, and from me. This involved learning a new language and economic logic—the very weakness that predatory lenders are quick to exploit. Foremost, the information that Julio and Clara needed to learn, or the cultural capital they were lacking, was not simply about *how* to buy a home. They also needed to know the motivations or reasons for *why* middle-class families buy homes. For people like Julio and Clara, who grew up poor, home ownership is a symbol of success, a testimony to their class mobility; it defines working-class respectability, and is an end in itself. But for people who grow up in the middle classes, home ownership is the harbinger of intergenerational privilege, the institutional mechanism through which middle-class advantages are secured and reproduced, a means to an end.[13] Understanding this dynamic meant that Julio and Clara had to confront the last component of their disadvantage in this process—their race and ethnicity.

The privileges associated with middle-class home ownership are organized by race and ethnicity. As Julio and Clara's early efforts to buy a house suggest, home ownership is by itself not enough to preserve economic and social advantages. This requires buying a home in a neighborhood where the value of the home will appreciate at a rate greater than inflation, and a home located in a neighborhood where the schools and other services provide the children of middle-class households educational advantages as well as salient social networks that are likely to expand future opportunities. Any of the three homes that I looked at with Julio and Clara in 2004 would not have been good investments into the middle class. Of course, these housing values were based solely upon Clara's salary, and eliminating Julio's debt expanded neighborhood housing opportunities considerably. However, Springfield neighborhoods are not only defined by household income, but also by race and ethnicity, as are most neighborhoods in U.S. cities.

Historically, banks, Realtors, governmental lending institutions, and white homeowners created racially segregated neighborhoods, through which privileges and advantages are derived.[14] The wealthiest neighborhoods in the Springfield metropolitan area are all white, and as David Rusk has shown, eight of ten poor blacks and Hispanics in Springfield live in poor neighborhoods compared to only two of ten whites, who are scattered throughout more stable neighborhoods.[15] Moreover, in 2000, Springfield had the highest level of Hispanic residential segregation of all cities in Massachusetts; in fact, for Hispanics to be completely integrated into neighborhoods in the metropolitan Springfield area, 63 percent would have to move into white areas.[16] Because of this high degree of residential segregation and because of Julio and Clara's ethnicity, buying a home in a neighborhood that would secure middle-class advantages would be difficult, irrespective of their understanding of market dynamics. Hence, their disadvantage was defined not only by poverty and incipient cultural capital but also by the discriminatory structure of the housing market.[17]

The problem, as Thomas Shapiro demonstrates, is the "silent and invisible way race is built into our logic and structures" in the United States. Housing values are themselves inextricably related to racial and ethnic segregation, and the more segregated an area, the more segregation will affect home values. Shapiro refers to this as a "segregation tax" and shows that homes in communities that are at least 10 percent black lose 16 percent of their value compared to all-white communities.[18] The historical patterns of white flight are based upon racist attitudes that as people of color move into neighborhoods, the quality of schools will decline, crime will increase, and properties will not be maintained. Once the pattern of housing segregation has been established, it becomes integrated into the market logic—it fosters a cultural psychology of home buying that, combined with tax policies that encourage home buying and selling, results in whites pursuing economic and educational advantages by buying homes in economically and racially homogenous communities.

Racial minorities moving into white communities will be tolerated, as long as not too many move in; but if minorities begin to move into the neighborhood in larger numbers, white homeowners, irrespective of their racial prejudices, may move out in order to preserve their home equity, especially in highly segregated metropolitan areas. It is in this sense that the housing market has become what Shapiro refers to as color-coded. Moreover, a color-coded housing market in highly segregated areas creates a dynamic in which minority homeowners desire racially and ethnically mixed neighborhoods that are at the tipping point for what most whites will tolerate as acceptable levels of racial diversity.[19] In other words, just at the point in which most minorities find neighborhoods to be ideally racially and ethnically integrated, whites begin moving out, re-creating the patterns of racial leapfrog that have resulted in urban sprawl; in a robust housing market enriching developers, lending institutions, and real estate companies; and in an entrenched segregated housing market.[20] This dynamic, evident in Springfield, affected Julio and Clara's choices for buying a home.

Julio and Clara wanted to buy a home in a racially integrated area, where they would feel comfortable and welcomed. Buying in an all-white area—assuming that they could have acquired a mortgage to do so[21]—was not their preference. Their experiences with whites in Springfield left them leery of white homeowners and white neighborhoods. Julio and his brothers are big Puerto Rican men and their presence instills fear in the eyes of many whites. I have witnessed this on many occasions, just as I have noted the apparent relief that white shop owners, for instance, express when they see that I am with one of the Rivera brothers. And inevitably, I am the one whom they engage, even when it is clear that our purpose for being in the shop has nothing to do with me. Further, Julio, his brothers, and friends have been pulled over by police on numerous occasions for no reason other than being a carload of Puerto Ricans, and all three have had the police call on them for simply being in a white neighborhood. Working as a security guard in a shopping plaza, Julio was approached on more than one occasion by naïve whites and asked about the gang problem in Springfield. And, as we have seen, Julio is constantly on guard at work, where racial and ethnic differences shape interactions. Like many racial and ethnic minorities, Julio and Clara wanted a nice home in a safe, quiet neighborhood, and, ideally, in a tolerant racially and ethnically mixed neighborhood. But given housing conditions in Springfield, this was not only unlikely, it was almost certain to diminish the value of their home equity if the racial diversity of the neighborhood they desired gave way to typical patterns of white flight.

Julio and Clara bought a house in 2006, and as Fausto put it a few months later when he was staying at the house: "A white person in this neighborhood would scare the hell out of everybody. In fact," he bellowed, "when we found out you was coming up, we put the word out—white man in the neighborhood!" After looking at several houses, Julio and Clara found an attractive three-bedroom colonial within their price range ($120,000) in an African American and West Indian working-class community. Their infatuation with the house, however, did not prevent us from scouring the inspector's report, which noted several structural problems and of making numerous demands on the seller to remedy the problems. Most were met, but they were less successful in finding a good interest rate. Unfortunately, Julio and Clara had avoided the difficulty of finding a mortgage lender by selecting the company that figured their taxes for them. When I pointed out that their interest rate was high, they decided that, since they had been approved and were already in the process of searching for a home, it was too overwhelming to back out and find another lender. The company representative had explained to them that because it was their first home and because they still needed to establish a good credit record, their best option was to go with a variable interest rate in order to get the lowest rate possible, and then remortgage in a few years after they had built some equity in the home. The rate was still high—9.9 percent at a time when my professional friends were refinancing at fixed rates in the 5 percent range and when forecasts were predicting a softening housing market and increasing interest rates.

Julio, Clara, and Iris moved into their new home just as the New England crocuses were marking the beginning of spring. While the maroon furniture fit nicely into their new living room, the large-screen television was oversized for the room, as were the table and chairs, china cabinet, and stereo squeezed into the dining room. But the new chandelier they hung over their table symbolized the pride of first-time homeowners. The house was a marker of class mobility and Julio was the only man from the block to buy his own home.

Getting ahead was another matter. By 2008, housing forecasts proved accurate—interest rates were increasing and the housing market was collapsing. Julio had attempted to refinance to lower his interest rate and was refused. He was bracing himself for an increase in the rate to 11.9 percent in March of that year. Consulting a Realtor, he found that the market value of his home was already declining. The house sits on a street with other small, attractive homes, with well-tended yards, but just a few blocks away the ravages of poverty and street life were evident. Julio reported that a rash of shootings two blocks away had closed down the housing market in the area and had crowded the streets with "walking police." The Realtor told him that nothing had sold above $100,000, that most homes in the neighborhood were left on the market unseen, and that foreclosures in the area were increasing. Despite Julio and Clara's high income, converting their income into middle-class stability was circumscribed by poverty, race, and ethnicity and, consequently, their continued success remained unclear.[22]

In looking back over Julio's biography at the age of thirty-three, he was certainly the most successful of the Rivera brothers, and in many ways always has been. Julio graduated high school and now has a career that pays a good wage. His new home is at the center of family holidays and has provided shelter for other family members from time to time, including a niece, his father, and more recently his drug-dependent brother Fausto, who promised sobriety in exchange for the comforts of Julio and Clara's home.

In 2000, Julio and Clara were formally married, an unusual status among the men I have known on the streets. By 2006, Julio had finally cut most of his ties to the streets. Julio's success is attributable to many factors—his strong determination, Clara's contributions to the family wage and her emotional support, the high school coach who reached out to him, the job information he acquired from Carmello while hanging out on the block, a changing employment opportunity structure in the 1990s, access to a prominent law firm at a critical moment in his life course, and a lot of luck. Julio, perhaps better than any of the young men I've known, reminds us that people are not good or bad, decent or street, deserving or undeserving. People muddle through the complexity of their worlds based upon myriad changing influences and circumstances.

Julio's life trajectory was, however, distinct from that of many others on the block in one important way. Julio had never done any prison time. He had been locked up with his father for several weeks awaiting trial, but he had not served time in state prison. And nothing was as salient in shaping the life trajectories of these men as doing prison time.

PART THREE

Living Through the Urban Drug War

I say that doubling the conviction rate in this country would do more to cure crime in America than quadrupling the funds for [Hubert] Humphrey's war on poverty.

—Richard M. Nixon

Now those who commit crimes should be punished. And those who commit repeated, violent crimes should be told, when you commit a third violent crime, you will be put away, and put away for good. Three strikes, and you are out.

—Bill Clinton,
1994 State of the Union Address

EIGHT

The Prison Pipeline

IN THE MIDDLE of the twentieth century, streams of African Americans and Latinos poured into U.S. cities to find work in America's industrial core. Forty years later millions would be returned to rural America in leg chains, handcuffs, and orange jumpsuits. Job opportunities in working-class communities reflected these changes, as Springfield defense attorney David Hoose was reminded each time he visited the local prison:

> Isn't it sad? I know when I go out to Ludlow [prison] . . . it is always a depressing experience for me because I sit there and as I'm waiting to be processed in, I see all these young men and women with spit-shined boots and pressed uniforms, and I think these were the people that in prior generations went to work in factories, who were productive workers.

Born in the 1970s, the Rivera brothers and others from the block would know only one side of this history—the side in which urban communities like the one they grew up in would be whipsawed by the loss of entry-level industrial jobs and the unprecedented growth in state prisons, where surpluses of the unemployed swept up by aggressive drug enforcement would become warehoused. Federal and state prisons as well as local jails were all growing, but the increase in the state prison population was stunning. Between 1980 and 2001, this population grew from 130 to 422 inmates for every 100,000 residents and became the home for nine out of ten prison inmates nationwide, for a total of 1.25 million state prisoners.[1] Forty-five percent of this increase was attributable to drug arrests.[2]

STREET-LEVEL DRUG ENFORCEMENT

For many young men leaving school, hanging out on the streets, or entering the drug trade, the growth of the criminal justice system created a school-to-prison pipeline. During Fausto's tenth-grade year, he followed Sammy to Franklin Street and was initiated into the game of cat and mouse. " 'Don't let this fuckin' detective catch you,' they used to tell me. 'He'll beat the shit out of you.' " Fausto was still learning the game, when one afternoon he heard Sammy yelling, "Fausto, throw it away, throw it away!" Too late. Clark Kent and Blondie—names the young men had given to the two most feared detectives—were descending on Fausto, Sammy, and another young man, Basilio. Fausto's story was similar to the stories others would tell over the years:

> First one grabbed fuckin' Basilio and threw him up against the wall. The other one grabbed me, and he's tellin' Baz, "Look up!" And every time Basilio would look at his face, he'd go, pow! Smacks him in the face. . . . In the meanwhile, this one fell with me, right. He dropped me on the [ground], right, and since he fell with me he got up real fast and he went like this [making a fist] . . . and Sammy yelled, "He's only fifteen! He's only fifteen! Don't touch him! Don't touch him! He's only fifteen!"

The officer did practice restraint, but Fausto had made a sale to an undercover cop, was arrested, and taken to the precinct, where, according to Fausto, the officers attempted to "scare him straight."

> They own you when they take you to the precinct—that's what they said, "We own you." There's nothing but cops in there. There's nobody watching you whether your rights are getting violated in there and no cops is gonna go against no cops, you know. . . . So he takes out his clip [from his gun] and he goes like this to me, "I'll blow you the fuck away." Right? So I seen the bullet, the big-ass bullet like this and he clipped it back and he put it in his waist. "I'll waste it. I'll fuckin' waste it. Give me a reason.

Just me and you here." You know, he just kept fuckin' with me. They took off all my clothes, had me naked . . . trying to harass me. One of the cops says, "Oh! You don't know what we do with the grown-ups around here. We beat the fuckin' livin' shit out of 'em. You're fuckin' up." And one of the white dudes is tellin' the other one, "He looks big enough. He looks big enough. We think he could take it, you know. Give him a couple smacks, you know." And throughout all this I couldn't help but lookin' at one of the detectives that was a narcotics detective and he was Spanish. He was agreeing with this type of shit and this type of behavior, you know, and it just blew my mind how he would agree, you know.

Fausto's mother bailed him out for $25 and he returned home to her wrath and his father's lecture. Fausto was back in school the next day, after having what the men on the block would call "his cherry busted."

Just about all the men I met on the streets had similar stories of police intimidation and harassment. Most were defiant and hostile toward the authorities. Sitting in lawn chairs on a relatively quiet evening, Benedicto would suddenly scream, "What you looking at, motherfucker?" as an unmarked police car passed by slowly. Throughout the years I have heard a multitude of stories, some from drug dealers, but many from others who were victims of mistaken identity or simply interrogated because they were Puerto Ricans standing on the streets in poor neighborhoods. Many of the men on the block pieced together different strategies to make their living, utilizing drug dealing at times as well as on- or off-the-books jobs. Similarly, drug preferences varied as well, from alcohol to marijuana and cocaine. Police were often unable, or unwilling, to distinguish among these nuances, and the mission handed the criminal justice system to "clean up the streets" gave police carte blanche authority, with little accountability.

A conversation in the spring of 2001 with Tito, a young Puerto Rican man, provided an insider perspective that was instructive. Tito had served several years in prison, was working as a dishwasher for a restaurant close to a suburban shopping mall, and was the father of two young children. He and his friend had just finished smoking a blunt and were talkative. An angry but engaging storyteller, Tito told stories that moved from one topic to the next, but police harassment was clearly one of his preoccupations.

TITO: Ah man, you hang around here enough you'll see what I'm talking about. Look, I work, I go to work, you know, and it's my day off and I'm sittin' here and I wanna sit here and smoke a blunt and enjoy myself. But pretty soon these guys are gonna roll up here and they're gonna get down on us.

TIM: What do they do when they get down on you?

TITO: Yeah, well, they go through our pockets, but that's not what the problem is. The problem is, you know, when they get up on you and they make you feel this small. Uh, when they squash out whatever ego you have in you. When they get on top of you and tell you what a piece of shit you are. That's what I'm talkin' about. That's why I hate the fucking police.

Tito had an interesting analysis for why they were treated this way:

People talk about gangs down here on the streets but, you know what, the police are a gang—they're a fucking gang, I'm telling you! Right, they a gang, you know they working to fuck up niggas like me. But you see the police, they answer to the mayor, and the mayor, you see, answers to the governor, and some shit like that. But here's what I want to know, bro, I want to know who the man is behind the last door! I know he's a white man, but I want to see that motherfucker's face.

TIM: Does it matter if the cops are black, Spanish, or white?

TITO: The cops, man, they just doing their job. When they put their knees on my back, when they making us feel like fucking lowlife shit-eating Dumpster divers, they doing their jobs for some motherfucker who's out there and I can't see. I want to see that motherfucker!

Like Tito, several of the young Puerto Rican men left on the block in 2001 worked in low-wage service sector jobs and some sold drugs to supplement their income, while a new generation of youths was rapidly learning the ropes and replacing many of the men who had left the streets. Those who remained all struggled to assert their masculinity in an unforgiving social and economic environment and many were involved in the criminal justice system, either on parole or else simply in between prison stints. Tito believed that the world had failed him and he struggled to figure out who the culprit was—the white man behind the last door. A restructured economy, a burgeoning prison system, and a public preoccupied with the moral degradation of a black urban underclass created a largely lock-'em-up environment, in which a mandate to manage the lives of unemployed black and Latino men was given to district and state attorneys and increasing numbers of police.

PRISONS AND THE BLACK UNDERCLASS

In the 1970s the world shifted on its political-economic axis. Declining corporate profits, saturated global markets, and the strength of organized labor and social movements signaled a crisis in capitalism. While the advantages of mobile capital had been evident to U.S. corporate leaders as far back as the 1950s, advances in computer and transportation technology facilitated the movement of capital to an unprecedented degree, and along with policies that deregulated the economy, reduced social spending, lowered taxes on corporations and the wealthy, and protected investments through inflation-controlled interest rate adjustments, a neoliberal model was created that would reach across the globe, drawing the strings of world politics in a post–Cold War era more tightly around free markets. Corporate leaders in the United States searched and found the right political candidate to carry the mantle and, in 1980, Ronald Reagan was elected president.

In many ways, Reagan picked up where President Richard Nixon had left off. From 1968 to Watergate, Nixon began laying the track for draconian crime measures that would expand in Reagan's presidency and crescendo in President Clinton's 1994 crime bill. Nixon increased law enforcement funds, curtailed civil liberties, and legalized secret special grand juries.[3] Three crime bills were passed under Reagan's War on Drugs that dramatically increased law enforcement funding, established harsh mandatory minimum sentences for drug felonies, expanded asset forfeiture laws, increased the military's role in training and equipping local law enforcement officers, and created a new "drug czar" position to coordinate efforts between the military, law enforcement, and intelligence agencies.[4] As Mark Mauer of the Sentencing Project points out, while spending on federal employment and training programs was being reduced by one-half between 1980 and 1993, corrections spending grew 521 percent.[5] And this was before President Clinton's $30 billion 1994 crime bill.

Clinton further abetted the public's appetite for harsh criminal punishment by increasing prison construction, extending prison time through truth-in-sentencing laws,[6] eliminating prisoners' access to federal Pell Grants to fund prison college education programs, tacking on two years of prison time without parole for anyone manufacturing or selling drugs within one thousand feet of any type of school, increasing sentences for gang members, and providing life sentences for anyone committing three felonies. When Reagan came into office, one in four federal prisoners was sentenced for drug offenses; when Clinton left office, the ratio was one in two.[7]

The increasing reliance upon incarceration to address the devastation visited on urban areas in the wake of deindustrialization was reinforced by the public's preoccupation with the "black underclass." President Nixon capitalized on the white public's economic fears in the late 1960s and early 1970s, but also their racial fears as his law-and-order rhetoric publicly condemned urban race riots, while his efforts to dismantle the War on Poverty stirred the public's wrath toward the growing numbers of black single mothers on the welfare rolls.[8] Further, Nixon publicly excoriated the Democratic Party for edging too close to the civil rights movement and succeeded at luring white Southerners and white labor union members from its electoral base.

Nixon's racial politics was evident in his hostility toward the War on Poverty architects and his efforts to wrest control of social welfare away from Washington and devolve authority to the states. His antipathy toward welfare liberals was advanced by conservative scholars George Gilder, Charles Murray, and Lawrence Mead in the 1970s and 1980s. Their exuberance for free market economics depicted white liberals as misguided social engineers whose generous and permissive welfare policies had created a mess in U.S. cities by refusing to coerce the poor, and especially the black poor, to take whatever jobs were available, irrespective of the wages they paid. For these scholars, joblessness represented a moral rather than economic crisis. These accounts of urban poverty, however, failed to acknowledge the brutal political-economic forces that were transforming postindustrial U.S. cities, but they gained political currency nonetheless, especially in a society that had become preoccupied with the ravages of black urban poverty.

In *Welfare Racism*, Ken Neubeck and Noel Cazenave demonstrated how the black urban rebellions in the 1960s changed the face of poverty on the covers of popular magazines. Not only did the complexion of poverty darken, they explained, but as poverty became associated with urban, inner city blacks, the portrayals of the poor became increasingly negative and unsympathetic, signified by the term "the underclass."[9] The concept made its public debut in a cover story in *Time* magazine in 1977, but it was Ken Auletta's series in *The New Yorker*, which later became the basis of his 1982 book *The Underclass*, that gave the term public currency. Auletta represented the shift that had taken place, even among liberals, from a more empathetic perspective of the poor that emphasized social responsibility to a reformulated culture of poverty perspective focused on individual behavioral pathologies. Despite his claims to balanced reporting, Auletta adopted a framework that demeaned the underclass as antisocial, deviant, welfare-dependent, and violent, with "bad habits" and a "welfare mentality"—and even at one point profiled a welfare recipient with twenty-seven to twenty-nine children (she had lost count), as if this was a consequence of state generosity instead of mental illness.

Preoccupation with the black underclass spilled over into the scholarly and foundation funding worlds as well, as scholars such as Isabel Sawhill, then at the Urban Institute, attempted to categorize and measure the underclass. Providing more sophistication than Auletta before her, Sawhill nevertheless hammered home similar points that portrayed the underclass as morally culpable for their own poverty, emphasizing for instance a maladaptive underclass culture that produced "actions most likely to inhibit social mobility, to impose costs on the rest of society, or to influence children growing up in an environment where such [underclass] behaviors are commonplace."[10]

Liberal scholars attempted to salvage the black underclass debates and keep the focus on the social and economic forces that were ravaging black urban communities. In his 1980 book *The Black Underclass,* Douglas Glasgow examined the aftermath of the Watts riot, and reflected on the lives of young black men who had become economically obsolete and institutionally resegregated in a postindustrial world. Glasgow poetically described the world of the black underclass:

> Being broke, hustling, jiving, stealing, rapping, balling; a fight, a bust, some time; no job, lost a job, a no-paying job; a lady, a baby, some weight; some wine, some grass, a pill; no ride, lost pride, man going down, slipping fast, can't see where to make it; I've tried, almost died, ready now for almost anything.[11]

William Julius Wilson followed suit in his seminal 1988 book, *The Truly Disadvantaged,* attempting to restore the debate to its structural causes by emphasizing joblessness and the class bifurcation of the black community that had left the black ghetto more socially isolated and mired in concentrated poverty. Still, Wilson's appropriation of the term "black underclass" and his descriptions of "ghetto-specific culture" as socially disorganized and pathological inadvertently reinforced the public's preoccupation with poor urban blacks.

Social scientists notwithstanding, efforts to craft a political response to black urban poverty seemed to be embedded in the white conservative backlash to the civil rights movement, the Great Society, and affirmative action initiatives. Liberals had been pronounced dead in Washington and in statehouses throughout the country, and racist political language fed the fears and insecurities of whites eager to reclaim privileges they were led to believe liberals were taking away from them. As if Ken Auletta had written his script, President Reagan railed against the excesses of the welfare system by publicly excoriating a Chicago woman with eighty names, thirty addresses, and twelve Social Security cards, anointed the "welfare queen," who became the symbol of black indolence and white liberal acquiescence. George H. W. Bush followed in the 1988 presidential campaign by plastering the face of Willie Horton across the public media next to his opponent Michael Dukakis—one a black man serving a life sentence who had raped a woman while out on furlough, the other a white liberal who hailed from the liberal state of Massachusetts and had supported the furlough program.

Democrats were not missing the political lesson either. Since 1968, the Democrats had managed to elect only two presidents, both white Southerners. Despite his popularity among African Americans, Bill Clinton reassured white voters in his 1992 presidential campaign by pushing Jesse Jackson to the campaign margins and staging a high-profile public relations fight with rapper Sister Souljah. Further, using color-coded language himself, he promised "to end welfare as we know it," and expounded on his support for "three strikes" legislation in his 1994 State of the Union address. Later in 1994, when his first term in Washington seemed to be coming undone, Clinton delayed the release of a governmental study showing that more than one-third of imprisoned drug dealers were small-time, with limited criminal histories, arrested for nonviolent crimes, to minimize its effect on the debate of the Violent Crime Control and Law Enforcement Act, which he pushed through before the midterm elections.[12]

At the heart of Clinton's crime bill were antidrug law enforcement and prison construction. Despite the $7 billion that the Black Congressional Caucus wrestled into the bill for varying prevention programs, the new law appropriated $8.8 billion to hire 100,000 new police officers and $7.9 billion for states to build new prisons. In fact, Clinton made Reagan's law enforcement budget look like the minor leagues, increasing annual spending to twenty times the amount the War on Drugs guru himself had spent.[13]

What was perhaps most significant about the Clinton administration's actions was its insidious endorsement of racial politics. Indeed, the world had shifted dramatically since the hopeful civil rights era only thirty years prior—the political and cultural distance between Democrat Lyndon B. Johnson's mid-1960s administration and the 1990s Clinton years was vast and the Clinton administration symbolized this transformation. The Democratic Party gave its imprimatur to racial politics at the state level, where getting tough on black urban crime had become the centerpiece of electoral strategies and where many more states followed the federal lead in creating their own mandatory minimum drug sentences, asset forfeiture laws, truth-in-sentencing policies, and "three strikes" legislation. Vijay Prashad reports that in the mid-1990s, $27 billion of state monies was spent on building 3,300 new prisons across the country, while another 268 had been designed and estimated to cost an additional $2.4 billion.[14]

Further, harsh penalties for drug offenders, increased police surveillance in urban minority areas, and prosecutorial instruments used to speed up judicial processing greased the wheels for the burgeoning prison industry. The federal government provided technical and logistical support to the states, as well as extensive drug enforcement personnel to partner with state and local police forces to "clean up" the urban drug trade. The consequence was an "anything goes" environment where police and the federal Drug Enforcement Administration were given financial and tactical support, prison capacity, and political license to get the job done.

Mandatory Minimums

The War on Drugs focused primarily on black and Latino urban neighborhoods. Attempts to organize the drug trade through street gangs increased violence in urban areas and drew more attention to urban neighborhoods already on the verge of collapse. Increased law enforcement in these areas followed and violent gang members were removed from the streets in police dragnets, but so were nonviolent drug offenders, drug addicts, and the mentally ill. Police vigilance in the inner city turned prisons into black and Latino stockades, and the numbers tell the story.

While the rate of imprisonment increased for all groups during the last quarter of the twentieth century, in 2003, 81 white women for every 100,000 were behind bars compared to 359 black women. Similarly, 717 white men per 100,000 were locked up compared to an astonishing 4,919 black men. Latino men and women fell in between these two groups with 143 Latinas and 1,717 Latino men per 100,000 incarcerated in 2003.[15] Further, to illustrate the racially discriminatory nature of drug policies and law enforcement practices, sociologist Bruce Western examined self-reported drug use among high school seniors and adults, as well as data on drug-related emergency hospital room use, and concludes, "There is little evidence that mounting drug use or relatively high rates of drug use among blacks fueled the increase in drug arrests during the 1990s."[16]

The primary tool used to increase drug-related incarceration was mandatory minimum prison sentencing, which gave unprecedented power for determining the outcomes of arrests to district and state attorneys. As Springfield criminal defense attorney David Hoose put it, "This is the best thing DAs could've dreamed of, you know, a system where they basically can ignore the judge and do whatever they want."[17] Mandatory minimums largely moved the deliberations of justice from the courtroom to the DA's office, where 90 percent of cases are resolved through plea bargains.[18] Establishing harsh mandatory sentences enhanced the power of the DAs because only the DAs have the prerogative of lowering the sentence beneath the mandatory limit. The explosion in drug arrests that occurred between 1980 and 2000 would have been impossible to prosecute within the limited capacity of the courts. Harsh sentences gave the district attorneys a lot of leeway in determining the outcomes of arrests, and because of the risk of being found guilty by a jury and receiving the full mandatory sentence, virtually all defendants plea-bargained their cases.

In Massachusetts, a drug dealer caught with two hundred grams of cocaine or heroin—less than a half-pound—receives a mandatory sentence of fifteen years in prison, the equivalent to sentencing guidelines for aggravated rape or manslaughter (if caught with one hundred grams, the mandatory sentence is ten years). For a first offense, irrespective of the amount of cocaine or heroin, the mandatory sentence is five years, with an additional two years if caught within a school zone (which covers most of the area of a city, since schools include day care, nurseries, Head Start, and both private and public schools). DAs routinely commute the sentence through a plea bargain process, but this often depends upon the willingness of the offender to give up information or, even in some cases, to wear recording devices on the street. Mandatory minimum sentences have greatly altered the power constellation between judge, prosecutor, and defense attorney, as attorney Hoose laments:

> It cuts the tongue out of my mouth. I mean, I can't do what I think I do well, which is advocate on behalf of my clients, because there's nothing to advocate for. The sentence is set in stone. The judge has no authority to do anything other than what the sentence prescribed by law is, and it forces me to do something that I don't think I do very well and that is go into the DA's office and get down on my knees and grovel and offer up my client to do this and do that and, uh, you know, it's all very distasteful to me.

The exclusive power given to district attorneys to manage drug cases can be exploited when DAs are elected officials, as they are in Massachusetts, especially if getting tough on crime is their ticket to reelection. With the tools and resources given to the DAs to prosecute drug dealers, they can essentially decide on the day and time to do a drug sweep that will make headlines in local newspapers. They determine the flow of bodies through the courts, as one Springfield public defense attorney explained:

> They plan for [drug arrests] . . . so the amount of it is controlled by the government. You or I could walk down to the South End this afternoon and find five drug dealers in half an hour. You drive through and see them every day. So, of course, police could do the same thing. They can choose on any given Sunday to nail five drug dealers or choose not to. And so you can end up with a hundred people coming to court or you could wind up with nothing. It's totally in their control.

Anyone who has sat in a state courtroom in the past twenty years has seen the consequences of the lock-'em-up era. The sea of racial minority faces rushing through courtrooms and emptying behind concrete-fortified walls and barbed wire is extraordinary. In Massachusetts, in 1997, Hispanics were eighty-one times and blacks thirty-nine times more likely to be sentenced to prison for a drug offense than whites.[19] Moreover, from 1985 to 1995, the number of Hispanic inmates in federal and state prisons increased 219 percent. Nationally, Hispanics are imprisoned at twice the rate of whites; in Massachusetts, they are incarcerated at six times the rate.[20]

The transition that many of the men on the block were making from the streets to the workplace was, for others, precluded by prison time. Unlike Fausto, whose drug addiction and reckless robbing spree were almost certain to end behind the wall, the other two Rivera brothers entered the prison lottery. They were both dealing drugs on the streets, but only one of them would go to prison, while the other, as we have seen, would develop a successful truck-driving career. Going to prison not only disrupts adolescent-to-adult transitions, it often generates a trajectory of its own.

SAMMY'S ARREST

Sammy had done a short stint in a local prison before his drug arrest, but on unusual terms. After his brother Fausto was arrested and awaiting trial for bank robbery, Sammy decided to follow him into the prison for two reasons—one, to show solidarity with his brother and to be there in case Fausto needed his help, and two, to break his own drug habit. Detox had not worked in the past—"I got in and out," says Sammy, and, at least in prison, "I can't go nowhere." For a week, Sammy showed up each day at the courthouse to turn himself in for a couple of arrest warrants for driving without a license. The court clerk sent Sammy away the first two days, because they were unable to locate his records. The DA's office then said they would give him six months' probation. This wasn't what Sammy wanted. "So I went back and the last time that I went, the judge seen me there again. He goes, 'Why the heck is this guy here again,' you know. 'He wants to go to jail, put him in jail.' So they brought me downstairs." After a week in jail, Sammy received a letter indicating the DA's office had located his records and was giving him six months of jail time. He continued, "They brung me back to court and the judge just

221

told me, 'I don't know why the heck you doing this. You had enough chances so they could give you probation. You didn't take it, but it's your choice.' " For four months, Sammy occupied a cell not far from where his brother was locked up in the facility.

After his release, Sammy was back on the streets using drugs and dealing. He managed to avoid arrest for the next four years; as described earlier, he moved in with María in Hartford after Jorge went to prison, had a son, and worked in a series of mostly temp jobs. As Sammy and María settled into the new millennium, they were paying their bills, while Sammy was managing his addiction with methadone and occasional trips to Springfield to get a dose of euphoria and to remind himself of why he would always be addicted to heroin.

Sammy's and María's daily routines were challenging. They woke at 5 A.M. to start getting three children ready for school; one walked to school while another took the bus. María sometimes took the bus and other times caught a ride with Sammy, before he drove over the mountain into the distant suburbs to his son's day care and then to his workplace. After work, Sammy picked up his son from day care, had dinner at home with his family, and then drove to his second job, whenever work was available. Their dependency on a twelve-year-old car was apparent, especially when one snowy night the car slid off an exit ramp as Sammy was returning from work. The car was totaled and Sammy and María were confronted with the morning reality of getting their son to day care and themselves to work. They called friends and patched together rides until the weekend, when Sammy hatched a plan.

Neither Sammy nor María had established good credit, so taking out a loan to buy another car was out of the question. Theirs was not an uncommon predicament for low-income inner-city families, whose livelihoods have become dependent upon varying sources of transportation to get them and their children to and from jobs and schools in expanding metropolitan areas. Keeping a car on the road is oftentimes key. But this can be difficult—old cars break down, car insurance is expensive, and buying a car without the benefit of credit is often prohibitive. In Hartford, the second poorest city in the United States, more than one-third of all households and nearly one-half of renters are without a car and must therefore rely on public transportation that is sometimes inadequate in meeting both child care and employment needs.[21]

Sammy turned to the source of income he was most familiar with and that was most readily available to him to "double up" his paycheck. Sam contacted Alexander in Springfield, who arranged for him to buy a car for $600. Sammy went to Springfield on a Friday night, cashed his paycheck and invested it in cocaine, with the expectation that he would earn double the amount of his check, pay for the car, keep a little coke for himself to party during the night, and return home with the full amount of his paycheck to give to María. Sammy went to a bar to conduct his business and drove the car that he intended to buy and drive home that night. All was going according to plan, until an undercover detective walked into the bathroom, identified himself, and placed Sammy under arrest. The officer had sent a user, who had been arrested previously for possession, into the bathroom to make a buy with a marked $20 bill. Sammy sprinkled a small amount of cocaine in a dollar bill for the guy, who promptly left the bathroom and the bar altogether after he handed the officer the bill. Sammy was busted and looking at a seven-year mandatory minimum sentence —five for possession with the intent to distribute, and two for selling within one thousand feet of a school building. The school was a day care facility, which was, of course, closed at midnight, but the law did not discriminate by time of day.

The next day, I went to the prison and paid Sammy's $2,000 bail. He returned to his family and to work with prison time awaiting him in the not-so-distant future. Sammy's case would not be tried for another eight months. During this time, he resumed his usual routines, working two jobs, taking care of the children, and managing his urges to use heroin with methadone. Later in the spring, he called his designated attorney, but the attorney didn't return his call. His first court date was approaching and he was getting anxious to find out the facts of the case and his prospects. I also called the attorney, and although his secretary promised a return phone call, it never came. A friend told Sammy about another attorney, whom he promptly called and arranged to meet at his first court appearance. Sammy agreed to be represented by the attorney, but was told to bring a $2,000 retainer to the next court appearance, and then later pay the remaining balance of $3,000.

Sammy asked me to meet his attorney and I didn't like what I saw. The attorney was angry when he found out that Sammy didn't have the money. He made promises about reduced sentences and grandiose comments about motions he would file to discredit the evidence, but stressed that he couldn't do any of this without the $2,000 retainer. When introduced to me and asked by Sammy to repeat what he had said about the case, the attorney appeared uncomfortable, failed to make eye contact, and shifted from one foot to the other, before abruptly departing. Sammy again changed attorneys, this time going back to the defender originally assigned by the court. With each of these changes, his court dates were postponed, slowing down the process.

Not long after, Sammy and I went to Springfield for his next court date. We met his attorney for the first time just before entering the courtroom. Sammy immediately confronted him about not returning his calls. The attorney was dismissive of Sammy, saying that he had received a call only from a college professor. I then introduced myself and repeated Sammy's assertion, "We've been trying to reach you for months." Without apology, he did promise to get the case continued, discuss it with us, and then to conference with the DA. Later that morning, after the attorney had read the police report, Sammy told him his story. The attorney said there was no sense taking the case to court, because the evidence was irrefutable, and that these types of drug busts had become so formulaic that there was little room for negotiation. He explained that Sammy's mandatory minimum sentence would be five years, with two years added because he was arrested within one thousand feet of a school zone. The attorney expected the DA to lower the sentence to five years total if Sammy pled guilty and saved the state the money of prosecuting the case. Beyond that, he explained, the only way to lower the sentence would be to give the DA names of other drug dealers—the bigger the fish, the more the sentence reduction. "You could get it knocked down to three or four years if you give the DA some information about the drug deal, where you got the stuff, and so on. If you give him information and some names about the Springfield drug trade, you might even get probation."

The attorney went on to say that making the case he was a "good citizen" was not likely to get Sammy a sentence reduction, that the DA was simply not sympathetic to these arguments any longer. I pursued this line of thought, describing Sammy's life over the past few years, arguing that the incident in the bar was an anomaly. Sammy was working, maintaining his drug recovery, contributing to the family wage, and taking care of children. Sammy then asked if he and I could talk alone. Sammy was incensed by the exchange with the attorney. "Who the fuck does this guy think I am, a fucking rat! Tim, you know, that's not what I'm about. Why would that motherfucker even say that shit to me?"

When the attorney returned, Sammy told him he wasn't giving the DA any names. We asked the attorney to explain the circumstances of the case to the DA and to let him know that there were several professionals, like myself, willing to testify in Sammy's behalf. Later in the morning, the attorney indicated he had spoken to the DA's staff attorney, and that he agreed it sounded like "Sammy had a life. He wasn't just lost like most people who come through here." The staff attorney suggested that we put together a packet of supporting letters and that he would "take it to his boss and see what we can do."

At this point the demeanor of Sammy's attorney abruptly changed—his stiff, distant professional manner melted as he removed his jacket, loosened his tie, and launched into a long critique of the system. He explained that with mandatory minimum sentencing, "judges no longer had any discretion," that the court was "simply a mill," and that he "is a part of it—a cog in the machine." He explained that there was little flexibility and that the power rested entirely with the DA. Nor did he expect these policies to change, "because politicians get elected on these issues" and because "tougher prosecution of drug cases has created a lucrative industry." Sammy's attorney critiqued the police, who "are making money. Making busts is easy. Christ, you or I could go into [Sammy's bar] and make a bust, it's not rocket science. These guys [the police] do this as overtime, they get overtime pay. They just go up and down the streets busting kids. Then they sit in court all day and draw overtime for that too. They're making a killing. Then you got the prisons themselves." We had unknowingly created an opportunity for Sammy's attorney to let off steam. He had a sympathetic audience and he clearly no longer liked his place in a system largely governed by drug enforcement, mandatory minimum sentencing, and the prison-industrial complex.

Sammy and I put together a packet of letters from employers and from a few other professors who knew him because of my relationship with him. Upon reviewing the case, the DA agreed to a sentence of three years. All that was left now was the waiting. During the next two months, Sammy continued working. In the waning weeks before the trial, he made a few more trips to Springfield to get high with his old friend Roberto, whose drug business was thriving. He and María were fighting over money and his Springfield escapades. I gave him a ride to work one morning not long before his trial date and the stress of his impending incarceration was obviously mounting. Sammy and I argued about his plans to emotionally separate from María while he was locked up.

SAMMY: Besides, I'm going in and I need to be free.

TIM: What do you mean?

SAMMY: Oh, you won't understand. White people don't know the same jealousy that Puerto Ricans know. It's better to be free and clean when you go in, so your mind, you know, your mind isn't fucking with you.

TIM: You're right, I don't get it. Are you trying to tell me that you want to break up with María because you don't want to worry about whether she's going to start seeing someone else?

SAMMY: Exactly.

TIM: What? You don't think you're going to think about her and wonder about her even if you break up? You don't think she's going to come see you even if you leave like this? You're right, man, I don't get it . . .

SAMMY: Tim, man, that's what I'm saying. Us Puerto Ricans
are jealous types, man. Ask Fausto about this. It's better to go
in free and clean, not to have to worry. You got to deal with a
lot in there and you want to have your mind clear. Women
can fuck you up, you know. You always worried about what
she's doing and shit. Ask Fausto, he can explain it to you.

Sammy was right. I probably couldn't understand. Nonetheless, he
and María did patch things up. Sammy spent his last night, first with
the whole family, then with María, and then by himself drinking a
twelve-pack of beer and a pint of Bacardi rum. He was "really emotional" that night, María would tell me later. The next day, sitting in
the courtroom, Sammy leaned over and whispered, "Man, I got a big
fucking hangover!" Why, I thought, would you go to prison any
other way?

The sequence of the court proceedings that morning emphasized
the absurdity of our drug laws. The case just before Sammy's
involved a man who had hit and killed a woman with his car while
intoxicated at the .21 level. The defending attorney argued that his
client had felt extreme remorse due to the accident. After reviewing
the file, the judge noted that the defendant had been arrested twice
before for driving intoxicated and proceeded to sentence the man to
four to five years in prison for killing a person. Sammy's case was
called next. The judge took a few minutes to read the file. He then
berated Sammy for making a bad decision and explained that his
three offenses—distribution of narcotics, second offense of distribution,[22] and selling within one thousand feet of a school zone—carried
a maximum of thirty-five years in prison. The contrast to the previous case was jarring. Referring to the letters we had gathered, the
judge emphasized that Sammy had disappointed several people for
his poor judgment. He stated, however, that he was willing to accept
the plea arrangement with the DA because it was obvious that he had
a number of people who would be supportive of him when he was in
and then released from prison. "Unhappily," he continued, "I must
tell you that I do not see this kind of support for most people who
come before me on these types of charges." Sammy received a three-

year sentence and waved to María over his shoulder as he was led away from the courtroom.

THE MASS INCARCERATION of economically marginalized men of color involved in the drug trade creates a trajectory that is difficult to alter. Slightly more than two-thirds of state prisoners are rearrested within three years of their release, and nearly one-half of those re-arrested are apprehended within six months of release.[23] Given the increase in the state prison population over the past twenty-five years, more than 600,000 inmates are returning to their communities each year, where the prospects for reintegration are poor.[24]

Sammy served three years. Most of his time passed without inci-dent. At a prison facility just outside Springfield, Sammy felt like an old-timer, commenting frequently on how young the inmates were, how "crazy" and "hardheaded" they were, and how many of them left and returned within months. He spent a lot of time in programs learning about drug addiction and "poor choices." For a short time he was transferred to a facility in Hartford to clear up a warrant he had there for driving without a license and failing to appear in court. This time was rough. At one visit, Sammy looked wide-eyed and shaken. He had just come from a fight and was finding himself regu-larly involved in similar altercations. His efforts to earn the respect to be left alone were leading to more and more fights. He was relieved to return to the Massachusetts facility, where his reputation in Springfield provided him with self-affirming respite and safety.

After two and a half years in prison and six months in a community-based transitional facility (referred to as a "three-quarters house"), Sammy returned home to María and the kids. He spoke the language of drug recovery and began looking for a job. After months of rejection, he walked into a small shop that did light assembly work and had a reputation for hiring former prisoners, and threw down the gauntlet. "I told the guy, this is it, I'm tired, dawg. I'm tired of putting in these applications and never getting a call. Either you give me a job or I'm going back out there and doing what I do." He started Sammy at $8 an hour without benefits, and despite a forty-minute drive to work, Sammy appeared greatly relieved. In a workplace marked by frequent worker turnover, Sammy earned a reputation as a reliable worker willing to put in overtime when job deadlines were short. Within two years, he was making $11 an hour.

Sammy's life had reached a fair degree of stability before he was incarcerated, and his prison time had been short and relatively easy. In contrast, urban minority men who enter prison without jobs, who are more mired in drug addictions and the streets, and who spend a longer time incarcerated are not likely to fare as well as Sammy. Further, for many men like Sammy's brother Fausto, prison does not provide a space for rehabilitation and many, also like Fausto, will leave prison in worse condition than when they went in.

NINE

Rebel Without a Cause

FAUSTO WENT TO PRISON young and angry. At nineteen, his anger seemed free-floating, moving from one target to the next with some rapidity. At times he was angry at his attorney, who, as mentioned earlier, had made the comment, "If it makes you feel any better, you should know that all of my clients do time." At times he was angry at the judge: "He didn't even try to understand me and my life. He didn't ask me one question, yo, he just gave me years." At times he was angry at school authorities: "The principal didn't give a fuck. They should've put me in bilingual, I could've been something at that school." Most of the time, he was angry at himself, for either botching the robbery ("Greed, that's what they say. You always make mistakes because of greed, because you want more and more and more") or for making bad decisions ("Drugs fuck you up, bro"). In prison, Fausto's anger became less diffuse and more focused on Department of Corrections authorities, who Fausto believed took their marching orders from political leaders.

As we have seen, the neoliberal transformation of the economy, the erosion of working-class wages and living conditions, the white backlash toward civil rights legislation and court rulings, and the public preoccupation with a black underclass created a political culture in which the fears and uncertainties of the white public were amenable to punitive lock-'em-up rhetoric. Moreover, urban deindustrialization along with racial segregation rendered many black and Latino youths economically superfluous in the 1980s and early 1990s as the urban drug trade flourished. Getting tough on urban crime was an institutional response to the economic dislocation of urban black and Latino youth, and political leaders made careers by exploiting these conditions—Presidents Nixon, Reagan, the first

Bush, and Clinton all benefited from this rhetoric and the subsequent imprisonment binge.

Similar political dynamics were occurring at the state level, where getting tough on crime as well as cracking down on welfare "cheats" became an instant formula for electoral success. Pete Wilson made his political career in California by excoriating welfare recipients and illegal immigrants, but his administration also endorsed harsh drug sentencing and passed one of the first "three strikes" laws.[1] From 1991 to 1998, Governor Wilson managed a prison increase that had begun in 1982, when thirty thousand inmates were in California prisons, but would number 150,000 by the time he left office. From 1992 to 1997, under Wilson, an average of 270 inmates were added to the prison population each week.[2]

In Massachusetts, Wilson's friend William Weld followed a similar script. Weld's tenure as governor from 1991 to 1997 paralleled Wilson's, but Weld came into office more prepared for prosecuting the War on Drugs. As U.S. attorney for the District of Massachusetts in the 1980s, Weld had pushed for mandatory drug sentencing, earning him a position in the U.S. Justice Department in the Reagan administration in 1988. In Washington, Weld crafted the 1988 National Narcotics Prosecution Strategy for fighting drug trafficking. As governor, the state prison rate nearly doubled during Weld's six years in office.[3] He also established himself as one of the nation's leading voices for increased prison punishment, insisting that prisons become a "tour through the circles of hell" and that inmates learn the "joys of busting rocks."[4]

Between 1980 and 2001, the rate of prisoners incarcerated in Massachusetts more than quadrupled, increasing from 56 to 243 prisoners per 100,000 residents, with the largest spike occurring between 1993—the year that Fausto was arrested—and 1997.[5] Nationally, Hispanics were being incarcerated at twice the rate of whites, but in Massachusetts, they were going to prison at six times the rate.[6] Fausto donned an orange jumpsuit and was placed behind cement and barbed wire with many other young men of color. They entered overcrowded facilities where the goal of rehabilitation had been replaced by a prevailing belief in punishment—William Weld's circles of hell.

ENTERING THE FRAY

When prisoners exchange their names for numbers, they enter a world in which they have few remaining civil rights, and where exercising their rights depends on gaining the attention of prisoner rights groups or criminal defense attorneys willing to hear their complaints. Fausto got a taste of this before he even stepped foot in a state prison. After he was arrested, he was taken to the police station, where he reported "they beat the fuckin' crap out of me." Cuffed and shackled in his underwear, Fausto's interrogation began as "a big lieutenant with a white shirt and a gold badge just came in and whaled on me." Fausto claimed that the lieutenant identified himself as a friend of one of the jewelry store owners whom he had robbed and, as the officer reached back to swing, declared, "This one's for Petey." Fausto described: "He just went—boom! My face went like that. I just got mad, right, and I looked at his badge and his name. He just whaled at me again." Fausto was particularly incensed that while the white officer beat him, the black and Latino officers stood by passively. The officers of color took him to the hospital after the beating and upon return did offer words of advice: "Don't act up," they insisted, because "they're lookin' to come in here and beat the shit out of you."

Fausto was placed in a local prison where he awaited trial. During this time, he joined Ñeta, a street gang that had started as a prisoner rights organization in a Puerto Rican prison. Fausto spent hours at the Ludlow facility listening to an "old timer" talk about Carlos Torres Irriarte, known as La Sombra ("The Shadow"), who founded Asociación Ñeta at El Oso Blanco prison in Río Piedras to fight against the injustices of prison guards and gangs.[7] Torres Irriarte was described as a revolutionary who had spent most of his life fighting for Puerto Rican independence. Fausto became a quick study.

> The rules that I was supposed to follow was very honorable . . .
> the Ñeta was to help—it was invented in prison. It was to help us
> live amongst each other with certain rules, you know, certain
> things that we couldn't do to each other. It was good. So, I felt

called by that because I always been a little bit of a revolutionary. . . . So I learned it all and I liked it and I joined.

In prison, gangs provide security, access to resources, and an intense network of brotherhood.

Arriving at the Concord facility where he was processed after his conviction, Fausto made his first stop in the world referred to as "going upstate."

When I showed up to Concord, the gang activity was very alive. Once I got to the joint, I heard people callin' my name, "Yo, Fausto!" It's a big fuckin' unit . . . they have a hundred cells, three floors, and it was like huge, right! . . . I'm lookin' at these faces, right. So somebody yelled, "Yo! Who you down with?" "Ñeta!" "All right. All right. What's up, Fausto! What you need?" I said, "I ain't got nothin'. I just showed up." So somebody sent me some tobacco and another guy sent me some rollies and toothpaste.

His gang affiliation helped him to manage the fear of the unknown.

Fausto settled into Concord. Angry, scared, and facing ten years, he wanted to prove himself, and his involvement in Ñeta gave him the opportunity to do so. Proving yourself on the streets is different, however, from proving yourself in prison. To use a sports cliché, it's a little like going to the big leagues—the level of street skills is higher and the competition for status more intense. Fear and vulnerability are often masked by toughness and violence, and physical violence in prisons is often an attempt to penetrate the façade of toughness and to expose fear. Men who can withstand these challenges and do what needs to be done in order to extinguish or at least hide weakness are considered to have heart. When these dynamics move from the personal to the gang, having heart means putting yourself on the line for the gang, and a collective heart makes the group stronger. Violently protecting oneself may afford some safety from future challenges, but violently protecting the interests of the gang raises the stakes to struggles over resources, reputation, and ultimately power.

Fausto admired the "old timer" at Ludlow because "he didn't

take shit from nobody," and his connection with this revered member of the gang enhanced his status. He also enhanced his status through his willingness to carry out extreme acts of violence for the gang. Fausto describes one violent incident that targeted an inmate who had openly proclaimed he was a member of the Puerto Rican Group 27—the ones responsible for the murder of Ñeta's founder, La Sombra—and was making provocative statements about Ñeta.

> I got this guy in the shower and they gave me, you know, the shaving creams? You know, they're heavy and a couple tuna cans, they're very heavy. They wrapped 'em around a towel for me. They made that thing like a hammer and that hurts. He was a pretty big guy. He weighed like almost three hundred pounds, this guy. So I kinda, like I said, I did things I had to do, you know what I mean? I'm not proud of it but I ended up beatin' him with that thing over the head. . . . I remember they locked the prison down and we left him there. We heard stories. I don't know. If they took him somewhere, I don't know. I never heard from the guy again. I never wanted to know. I kind of asked for forgiveness that night. You know what I mean? I got on my knees and asked for forgiveness.

Fausto moved up rapidly in the gang hierarchy because he demonstrated heart, but he possessed other appealing leadership characteristics as well, particularly the ability to articulate the gang's ideology. "They liked the way I talked, I always been good at that," Fausto remarked. In many ways, Fausto bridged the contradiction that often divides gang members, between those who believe gangs can broker justice in a predatory environment and those who recklessly seek power through gang violence. Fausto was smart and compassionate, with a genuine drive to protect the vulnerable and establish justice, and yet was also willing to engage in extreme instances of violence to further the interests of the group.

Many of the missions that Fausto described, however, were not ordered against other gang members or non-gang-affiliated inmates, but against members of his own gang who violated rules. Gang members who accumulated gambling debts or who became drug-dependent in prison placed the gang at risk of retaliation by other gangs. Further, stealing, raping, and snitching were cardinal sins that would result in "beat-downs" or even "exterminations" (expulsion from the gang after the beating).

At Concord, Fausto molded his anger into disciplined forms of conduct and, as he did, developed leadership qualities and charisma that moved him up in the organization. When he first entered Concord, assigned to a dormitory, he and a few others ran drugs in the prison. But by the time he was classified and headed to a medium security prison at Gardner a year later, his drug involvement had dissipated and his conversations focused more on the virtues of "the organization." He increasingly saw himself as a revolutionary who was fighting for the rights of prisoners against a repressive administration and stressed the importance of being organized.

> But the prison system in Boston was not gonna accept that . . . we was becoming very organized, very quick. And we were growing one hundred fifty to three hundred in the summer and we all were so organized that it scared them in a way, you know . . . it's always been the thing here in the United States, [politicians] fear people coming together and raising opinions.

At Gardner, Fausto was promoted into the leadership ranks of Ñeta.

LEADING ÑETA AT GARDNER

The administration at Gardner had already begun cracking down on gangs when Fausto arrived. Several leaders of Ñeta had been transferred from the prison, creating a vacuum in leadership.[8] Fausto received "the blessing" of the gang's leaders located at the Walpole facility and was made "sergeant of discipline" at Gardner, which was no small task. Fausto found the organization in disarray—he described members as lacking discipline, initiating needless violent missions, running up gambling debts, and pushing rival gangs to the brink of war. "Things were jumping off the fucking roof."

Fausto took his charges seriously and implemented a strategy to evade the administration and clean house. As sergeant of discipline, he declared a moratorium on missions and started a recruitment drive that included gathering information to do background checks on new recruits. Fausto said he threw several members out of the organization because of gambling debts or refusal to adhere to the new strategies, and demoted others. His initiatives were risky, so he surrounded himself with two bodyguards. "This one on my side, he's like six seven, almost a giant. He's got AIDS, he don't give a fuck. . . . This one over here, I think it was his cousin and he had AIDS. . . . They was like down for anything. . . . They were crazy puppies." He referred to his plan as "Operation Ghost": "We became like ghosts for a while because we were too hot. We need to grow . . . so we're gonna have to become very quiet for a while." Missions were later reinstated, but were done "more secretly." Fausto wanted to frustrate the administration by making it impossible for them to track the gang's actions and he wanted to increase the gang's membership— but he needed group discipline to do so, which is difficult to accomplish for a couple of reasons.

First, despite popular characterizations, prison gangs are rarely tight organizations. Phillip Kassel, an attorney with the Massachusetts Correctional Legal Services who has represented prison gang members in court, explains that they usually consist of a small subset of core members who make up the gang leadership, surrounded by a larger, more peripheral group of members who often act semi-independently and, sometimes, even defiantly toward the leadership.[9] Fausto claimed that the leadership had attempted to address gang unity by flattening out the hierarchy and making decisions by consensus:

> I ran everything as a democracy. Every time I made a decision I made it so that everybody was okay with it. Not like before— whatever I say goes without asking anybody. What I used to do was sit everybody down, discuss the problem whatever it was, take opinions, come up with a decision, and that decision . . . everybody had to be okay with it and . . . whoever was disagreeing, we'll try to iron that out. . . . Everybody had power. . . . Everybody had a right to express their opinions and collectively we came up with decisions. When disciplinary things needed to

be dealt with, I had a disciplinary board . . . they ran all the disciplinary problems that we had.

While Fausto and other leaders may have attempted to be more inclusive, as newcomers filling a vacuum of positions and attempting to shore up group discipline, they were making decisions that evoked defiance and created enemies within the organization. Fausto recalled:

> I tried to do as best as I could. And I had some good people who showed up later from Concord who helped me run it. I didn't run that thing by myself. . . . I got pretty liked immediately by people. I was hated too, you know . . . you're always gonna have your critics.

The second and perhaps more important reason it is difficult to sustain gang discipline in prison is attributable to administrative intelligence gathering and strategic actions. Snitches are detested and feared by inmates, and used by the administration to manage the prison. Prison authorities acquire information by exploiting the vulnerabilities and deprivations of inmates—by offering privileges or better treatment, or by issuing threats. As Fausto described, choosing friends and gang associates in prison requires a shrewd assessment of character—of determining who is and is not likely "to be flipped by the IPS," the Internal Perimeter Security team.[10] Fausto initiated Operation Ghost so the gang could become invisible to prison authorities and reorganize, but not long after he assumed a leadership role in Ñeta, his identity was exposed to prison authorities.

> I had a CO [corrections officer] come up to me—'cause I worked at the kitchen and lieutenants and everything were there, and they came up to me and said, "Oh, so you're the one." I said, "I'm the one what?" They says, "Oh, you're the number one head in here for the association group?" "No *inglés,*" [I'd] throw it right back. But they laughed it off, but they knew, so I got ratted out. . . . I know somebody had to give me up.

Loyalty is the sine qua non of prison relationships and networks, just as betrayal is for prison management.

In the spring of 1995, the Massachusetts Department of Corrections (DOC), conducted a sweep at Gardner, removing the leadership of the gangs, particularly the Latino gangs. Fausto was among the prisoners removed and placed in solitary confinement at the notorious Walpole facility.[11] After Julio called to tell me that Fausto had been taken out of Gardner, I called a friend who was working in the research department of the DOC at the time and someone I relied on regularly for information about Fausto. My friend explained that Fausto had been identified as a gang leader and that the DOC was adopting a militant strategy to remove the leaders of Latino gangs throughout the prison system, break their will to resist and organize, and throw the gangs into a state of disorder and anarchy. Moreover, he claimed that the administration had been tipped off that some of the gangs were planning a hostage takeover at the Concord facility. Prison authorities at Gardner described Fausto to my friend as a charismatic guy whom many in the administration liked. He was relatively successful in maintaining order within the gang, was reasonable, and not a "gangbanger." He was the type of leader that administrators like because he could help establish order within the prison—not an easy task to accomplish within gangs.

Fausto did not believe there was ever a planned hostage takeover, but instead argued that the administration had used this as a justification for the sweep. Fausto claimed that the real threat was interracial gang unity. At Gardner, gangs were talking to one another more, while blacks and Latinos were attending one another's cultural activities.

> It was getting good [between the gangs]. It was getting good for a while between all of us, but they [the administration] hate that. Right? They would be, like I said before, their motto—divide and conquer, right? They never like to see unity within inmates because to them unity means power and power means we're gonna demand things. You know, after a while it's gonna become political, right?

238

On Springfield streets and in school, Fausto's engaging personality had allowed him to make friends with people across racial and ethnic and, sometimes, class lines. In prison, where identity and status are tightly wound around race and ethnicity, Fausto learned early that he had to carefully manage his interracial personal associations.

You know, there's certain rules that you have to apply to yourself when you go in prison . . . in my race . . . Latin people didn't talk to whites. I treat everybody the same way, you know . . . but I couldn't be with [whites or blacks] because then my people will start looking at me like, wait a minute . . . they would worry about me in case of a racial riot or anything like that, that [I would] give up where the shanks are or anything like that. But I talked to people [of other races and ethnicities], you know, but there were certain things that I had to do. There's a certain way that I had to carry myself in order to get the respect that I needed in order to survive in there.

At Gardner, however, racial dynamics had taken an interesting turn.

Even though the administration was cracking down on gangs when Fausto arrived, he was surprised by the liberties that inmates had. He commented, "Gardner had a lot of privileges . . . they had Latino community, Latino stuff. They had a lot of stuff that, really, I didn't see a need for the association really, because Gardner already had the things that the inmates needed." An older inmate, a Puerto Rican *independista*, was central to the Latino cultural activities, where he worked with Puerto Rican inmates to acquire an understanding of their cultural histories. Fausto enjoyed long conversations with "the Doc," as they referred to him, and arranged for me to meet with him on a few of my visits to the prison.

The Doc and I would talk about his political consciousness-raising prison initiative, based on the ideas of Brazilian educator Paulo Freire, while Fausto listened intently. Fausto's leadership of the Ñeta and the Doc's work in the prison's Latino club made an interesting alliance, and there was potential for a more politically informed group to emerge. I suspect that some of Fausto's ideas on democratic leadership came from the Doc, but the Doc did not have much influence among many of the gang members. The gangs were organized around violently instilled discipline and paramilitary control of meager prison resources, and, in fact, they often used the Latino club as a cover to plan gang-related actions. Besides, as Fausto pointed out, the Doc was viewed by many as just "a weirdo" who talked with big words. Nonetheless, the Doc pushed at the racial and ethnic boundaries within the prison by attempting to reach out to African American groups and by articulating the African heritage in Puerto Rican history. He argued that African Americans and Puerto Ricans shared a similar status as people of color in the white-dominated United States. These ideas appealed to Fausto and he saw power in unity.

According to Fausto, despite the racial boundaries marking identity and territory, rival gang leaders were making efforts at Gardner to establish peace and to unite against a common enemy, the administration. Fausto admitted that controlling the behavior of Ñeta members was difficult and seemed to continually dissipate into squabbles that threatened brokered peace and interethnic unity. On the other hand, more formal cultural exchanges crafted by inmates like the Doc and informal networks established by gang leaders set the conditions for more unity within the prison. Fausto claimed that gang leaders met regularly:

> We just talked things out . . . sat down at a table at the library with some families [gangs] every now and then and talked. I had it to where we meet at a certain day all the time . . . and we'll talk, and whatever needed to be said, was said. And that's how we kept relationships flowing.

Even if Fausto's claims about gang unity are overstated, any semblance of inmate organization within prison must threaten prison authorities, because, as Fausto said, "after a while it's gonna become political, right?"

Fausto may have stumbled upon an important contradiction that prison administrators create for themselves. On one hand, in order to maintain order within the prison, administrators need the cooperation of inmates, or some mechanism for managing the population. Gangs can serve this purpose. The organization of gangs by race and ethnicity, of course, reflects societal racism, but, more important, it also institutionally entrenches and facilitates racist behavior among inmates and guards. Prison administrators can benefit from this arrangement—gangs produce some degree of order and discipline among the population and, as Fausto recognized, keep the inmates divided and fighting one another. On the other hand, gangs are also violent organizations that can threaten the safety of prison guards and the institutional order.

Whether there was a planned hostage takeover, fear about gang unity, or a broader institutional anti-gang mandate deployed, a gang sweep was ordered to separate the leaders from the membership in the spring of 1995. Attorney Kassel, who represented the inmates in court, explained that prisoners were placed in solitary confinement, allowing for only one hour of release outside their cells four days out of every five-day cycle, with no release on the fifth day. On average, prisoners removed in the sweep were subjected to these conditions for a year.[12] Fausto was among them.

Gang Sweep

Fausto was awakened around six in the morning by special police units in riot gear.

> I jumped out of the bed ready to fight somebody and then a guy pulled up his helmet and he says, "It's me, sergeant. Calm down." So I go, "What do you guys want?" He goes, "Cuff up. We're taking you." . . . They put me in the leg shackles and got me the fuck out of there. So by the time I made it up to the administration building, they got about fifty of us up there. We thought we was getting shipped out of state 'cause that was the rumor. . . . We got this big convoy of fuckin' vans, right, all fuckin' guards with fuckin' guns outside and fuckin' crazy shit, right? Guns, a lot of guns, a lot of M-16s, right, big convoy, a lot of vans and a lot of people in fatigues like. It was like a big extraction team, right? They're loadin' us up in these vans and they're takin' us outta there. A guy says, "Yo, where the fuck you takin' us?" He

says, "I can't tell you that." Man, as soon as we saw that white wall, I seened it from far away, I said, "Oh fuck. We're in Walpole, guys. Walpole!" Oh man, as soon as they opened up the fuckin' back, fuckin' guys were comin' runnin'! De-de-de-de-de. Draggin' us, right? Runnin' with us. Runnin', "Move! Move! Move!" Like a line of motherfuckers. If you trip, they had fuckin' batons. They were runnin' with us. I got shackles on me, right? And these two big guys practically in the air with me, runnin' with me. Right? All of us at the same time runnin', runnin'— "Move! Move!" All of 'em yelling. Then they got us all down to the basement—"Strip!" They were like, "Give me a fuckin' reason! Right?" . . . Then I got three of 'em around me. "Strip!" So I stripped. We stripped. They made us go butt-naked. Then they said pick up your clothes. Now they were doin' the same thing again. They put my shackles on my legs real tight so that when I was walkin' they were hurting like a motherfucker. So then they brought us to the units. . . . They brought me up the stairs. They brought me up to the second floor, Cell 42. Boom! Lockup! Single cells for everybody, right? Now we're in Walpole!

Attorney Kassel estimates that at least 90 percent of the members removed in the sweep were Latino and that the net had been far too broad, transferring inmates who were not gang-affiliated.[13] Fausto saw the same on the inside:

They had people in there that were not even gang members. Just suspected of bein' a gang member, you were gone. That became the thing—after we left, if I didn't like you and I said I want to do you some harm, I just go up to a CO [corrections officer] and say he's a gang member. He'd be gone. And he's just a guy minding [his] own business.

The Department of Corrections' intelligence may have erred on the side of being too inclusive, but the sweep captured many of the leaders from the Latin Kings, Los Sólidos, La Familia, and Ñeta.

Prisoners fought back with whatever they had at their disposal to resist their treatment. Riot conditions existed for an extended period of time, as members from different gangs, thrown together in prison blocks in one of the state's oldest facilities, joined ranks. "We would just war with 'em," Fausto described. "I mean war!"

> Everybody started screamin', throwin' shit out there. It was fuckin' wild! I mean, they had to pick up trash. Everybody was goin' crazy. Yellin' out "Ñeta" and the fuckin' Latin Kings were yellin' their signs, Familia were yellin'. . . . It was crazy! We went to war with these people for the whole months that we were there. Remember the time that nobody could come up and see me, Walpole was locked down? We were goin' to war with 'em. I mean war. I mean they couldn't come in and calm us or nothin'. Any CO that came in was getting . . . something thrown at him, shit at him, 'cause there's no Plexiglas. It's bars. There were fires takin' place everywhere. We had lighters, so you know all the sheets went up in smoke.

According to Fausto, the administration responded to the prisoners' rebellion with systematic deprivation and provocation. He claimed that their food was tampered with, inmates were beaten, doors were left open in the winter, water was turned off for days, inmates were refused their daily one-hour release from their cells, and guards used racial epithets regularly to provoke them. Moreover, Fausto claimed that guards were at liberty to do whatever was necessary to subdue the population.[14] When guards would enter the unit to clean up a mess the inmates had made, Fausto and others would taunt them. Guards would promise retaliation and, according to Fausto, would later respond with impunity.

> The beatings . . . took place a lot. . . . Anybody that got extracted from their cells got beat up. Everyone knew you were going to get beat up. A lot of 'em ended up in the hospital. They don't document that, they don't feed that out there.

For Fausto, living in these conditions required self-discipline— focusing his mind, refusing the provocations of guards, maintaining a physical exercise regimen in his cell, and collectively strategizing with other inmates across cells. Many inmates could not endure and Fausto describes moments when he cracked. He was close to an older inmate, Christo, who was widely liked and respected behind the wall. He was serving fourteen years for stabbing a driver who transported Puerto Rican and Jamaican laborers to the tobacco fields and, according to Christo, repeatedly mistreated them. Christo was only a few cells down from Fausto's when several guards entered his cell. Fausto continues:

> Look, they grabbed Christo, shut off the camera,[15] beat his ass, Maced him to the point where the guy was gonna lose his eyes, leave the cuffs on, shut off the water, threw him in DDU [Disciplinary Detention Unit], beat his ass on his way down there, left him with all that chemical on his face and didn't let him wash his face for like four or five hours. They did the same thing to me, right, 'cause I started screamin' about him bein' beat up. All I saw was a boot hit me right here [points to a scar on his face] and I remember my feet draggin' from cement into dirt. That's how I knew I had left the building [chuckle] and gone to another building, that was DDU but over there you don't have a bed. You got a slab . . . and they fuck with you there. The COs are always dressed in fatigues. They're ready always for action. Big motherfuckers, you know, almost three hundred pounds, and half of the COs up there are on the juice [steroids].

Fausto developed survival techniques to deal with solitary confinement. He described a disciplined routine of reading a Bible, doing push-ups and sit-ups, and, most important, keeping a clear mind about who the enemy was and what could be done to resist them. He spent a lot of time "just observing, always thinkin' about what the administration's next move was gonna be." For some, however, the physical and mental deprivation without apparent end became unbearable.

> I had a dude . . . Carlos who I was talkin' to at ten o'clock and he was tellin' me, um, "Damn, Fausto, I can't take this shit no more." I said, "Yo, what are you talkin' about? We've only been

here for a while." And I said, "Calm down, bro . . . they're gonna have to let us go." . . . At eleven o'clock, CO did his count, I don't know, between eleven o'clock or twelve. . . . The fucker had hanged it up.

Physical and psychological deprivation also created personal agitation and fierce aggression that inmates turned on one another.

Oh, guys started turnin' against each other. Real friends. I started noticing that, the psychotic part. Like one little thing you said to me will tick me off. Like people were in such a bad fuckin' mood. There was, you know, one little argument, somethin' that you could blow off. "I'm gonna kill you, motherfucker, as soon as they open my cell!" Shit like that!

The prisoners attempted more organized forms of protest as well. For example, they attempted a hunger strike and sustained it for four days. They also received legal assistance from prisoner advocacy groups and public counsel, who filed suit claiming that due process was being denied the prisoners and that long-term segregated confinement was illegal. External pressure resulted in immediate minor improvements—for instance, twenty-four-hour daily lockdown was prohibited and prisoners, especially AIDS prisoners, were better able to obtain their medicine.[16] Four years later, the Massachusetts Superior Court ruled on behalf of the prisoners, arguing that the confinement was "atypical" and that due process had been denied.[17] The decision, however, was stayed pending review by the Supreme Judicial Court. In October 2002—two years after Fausto had been released from prison—the Supreme Judicial Court upheld the Superior Court decision; however, the court refused inmate compensation.[18]

THE BARGAIN

For Fausto and others held in segregated conditions in 1995, maintaining their fierce resistance was difficult. Further, conditions gradually improved—the food was better, inmates were let out of their cells three at a time for an hour each day, and cell assignments allowed for members of the same gang to be together in the same block. Months later, the administration approached the prisoners with an offer to be moved back into regular population provided they signed statements declaring they were gang members, or members of a Security Threat Group, renounced their gang affiliation, and completed an anger management program. Moreover, by signing, they also agreed that if at any time during the remainder of their sentence they were found to be associated with a gang, they would be returned to Walpole and serve the remainder of their full sentence (without parole) in solitary confinement. According to Fausto, the prisoners refused to sign. The DOC and the inmates struck a compromise that they would proceed with the program on a "good faith" basis without signing the document. The first half of the anger management program was to take place in Walpole and the second part in a different facility at Old Colony. Halfway through the program at Walpole, the prisoners were again approached to sign the document as a condition for transferring to Old Colony. Fausto said that the group debated the administration's demand and then staged a walk-out of the program.

The administration, however, was not to be denied. According to Fausto, a few months later, the administration again offered a "good-faith compromise" that allowed inmates into the program without signing. This time the inmates finished the first half of the program at Walpole and, without signing, were transferred to Old Colony for the second part. At Old Colony, the anger management program was run by Spectrum, a group that specialized in drug and alcohol treatment. The program focused on individual responsibility, stressing that inmates had made bad choices in their lives, but Fausto struggled with the message of blame. On one hand, he acknowledged that he had made bad choices—after all, nobody forced him to walk into the bank on that fateful morning. On the other, however, he wondered how the young Latino college student who taught the course could understand the choices that he and others like him had been given, or the anger and humiliation associated with the experiences of school failure, family poverty, racism, or social marginalization more generally. Fausto tried to argue a social justice perspective:

I always went into it deeper, how politics played a role in order to fuck minority communities and shit like that. . . . How the fuck you expect me to have a choice when you're not creating what is best for me to succeed in life . . . inventing laws . . . aimed at destroyin' me . . . and things like that [laugh]. . . . And they're tellin' me, no, shut up, I almost got kicked out once [laughs].

Fausto and others, however, did pass the class and complete the program and, for the first time in nearly two years, were permitted contact visits with their families.

According to Fausto, however, the Department of Corrections had another trick up its sleeve. On the morning they were anticipating their first contact visit, the inmates were, again, presented with the document declaring they were a security threat and renouncing their affiliation with any gang. The ultimatum was clear—sign or be returned to Walpole. The good-faith compromise was shorn of its good faith. Fausto was incensed.

Everybody wanted to be able to touch their families again, and then [the administration] come up with that paper and say you either sign here or you go back to Walpole. But what about the skills that you just taught me that was supposed to be preparing us to go to that [next] level, right? So that means this is bullshit and it all came down to signing that fuckin' paper. That's hard, you know. You got a choice to make. Your family is beggin' you— "Hey, uh, we need to see you." Your son is mad 'cause he never touches you or your wife, your mom, your grandma.

Everyone signed except three members of the group that had been transferred with Fausto to Old Colony. Those three were sent back to Walpole and placed in solitary confinement.

Fausto signed. In an animated conversation with Julio and me, he tried to maintain some shred of dignity in his decision.

I wanted to see my mother. I wanted to go to Norfolk and work and make some money or something, you know. The gym was nice [there]. I hadn't worked out for years. A lot of people did the same thing. They wanted to touch their sons and daughters. It's hard, yo . . . the next day they're comin' to pick you up to take you into population. You haven't stepped out in a yard for two or three years, 'cause all you do is walk from here to here in your room.

Fausto's anger crescendoed as he recalled putting pen to paper:

Fuck what they think! . . . I'll sign your piece of shit paper. I never cared what the fuck you think. I don't care what the fuck you think now. And I wrote down, I'm thinkin' about becomin' a born-again Christian [laughter].

Fausto signed, saw his mother, and was then sent to "the hole" in Norfolk.[19]

The experience at Walpole increased Fausto's anger toward the administration and he was now faced with the dilemma of managing that anger. This was the true test. Before he would be released back into civilian life, he would have to demonstrate submission to unrestricted, ubiquitous power. This is what breaking the will of angry, defiant young men meant, whose resistance to authority had been shaped long before they walked through the prison gates. Prison was an incubator of larger societal dynamics. Breaking the will of inmates was an attempt to eviscerate their deviant identities, to pacify them, to leave them impotent in the face of social and economic conditions that rendered them invisible, unworthy, or superfluous. Oppositional or deviant identities are shaped over time from efforts to find dignity in circumstances that deny it, or in other words to make the socially invisible, visible. Gold chains, expensive Timberlands, slow-moving, bass-booming, Ford Explorers with shiny rims scream for visibility, as if to say, "See, motherfucker, and you thought you could make me invisible!" Oppositional behavior solidifies into oppositional identities when the meaning of these behaviors become articulated and valued by a larger group of marginalized people (whose symbols then often become commodified and produced by the market for profit).

Gang organization was one attempt to harness and give form to oppositional anger, but the paramilitary form it sometimes took was no match for the repressive arm of the state. After fighting the DOC for nearly three years, Fausto recognized the futility in the strategy.

We had heard rumors that they had done a raid again, right? People who had left the program before us, two months before us, they were already gathered up again and sent back to Walpole, because three or four of 'em were talkin' in the yard one day and they used that to ship 'em right back to Walpole. They wasn't giving out no jobs to the gang members, ex–gang members. There wasn't anything but shit while you were there. No jobs in the quad, no nothin'! They wanted you to get in trouble again so they could ship you back out. They had a vendetta. You know what I mean? So they were out to fuck with you, so you really had to really hide from these motherfuckers throughout the whole time you were there because they were out to hunt you down and ship you back, you know? . . . Now they had a fuckin' paper justifyin' that you're admitting, right. . . . A lot of people got shipped back to Walpole.

Of course, whether the Department of Corrections wanted Fausto and others to "get in trouble" is dubious, but what is clear is that their strategy to isolate and repress gang leadership was harsh, and at times brutal and unlawful, and that while inmates like Fausto may have eventually submitted, they did so with renewed hostility toward the DOC and the larger society it represented. The challenge then for Fausto and others was to manage their rage and hostility in order to "do their time."

INMATE TO CONVICT

As Julio and I made our regular visits to Fausto over the years, it became clear that Fausto didn't keep track of time. One way of "doing time" was to forget time, to allow it to pass unnoticed. Fausto felt the passing of the seasons and holidays in the cafeteria, but months rolled by unrecognized. Routines carved up the day, as Fausto learned to abide the minutiae of time—two trips to the gym a day, push-ups and sit-ups in the morning, a computer class in the afternoon, a few hours of work in the afternoon, and so on. Routines passed the time; in fact, they became the time, and beyond this, time was a vague abstraction whose oppressive weight was to be avoided, if possible.

Fausto bumped up against this oppressive weight occasionally. For instance, visits from outsiders reminded him of time—his daughter's birthday, approaching holidays, the discussion of children growing up. Moreover, time was marked by the differences in sentences among inmates. Fausto preferred hanging out with lifers, inmates who would never be released from prison, and there were several locked up at the medium security prison at Norfolk. He preferred lifers because they taught him how to manage time, but also because they reminded him that there was a clock out there ticking that privileged him. On his chart he had a specified release date; on their charts, the release date was stamped "death."

For Fausto, learning the "culture behind the wall" was learning how to do time, and at Norfolk he realized that he had not been "doing time," but had been "fighting time." When Fausto entered prison, he challenged the efforts of the Department of Corrections to "break him down"—to make him obedient to state authority, culpable for his crimes and lifestyle, and impotent in changing his life circumstances. When Fausto and others pushed, they got smashed by the power of the state—and the powerlessness of their social marginality became perhaps clearer to them than ever before. Learning how to do time meant learning how to manage himself in relations with both prison authorities and the population behind the wall. For Fausto, the former was more difficult than the latter, in part, because it meant succumbing to state power. Prison authorities had not only demonstrated their repressive capacity, but at Norfolk they maintained their authority by insisting that Fausto demonstrate daily that he was no longer gang-affiliated. Fausto felt their eyes wherever he went—in the yard, the gym, in his cell, and in the chow hall.

Managing himself among inmates was easier for Fausto because he shared a life world with many of them.

You communicate a lot. 'Cause that's all you do, you talk . . . I mean, you got some characters in there, but we so much the same. . . . I didn't know 'em personally but I knew their story. I knew what led 'em to do what they did. Pressure, you know, the pressures of life. . . . Drugs played a big role in a lot of crimes. . . . Money—people needing money to support their families or support their lifestyles. . . . Everybody in there can relate to each other. . . . I was familiar with the poverty thing, so I fit right in. . . . I already knew violence, abuses, drug addicts, just havin' a rough upbringing from different parents, single parents, divorced parents, uh, moms that was a whore, uh, bein' raised by two junkie parents and shit like that. Stories like that I already knew 'cause I seen them. You know, all my life, we never lived in no rich neighborhood. . . . I was seein' already junkies . . . since I was young. . . . Crack had started to come in the scene when we were growin' up, but heroin was always out there. Drugs played a big role, so goin' into prison I already knew these stories. So, I fit right in. The only thing that I had to learn was the ways, the ways that you carried yourself in prison, the things that you had to look out for to avoid certain people. You know, problems, to learn how to see problems comin' from a mile away, you know what I'm sayin', and avoid them. I wasn't so good at that when I first started.

Of course, it was this shared life world that allowed Fausto to become a leader.

As Fausto settled into Norfolk, however, he became increasingly critical of both the state and prison gangs. Toward the state, he and others were all too aware of the "get tough on prisoner" policies that had been heralded by Governor Weld and his successor, Paul Cellucci. "Weld's a stupid son of a bitch," Fausto decried. "He's a hated motherfucker around here." He wants "to take everything away from us," Fausto continued, "that's how he gets elected. Take it away from the inmates, get tough on criminals." Fausto saw the strategy as misguided, that while it may have succeeded in getting Weld and others elected, it was a poor way of controlling the burgeoning prison population. He argued that "people have to have something to lose, or else you can't control 'em."

Fausto also became disillusioned with organizing inmates. One visit when Fausto was particularly despondent, he lamented that the gang was too difficult "to hold on to and try to unite." He reasoned that people did not want to unite, but instead wanted to do drugs and gamble, or do things that were not in the interest of the larger community. Moreover, he believed that the administration was too adept at manipulating inmates, turning them into snitches or dividing and provoking gangs into internecine warfare or racial conflicts. He also believed that gang rules were repeatedly broken to protect members who were part of or favored by the leadership—what he referred to as "towel throwing," which created internal gang divisions and conflict. Fausto left the gang, but insisted that he did so on his own prerogative rather than conceding to the DOC's success in creating conditions that made it nearly impossible for Fausto to continue his gang affiliations. "I don't agree with what [the DOC] did to us," Fausto explains, "but it was time for me to move on. And a lot of my friends saw it that way too, and we did. We moved on. No extermination. No hard feelings. You know, basically, nobody touched me. So I moved on."

Of course, Fausto "moved on" for many reasons—his disenchantment with the gang, his weariness from prolonged solitary confinement, his yearning for contact visits with his family, and his desire for simple pleasures, like breathing outdoor air, eating with the inmate population, lifting weights, or just having a laugh with the boys. Looking back on his experiences during the first four years of his incarceration, he concluded that he had been a "rebel without a cause," that his defiance had never gained enough traction to challenge the power of the authorities and that his desire to organize and be a leader were mere fantasies. Settling into a new stage in his incarceration, Fausto articulated what he considered to be the difference between an inmate and a convict:

> An inmate when he comes in, right, he's wild, uncontrollable. He still thinks he's on the street. He's operating with the mentality of a street person. That's an inmate. He wants to be in everybody's business. He doesn't know how to conduct himself in prison. And you have to survive in prison and get yourself out of trouble with

the guards, all the inmate population, you have to conduct yourself in a certain way and that comes with time. The more time you do in prison the more you're gonna learn about doin' time. By then you have become a convict, a person who understands who he is, what he's done and what he's there to do, which is to do his piece of time and get the fuck out or to do the rest of his life in there. . . . [But] an inmate . . . the ones that . . . don't give the respect. . . . Usually, those guys, like me, get in trouble their first years that they're there. They make a lot of trips to the hole. That's when you are your most dangerous when you're an inmate because you don't know how to act. There's certain things you have to do in prison in order to survive.

Learning to, as Fausto put it, become a convict meant learning the "culture behind the wall." Some of these lessons were readily apparent:

Don't gamble. Don't take drugs unless you can pay for 'em. Don't gossip. Stop hangin' around the yard so much 'cause the yard is like the streets. There's a lot of things goin' on out there and you don't want to get caught up in any of that shit. Um, keep your fuckin' comments to yourself.

Some of the lessons were about physical survival:

Don't say you're gonna hurt somebody if you're really not gonna do it. There are certain rules, you know. Play the fence. Put your back up against the wall. Don't sleep with your head toward the bars. Simple shit, but survival. Everything is survival.

Some of the lessons were about suffering the abuse of prison guards:

Then you got the fuckin' guards you gotta deal with, the most prejudiced fuckin' force on earth. They let you openly know that you're a fuckin' piece of shit. You're worth nothin'. You're gonna do as we tell you. You're gonna get up and move when we tell you

253

to move, and I will call you a fuckin' nigger or a spic in your face and there ain't shit you can do about it. You know what I mean? Basically, you're reduced to nothin', to bein' a fuckin' number. That's what they want you to feel like.

But then there are the more nuanced lessons that require empathy and a respect for human deprivation:

Your body's in prison but your mind ain't . . . your mind could go further than what you are in here. . . . That's why there's certain things that are very respectful in a prison. Never wake up a convict when he's sleeping 'cause . . . sleep is very sacred in there. *You don't go wake up anybody if you see 'em sleepin' 'cause that's the only time you're free.* You're not in there. You know what I mean?

Fausto concludes:

After a while, you start learnin' how to live and you start learnin' the rules . . . so now you're not an inmate anymore. . . . Now you've learned how to act. Now you're calmin' down. Now you're getting into doin' your time, acceptin' it and tryin' to get out. That's when you become a convict.

Behind the wall, a code of honor is observed and boundaries are established so that oppressive conditions can be inverted into routines of dignity. In prison, unpredictable emotional eruptions occur frequently, as everyday frustrations and irritations swell into potential confrontations. The codes of honor and respect are attempts to deal with these eruptions—to remind prisoners where the lines are drawn, where provocation is and is not tolerated. Transgressing these boundaries happens frequently and the consequences can be severe, often taking the form of brutal violence. Avoiding these encounters may not be possible, but learning the codes, learning the practices of mutual respect, and learning to discipline both body and mind increase one's chances.

A Special Viewing in Leg
Irons and Handcuffs

Like others, Fausto struggled with the world outside the prison wall.
Sometimes it seemed as if the rigidity of his daily routines not only
protected him against the ticking clock, but also hermetically sealed
him away from the outside world. I observed his ambivalence. On
one hand, he desperately wanted to be visited, called, written, and
sent money and gifts. On the other hand, these visits were sometimes
agonizing, especially when he learned about family problems that he
couldn't do anything about. Relinquishing power and control over
outside matters is difficult and feelings of impotence can lead to mis-
directed violence inside prisons. Fausto especially saw this among
men with partners and children. Having emotional connections outside the prison walls provided an important lifeline for many prisoners. They stayed connected to children and they remained hopeful of
a life—often an imagined reconstructed life—after prison. Moreover, the comfort of being loved, which usually took on a different
form and meaning when one was locked up, helped inmates cope
with the isolation and deprivations of prison life. If nothing else, it
allowed them to imagine, to fantasize, to leave the moment. But relationships were difficult to maintain and men were forced to recognize
the limits of their control.

Fausto entered prison romantically involved with two women,
but quickly learned that managing relationships inside prison was too
painful. He explained this to me the way Fausto often explained
things to me—by telling a story. He described how one of his friends,
when bored, would sit close to the prison phone to indulge himself in
voyeuristic entertainment. One time he invited Fausto to join him.
The friend set up two chairs at a safe but manageable distance from
the phone, brought food purchased from the commissary, and settled
in for the show.

And so we sat down with our back toward the phone, right? . . .
First customer was a Dominican guy, right? Picks up the phone,
dials home, and next thing you know the conversation started

from, "Hey! How ya doin', baby? I love you, blah, blah."
[laughs] The conversation went from that to, "You fuckin' bitch!
Hah? Hah? You will? He's there? Hah? He's fuckin' there! You
got some fuckin' balls! When I get outta here, I'm gonna fuckin'
kill you! You fuckin' bitch! You die!" He hanged up. [laughs] I
was tryin' to hold myself. The next one came over, right? That
phone was evil, bro. . . . That's when I picked up, though it was
funny, I picked up that I could be one of those guys and I didn't
want to go through that the rest of my sentence. Guys go through
hell when they're married [or in a committed relationship]. You
know what I mean? Especially the ones that left their wives and
been with her for ten years and then now they're getting ready to
do a twenty-year bid. You know he's gonna lose that. . . . That's
one of the worst traumas you're gonna see in prison, the fact that
you're gonna lose your wife. I don't give a fuck if you've been
married for thirty years, very rare does the woman stick with the
man. You know what I mean? They don't wait. . . . They can't
wait. You know, and you can't blame them for it but a lot of men
don't want to depart from that, right, and, uh, second customer . . . he started sayin', "Babe, what's up?" and, you know,
"Where you went Friday?" "I called." "I called three times."
"No, you wasn't. You wasn't home. You're lyin' to me!" [laughs]
You know, so I guess she broke down on the other side, said,
yeah, she wasn't home. Some guys didn't take it. Some guys
accepted it. Some, in order not to lose that little $20 a week
[money from outside deposited in commissary accounts for an
inmate's use], went on with it and said, "But all right, baby.
Once." The smarter ones is like, "All right. You could fuck him
but, but keep me straight here. You know what I mean? Keep
bringing me money." And shit like that, you know . . . it taught
me that I had to let go of the relationship that I had 'cause I wasn't
gonna be one of these guys—you do some bad time like that. You
know, worryin' about your fuckin' wife and who's she seein'. . . .
You get those signs, those Dear John letters, you know.

Most of what happens on the outside is uncontrollable, and men often
have to learn to manage rage or guilt as events unfold beyond the

wall. Fausto's most difficult moment came in late fall 1996, with the death of his daughter.

Fausto's daughter, Melinda, was born with heart and lung defects. As Fausto often said, "I owe my little girl's life to the doctors at the hospital." Indeed, Melinda was in the hospital much of her first two years of life. Her sternum had been cut and never reattached due to yearly operations that were necessary to adjust internal tubes as she grew. In her seventh year, her heart gave out. Melinda had been taken to a local hospital in Springfield after she fainted on a hot summer afternoon. She was given oxygen and then released when her vital signs appeared strong. She died within twenty-four hours of her release. Juan and Angela were living in Puerto Rico when they heard about the hospitalization and immediately flew to Springfield. Their sadness was lessened slightly by the thought that Melinda had waited to see them one last time before she died.

At the time of Melinda's death, Jorge and Julio organized a local "fund-raiser" to pay for the funeral. A group of guys gathered in Jorge's basement where they cut up a couple of ounces of cocaine and fanned out across the bars in Springfield. At the end of the night, they delivered their profits to Melinda's mother, Virginia. They provided well—bright flowers adorned the casket where Melinda's body lay. Throughout the visitation, the story of Melinda's determination to defy death until she could see her *abuelos* one last time was told repeatedly. Conspicuously missing from the evening, however, was Melinda's father, who was suffering Melinda's death behind bars.

On the morning of the scheduled visitation, Fausto had been transported to the funeral home in handcuffs and leg irons to view the body alone. Fausto later reported that the guards had refused to remove his handcuffs. "Can you believe it, bro, they wouldn't even let me touch her, my own girl, they wouldn't, I'm telling you, they wouldn't undo the cuffs. I went off on those motherfuckers. They didn't give a fuck." Fausto returned to the prison that afternoon without sharing a word of consolation, a memory, or a tear with other members of his family.

Fausto didn't talk much about it when Julio and I visited. Tears rolled down his cheek and he closed his eyes at one point as he expressed guilt about not being there when she died. Melinda was his only daughter and her loss removed one of the inspirations he had to change his life. Even now, Fausto rarely talks to me about Melinda, but will on occasion say that his brother Sammy, who also struggles with heroin addiction, has one reason that he doesn't to stay clean— his children. I surmise that in the deep recesses of Fausto's conscience looms a demon that today contributes to his sensory-numbing acts of self-destruction, and within that demon lies the innocent smile of a seven-year-old girl.

PRISON VIOLENCE AND ITS CONSEQUENCES

Fausto's struggle today is attributable to many factors, his daughter's death only one of them. The wounds suffered during the seven years he spent in prison have not healed well. His exposure to and partici-pation in prison violence returns regularly in nightmares four years after his release, and the medical profession has labeled him with a diagnosis reserved, until recently, for war veterans: post-traumatic stress disorder.

Violence in prison is poorly documented. Prisoner rights organi-zations scoop up some of the cases and attempt to publicize them in the media, but most violence goes unreported. A 2001 Human Rights Watch report revealed that prison rape was common and predictable where "prison and prosecutorial authorities do little to prevent and punish it."[20] Based on the report, attorneys Robert Weisberg and David Mills conservatively estimated that around 200,000 current inmates have been raped and a million sexually assaulted during the past twenty years. They concluded, "The truth is that the United States has essentially accepted violence—and particularly brutal sex-ual violence—as an inevitable consequence of incarcerating crimi-nals."[21]

Some of the most egregious cases of violence do make the news. In the 1990s, the Corcoran prison administration in California adopted an integration policy in the prison yard ostensibly to teach prisoners racial and ethnic tolerance. Christian Parenti reports that when fights broke out in the yard, the administration shot live rounds of ammunition to quell the violence. From 1989 to 1994, 175 inmates were shot and twenty-seven killed. Despite public protest, the policy continued and another thirty-two were wounded and twelve killed between 1994 and mid-1998 (in only one case was a prisoner armed with a weapon). During this same time period, only six inmates were shot by corrections officials in all other prisons in the nation, and all six cases involved an escape attempt. The hollowness of the integration policy was also exposed by the entertainment value that the yard provided some of the guards, who tape-recorded several of the fights and made gladiator-style bets on them.[22]

While the events at Corcoran prison may be extraordinary, the U.S. military interrogation techniques exposed at Abu Ghraib in Iraq that disgusted and shamed Americans prompted several journalists to draw comparisons between these abuses of power and treatment of inmates in U.S. prisons. *New York Times* journalist Fox Butterfield, for instance, pointed out that in 1999 a Federal District Court judge imposed a decree at a Texas facility, while George W. Bush was governor of the state, citing guards' complicity in a gang-organized sex slave trade in the prison. The judge concluded that the prisons in Texas had become a "culture of sadistic and malicious violence."[23] Butterfield also noted that more than forty state prison systems have been under court order at some point during the past twenty-five years due to brutality, overcrowding, poor food, or lack of medical care.[24]

Human Rights Watch, having documented prison abuses in the United States for some time, reported that while Americans were shocked by the Abu Ghraib photos, these incidents were not surprising to those familiar with abuses in U.S. prisons. Jamie Fellner of Human Rights Watch asserts:

> In recent years, U.S. prison inmates have been beaten with fists and batons, stomped on, kicked, shot, stunned with electronic devices, doused with chemical sprays, choked, and slammed face first onto concrete floors by the officers whose job it is to guard them. Inmates have ended up with broken jaws, smashed ribs, perforated eardrums, missing teeth, burn scars—not to mention psychological scars and emotional pain. Some have died.[25]

Kara Gotsch, public policy coordinator for the national prison project of the American Civil Liberties Union, forced the issue:

We have clients who have gone through extreme emotional trauma and physical pain because of the abuses they've endured here in the United States. When the president and officials in Congress say they are shocked and embarrassed by what's going on in Iraq at the hands of our U.S. military, I have to point the finger and say, "Why aren't you expressing the same outrage and shame at the same conditions going on in your home states?"[26]

And Julian Bond, chairman of the NAACP, reminds us that blacks and Latinos are often the targets of prison mistreatment in the United States:

Sadly, there is no real surprise in the horrific photos from Iraq. Americans of color are all too familiar with incidents of prisoner abuse stretching from the distant past to the present day. It begins when the person held prisoner is considered less "human" than the prison guard; it happened in Iraq and it happens all too often here.[27]

These arguments were bolstered by reports that several soldiers participating in the Iraqi abuse had worked in U.S. prisons in Virginia and Pennsylvania, and in a few cases had been investigated for prisoner abuse. Journalist Scott Christianson points out that the assistant director of operations for U.S. prisons in Iraq, John Armstrong, was accused of two prison deaths in lawsuits filed in the United States, and Lane McCotter, one of the architects of the reconstructed Abu Ghraib prison, had headed a private prison company in New Mexico that had been cited for abuses by the U.S. Department of Justice.[28]

The War on Drugs granted state authorities extreme liberty in subduing and managing an angry, marginalized population of mostly racial minority youths—whether on the streets or in prison. Under these conditions abuses occur, and the failure to adequately respond turns transgressions into systemic practices. Some of the abuses occurring in Massachusetts prisons have also made it into the media. The more notorious cases include a mid-1990s incident in which a prison guard threw a bucket of acidic detergent on an older black psychotic inmate and a December 2000 incident in which a shake-down at one of the state facilities resulted in prisoner burns and dog bites. Further, a 1994 *Boston Globe* article reported that the Massachusetts Department of Corrections was using rape as a form of social control. In this case a psychotic rapist, referred to as a "booty bandit," was used to discipline newer irreverent inmates by assigning them to the rapist's cell.[29]

The most widely publicized incident in Massachusetts involved a white priest regularly abused by prison guards from April through September 2002. Sixty-eight-year-old Father John Geoghan, accused of sexually abusing more than 150 children, was serving a nine- to ten-year sentence in Concord for molesting one of his victims, a ten-year-old boy. He was struck in the face by a guard just outside the prisoners' visiting room where inmates are strip-searched.[30] In addition, Geoghan claimed guards posted newspaper articles about him around the prison, interfered with his mail, called him "Lucifer" and "Satan," and defecated on his bed. Geoghan's complaints were ignored and, against the recommendation of the classification board, he was moved to a maximum security prison in Shirley and placed in a protective custody unit reserved for Massachusetts's most violent inmates.[31] Abuse from guards ceased at the new facility, but Geoghan became the target of fellow inmate Joseph Druce, who was serving a life sentence for murdering a gay man. On August 23, 2003, Druce followed Geoghan into his cell, jammed the door with a paperback book, a nail clipper, and a toothbrush, and strangled Geoghan to death with stretched-out socks, a shoestring, and a pillowcase.[32]

A five-month investigation ordered by then Governor Mitt Romney exposed a prison system with "major administrative breakdowns."[33] The Concord prison where Geoghan and Fausto had been initially held was considered the most poorly managed and described as "insular and beyond control of the correction commissioner's office."[34] The report confirmed what attorneys from the Massachusetts Correctional Legal Services, such as Leslie Walker, had been saying for years: "The classification system is corrupt and the inmate disciplinary system is corrupt and . . . there are layers and layers of problems in this very expensive system that is out of control."[35] Of course, in a more remote area of the prison system, far from the attention of the governor and the media, Fausto and others like him had made the same claim. Their credibility was bolstered by the report, but few people knew their stories, or knew the violence they had experienced or the scars it had left. It took the death of a sixty-eight-year-old white priest to provide a window into a world Fausto knew all too well.

Fausto saw the worst of prison guard behavior because of his gang involvement, the gang sweep, and the riotlike conditions that ensued. Fausto states that many corrections officers he encountered were decent people just doing their jobs, but he is not lacking stories about those who were corrupt, sadistic, and racist.

> They'll fuck with your food. They'll come and pee on your bed. These are the things I've seen done. . . . Um, like I had this one come up to my face and spit in my face just so I would hit him. You know what I mean? Really push your buttons so you could act up. Or they'll have all the convicts fuck with you. Pay a convict off and have him come fuck with you. They're crooked motherfuckers inside. Once they get you in the hole, then they really fuck with you. The guy will get a couple of buddies, come and team up and beat your ass, right? Um, they get you to a point where you snap, right? . . . They have breaken many people's arms and then they call it self-defense, it's always their word against yours, and you're gonna lose in the eyes of the public, right?—you're the convict.

In one case, according to Fausto, a prison sergeant was brought up on charges:

> There was a case in Gardner . . . where there was a sergeant that was having sex with his buddy and Bruce found out about it and they took Bruce to the hole. But this sergeant got caught 'cause he had Bruce tied up to the bed and he was gonna rape Bruce and they were kinda watchin' him and they caught him tryin' to rape Bruce.

In our discussions of his prison experiences over the years, Fausto frequently referred to the racist attitudes and behaviors of prison staff. Phillip Kassel reported the same from his interviews with Latino prisoners incarcerated in segregated units at Walpole.[36] Fausto recalled:

> Oh, I had them call me all kinds of names. This motherfucker called me a spic one time. "Get in your fuckin' cell, you fuckin' spic." One time, one grabbed a rosary bead that I had on my neck and ripped 'em out of my neck, sayin' . . . "What, you know God? You Puerto Rican motherfuckers don't know God."

Because most of the prisons were located in white rural communities and the majority of prisoners were black and Latino, Fausto argued that racism pervaded the entire system:

> The majority of the staff in the prisons is predominantly white . . . mostly from these hick towns, right? Look where they built the prisons, in Norfolk, Gardner, Shirley. Go see who lives in Shirley, these hick motherfuckers, redneck motherfuckers, right, who hate everything. There's hardly no blacks livin' in these fuckin' towns.

Fausto explained that inmates could file grievances against the guards, but rarely did because "if they leave him in the same unit, he's gonna come back at you with his buddies and he's gonna make your life impossible. He's gonna be shakin' down your cell every chance he fuckin' gets. So he's gonna get you to the point where you can't take it anymore and you're gonna snap." Moreover, Fausto insisted that the guards stick together in what emerges as a strict us-versus-them scenario.

> And then he'll tell the second shift, "Hey, we got a troublemaker on Number 42, make his life miserable." Right? And second shift'll tell third shift . . . "Make his life impossible, he's a piece of shit. Gave me hell all day." "Really? I'll take care of him." So you got three shifts makin' your fuckin' life miserable. You know,

you're gonna snap. You know, fuckin' with your mail, fuckin' with your visits.

Fausto made frequent references to inmates "snapping" or "going off," and he attributed these incidents to oppressive conditions, and argued insightfully that prison policies made prisons unsafe for guards and inmates alike.

> You know who kills COs? The administration does. The administration is the number one killer of COs in there, 'cause they're the ones that come up with the laws. They're the ones that come up takin' and takin' and takin' and takin' from the inmates. But you can only take away so much from a man and you can only humiliate a man so much and he's gonna snap. The lieutenants and all that shit comes from higher up there. "I want you to do this to them now." COs are left to enforce that. Inmates are gonna rebel against that. So who's jeopardizing whose life here? Is it us? Is it the administration? Don't blame us for fuckin' fighting for our rights or fighting to a point where we say it's inhumane what you're doin' to us. Blame your own fuckin' administration for what we're gonna do to you when we get our hands on you.

Fausto articulated what the investigative report ordered by Romney had found—a system that was corrupt, insular, and out of control. And because of Fausto's self-described identity as a "rebel" or "revolutionary" in his role as gang leader, he experienced the worst of state violence.

Fausto's narratives about his prison experiences often seem like self-searching endeavors to understand how he was socially and emotionally transformed during these seven years. And while most of his focus is on prison guards, the Department of Corrections administration, and even state governors, his narratives are replete with stories of violence. Inmate-on-inmate violence was common behind the wall and Fausto witnessed several gruesome incidents— images that I suspect are much like the memories that war veterans carry with them. I offer brief descriptions of three to illustrate.

One time, this faggot, right, I guess he gave AIDS to another guy. The guy knocked him out, stuck his whole fist in his ass, right, in his ass, grabbed whatever insides he had in him and pulled them out like that. So he was walkin' around with all kinda fuckin' intestines shit hangin' out. They put a bag on him. When they brought him out they had all his insides in a bag. He did that shit to that guy 'cause he gave him AIDS, right?

And:

Then I saw, um, the old man that was always prostituting the fag-gots, right? He's like a big pimp. Somebody took a lock and kinda like buried the lock inside his brain, you know? Hit him so hard with the lock that the lock was still inside his head. You know what I mean? That was some bad shit.

And:

So I was in the line to go get my dinner and there was this black guy that had gotten some drugs from this Spanish dude and I guess he didn't pay. You owe somebody, you're gonna pay that person or that person's gonna come at you. . . . So I'm in line with, with Rolando . . . he said, "Fausto, put your back up against the wall." So I put my back up against the wall, so the guy passed right by me and grabbed the black dude and went like that to his stomach—boom! And opened him up so when he pulled that shank out, the shit just fell off. Oh! Man, it was ugly. Damn! That was fuckin' ugly.

Initial consequences of prison violence and repressive measures were extreme—some inmates had psychotic episodes, some commit-ted suicide, some directed their rage toward one another, while oth-ers spent long periods of time planning revenge. In the following story, Fausto describes losing a friend:

The guy gave me all his canteen one night, gave me some Cokes, some candy bars and stuff like that and I was like, I asked my

Colombian buddy, I said, "Yo, what's up with this dude givin' me all this shit? He still got five years left." "I don't know, just take the shit. He gave it to you." So he was across the hall from me. So by eleven o'clock he hanged it up, when they cut him down he landed right in front of me, man. I seen 'em trying to give him first aid, tryin' to revive him. He was purple. His tongue was purple. I heard him kicking because when he broke his neck, when he realized he was done, he tried to get himself out, but he had broken his neck already, you know, so he was gone. That guy died.

Violence experienced by Fausto was instigated by the Department of Corrections, by gang activities, and by inmates within an institution that has become an incubator of violence. War analogies are not as far-fetched as the tendencies among mental health professionals to label former prisoners as victims of post-traumatic stress disorder would suggest. Memories floating around in Fausto's twilight of consciousness reveal the disturbances that violence has engendered.

As Fausto's efforts, after his release, to integrate himself back into civilian life have failed, he has searched for answers. He frequently bumps into or hears about friends he met in prison who have suffered the same consequences. "They are either addicts, back on the streets doing stupid shit, got AIDS, or dead," he says. While the answer to his question is complex and can't be reduced to a single factor, Fausto has certainly discovered part of the answer:

When you come out here, it's hard to turn things off because they come at you in your dreams. . . . The effects of prison, you don't see 'em right away, you see 'em afterward when you're back out into society. Why hasn't prison left you? You know what I mean? . . . So a lot of those things really break you, right, they disturb you—they disturb a part of your brain that's not meant to be disturbed.

TEN

When a Heart Turns Rock Solid

TIM: I was thinking, you know, when we were talking to Tito [a friend from Angela's neighborhood] the other day . . . and when he was saying things like you gotta teach these kids growing up how to block away their emotions, [like when he was saying that he had to teach his] one-and-a-half-year-old daughter how to be tough, to fight back, [and teach his] twelve-year-old nephew how to have sex without feeling . . . because feeling hurts you and feeling gets you in trouble, right? So, I'm thinking, where does that come from?

FAUSTO: It comes from things that happen. Things that have to happen to make *a heart turn rock solid*. . . . It ain't just Tito, it's Bolo [another friend from Angela's neighborhood], it's everybody out there . . . people in minority communities. They got us living like this, you know, a separate place, in a controlled environment, if you wanna call it that way. . . . It's poverty and like a twelve-year-old kid will come behind you and shoot you in the head just to claim gang colors, just to, to throw in a name for himself. It's a war. . . . And for that person to die, or for any kid to go out there and shoot anybody, there's a series of things that have to happen in his life that he saw, that he learned, you know, and made him hard, made him finally say, in order for me to survive out here, I have to be this way. . . . For me, it's like prison.

Criminologist Jeremy Travis asserts that in the retributive era of making prisoners pay heavy penalties for their crimes, policymakers seem to have forgotten the iron law of imprisonment—"they all come back."[1] In fact, 93 percent do.[2] Travis points out that, in 2002, approximately 630,000 prisoners returned to their communities, more than four times the number of reentries thirty years ago. Moreover, in these thirty years, the prison environment has shifted from rehabilitation to punishment and former prisoners are not only poorly prepared for reentry, but are still facing penal sanctions after they are released. These collateral sanctions constitute what criminologists refer to as "invisible punishment," or policies that prevent formerly incarcerated felons from accessing welfare and housing benefits, jobs, and in some cases even their families. Considering the abandonment of rehabilitation efforts, the effects of collateral sanctions, and the poor community conditions to which many former prisoners return, we should not be surprised by the extraordinarily high recidivism rates. In fact, one-third of released prisoners are reincarcerated within six months and nearly one-half (44 percent) within a year.[3]

There is some evidence that the criminal justice pendulum is beginning to swing back in the direction of rehabilitation and community reintegration as a response to the bankrupting costs of mass incarceration and widely publicized accounts of negligence in state prisons. Alternatives to incarceration are being instituted alongside the stirring of justice reinvestment movements, which argue that the money saved from developing alternatives to incarceration should be reinvested in poor urban communities that have paid the heaviest price for mass incarceration.[4] The pendulum swing is perhaps best represented by two Supreme Court justices. Justice Harry A. Blackmun, a Nixon-appointed conservative turned liberal on the court, wrote the majority opinion in *Roe v. Wade* legalizing abortion, was opposed to the death penalty, and had been influential in eliminating cruel and unusual punishment in the prisons. Nonetheless he sided with the status quo in his 1989 defense of federal sentencing guidelines by declaring prison rehabilitation efforts, predominant in the 1970s, as "outmoded" and "failed."[5] Fourteen years later, a Ronald Reagan appointment to the bench, Anthony M. Kennedy, speaking before the American Bar Association, asserted that our criminal justice "resources are misspent, our punishments too severe, our sentences too long." More strikingly, Justice Kennedy referred to our prisons as a "hidden world of punishment" that would startle the public when fully exposed.[6]

For those behind the wall, however, the so-called twenty-five-year experiment in getting tough on prisoners is not a theoretical issue, nor is its failure particularly striking. Fausto explains:

Man, what are you gonna do with a so-called animal? You keep calling people animals. Educate them. Teach 'em something. You know, not everybody is gonna be in prison for the rest of their lives. Majority I'd probably say . . . are people who are eventually gonna come out back into society. Back to what? What kind of skills did they learn while they were in? This could be the perfect setting to teach somebody something . . . half of 'em don't even know how to write. Teach 'em how to read, teach 'em that there's another way of life than crime. Teach 'em some humanity skills, some self-esteem, 'cause a lot of them are abused kids, you know, and drug abusers. If you could do that, then you're lookin' at a halfway population who's gonna come out with some sort of fuckin' decency and some sort of wanting to try somethin' else besides that life of crime that the legal system likes to portray so much when they want to portray you in front of society as career criminals. To make laws like the three-strikes-and-you're-out laws, right, these are made for habitual criminals, but what is a habitual criminal? You ask a habitual criminal, a guy that keeps on committing the same crime over and over again, why does he keep on committing the crime over? 'Cause he likes it or because he never learned anything else? You never even bothered teachin' him when the first time he went into the prison system. Half of 'em were in and out of prison. There has to be some intervention and the Department of Corrections doesn't want to intervene. They want to punish. They want to warehouse. They want to keep on providing jobs . . . for hicks in these unknown fuckin' little towns who accept it because they don't have no factories. They have nothing.

PRERELEASE: THE LAST STOP

The wall separating Fausto and civilian life was removed when he was placed in a prerelease prison facility. Prerelease is the first step in the cultural transition from prison back to the community. Fausto had spent more than five years in medium and maximum security prisons and had internalized the culture of survival behind the wall—how to develop self-enabling routines, how to sense trouble, where to draw lines of interpersonal tolerance, how to deal with COs, and how to respond to bad news from home. Moving to prerelease was disorienting. The same rules no longer applied. He talked to Julio and me about the difficulty of interpreting gestures, behaviors, and assertions. At times he would be ready to fight, and someone would have to tell him that he was misinterpreting the situation, that he was overreacting. Fausto was placed in a dormitory with prisoners who were working off-grounds during the day and he felt overwhelmed by their liberties—there were too many temptations for a young man who had learned to recoil from the pleasures of life. His first job was in the kitchen and he wasted no time in persuading his supervisor to help him move into a more restrictive dormitory where there were men more familiar with his path through the system. His supervisor complied and Fausto was moved.

Fausto slowly adjusted to his new environment. There were jobs, freedom to associate on the grounds, fellow inmates coming and going from the civilian world where they worked and shopped, and there were women in dormitories on the other side of the grounds. Fausto's five-year pent-up libido led him out of his guarded personal cocoon to test the limits of his newfound liberty.

So the security was not as tight as it is behind the wall. So I saw myself very free but yet confined, you know. I said, wow, no wall, no nothin'. Within a few months I had gotten some pussy already. I was jumpin' out the window and it was too easy for me. You don't put a guy in a place and show him candy and tell him he can't have it after years of bein' locked up and pussy's right next door to me . . . all I got is a window and nobody watchin' the fuckin' grounds at four o'clock in the morning. I could've gone to a club and come back, you know. . . . I worked in the kitchen, so I knew who was sick, who wasn't, 'cause I do all the diets for the fuckin' HIV people and everything, so I had all the names of the women that were sick. So I checked the girl out real good, you know—she was a Portuguese chick. . . . But I still didn't take any chance, I told the guy in prerelease bring me back some condoms. He brought me like sixty of 'em. [laughs]

According to Fausto, the liberties at the new facility also produced several sexual relationships among the prison staff themselves and between staff and prisoners.

It was a big change, right? The only thing that stops you from leaving is the rules. There were a lot more rules, 'cause there really wasn't any wall. You want to take off, you take off. These guys over there, the staff were fuckin' each other, fuckin' the inmates, the inmates were fuckin' them—sexually, right? A CO kinda told me before I left Norfolk, "You never heard? Yeah, you're goin' to a place where there's a lot of shit goin' on."

Eventually Fausto moved back into less restrictive housing and his first off-site job was in a local factory making phone adapters. Here he met Lynne, a meek, third-generation French Canadian left with the responsibilities of raising a teenage son after her husband, a heroin addict, had left her several years before. With her son on the verge of dropping out of school and her failed relationship to a heroin addict, she had become a disappointment to her father, the patriarch of the family. Starting a relationship with a prisoner was not about to change this. Fausto saw Lynne differently. Lynne had her own apartment in a white neighborhood and a job. From where Fausto sat, she symbolized stability. She relied on Fausto for advice on how to deal with a scrutinizing aunt, a disgusted father, and a rebellious son. In turn, Lynne helped to soothe the fears and anxieties that "being short"—or close to release—produced in Fausto.

As he neared the end of his seven-year journey through the Massachusetts state prison system, Julio and I noted Fausto's growing anxieties, his irritability, and his self-destructive tendencies. Sitting at a picnic table on the prison grounds, Fausto had often talked about his plans after release, which included getting a job, an apartment, a car, and remaining single ("women fuck you up, bro"). These are fantasies of hope that help prisoners survive their confinement. No longer behind the wall, Fausto experienced time differently, and as the clock wound down, time became oppressive. Fausto was involved in more fights and began snorting heroin. He talked about how he was "going to fuck this dude up" who had disrespected him in the cafeteria when he was serving food, and asserted, "I don't care if they send me back behind the wall."

On our rides home, Julio and I wondered if Fausto would make it to the end—he had become the greatest barrier to his release. As the reality of getting out was seeping in, he talked more about his old playground, and "his boys who were still out there doing their thing." He worried about Juan and Angela, who had recently separated, and how he was going to deal with his mother talking about his father and vice versa. He even mentioned the loss of his daughter on one visit and how he feared this would affect him when he was out. Fausto was scared and was fighting self-doubt.

A few months before his release, Fausto started working for a plastics company. He stood on a platform, emptying sixty-pound bags of chemicals into machines. He was paid $10 an hour for a job that few civilians wanted. Temperatures on the platform reached 130 degrees, unbearable in the safety clothing that he was required to wear. Despite the toxic warnings on the sides of the bags, Fausto removed his clothing by midday and wrapped himself in an apron, hoping for the best. The job allowed Fausto to save a few thousand dollars, after paying the state for his involuntary room and board. On the day he was released, after nearly seven years of confinement, he unceremoniously walked through the front gates, tossed a duffel bag and a money order in the backseat of Lynne's car, and headed to her apartment in a small town in central Massachusetts.

COMING HOME

The personal adjustment that Fausto had to make when he moved from behind the wall to prerelease provided an inkling of the transition he would need to make to reintegrate into civilian life. His initial experiences on the outside were even more culturally disorienting and he left prison without the guidance or support of a parole officer.[7] The day after Fausto was released from prison, he came to Hartford to visit his mother. I arrived later in the afternoon and Fausto did not look like a man enjoying his newfound freedom. Sammy, Angela, and

a few of her friends had taken Fausto to a neighborhood bar to celebrate his release, but Fausto did not last long. "I almost took a swing
at someone, bro. I had to get out of there, I was ready to go off. This
motherfucker was standing this close to me, man, talking shit about
my mom right in my face. I was like, what the fuck, you know, I was
gonna knock this motherfucker out. I'm like, Sammy, get me the fuck
out of here."

People in the bar unknowingly violated the cultural norms that
Fausto had internalized in prison—they stood too close to him and
appeared careless and undisciplined in their conversation and in their
laughter. Fausto felt culturally dislocated—he couldn't read the signs
or the codes of ordinary conversation, he couldn't participate in the
celebration. Instead, he felt disrespected, taunted, and personally
challenged. Sammy took me aside later: "He just ain't used to it, you
know what I'm saying? He thought people were like looking at him
funny, you know, fucking with him and shit. They weren't doing
nothing. But, man, he was sweating like crazy. I had to get him out of
there before he got stupid."

Fausto was also not prepared to see his mother's living conditions.
His brow knitted and his eyes darted around anxiously as he confided, "Things are bad, bro. Look at how my family is living. You
didn't tell me this, bro. It's worst than when I left. Poverty, yo, it's
poverty, it fucks people up." Further, because his parents had split up
while he was in prison, he was not prepared to see his mother's new
life. To Fausto, Angela's place was at home, cooking, cleaning, and
tending to the needs of the family, not dancing, carousing, and
spending time with the stream of new friends pouring into her living
room to say hello to her newly released son.

Fausto was relieved to return to central Massachusetts, where he
attempted to start a new life with Lynne. He was hired as a machine
operator at the same factory where Lynne was employed and paid
minimum wage. The job was a daily reminder of his post-prison status and, again, Fausto felt disrespected.

And what am I doing now, working some shit job for minimum
wage? I am nobody where I work, I'm lower than the fucking
janitor. And the people there are prejudice, bro. I mean, they

don't say anything to me, they know better than to do that [laughter]. But I see the way they look at me and shit. You know, they talk about me, never to my face, but I know they prejudice. They say shit about black people around me, so I know they talking about me behind my back, you know.

Soon after this conversation, Fausto relapsed—he ran into a former prison buddy and started using heroin again. At first, they used the drug sparingly, but then hatched a plan to go to New York to cop an ounce so they could sell enough to make their money back and have their own stash. As this occurred, Fausto's drug use escalated. He was still working and paying half of the bills, but his drug use had become habit-forming and he feared where this was leading. He called his brother Sammy, who helped him get into a detox unit and drug rehabilitation program. But Fausto stayed only long enough to detox. He claimed the confinement in the hospital made him anxious ("it felt like prison, yo") so he checked himself out, much to Sammy's dismay.

I met Fausto at his mother's house in Hartford the same afternoon he left the clinic. We took a long walk and he talked about his drug use. Fausto was filled with shame and guilt:

I feel like the family fuck-up, Tim, that I'm worthless. It's these voices I hear in my head—you wasted your life, you haven't accomplished anything. I mean, both of my brothers are doing good. Julio's driving and Sammy's doing culinary school to be a cook. And what am I doing? I feel like I wasted my time in prison, you know. I'm the family fuck-up. I feel guilty, bro. I mean, I was in prison when my little girl died. What kind of father is that?

Neither was Fausto's relationship with Lynne satisfying—it appeared to be driven by the transitional stage he was in and about the stability her home provided, rather than intimacy. Efforts to mentor Lynne's son, Jerry, were also not working. Jerry was doing poorly in school and spending time on the streets, and despite Fausto's interest in being a surrogate father, he and Jerry mostly argued as Fausto asserted his authority in the house, insisting, for instance, that Jerry treat his mother with more respect. Beyond this, there was little romance in the relationship, and as Fausto's heroin use escalated, there was even less.

Fausto was seeking a way to fit in outside prison, but continued to feel marginalized and alienated. While many of his memories of living behind the wall were excruciating, he longed for structured routines, something that prison provided.

> I hated those motherfuckers and I will never forgive what they did to me. But at least when I was behind the wall I knew how to live, Tim. Out here, I don't feel like I know how to do it. I mean it, I feel like a loser, like I don't know how to live out here. Everything is so different than before I went in. . . . Everything is moving so fast, I can't figure it out.

Later in the day, after our walk, people gathered in the backyard of Angela's house for a cookout. Julio, Sammy, Fausto, and I huddled in the far corner of the yard to break the news to Julio about Fausto's relapse. Julio struck an unforgiving big brother pose: "You did what, you stupid motherfucker?" Tightening his fist, he added, "I ought to fuck you up right now. You stupid, you know that? That shit got you thrown in jail and you doing what? What! What the fuck's the matter with you?" Looking chagrined, Fausto weakly retorted, "Fuck you, Julio, you don't know nothing about me." "I know that you fucking up," Julio shot back. "What else I got to know? I know I ought to kick yo ass."

Julio did eventually calm down and agreed to take Fausto on the road with him cross-country for two weeks. This way, Fausto could get healthy and big brother could keep an eye on him. Moreover, it would give Fausto an opportunity to see if he was cut out for truck driving. When Fausto returned, he moved in with his mother and began searching for work in the Hartford area.

THE FORMER PRISONER'S DILEMMA

A consortium of Hartford community and human services groups and union locals developed a construction jobs initiative in the 1990s to help urban youths acquire the training for jobs in the building trades. I helped Fausto, who had just turned twenty-six, make contacts with program staff who arranged placement tests for him. Fausto didn't score well on the tests and was told he needed to enroll in a remedial education program to meet program standards, especially in math. Fausto began attending classes and I tutored him in the evenings. The program didn't pay a stipend, so Fausto and his mother survived on her Supplemental Security Income (SSI)—medical disability payments received as a result of recurring seizures—and food stamps, and on the monthly rent paid by a boarder who lived in one of the two bedrooms in the house. Fausto slept on the couch, which became a problem because his mother's schedule conflicted with his own—she was up late at night, often with friends in the house, while Fausto had to be at school at 8 a.m.

Fausto continued attending his classes and I continued tutoring him, but the need for income was apparent, although no more apparent than the scarlet letter that identified him to prospective employers as a former felon. Submitting applications was useless, so Fausto relied on other former prisoners to locate off-the-books jobs. One of Fausto's contacts suggested a bricklaying company, often in need of laborers with strong backs. Fausto fit the bill and began working for $10 an hour carrying buckets of cement and building scaffolding for skilled bricklayers who had plenty of work in the suburbs erecting new shopping centers in the late 1990s.

Because his intellectual capacities exceed his reading, writing, and arithmetic skills, digging himself out of his literacy hole has always been daunting for Fausto, and as his enthusiasm for learning a trade increased, he slowly lost interest in continuing his remedial schoolwork. While I continued to show up to tutor him in the evenings, conversation often shifted to the new skills he was learning and to his efforts to convince the masons he was worthy of an apprenticeship. He was asking the masons questions, watching carefully as they laid the bricks, learning about the union, and inquiring about career opportunities. He took pride in his work, taking me on several occasions to a work site to show me the scaffolding he had built and to display his growing knowledge about the craft. Moreover, the masons told him that they made around $1,000 a week, a further enticement. The bricklayers, however, showed little interest in Fausto beyond his keeping the mortar troughs full and climbing the scaffolds with heavy buckets of mixed cement for $10 an hour off-the-books pay.

Over time, his hope dwindled. The money Fausto made didn't last long. He cashed his check, often paid a portion of his mother's rent, bought something for the household (like a clothes dryer on one occasion), purchased groceries, bought a carton of cigarettes, and was then broke until his next paycheck. Further, his living conditions were stressful. He purchased a small mattress that he slept on in the dining room and argued with his mother constantly about her late-night routines and her failure to meet Fausto's expectations of cooking, doing laundry, and cleaning the house. Fausto was not sleeping well and, in fact, had not slept well since he left prison. Conflicting household routines made it even more difficult for him to get rest. He discontinued our tutoring sessions, determined to take them up again at some point in the future. After several months of working for the masons, he concluded that an apprenticeship was not likely. He heard, again through informal neighborhood networks, that a construction company was looking for laborers and pursued the tip.

Fausto was finding that there were many off-the-books jobs available at the end of the 1990s for persons like himself who had little education and were not likely to be hired in the formal labor force because of their former prison status. His new job was with a large family-owned building contractor, but the main office was a forty-minute drive from Hartford. Moreover, the position required transportation to varying locations throughout the state. As Fausto's father, Juan, had done so many times before, he purchased a fifteen-year-old Buick for $300 and, after several long days of crawling over and lying under the engine, Fausto was on his way to his new job.

Upon completing his first job in a wealthy Hartford suburb, Fausto went to the main office to pick up his check and ask about his next assignment. His timing was fortuitous—the company owner had just lost a driver and, in a state of desperation, asked Fausto if he had ever driven a flatbed truck. Fausto assured him that he had and told him about his two-week trip across the Rockies in his brother's eighteen-wheeler. The owner tested Fausto's skill by asking him to drive the truck around the block. Fausto satisfied the owner and was immediately assigned to a more experienced driver to learn how to move heavy equipment to construction sites throughout the state. The company's risk was striking—Fausto didn't have a Connecticut driver's license, let alone a Commercial Driver's License.

When there was no need to transport equipment, Fausto either prepared mortar in large mixers at construction sites or else stayed at the main office and worked in the garage, where he was more likely to come in contact with the company's managers. His eagerness to impress contrasted sharply with the dispositions of others who worked in the garage, all of whom were older white men. Most of these men had worked at the company for several years, were relatively job-secure, and none of them, according to Fausto, showed a particular loyalty to the company or an enthusiasm for the job. The company was a nonunion shop and Fausto desperately wanted to be made a full-time, on-the-books employee, which he assumed would increase his salary beyond $10 an hour. He often asked the managers for extra work while he was waiting for an assignment and even suggested projects to them, like removing rust from the equipment and repainting it. Tensions developed with his white co-workers, especially with the man responsible for training him. Fausto felt his trainer was prejudiced; moreover, the man drank and smoked pot on the job and Fausto was afraid his behavior would reflect poorly on him.

Fausto had a lot riding on these under-the-table job opportunities. He was searching for a job that paid a living wage, in which he could learn a marketable skill and be valued by his boss and co-workers. But more important, I believe that Fausto was testing whether his seven-year incarceration had permanently marginalized him, or whether there was some hope that he might reclaim lost time and find a place for himself in the social mainstream, where Julio was established and Sammy was circling.

THE LAST STRAW

The pressures at work were compounded by problems at home and on the block. At home, Fausto felt responsible for taking care of his mother, who was going out to clubs every Thursday, Friday, and Saturday night with her friends, defying Fausto's image of a respectable woman, let alone a mother.

> As her son, I worry. So that's what's been killing me, and it's getting to a point where it's getting very disrespectful. She's disrespectful to me when she talks and I've gotten to a point where I said a few things that I don't like saying to her [like] you're coming to be just like your friends, you know. What are her friends? Bitches.

Managing relationships with some of the men on the block was also becoming stressful for Fausto. Street activity on Angela's block was lively and Fausto quickly learned who the players were. He developed friendships with a few guys and was closest to two young Puerto Rican men, Tito and Bolo. Tito was working as a dishwasher at a restaurant in a suburban mall several miles away from the block, and Bolo worked at a fast-food restaurant, a similar distance away. Bolo supplemented his income by selling cocaine in order to provide for four children. Tito had served several years in prison and was now living with his girlfriend and their daughter.

The three of them spent evenings playing chess and Fausto enjoyed late-night conversations with them about the world. Hanging out with Bolo and Tito was fine, but others were not as easy to get along with, especially while Fausto was attempting to "go legit" and avoid the street economy. Fausto was new to the block, where a hyper-masculine culture prevailed, and the status wedge driven between men employed in the low-wage economy and men employed in the drug trade at times created tense interactions. Fausto associated mostly with men who worked, and they talked about finding better jobs or learning a trade. But Fausto also had enough street experience to manage relationships and maintain respect among men more street-involved, while keeping his distance from illegal street activities. Managing these status tensions was nonetheless difficult.

One night during a chess game, one of Tito's friends challenged Fausto's street reputation and prowess. Fausto had just lost a game when Tito's friend arrived. He looked high and was fidgety. Fausto gave him his seat at the board. The friend then demanded aggressively that Fausto move out of his light. Fausto let it slide and moved. The friend then asked if Fausto was Tito's new bodyguard, insinuating that he had served as Tito's bodyguard in the past and drawing attention to both Tito's skinny frame and his own muscular build. Fausto said they were just "boys" and again let the comment pass. The friend then launched into a long account of his street life—he talked about being locked up for thirteen years and about a number of things he had done to cultivate a street reputation. He abruptly turned to Fausto and asked him if he had heart. Annoyed, Fausto told him, "Yeah, I got heart, don't you worry about it." The friend told him he would test his heart someday, that they would go out together and start a rumble somewhere to see if Fausto really had heart. At this point, Fausto lost his composure. "Jail is for suckers, bro. I did my time and one thing that I learned is that jail is for punks. I don't care about the things you did—that's the easy way, bro, that's easy shit. But you want to talk about heart, well we can settle that one right now, right here. Empty your pockets, motherfucker, and we will go behind the house and see who's got heart." Tito had gone across the street to get some marijuana before this heated exchange and returned in the midst of the argument. He quickly intervened, telling his friend that Fausto was his "boy" and that he needed to calm down. Fausto was more insistent: "Game's over. Take your board, Tito, and go home and get this motherfucker off my property."

Anxieties at work, home, and on the block challenged Fausto's determination to overcome his post-prison status. Further, prison memories were haunting him. He talked about recurring nightmares and about how the Department of Corrections had wanted "to find a way to breaking you, right? That terminology, I heard it referred to a lot of times," he recalled. "We need to break 'em in, right?" Now Fausto wondered if he had been "broken." "'Cause, you know," he described, "you keep on functioning. You keep on going through life like nothing's going on, but I can't quit smoking. I can't stop and it's my nerves. You know what I mean? More nervous person than I ever was before. More jumpy. Ah, when I came out, I was like this."

Feeling overwhelmed, Fausto had turned again to heroin, the ultimate painkiller. At first he denied using, claiming to me that he was walking to the bar and drinking beer when he was feeling forlorn, but he finally confided his secret, largely from guilt, but also from the fear that he would lose control of his drug use. He was using occasionally, mostly after he got paid, and his mounting anxieties along with the shame associated with his increasing drug use left Fausto surly and short-tempered.

One night his boss made his nightly call to Fausto to give him his assignment for the following day. The conversation began jovially but Fausto soon exploded in anger. Apparently, Fausto's trainer, toward whom he already harbored ill feelings, told his boss that Fausto had been driving too fast and had refused to slow down even after he pointed it out to him. Fausto screamed into the receiver, "That guy is the biggest fuck-up. Did that motherfucker also tell you that he lit up a joint in the truck today and that he had a stash of beer behind the seat? I don't want that asshole in my truck again, you understand me? I'm out there trying to do my work. The reason we didn't make all our trips today is because of that lazy motherfucker. Fuck him!" After he hung up, Angela scolded him for his temper, which triggered another argument. Fausto suggested we take a walk. Outside he asked me for money. I refused and explained that I didn't want to contribute to his drug use. Fausto was angry at me, but didn't deny his intentions. He told me he had a few things he needed to do, giving me the brush-off. As I drove away, I saw him walking up the street to find a more generous friend.

Fausto didn't return to work, and perhaps it was just as well. Illegally driving a flatbed truck with heavy equipment across the state was one thing, but driving while his heroin use was escalating was quite another. During the next few weeks Fausto fully gave in to his cravings. When his mother went out to celebrate Christmas Eve, Fausto stayed home by himself and spent the night getting high. On New Year's he went to see Lynne and spent a few days visiting old haunts. To untangle his thoughts and emotions associated with drug use, I encouraged Fausto to carry a tape recorder and speak into it whenever he wanted to reflect on his heroin use. One cold winter night, a few days after the new year of 2001, Fausto recorded the following while high on heroin:

I want to get my thoughts [down] on drug addiction. This is something that has played a big role in my life and continues to play a role in my life. Actually, it has destroyed my life completely. It continues to destroy my life. I don't know when is it gonna end. I don't know why. I ask myself, why me? Why I continue to destroy myself? Why am I in so much pain? Why I feel so alone? Why is it that things are not the same from eight years ago when I left . . . when I was put in prison for ten to twelve years according to a man who knew very little about me. . . . I needed some help. He didn't see that. He didn't see who I was. He didn't know me. I don't want to blame him, but I feel very angry. . . . I am part of the society. I am human, although I had a drug problem and robbed and stealed to support the habit. . . . But I fell into that trap. They put me away, calling me a menace to society. . . .

I'm angry. I'm in pain because anger is no good for nobody. Anger destroys people. Anger destroys me. . . . But there are thousands just like me who are going through this now. . . . But I'm in pain because anger's not healthy. It destroys your soul and destroys everything you believe in. You no longer look at humanity, at people who you love, who you have shared so much with, with the same eyes anymore. You no longer trust. You feel uncomfortable. . . .

Drugs to me help escape temporarily that pain. The pain of losing my daughter. The pain of seeing my mother going from somebody who never went out, to a woman who be in a club dancing with friends who I realized as being no good. . . . My father, who has a gambling problem and drug addiction, I come from a very dysfunctional yet loving family. Very confusing, my family, they're very confusing. But deep inside I love both of them. I would give my life for them, for all of them. I'm the middle of three brothers. I'm the middle one. Why am I going through this? Why do I feel so alone? Why do I be so hard on myself? I keep telling myself things are gonna look up. . . . I'm gonna find a way to fight this addiction. I will find a way. . . .

[Prison] controlled me, my moves, the way I talked, the way I walked, where I had to go, where I had to sleep. I wasn't allowed anything. They took the normal things from me. Things that a child, a teenager needs to grow up strong with a sense of respect and self-

respect, self-worth, like you're worth something. I was led to believe that I wasn't worth nothing, a number at an early age. You think about that. Led to believe that you no longer count. That your thoughts don't count, that what you say don't count. All you are is just a number, a letter and some numbers. That's all you are. You have no rights. No rights whatsoever. You're a nobody. You're a nothing. . . .

So much I missed out on which I now regret. I regret not being there. I blame myself. . . . Sometimes I think if I would've stayed in Puerto Rico and grown up in Puerto Rico maybe I would've became something. . . . My thoughts of Puerto Rico and growing up there is like the Bible says—paradise. Those were my thoughts of Puerto Rico at one time. . . . But like Adam and Eve, your parents or something, somebody had to commit a sin for me to be taken away from paradise and to be thrown out into this world, you know, United States. . . .

Never been comfortable with who I am today, who my family is, what part in society we play and all my fellow Puerto Ricans, all my fellow Latinos, what part we play in society. I want equality. I want equality but I might not see it in my lifetime. Yet, I'm going through all this hell. I'm in hell within me. . . . There are thousands just like me who probably are going through this, who I've seen going through this. I am in pain. I'm in solitude. I'm by myself sometimes within me. The hope is almost gone. I once told Tim that hope moves mountains and I wonder. I always wonder how are we gonna move these mountains, these obstacles. . . . People like me were to be kept down and not allowed to succeed in life. . . .

Why my addiction to drugs? Then you ask me why you have an addiction to drugs? My brother doesn't have an addiction to drugs. My oldest brother never did. Just me and my younger brother who fell into this life. I had talked to my little brother. I had seen his addiction. . . . Yet, he's so kind. We have good qualities. Good respect . . . taught to us by our parents. This is who we are. . . . I can't be selfish. I can't just talk about me because there are so many just like me who are going through the same thing that I am going through today. The hope is there. I'm not gonna let it go away. I'm gonna keep hope until the day I die, because my faith, the stories and the Book tells of men going through hell and yet, they never, they never lost their faith. . . . That's what keeps me going because while I was in prison I had a chance to read the Bible for the first time in my life. I got to read it and I learned from some of the stories in there. Like I said, poor people have to have faith. Poor people have to believe in God. That's what keeps us sane. That's what keeps us with a state of mind that there is hope in life. That's one of the very few things that we have to attach ourselves to. Poor people have to believe that there's a better life than this. . . .

So many things that I see that are wrong with this society, that are wrong with me, the things that I have done. . . . When is it ever gonna stop? When is the cycle ever gonna be broken? Who's gonna help us? My faith leads me to believe that there is a God and for poor people, people who sin. My faith leads me to believe that one day I will see the good things. I will get peace. My mind will be at ease. The pain will go away. The suffering will go away. My family will unite. The love will once again be there. One day. One day I will get to see it again. My faith leads me to believe that one day I will see all those things again. The hug of my mother, my father, my brothers, their friends. My faith is there.

My thoughts on addiction. Fausto Rivera.

Shortly thereafter, Fausto moved back in with Lynne. I knew this was not a good sign. Lynne's place provided Fausto with the security to pursue his drug life. Removed from street activities, her neighborhood provided Fausto with his getaway, a place where he could do heroin and mold himself into the couch in front of the television. In a classic psychological sense, Lynne was an enabler. As long as Fausto was with her, she would tolerate his drug behavior and Fausto knew he could manipulate her. Moreover, Fausto knew many of the street players in town—he had done prison time with several of them. Moving in with Lynne meant that Fausto was done trying to make it in the "legit world," at least for a while.

The previous summer, I had moved to central Massachusetts, which located me just down the road from Fausto. In fall 2001, I was granted a one-year sabbatical to begin writing this book. As it turned out, the book would be put on hold and I would see a lot of Fausto over the next two years. For the first few months after Fausto relocated, however, I didn't hear from him at all.

WHAT'S AN ADDICT WITHOUT A HUSTLE?

Fausto moved into Lynne's second-floor apartment in a two-family home built in the 1920s. Lynne's father, now retired, migrated to New England in the 1950s from Canada and worked as a machinist at a wage that allowed his wife and him to raise three children. Indicative of the restructured economy in the 1970s and 1980s, Lynne worked for a plastics factory in 2001, where she made $8.23 an hour. Her work had been cut back to four days a week as the company began expanding their production in China, and they eventually closed their shop in 2004. Lynne preferred her working conditions in the plastics factory, however, to the non-air-conditioned molding plant where she had previously worked for $7.33 an hour—a "real sweatshop," she pointed out.

After he moved back in with Lynne, Fausto's drug use escalated. To afford his drug lifestyle, he turned to an old prison buddy who was dealing drugs. His friend was strictly a businessman who didn't use drugs himself, but was well networked among street criminals. He hooked Fausto up with Raúl, a crack addict immersed in the drug life, and, according to Fausto, "a crazy motherfucker like me. This kid is wild, somebody I could really do shit with." Fausto and Raúl began by robbing drug dealers, mostly Dominicans, whom they loathed as ethnic rivals in both the legal and street economies.

In the first robbery, Raúl went into an unfurnished apartment, controlled by Dominicans, to case the drug spot. He found only two men in the apartment and didn't see any guns. He signaled Fausto, who came in on the pretense of making a buy, but then pulled out a fake gun and put them on the floor, leaving with money and drugs. When I asked about the risk of using a fake gun, Fausto explained, "It's not about the gun, it's about the attitude. You show them the attitude and they don't even look at the gun."

In a second robbery, they worked with a woman who was being beaten regularly by her boyfriend and was therefore eager to set him up. He was dealing drugs out of their apartment. Fausto and Raúl borrowed a .45 caliber handgun, held it to the guy's head, and walked away with $600 and drugs. In other street robberies, Fausto would allow himself to be "victimized" by his partner. He would set up a drug deal between a dealer and Raúl, and during the exchange Raúl would turn on both Fausto and the dealer, forcing them to the ground with a gun and in one instance using the gun to knock Fausto unconscious. Raúl would then make off with the money and split it with Fausto later.

Robbing drug spots, however, had its limitations. Fausto and Raúl usually made off with only a small amount of money and some drugs, and the number of spots in the city was limited. Besides, they were likely to be known by dealers sooner or later and retaliation was almost certain, even though Fausto maintained that "no one will fuck with me because they all think I'm carrying [a gun] and they're all scared of me, yo, think I'm crazy. It's the way I present myself."

Meanwhile, Fausto's drug life was taking its toll on his relationship with Lynne. She was continually doling out her meager savings to Fausto to prevent him from doing more crime. She soon exhausted her savings and was behind on the rent. Fausto felt guilty and kept promising to check himself into detox. Each morning for some time he woke up with these intentions, but the organization of his day around getting high would consume him as soon as he searched for his first fix to stave off physical discomfort, and yet another day would go by without following through on his promise. In the spring of 2001, Fausto arranged for me to drive him to a detox unit. Before leaving, Fausto and I drove around town as he pointed out the places he had robbed and was thinking about robbing, as well as the spots where he "copped" (purchased drugs). Fausto agreed to have the discussion tape-recorded, although at first he expressed shame that this part of his life would be exposed.

Just before we left the apartment, however, Fausto had received a call from Raúl, who had staked out a robbery for that night. Although he told Raúl he was going into detox, he was clearly ambivalent about the decision.

I can roll with him tonight. He told me to call him tonight. He's got something for $10,000 tonight, 'cause I told him I'm not doin' any more nickel-and-dime shit, I'm tired of that, you know.

Somebody fuckin' shoot me for nothing. So, tonight he says, "Call me tonight, I got somethin' for $10,000." And I said, "What—Dominicans?" He says, "Yep." I think it's the same ones he's workin' for, 'cause he's workin' at a spot right now. You know, he's taking care of the door. You know, he opens the door and he lets people in. So he called me up. He wants me to do it with 'em.

The excitement in Fausto's voice rose as we drove by his prison buddy Benzie's house (the guy that Fausto had gone to New York with to cop heroin shortly after he had come out of prison) and he recognized his girlfriend's car in the driveway. "She's fuckin' loaded, yo," he exclaimed, "she got money. She's got drugs inside that place. She's got a lot of shit! These people are large." At this point Fausto turned to me as if I were the only thing holding him back. "Ah, how come you don't do drugs, yo?" We circled around the block and passed by again. Fausto continued,

That's where I hang out, right there. I did time with him. . . . That's her car right there. She works for a Spanish guy. She does deliveries right there. All you gotta do is beep 'em and they come in. She's fuckin' loaded right now, loaded! But that's Benzie's connection. Benzie's a weasel. I don't trust Benzie. He's got a real gun right now so he and I just gotta be real. . . . He's a piece of shit now. He's shooting up dope. . . . Benzie's changed a lot. He was a different person. He used to be my workout partner in there too. I used to work out with him in prison. Now he's like all fucked up. He's always trying to scam off his old friends, you know. He's like, "Fausto, if you ever need to talk or deal, you know, all you gotta do is give me a little percentage, you know, for whatever, you know." Everything's about what they can get from people, you know.

The churning of Fausto's mind—the "criminal mind" as he referred to it—reflected the daily work of copping and using drugs. He was immersed in daily routines that began when he woke up "drug-sick," suffering withdrawal symptoms, and in need of a fix to eliminate his discomfort. Fausto's and my relationship had been largely organized around what he might become in the so-called legitimate world, and exposing this part of his life to me was difficult for him, but his drug addiction and his immersion in daily drug life fostered obsessive thinking and my presence did little to derail this process. Riding around town, I listened to Fausto indulge in "robbery dreams."

> I was thinking of doing a nice robbery, nice one that I know I'm gonna come off with like $40,000 if I come off. Check into a hospital and then come out and have that money waiting for me. . . . That's gonna bring the heat on me, though. And I don't want to deal with fuckin' cops after me. But even though the shit that I know already or the mistakes that I made in the past, I don't want to make 'em again, you know. If I'm gonna come off, I'm gonna come off lovely. No fingerprints, no nothing. . . . [pointing out the window] That place is loaded, man. They cash checks. They got close to $50,000 in that place and they cash checks from everybody.

I listened to similar narratives sitting in Lynne's living room or on my balcony during this period of time. Fausto fantasized about pulling off one big robbery and then going to Puerto Rico, getting clean, and living happily ever after on his loot, or getting on a bus and going anywhere—it didn't matter because he would have $20,000, $40,000, $50,000, or maybe $100,000 with him. First he would take care of Lynne and his brothers, his mother, and even his father, and then he would ride off into the sunset. The fantastical nature of this thinking was striking. Fausto would become animated, his eyes excited, his voice raised, his resolve determined. He was going to figure out his escape—his escape from the exhausting cycle of using and hustling, and his escape from the guilt he felt in betraying and disappointing those who cared about him.

The hurdles to check himself into detox were high—Raúl was tempting him with a $10,000 robbery; the check-cashing place and a Dominican bodega had their own appeal; and Benzie's girlfriend was carrying bundles of good-quality heroin. Fausto's ambivalence was apparent, but checking himself into detox had also become part of the routine. In the previous five months, Fausto had checked himself in three times. Detox held out its own set of hopes—the hope of overcoming daily sickness, the fantasy of getting a job and living a regular life, the prospect of having a satisfying sex life again, and the hope of figuring out why he continued to relapse.

As we got closer to the detox unit, Fausto became irritable and sullen. He began preparing himself for the transition by talking about the recovery process:

> You hear other people's stories, some of the shit they've done, you know. Sometimes I think I got it bad, man, the stories I heard in there, you know, they got people in there that are worse off than I am. People that spent all their life in prison and they're still doing drugs, you know. I'm just tryin' to figure out why . . . I keep doing drugs and how is it I keep falling into the same shit.

Fausto stayed for three days before he was back on the street again.

In observing Fausto's relapses over the years, there are a few salient dynamics that have repeatedly undermined his recovery. First, when he gets clean, there is a strong inducement to get high again because he can acquire a sensation from the drug that he lost when he was immersed in the daily struggle to stave off physical withdrawal symptoms. This temptation is powerful, and Fausto has described on numerous occasions the "mind games" he plays to convince himself that he will use this one time and then stop, or that he is disciplined enough to manage casual drug use. Second, it has been extremely difficult for him to develop a new identity, a set of routines, dispositions, and life skills, or to find opportunities that allow him to break away from more familiar and embedded life patterns of drug use. As we will see, there have been interludes in which this has occurred, but sustaining it in the context of physical addiction and limited alternatives for providing supportive, self-validating routines has proved futile.

Third, Fausto's relapses often occur as a way of dealing with guilt. Getting clean forces him to recognize the pain that his addictive lifestyle has caused others, especially Lynne and his family—pain that is often difficult to acknowledge. The self-loathing that results, ironically, fuels an emphatic reimmersion in the routines of using and hustling. His addiction routines allow him to close down the larger world around him and instead engage a narrower slice of it as he shoots up in the morning and then spends the rest of the day strategizing about ways of making money to shoot up again. The rest of the world melts away, including his obligations to others and his related feelings of shame, guilt, and failure. But never entirely. Fausto is not able to totally shut out the larger world, which he still relies on to meet his own needs—including his addiction needs—and to which he also remains, at least, minimally attached emotionally. Lynne needed to talk about paying the bills and about problems with her son, his mother wanted to know why he wasn't calling, I was searching for him at home and on the streets, and Sammy called regularly to talk about the virtues of methadone maintenance.

Unable to fully engage his drug career, to throw himself unreflectively into the world of using and hustling, Fausto described moments in which he would have "to look at himself in the mirror." In these moments, his self-loathing was at its greatest.

> You don't look at yourself in the mirror. It's like you don't want to accept reality, but every now and then you take a look at it. . . . It hurts to look. It hurts to look at what you've become, you know. It hurts to face it, but every now and then . . . you open your eyes, see what's goin' on, you know. . . . You want to live like everything is fine. Everything is under control. Nothing's going on. You tell yourself these things, you know. If I keep on doin' what I'm doin' and try not to get caught, maybe I'll find the perfect edge. Maybe I'll find the perfect, perfect case. Maybe I'll hit somebody up and come up with $20, $25,000, I'll be fine, you know. I'll have some money. I'll get Lynne a new car and I'll put up money in the bank that I've fuckin' blown already.

Three days after I had dropped Fausto off at detox, he resumed his street activities, and this time with even more reckless abandon. His guilt strengthened his determination to make a big score—to pay back Lynne and to show his family that he could take care of them.

Fausto still desired to "be somebody," but his social and economic dislocation exacerbated by his drug life had constricted his range of opportunities to the streets.

Shortly thereafter, working alone, Fausto did pull off a big robbery that netted him about $12,000. The money didn't last long, but it did enable him to live out his fantasy with Lynne and his family. Fausto distributed the money in a Robin Hood manner. He paid off both Lynne's and his mother's back rent, and gave his mother $1,000 to entertain his cousins who were visiting from Puerto Rico. He paid several hundred dollars to clear up his father's past driving violations and get his driver's license. He gave Sammy $2,500 to buy a car and even gave Julio $1,800. Julio had just returned a truck he was leasing-to-buy from his boss, and needed $1,000 to pay for expenses and taxes he owed on the truck to get him out of the deal and another $800 to pay bills he owed due to the truck ordeal (he had gone a month without making any money). At first Julio refused the money because Fausto would not tell him how he got it. But three or four days later, Julio relented. Fausto felt triumphant that his successful big brother had needed him and that he had provided—for one brief moment, he had inverted sibling status.

I saw Fausto soon after he returned from Hartford and he was feeling good. "You know me. I take care of family. I had this money and my family needed this money and I was there for them. I took care of them, you know. Nobody in my family is gonna go needing things. This is what it's all about. And they say money can't buy love and happiness, hah!" But money didn't buy love and happiness. Fausto's family took the money that they needed, but the next day, both his mother and father questioned his source. His father accused him of giving them drug money and lectured Fausto about how he was living. His mother wanted to know if he "was in some kind of trouble up there in Boston." Fausto was stung by their scrutiny and felt betrayed. He wanted them to appreciate him, to acknowledge that he took care of his family. Several times during the next few weeks, Fausto stated he wanted "to be somebody," and while he continued to talk about this in terms of going to school and being a leader in his community, his milieu had been reduced to the streets, and it was there that he was cultivating a reputation, something that his family was simply not going to embrace, whether he gave them money or not.

When Fausto's money ran out, he committed a few more small robberies, but then changed his hustle. This happened for two reasons. First, another former prison buddy that Fausto had hooked up with in town had been arrested and was awaiting trial, and he expected to go back to prison. He shoplifted merchandise from retail stores daily to support his drug habit, a practice referred to as "boosting." Fausto's friend taught him the "trade"—how to remove the electronic strip from the merchandise, avoid store detection, leave the store innocently, and get rid of the merchandise. When his friend went to prison, Fausto considered that he had "left me the business."

Second, boosting was a victimless crime; it didn't involve holding a gun to someone's head, only "stealing shit from rich motherfuckers," Fausto rationalized. Fausto was determined not to return to prison and he was concerned that, regardless of how well he planned his robberies, one mistake would send him back where he feared he would become an old man. Further, Fausto may have developed the nerve—or heart—to rob, but the numbing effects of heroin and the hyper-masculine sense of power did not entirely obliterate his conscience. He could easily rationalize robbing drug dealers, especially rival Dominicans—"they're pieces of shit," he would insist—but Fausto's robberies had moved away from the streets to legitimate retail business, and putting store clerks on the floor while he cleared out a register was difficult, and something that Fausto would agonize over for days, irrespective of how much heroin he shot up his arm. Boosting was not only safer, it eliminated the moral agony. I realized at this point that Fausto robbed because this is what he knew, it was really his only hustle, and as Fausto would say many times during this period, "What's an addict without a hustle?"

TIM: So what does it take to do this shit?
FAUSTO: Guts.
TIM: Where does that come from?
FAUSTO: Guts?
TIM: Yeah, where do you get that?

FAUSTO: Guts come from fuckin' desperation, yo. Being
   desperate, from being dope-sick, to needing stuff. Look at
   me! I got fuckin' bills up the fuckin' ying-yang at home that
   haven't been paid. I think the cable needs to be paid. The rent
   gotta be paid, okay. . . . The car's acting up, you know, and
   the only one that's working in my house is Lynne.

At the time, Fausto didn't have the skills to be a drug dealer—he
wasn't good with money, nor did he have the self-discipline to hold
on to the drugs long enough to sell them. He was often hired by drug
dealers as an enforcer. For instance, around this time, he was
recruited by a former prison contact who controlled drug dealing in a
public housing project in a nearby city and wanted Fausto to work for
him, to collect money owed, and to help him keep competitors out of
the housing project. Fausto spent some time there, but considered the
situation too dangerous and declined the offer. Besides, he preferred
working alone, or with a partner who did what Fausto told him to do.
Boosting expanded his repertoire of skills and allowed him to
develop a different, less dangerous hustle, and one that he could do
alone.

While Fausto was boosting, his habit grew to around $200 to $300
a day. He was boosting daily at large retail stores located within a
three-state geographical radius. He walked out of stores with com-
puters, televisions, DVD players, Game Boys, car parts, and whatever else was in demand among his network of fences. There were
several close calls, especially in the beginning, when he set off the
alarms because he had failed to remove the electronic strip properly.
On one occasion he started toward an entrance door with a television
set, but stopped and turned around when he noticed a security guard
close to the door. His abrupt movements drew attention to himself,
so he got in line at the security desk and stewed about what to do.
When the clerk waited on him, he told her he wanted to return the
television but had left the receipt at home. She, in turn, told him
the store would not accept it without the receipt. Fausto assured her
he would go home and get the receipt and return shortly, and then
proceeded to push the cart out to his car without further notice.
Fausto was not, however, always so lucky. He had a few close calls

that required him to drop the merchandise and run for his car. On one occasion, a store clerk followed him out into the parking lot and wrote down his license plate as he drove off with several DVD players. Upon his return home, two state troopers were waiting and Fausto was busted.

Without a car, Lynne called and asked if I would take her to the courthouse to pick up Fausto. He had spent the night in jail and was waiting to be arraigned. Lynne was depressed and feeling lonely in the relationship. Fausto had totally withdrawn his affections, spending his nights in the living room shooting heroin. She needed $275 bail money and $90 to retrieve her car, and had sacrificed a day's pay by making up a story so she could get out of work. Fausto sent us to one of his stolen goods customers at an auto body shop in a neighboring town. The owner of the shop gave Lynne the money and told her that he "would take care of" Fausto when he was released. He too was a recovering addict and knew Fausto would be drug-sick. He seemed sympathetic and said he wanted to supply Fausto with drugs so he didn't act out of desperation. When we arrived at the courthouse, Fausto was waiting for us outside. He had been arraigned and released on his own recognizance.

Sitting in the front seat of the car, Fausto looked pale, sneezing and yawning as we drove to the lot where his car had been impounded. He seemed relieved that Lynne was now carrying an extra $275. He was angry at himself for being greedy. He had taken two DVD players from the store and had placed them in his trunk. Sitting in the parking lot, he reflected on how easy the theft had been and decided to go back in for three more. "They always said in prison, you make your mistakes when you get greedy. That's it, bro, I got fucking greedy." When he returned to the store, he was recognized and followed.

Upon release, Fausto immediately returned to boosting. Moreover, for the first time he acknowledged to me that he was using heroin with a hypodermic syringe—he was "busting his veins." Fausto had morally distinguished himself from other heroin addicts by maintaining that he would never bust his veins. While I suspected that he had been shooting up for some time, admitting this to me appeared to strip away the last shred of decency that Fausto could hold on to. It was becoming increasingly difficult for him to view others on the street as lowly "pieces of shit," without having to confront his own moral status. Those he disdained most, like Benzie, were becoming indistinguishable from himself. He was also smoking crack during the day to keep himself more alert while he was boosting, and then shooting up heroin through the night. Moreover, he was irritable, impatient, and prone to violence when things didn't work out. His "I don't give a fuck" attitude had reached a lethal level. Boosting and drug use had sealed him off from everyone—he was in a self-destructive zone that seemed to have two possible outcomes: prison or death. He was engaged in street fights regularly and was taking more risks. On one occasion, the tables were turned when an addict pulled a gun to rob him of his stolen merchandise:

I walked toward the dude and I told him, "Fine, but I'm gonna tell you right now I want you to take that gun and I want you to shoot me right between the eyes. I don't want you to shoot me in the leg. I don't want you to shoot me in the arm. I want you to shoot me right here [pointing between his eyes]. Because I want you to shoot me and I want you to kill me and to put me out of my misery. If you don't do that, if you shoot me in the arms or you shoot me in the legs, I'm gonna go to the hospital, and when I get out of the hospital, I'm gonna come looking for you and I'm gonna do to you what I'm telling you to do to me right now." And, yo, I start walking toward the guy, and I knew the guy wasn't gonna kill me. I knew he didn't have the heart to do it, I knew by looking at him, yo. I learned that in prison, how to look at someone and see what they are about. And yo, all three of those motherfuckers ran off.

I hadn't seen Fausto for three weeks when I picked him up to take him to court for his shoplifting case. His physical condition had deteriorated—he had lost fifteen to twenty pounds, his face was a pale, ashen yellow color, and his eyes were sunken, with dark circles around the sockets. He cried on the way to the courthouse and confessed that he was both "depressed" and was "fucking up." He claimed that he was using heroin to combat the depression, but then experienced even deeper depression when he wasn't high. He reiterated his feeling of shame about busting his veins, confessed that his life was "all about getting high," and mourned the loss of his sex life. Fausto talked about boosting, how he had worked with a female addict for a while before she was arrested for violating probation, and the number of close calls they had experienced. He admitted that he was suicidal and even asked if I thought his death would make my book a best seller.

As we drove to the courthouse, he attempted to revive himself through robbery dreams, describing in great detail his intention to rob a bank and to make up for the pain he had caused everyone in his life by paying them off, but then claimed he had postponed his plan because of 9/11 and the increased police surveillance he expected at the bank. He also fantasized about returning to Puerto Rico to "find the answers of what went wrong" in his life. Fausto continued, "I don't know, bro, I'm searching for the answers and something tells me that I might find the answers to my life in Puerto Rico."

We consulted with his public defender at the courthouse, who worked out a plea bargain with the district attorney's office. The DA offered a sixty-day sentence, without parole, if he accepted the plea on the spot. His attorney explained that if they delayed the case, filed any motions, and went to court, the DA was likely to ask for a stiffer sentence. Fausto didn't care; he had only one concern—to delay the case so he could take care of his immediate physical pain. The date was postponed and I took Fausto to the home of a former prison friend who lived in a nearby city. Fausto's friend had recently offered him a position in his drug operation and Fausto knew he would take care of his current physical malady.

I was introduced to the friend, who appeared high on cocaine but didn't seem uncomfortable in my presence. At this moment, I realized that my fieldwork might take yet another turn. According to Fausto, his friend was selling a high grade of heroin in a housing project, stamped with his product logo, "Money for Life," which had replaced his previous logo, "The King of Kings." The logo provided useful information to users about the grade of heroin they were getting and also marked the dealer's turf. The prospect of extending my study, however, was no longer appealing to me. It would take some time to build rapport with his friend and, frankly, I had seen enough of the streets. Moreover, I was tired of feeling helpless as I watched Fausto self-destruct before me. I cared about Fausto. I knew his potential, his gentle side, his intellect, the rebel that lived within him that would thrive in the right context. That night, I called Julio and Sammy and began to organize an intervention.

ELEVEN

Good and Bad

ON THE MORNING of the intervention, I called and reserved a bed at a detox facility in central Massachusetts. I had spent the week reading about interventions and talked to Julio and Sammy about the process on the way to meet Fausto.[1] Sammy primed himself: "We got to break him down, get right in his face. We can't let him cop an attitude with us. We gotta make him go in. We don't give him any options, we just keep saying, 'You're going in today!' "

When we arrived at the house, Fausto had just left. Lynne was agitated, pacing in the kitchen. "He had better not go boosting in my car. You guys just missed him by not more than ten minutes. He's got my car. He went boosting yesterday—he'd better not go today. My car doesn't have any brakes, the wheel's about to fall off." We asked questions, but Lynne was in no frame of mind to answer them.

We drove to Fausto's drug spot, identified his car, and pulled up behind him. Fausto jumped out of the car, visibly annoyed that we had "rolled up on him." He yelled at Sammy, "Man, you guys just don't do this to me." Regaining his composure, he greeted Julio with a handshake and partial embrace, but when he went to do the same with his younger brother, Sammy grabbed him in a bear hug and started sobbing. I too greeted him with a partial embrace, but he refused to make eye contact. In a moment of mutual discomfort, I suggested we go back to his apartment. Fausto agreed but as the three of us piled into the car, he ran over to two guys standing next to his car and copped a bag of heroin.

When we arrived at the house, Fausto jumped out of the car, ran up the stairs and into the bathroom, and shot up while we sat at the kitchen table. Fausto broke the tension in the kitchen by yelling for Lynne to bring him a clean shirt. When Julio later confronted him about his appearance, he remarked, "Man, I'm drug-sick, I don't care what I look like. I put anything on when I go out like that." Fausto came out of the bathroom looking better—hair combed, face washed, clean shirt—and headed for the door, barking over his shoulder, "Come on, let's get out of here." As we walked out to the car, his aging landlord watched from the third-floor landing. Agitated, Fausto yelled, "These are my brothers, you see, my brothers."

We piled into the car again and drove to a park, but Sammy had already started before I shut off the engine. "Man, you're going into treatment and you're going in today. You look bad, man." Sammy was crying and holding on to Fausto in the backseat. Fausto looked shell-shocked. Sammy continued talking as we searched for a place to sit. Finding a set of bleachers next to a baseball diamond, we sat down as Sammy cried and pleaded with Fausto.

We here for a reason today. Someone sent us here—God, a higher power, whatever, but we here for a reason. You got to stop this, man. You killing yourself. This drug is fucking you up. What you doing, Fausto, busting your veins? Let's see your marks, man—you got so many in one arm, you got to use the other? Look at yourself. When you gonna wake up in the morning and look at yourself in the mirror, really look at yourself and say, "Fuck, man, what am I doing to myself?" You got to face your problems. I know shit's not good but you got to face it. I know your daughter died and shit, but you still got family, man. But where you been, where you been? You don't come around, because all you can think about is sticking yourself, copping another bag.

It was my turn. "Fausto, look at me. I got something to say too. Look at me, man, don't look down, look me in the eyes, man. I want to say this to you. Look at me." He looked but couldn't hold the gaze.

I love you, man. I really do. I've known you for eleven years, we've been through a lot of shit together, and I really care about you. You got so much potential, but you're killing yourself, man. You look like shit. I mean it—you look like shit! You've lost fifteen pounds in the last month, your skin is yellow, man, fucking yellow.

Fausto was shaking his head affirmatively.

I'm here with your brothers, because we love you and we're here to tell you that this has got to stop. If it doesn't you're either going to end up dead or back in prison. There's no other way. I don't want to get a call, man, from Lynne that she found you dead in an alley somewhere with a fucking needle sticking out of your arm. I'm here to try to do something about this before it's too late.

Tears were running down my face as Julio began.

What the fuck's the matter with you, man? You fucking look like shit, now you got my tears. I don't like crying, but you got me crying. You look like shit. And where you been? You don't come around, you turn your back on the family. What's the matter with you?

Julio shoved Fausto to punctuate his words.

You know you don't have to stay here, you can stay with Clara and me. You know that, you always know that. Man, you shooting that shit up in your fucking veins, you crazy, man. We had a party at my house on Saturday and where were you, huh, where were you? That's family, bro, and you're up here busting your fucking veins instead of being at the party. Look at me, look what you're doing to the family.

At this point, Fausto exploded, "Fuck you, man, fuck both of you. Family, you say—what kind of family?" Crying, Fausto jumped up from the bench and yelled:

I spent eight years of my life, eight fucking years in that place and I come out and what do I find? I don't have no family. Mom and

Pops is fucked up. My family's come apart, it's all fucked up.
Where were you guys when I was away, how you let this happen?
The whole fucking family's fucked up. Where were you mother-
fuckers when the family was falling apart?

Julio yelled back, "That's them, man, that's Mom and Dad. What
can we do about them? They don't want to be together no more,
that's them. What we going to do about it?" Sammy interjected: "It's
all right, man, let him get it out, go ahead, bro, get it out." Fausto
continued, "And what about you guys, my brothers? I call you up, I
need money but you don't come through for me, after you call me
up and I'm like there. I come down and take care of you motherfuckers when you needed me. But you not there for me." Now Julio
exploded, "What you mean, we need you, what you talking about?
When we call you up and ask you for anything? That's fucked up,
bro." "Shit," Fausto continued, "Mom called me and said Sammy
needs this and Julio can't pay his bills and she's gonna get kicked out.
You think I got that money for myself, huh, is that what you think? I
gave all that money to you guys to help you out."

"That's fucked up," Julio countered. "We don't need your fucking money, you not doing this shit for us." Sammy continued: "Hey,
Fausto, I'm paying my rent, man. I pay my bills. You just be talking
that drug shit. You the one not paying your bills, you the one can't
pay your rent. Look at us, we getting by—you the one fucking up,
not us." I added:

Look who's here, Fausto. . . . You know, in the eleven years that
I've known you guys, you've been through a lot of shit. You've
all had lots of problems that you had to deal with, more than you
probably should have had to deal with. But what has always been
beautiful about you is how you did it together. . . . Look at who's
here. On Saturday, we were at Julio's for a birthday party and
everybody was there, your brothers, the kids, but there was
something missing, a big fucking hole in the party. You weren't
there and you should've been. We missed you, man, your laughter, your love.

Sammy pleaded with Fausto through his tears:

> You got to stop this shit, Fausto. You got to stop. You got to look
> in that mirror, man. You got to come back to us, to the family.
> You know how you used to be. You the life of the party, man.
> People say, that nigga's the funniest, man, he got us laughing
> 24/7, that nigga he's down with us, he's there for us. You got to
> get out of here, you don't got nothing here except drugs, and
> that's nothing. You don't owe nobody anything except yourself.
> The drug is shit, the people out there is shit. They don't care
> about you, we care about you. I've been there, I know, and there
> ain't nobody out there that cares about you, nobody, man. You
> better than that, man, you better than this fucking drug and those
> drug addicts you be hanging with. You better than that.

Sammy walked away sobbing. There was a moment of silence, while
Fausto stared at the ground. I entered the silence. "We got a bed for
you, for today. We're taking you in today."

Fausto continued looking down, smoking, nodding his head affirmatively, rolling the words across his lips slowly, "Today, today."
The wheels visibly turning, he finally said softly, "Not today, tomorrow." Julio and I exclaimed at the same time, "Today, man!" I continued, "There is no tomorrow, Fausto. Tomorrow never gets here. It's
got to be today, that's why we're here." Sammy returned and pushed
Fausto: "Today, nigga, today. We taking you in today. What you got
to do today that's so important?"

"I got bills, man, I got something planned, I got to do it first,"
Fausto responded. "Motherfucker," Sammy screamed, "you lost
eight fucking years of your life doing that shit, eight fucking years. Is
that what you want, to go in again for another ten years? That's what
this shit is going to get you. You stupid motherfucker, you not doing
that, you going in today, nigga. Today!" Fausto again nodded his
head affirmatively. Julio chimed in, "It's today, man. We here today
not tomorrow. What you got to do but bust your veins? You get some
money and that shit goes right up your veins and you don't pay
nobody. You still got bills." Sammy interrupted: "We're here today
for a reason, Fausto. God sent us here, or a higher power sent us here

today. You weren't supposed to do whatever you got planned. We're here for a reason." "That's right, bro," Julio said. "We here for a reason today. There's a reason for everything. You supposed to go with us today, not tomorrow." Looking down, Fausto again nodded affirmatively. He looked exhausted. Silence permeated the moment. Finally I interjected, "You ready to go?" Fausto nodded and we started walking slowly back to the car.

Just as I was beginning to believe that we had succeeded, Julio announced, "Trinidad fights tonight, bro." Felix Trinidad had become the welterweight boxing champion of the world the year before and was the pride of Puerto Ricans everywhere. Fausto quickly replied, "Oh man, that fight's tonight. I want to see that fight, man." Julio said warmly, "Well, you chill at my crib tonight, we watch the fight, and then you go in tomorrow." To my astonishment, Fausto had just gained another twenty-four hours. When we returned to Fausto's place and climbed out of the car, he leaned over to me and said, "Something tells me you are behind all this." I replied, "We're here because of your absence on Saturday—we all missed you and felt you should've been there." Inside, while Fausto was packing, I tried to talk Julio and Sammy out of the evening plan, but they were convinced that it would be all right, like a send-off for Fausto, a last night together to bond as brothers before he started a new journey as a recovering addict. I strongly objected, but Fausto won another day.

Before we left, Fausto and Lynne went into the living room to talk privately. She looked haggard and dangerously thin. When we told her we were taking him in, she was pleased, but at the same time intent on telling him what a disaster her life was because of him. "It's good you're going in," she said to Fausto, "but what about me?" As we left I heard Fausto tell Lynne that he would send her $1,000 tonight, that he knew somebody in Springfield who would give him the money. This was one more of his many promises that would go unfulfilled. Meanwhile, I glared at Sammy and Julio, still smarting from the afternoon's abrupt U-turn.

The dynamic between Lynne and Fausto was unhealthy, what might be referred to as a dangerous co-dependency. Lynne lacked self-confidence, did not have friends, was estranged from her father and sister, was struggling to raise a rebellious eighteen-year-old school dropout, and was working at a factory that had cut her work to four days a week. Even though she was aware of Fausto's burgeoning drug habit, she had pleaded with him to move back in with her and had refused to kick him out, even as he wrecked her life. Fausto felt guilty about the suffering he had caused her, but nonetheless enjoyed the comforts and protection that her apartment and neighborhood provided. Their financial crisis created another motive for Fausto to engage in street crime, but even when he gave money to Lynne, he inevitably asked for it back to feed his addiction. Lynne gave in to his pleas because she wanted to relieve the pain of his withdrawal symptoms and didn't want him to resort to street crime. This dynamic produced a deepening crisis in their lives. They were three months behind on the rent, Fausto had wrecked Lynne's car twice, the brakes were beyond repair, and the identification of her car in a robbery had implicated her son, who was then facing charges for larceny and attempted murder. Fausto's guilty feelings were apparent, but his addiction prohibited him from following through on any strategies to resolve their problems. Lynne, on the other hand, continued to demand that Fausto rectify the problems he had caused, which ironically became a barrier to his entering treatment. Later that night in Springfield, Fausto described the destructive dynamic: "She's a trigger, man. I need to call her, but when I do she's going to tell me about all her problems and I'm going to feel bad and then I'm going to be out there again."

FAUSTO LEFT for Springfield with Sammy and Julio, and my partner, Mary, and I agreed to meet them in Springfield later that evening to watch the fight. As they left, I heard Sammy tell Fausto, "I'll take care of you tonight, I'll score you a couple of bags to get you through. But tomorrow you go in." Fausto agreed, while I remained dubious. When Mary and I arrived later at Julio and Clara's apartment, Fausto and Sammy were at the bar. Sammy scored Fausto a few bags and they then joined the rest of us for the fight. That night, we ate Clara's cooking, talked boxing, and had a few laughs, as Trinidad was soundly beaten by Bernard Hopkins—an unfortunate ending to an exhausting day. When Mary and I left, Fausto was again suffering withdrawal symptoms, but was determined to make it through the night. I continued to remain dubious.

I returned to Springfield the next morning and was relieved to see Fausto. He had slept little during the night. Juan had shown up late and they had spent much of the night talking and crying together. "I never saw my father cry before," he said. To ease Fausto's withdrawal symptoms, his father left at one point during the night and returned with a bag of heroin. They apparently talked about their family's past. Fausto carried with him some deep, dark memories that he wanted to raise with his father. Fausto said they lay on the bed together for much of the night, while Juan rubbed Fausto's back and his hair, cried, and told him how much he loved him and how important his three boys are to him. Juan apologized for not always being a good father, but emphasized that his three boys were the most important things to him in the world—"his three hearts." The night was exhausting but important to Fausto—"my father and I poured our hearts out to one another."

By daylight, Fausto had slept only a few hours and woke drug-sick. The efforts by Sammy and Juan to sustain his habit through the prior day had fallen short. Fausto remarked, "The shit they have here is nothing, man, compared to what I get [upstate]. I mean it's bad. I got a $300- to $400-a-day habit and the shit didn't do anything for me." In the morning, Fausto took Julio's car and went to see his cousin Emilio, a fellow heroin user. Fausto found Emilio, but he was empty-handed, drug-sick, and, worse yet, an addict without a hustle. Fausto was aghast. "I told him, a guy with your habit and you ain't got no hustle! Get the fuck in the car. And then I asked him to take me to the nearest [big box retail store]." Fausto said he parked the car in a lot next to the store and then returned carrying a computer. Emilio reportedly asked in awe, "How the fuck did you do that?" Fausto repeated the familiar line, "What's a addict, bro, without a hustle?"

The next morning, I called again and was relieved to find that the detox facility in central Massachusetts still had a bed available. Meanwhile, Lynne had been trying to reach Fausto. She had left a message on my answering machine asking for Julio's number. While I went to Springfield, my partner, Mary, called Lynne to confront her co-dependency. Lynne told Mary she wanted to talk to Fausto to describe the awful circumstances he had left her in. Mary refused to give her the number, and instead talked about her inability to take care of herself or to protect her son. She extracted a promise from Lynne that she would not pick up Fausto from detox under any circumstances. Having done some homework earlier in the morning, Mary also gave Lynne several numbers to call for various forms of assistance.

Fausto and I arrived at the facility in mid-afternoon. Both of us exhausted, Fausto appeared ready to detox, a small but essential step toward living a drug-free life.

THE TREATMENT MORASS

After five days in the detox unit, Fausto was discharged for smoking a cigarette in the bathroom. Fausto called Lynne and asked her to pick him up. Maintaining her promise, she refused, and when Fausto threatened to call his friend who was dealing drugs in the nearby housing project, Lynne called me. I drove to the detox facility and found Fausto standing outside the front door. Lynne had told him to expect me, so he wasn't surprised, but was wiping tears from his eyes as he climbed in the car. "What up, dawg?" he bellowed. I later asked what was running through his mind while he was standing there.

> I didn't have nowhere to go. I went like this [taking two steps in one direction and then two steps back, then two steps in another direction and back, and then repeated the movement a third time]. I said, shit, I got nowhere to go. But then, Tim, I reached into my pant pockets and I pulled out two works [hypodermic syringes], and I'm standing there looking at them—I guess they hadn't checked my clothing [they give patients pajamas to wear when they enter the detox]. I started crying like a baby—even though the guys could see me from the window. I started bawling, 'cause I always said I wouldn't bust my veins. And I knew I had fucked up and I had to try to change, I couldn't go back to that. I threw them in the trash and I waited for you, dawg.

I took Fausto to my house and we began looking for a treatment program. This would be my first encounter with the drug treatment system in Massachusetts. I was familiar with state bureaucracies and didn't expect the process to be simple; however, by the end of the three-day weekend, Mary, Fausto, and I had spent more than fifty hours speaking on the phone and to people at several Narcotics Anonymous and Alcoholics Anonymous (NA and AA) programs. We were astounded by the complexity of the system and wondered how a street addict would be expected to negotiate it. After three days of copious note taking and long conversations, we finally felt as if we understood the rules governing the treatment system; nonetheless, the cynicism, incompetence, and bureaucratic intransigence we encountered left us feeling overwhelmed and exhausted.

Our first task was understanding the relationship between detox units and long-term drug treatment. We were interested in getting Fausto into a long-term residential treatment program, where he could address the sources of his addiction in a supportive environment of recovering addicts. Detox programs are short-term medical protocols designed to relieve physical withdrawal symptoms, but do not prepare addicts to return to their social environments where drug use flourishes. Drug addicts are encouraged to attend NA and AA programs, which are self-help groups designed to create an alternative community, lifestyle, and identity for recovering addicts. Remaining clean requires tremendous individual determination to avoid familiar routines and social networks, and to develop new strategies for managing a range of feelings, including stress, anxiety, depression, guilt, exuberance, and boredom. Creating alternative drug-free communities is difficult in social contexts where alcohol and drugs are commonly used to alter internal, emotional worlds and are a regular part of community life, and frankly I have yet to find a community in which drugs and alcohol are not common, even though the symbolism of their use may vary.

Drug treatment is easy to find if one can pay with private funds or insurance, but difficult to access if one does not have the financial resources—waiting lists are long and bureaucratic rules are often inflexible. The normal treatment track for dependent drug users like Fausto is to begin with detox, to move to a Temporary Support Service (TSS) program, and then into a residential treatment program. TSS programs are essentially supervised holding tanks to manage addicts until a placement becomes available in an inpatient treatment program or else a halfway or three-quarters house, where recovering addicts are slowly reintegrated into the community. Normally, when addicts complete detox at the facility Fausto attended, they are moved into a TSS program located at the same facility, where they remain for up to six months or until a treatment slot becomes available elsewhere.[2]

Because Fausto had been "administratively discharged," he was no longer eligible for a TSS facility anywhere. And because he was "medically cleared" of physical withdrawal symptoms, he was also no longer eligible for a detox facility, which was the feeder into the treatment system. Incensed by the dilemma, I confronted a staff member at Fausto's detox unit. "You're throwing a guy out on the street who had a $300- to $400-a-day dope habit because he smoked a cigarette in the bathroom?" She snapped, "Those are our rules, sir." She encouraged Fausto to go to the Salvation Army. Fausto had heard that there were "mad drugs at the Salvation Army," and that it was no place to recover. When I relayed this information to the staff member, she stated what would become a familiar refrain that weekend: "There are drugs everywhere, in every aftercare program. He has got to want to stay clean, it's up to him."

For the next few days, Fausto, Mary, and I called around twenty TSS units in the state, but all were full and none accepted people off the street anyway—indeed, they had to come directly from a detox facility. At the first AA meeting we attended that weekend, Fausto befriended a Puerto Rican woman who had been in recovery for several years. Her health was sadly deteriorating with AIDS, but she radiated hope, strength, and forgiveness, and reached out to newcomers like Fausto. She explained to Fausto what he needed to do to get through the weekend, gave him a list of NA and AA program locations, and agreed to meet him at some of the meetings. When we told her about Fausto's homelessness and his need for a treatment facility, she sent us to Andrea, a drug rehabilitation counselor at a local facility who attended meetings during the weekend and was also deeply committed to the recovering community.

Andrea knew the system well—she was an insider not yet defeated by the system's irrationality. "When people detox and aftercare is not available," she explained, "they're sent back to the streets. Then the only way to get into aftercare is to get high again and detox." "What should he do?" I asked. "Keep going to meetings," Andrea responded. "Maybe he should go back to detox," I suggested. "He's clean, he can't get in." "Maybe he should lie." "They'll know." "How?" "His blood pressure, his eyes. They'll just throw him out once they find out he doesn't need the medicine." I asked about residential programs in the state that accepted people directly from the streets. "There are only four in the state," Andrea explained,

> and they're all in Boston. They will have waiting lists. It's getting close to wintertime. Addicts are moving into these places for the winter. There's just not enough beds for what we need. I tell people that you got to pay attention and vote. I always vote for the candidate that talks about increasing drug treatment money. If you got insurance, you're all set, but the rest of these people, well, the system doesn't work for them.

Andrea's observations reflected a government report issued in 2000 that estimated that more than ten million drug abusers in need of treatment were not receiving it.[3] She suggested that we call her on Tuesday and she would inquire about openings at her facility. The agency where she worked ran an intensive six- to nine-month inpatient treatment program. Andrea was sure it was full, but would find out the length of the waiting list and would do what she could to move Fausto up on the list. Otherwise, Fausto's options were to enter a shelter or the Salvation Army. She gave us the name of a shelter that ran a drug treatment program within it, mostly organized around self-help meetings.

The weekend bordered on the surreal. At one point, I sat in our apartment talking to Fausto while I simultaneously listened to Mary calling around to get information.

> FAUSTO: They had some good speakers there, bro. This one
> guy, he's been clean for a year and he was just like me. He

was doing mad drugs and he didn't care no more, he was crazy on the streets . . .

MARY: But to get into a TSS [pause]—you don't have TSSs? [pause] What are TCFs? Are they different from TSSs?

FAUSTO: I know I can do it, bro. I'm tired of the streets. This guy, what you call it, inspired me. He gave me hope.

MARY: I already called that number; they're the ones that gave me the TSS numbers. What does a person do who's just been detoxed and is on the street? That's all I want to know [pause]. But I called there already [pause]. Okay, but what does he do between now and Tuesday? Okay, thank you very much. [hangs up]

FAUSTO: I got a number for a psychiatrist, they think I need a psychiatrist. I guess I need to deal with some of my problems. I get so depressed, man, that's the problem. I like get real down, you know.

MARY: [back on the phone] Are there any more TSSs? [pause] Okay, give me that number. Okay, there are two avenues. What exactly is outpatient? [pause] But he's already been detoxed [pause]. But he's homeless, what good is detox? [pause] The Hope Shelter. Where's that? Is it for drug treatment? [pause] Anybody from the street? How's he going to stay clean there?

FAUSTO: I guess I got a lot of anger, that's what they tell me. You know, at the prison staff, at my daughter's death, at my father . . .

MARY: But we heard that there's all kinds of drugs at the Salvation Army [pause]. Yeah, it's up to him, but he just got clean, he's vulnerable right now [pause]. They don't have any beds [pause]. Maybe they shouldn't have, but they did, they turned him out on the streets. They said they would send a referral, you know, his paperwork. They said it might work [pause]. Well, how does he get back into detox? He's already clean.

FAUSTO: Me and Pops made up, though. We had a good talk. But I'm still mad at what he did. I guess he did his best. You know, he doesn't have an education, he's done good considering he only has a second-grade education. I forgive him. I told him. He did the best he could.

MARY: Okay, I'll call there [pause]. Huh, where do I find out about the AA or NA meetings? [pause] Where? Can you give me that number? [pause] Okay, thank you, goodbye.

On Tuesday, we called Andrea and were told that the waiting list for the treatment program at her agency was short—she expected only a two- to three-week wait. Fausto was dubious about the program because it was run by the same organization that ran the anger management program at the prison where he was incarcerated, but, at this point, was willing to do just about anything. We were all hopeful until Andrea began to do the intake over the phone. When she found out that Fausto had an open court case for shoplifting, she explained that because the program required uninterrupted long-term care, he would have to take care of the pending court case before he enrolled. She suggested that Fausto call his public defender and ask for a six-month continuance. We followed her advice.

The public defender was not encouraging. Unlike with Andrea, we were encountering another jaded professional in the system, only in this case, the paradigmatic clash between the courts and drug rehabilitation created an insurmountable barrier. After speaking to his attorney for a few minutes, Fausto put his hand over the phone and commented with obvious frustration: "This guy ain't going to do nothing for me." I took the phone. "Yes, Dr. Black," he said disgustedly, "I don't have much time." He explained that these cases have a life of their own, a progression, and that putting off the case for six months would be out of the question. This particular judge, he insisted, would not go for it. "I base this on ten to fifteen years of experience before this judge," he emphasized. From the court's view, he said, this would be seen as a ploy, an attempt to avoid jail time. He questioned Fausto's sincerity and said that this strategy is frequently tried by defendants. I argued that I had known Fausto for eleven years and felt strongly that he was serious. "It doesn't matter," he shot back, the court won't see it that way. He's going to do time. If you're lucky, the judge might give him a longer sentence but then recommend him to a lockdown facility for drug treatment. But the DOC doesn't have to accept the recommendation, and given his past record of violence, they won't accept it. He's going to do time and the judge won't postpone the case.

The attorney went on to explain that there was a fundamental conflict between the rules of the court and drug treatment. Residential drug treatment facilities, he explained, will not treat people until their cases are cleared, while the courts will not suspend cases until treatment is completed. "That's the way it is," he asserted. "People like Fausto get caught in between."

I deferred to his expertise on the matter. "What should he do, then, in your experienced judgment?" I asked. "Off the record," he said,

if he's serious about treatment, I would tell him to default [to not show up for his case]. The court will put a warrant out for his arrest. When he finishes treatment he should come back before the court and then do his time. He probably won't get any more time if he can show that he defaulted because he was in treatment and that he completed it. He's still going to do the time. But at least he'll be clean then. If I file the continuance request, then not only will the judge deny it, they'll know where he is and they'll pick him up.

Fausto was stuck. He was outside the system and couldn't get back in, and the one option we had pried open was being closed by conflicting rules and expectations between the courts and the drug rehabilitation system.

I called Andrea back and told her what I had learned. "Okay," she responded, as if she already knew the answer. She reiterated that he would need to first clear up his court cases so his treatment would not be interrupted; in the meantime, she suggested that Fausto call her every few days to keep his name on the waiting list, even if he goes to prison. "The system is messed up," she said. "I see this all the time."

I asked, "What should he do now?" "Keep going to meetings," she responded before hanging up.

Fausto was left with two residential options—the Salvation Army or the Hope Shelter. We decided to learn more about the latter. Hope Shelter is a homeless shelter that runs a drug program. It provides an on-site drug counselor and space for AA and NA meetings. It is located in the middle of the city, in a neighborhood teeming with drugs. Walking toward the shelter, Fausto, Mary, and I were startled by a truck coming to a screeching halt in the middle of the road. Fausto looked over, "Shit, it's Freddy. What up, dawg?" Freddy was screaming out the window, but was caught in a stream of traffic that forced him to move on. "That nigga and I were locked up together, he's real cool," Fausto said as we watched Freddy drive off. Approaching the shelter, Fausto saw another former prison buddy. "Oh man, Nito, what up, dawg!" They hugged—the reservoir of affection between them evident. Fausto told him he was in recovery. Nito's eyes glanced away, far away. He was high, staying close to a nearby drug spot, and repeated, almost rhythmically, his greeting, "What up, Fausto, it good to see you." He drifted away from Fausto, who now looked distressed.

We reached the back of the building and walked into a sea of people, many leaning against the building with heads nodding. Cuts and bruises marked many of their faces, eyes were sunk deep into their sockets, glazed but hollow—bodies of the living dead. We broke up a drug deal as we walked more deeply into the dense gathering. Fausto was recognized by a dealer. "Hey, Fausto, what you need, bro?" "Nothing, I'm cool. I'm trying to find the, whatcha-ma-call-it, the Hope Shelter." "There's the door, bro," the dealer said pointing. "You sure you okay, man?" Fausto hesitated, "Yeah, man, I'm cool." We entered the back door and approached a white college-age student with a green Mohawk. "The Hope Shelter, we're looking for the Hope Shelter," Fausto stammered. The young man didn't have a chance to respond before Fausto turned to me: "Tim, man, can we get the fuck out of here? I'm getting real nervous." The young man shrugged as we turned to leave. On the way back to the car, Fausto talked about copping at this spot, about the "head nodders," about the dealer we had encountered. He shook his head and quickened his pace. "I don't want to go in that program and walk by that every day. What the fuck, man. Motherfuckers! That guy knows me, he knows because I copped from him before. Fuck, man," he said, as we got into the car, "get me the fuck out of here!"

We returned to my apartment and called the Salvation Army. They had a bed and did an over-the-phone intake with Fausto, only this time, when Fausto was asked about any pending court cases, he lied. After he hung up, he reasoned, "If I don't lie, I don't get a bed. And yo, pops, even if I'm only there three months, the judge will see that I'm serious. Maybe he'll let me do my time there or something." Fausto had an appointment with the major at the Salvation Army later in the afternoon. "It's really up to me," he said repeatedly. "I just have to find people who are clean. I can work there—they'll give me a job. Pops, maybe I'll be ringing one of them bells at Christmastime when you and Mom come out of the store."

THE HOUSE THAT BOOTH BUILT

Sitting in the lobby outside the major's door, Fausto and I read the institutional rules. The program provided a tight daily structure of meetings, work, religious meditations, and individual counseling sessions. "Yo, what does no frat-er-ni-za-tion mean?" Fausto asked, sounding out the long word. "It means that there are women here and you can't be messing with 'em," I replied. "Oh shiiiiit," Fausto groaned, "that's not good, bro." The door then opened and we were greeted by Mrs. Delaney. She and her husband were the Salvation Army officers who ran the facility.

Fausto introduced me. "This is Dr. Tim Black, he's a college professor in Hartford. He has known me for, what, I don't know, a long time, since I was a kid." Mrs. Delaney smirked. "Doctor, huh?" My secular title and status did not impress her. "Well, Dr. Black," she said derisively, "I don't let people in here during the interview. Is there anything you need to say?" Deferring to her authority, I asked if I could bring Fausto some clothes that evening even though the rules forbade anyone receiving personal items after the intake without a receipt. She assured me that it was not a problem. I asked Fausto if he needed anything else. "I don't think so," he answered, but looked at Mrs. Delaney for reassurance. "Do you smoke?" she asked. Fausto nodded. "Yeah, but I have cigarettes." "There is a canteen here. Do you have any money?" she inquired. "No." He looked at me. "Give me a few dollars, pops." Already reaching in my billfold, I handed him a twenty. I had considered giving it to him earlier, but was concerned about him carrying that much money around with him, enough to cop two bags. "Whoa," Mrs. Delaney said disparagingly. "What?" asked Fausto, looking askance. "Did I hear a thank-you?" she scolded. "Oh," Fausto said, looking relieved, "thank you, yeah, thank you, pops. But he's just like family, you know." "Still, I don't think a thank-you would hurt," she insisted.

The Salvation Army was the last-resort option for Fausto, but then, the Salvation Army has historically targeted the socially abandoned working classes for its soul-saving mission. Founded in Britain in 1865, the Salvation Army movement of open-air evangelical preaching, brass bands, and street theater reached into the corridors of urban wretchedness to save the working-class souls of nineteenth-century industrial capitalism. Its founder, William Booth, considered laissez-faire economics anti-Christian. He railed against the social Darwinism of his time, believing that the habits, customs, and laws of the burgeoning industrial, urbanized society had "greased the slope down which these poor creatures slide to perdition."[4] Reaching the United States in 1880, the Salvation Army also distinguished itself from the "scientific charity" movement, which repudiated public relief efforts that indiscriminately provided aid to the poor.[5] As Edward McKinley describes, the Salvation Army refused the underlying assumption that public relief would foster dependency and moral corruption:

> The Salvation Army believes, however, that some people—those who are hungry or lonesome, helpless or frightened, sick or poor, or too old or too young for others to care much about—must first be given practical assurance that God and his children love them and will not leave them in their want or despair, before they can be told of His grace and love.[6]

The Salvation Army did not, however, attempt to address the political-economic causes of poverty, but instead focused on saving individuals one at a time. Salvation Army workers, whom the organization referred to as "slum sisters," lived among the poor and ministered to their daily needs while attempting to facilitate spiritual transformation.

Today, the Salvation Army remains hierarchically organized around an order of command defined by military offices, which appears anachronistic—or as historian Lillian Taiz describes, conveys a nineteenth-century "crusader spirit" to "conquer this modern world of ours."[7] Despite its hierarchical and military symbolism, it nevertheless allows for considerable regional autonomy and democratic inclusion, and always has. It was the first agency, for instance, in Washington, D.C., to racially integrate its facilities in 1946 and it has encouraged the promotion of women into leadership positions since its beginning, when Catherine Booth, wife of the founder, began preaching the gospel in the streets of East London.[8] The Army's march through the twentieth century has, however, diluted its soul-saving mission. The early-twentieth-century movement to advance institutional planning, bureaucratic efficiency, and scientific rationality, along with the professionalization of social work, diminished the working-class religiosity that spiritually founded and guided the Salvation Army. Open-air revivalist meetings are virtually nonexistent today, and while lay staff are still recruited from the program's clientele, other staff members are likely to be educated in the counseling professions.

Current administrative demands are no small matter either and have also worked toward changing the image of the Salvation Army. It received the largest share of charity donations through much of the 1990s, and in 2003 received $1.37 billion in private support (second only to the Red Cross) and reported a total income of more than $2 billion.[9] Part of the Salvation Army's revenue is generated by its multitude of stores that sell used furniture, clothes, and other items. But even this has changed. Begun under the leadership of Frank Smith in the 1890s as the Salvage Brigades, the primary purpose of this operation was to provide temporary work for the unemployed.[10] Smith's Salvage Brigades took root and fostered an international movement of furniture and clothes recycling that has evolved into the hallmark of the Salvation Army (along with its red-kettle bell ringers at Christmastime). This popular vision of the Salvation Army, however, deviates from its original evangelical mission, as it has become more associated with its social programs rather than its soul-saving mission. Taiz suggests that these changes have required a subtle shift in the Salvation Army's ideological self-description: "Instead of featuring the spiritual power of individual soldiers working through the Army . . . social programs were the true investments of redemption and . . . Jesus, working through these institutions, gave the Army the power to transform derelicts into respectable citizens."[11] The Salvation Army's prominence as a charitable institution in the late twentieth century has redefined its relationship with the social mainstream, as it has "found its place, in the great stream of philanthropic endeavor . . . to become the great go-between, the national distributor, of the country's wealth, to the country's poor and needy"—far removed from its ragtag marching band of an earlier era.[12]

Fausto was enrolled in one of the Salvation Army's adult rehabilitation centers in Massachusetts, and his experiences took shape within these contradictory historical currents running through the institution, providing a reservoir of services that were infused with differing understandings and intentions. After a brief orientation period, Fausto quickly fell into a routine of work, individual counseling sessions, AA and NA meetings, and evening weight lifting. His first counselor had very little professional training, but was instead motivated by the Army's long-standing spiritual mission. According to Fausto, when he guardedly talked about street life, drug use, and his prison experiences, his counselor "would always say to me, 'Okay, let's get down and pray,' and we kneel down, bro, and pray together" [laughter]. Similarly, when Fausto talked about Governor Weld's prisons, "she said to me, 'I'm sorry you had to go through that,' you know, the twenty-four-hour lockdown. . . . So then she says that it was probably 'God's revenge' that he was no longer the governor and he was fired [as the ambassador] in Mexico [laughter]. She's a nice lady and all, but she's crazy, yo."

With the exception of Fausto's counselor and the majors who ran the organization, no other staff appeared to adopt the religious zeal that would have pleased William Booth, whose portrait was prominently displayed in the lobby. Successful clients who had been promoted to positions of institutional authority did not adopt such a pose, but rather focused on enforcing rules and managing a revolving door of men and women in need of shelter. But neither did the other counselors whose professional training defined their approach to the young men. According to Fausto, many of the more professionally oriented staff looked forward to the pending retirement of the majors, who were viewed as old-fashioned and were expected to be replaced by a younger, more progressive commanding officer. Indeed, the Sunday church services led by Mr. Delaney exposed the differences that he and his wife had with the professional staff, but also demonstrated the evangelical roots of the early Salvation Army movement.

My partner, Mary, and I became an integral part of Fausto's life during this period. We regularly visited Fausto at the facility and developed a fictive kin relationship, with Fausto referring to us as "pops" and "mom." Most of the staff at the facility were white and had little familiarity with fictive kin relations, more common in Latino cultures. Occasionally, someone would ask, "Are you really his parents?" While both Mr. and Mrs. Delaney were the majors who commanded the facility, I rarely saw Mr. Delaney, but would encounter Mrs. Delaney occasionally. Although she remained skeptical of my influence, she usually had nice things to say about Fausto and always encouraged us to attend Sunday services, a requirement for residents.

Mary and I attended one Sunday service. We sat in a pew behind Fausto and three of his friends, while Mrs. Delaney led everyone in song. Mr. Delaney then stepped to the pulpit, acknowledged family members visiting, and led us in prayer before settling into his sermon for the day. Dressed in military officer regalia, Major Delaney was hardly an inspiring orator on a pedagogical stump. His passion overwhelmed his linguistic skill and he appeared an anachronistic character, reminding me of some of the preachers I had heard at my grandmother's Primitive Baptist Church in rural Illinois in the early

1970s. I could only imagine what was going through the minds of the black and Latino residents sitting in the chapel.

Mr. Delaney's topic of the day was the evil of secular education and evolutionary theory. Mrs. Delaney's thinly veiled contempt for me was now evident. Over the previous month, I had been passing out books to Fausto and a few of the other residents, and Fausto, eager to adopt a student identity, was especially enamored by *Lakota Woman,* a book by Mary Crow Dog that describes the American Indian Movement's freedom struggle on an Indian reservation in South Dakota in the 1970s. Wherever Fausto went, he carried the book, even to work and to the chapel. Embracing the Salvationist roots laid down by William and Catherine Booth, the majors no doubt saw me as part of the problem rather than the solution. I searched the chapel for facial expressions as I listened to Mr. Delaney. "These little squiggly things were living in puddles of water," he uttered sarcastically,

> but they found themselves wanting to take to the great seas, but they needed gills. So one day, they just happened to develop gills. And then millions of years later, they decided that they wanted to come out of the water, but when they tried, they found they couldn't breathe, that they needed lungs and then one day, they found they had lungs . . .

The major's intent was to dramatize the absurdity of evolutionary logic, after which he asked the residents and their guests to call out their favorite book of the Bible. Several responses were forthcoming. Mary offered Song of Solomon, which the major ignored initially, but when Fausto and the young man sitting next to him yelled the same, he grudgingly acknowledged it. Fausto, sitting in front of us, turned and asked, "Hey, mom, what's Song of Solomon?" "Look it up," Mary coyly replied. Fausto and the three guys sitting in front of us all reached for their Bibles, as the major continued his sermon.

Extolling the virtues of the Book of Genesis, his favorite book of the Bible, Major Delaney reached the moral of his sermon, that God, the creator of all things, had made the world in seven days, not millions of years. He confessed that he had spent years unlearning what he had been taught in school by misguided educators and their schools. The answers to life's mysteries, he insisted, lay with God, not education. Raising his voice, he bore down on the homeless and alcohol- and drug-addicted residents before him, claiming that "Satan is present in this room today" and that "God has punished you for the bad decisions you have made in life." He railed against the power of temptation and insisted that the residents' wounds would never heal until they accepted God, renounced their sins, and were saved. He invited all of them to come to the altar to ask God's forgiveness and to pray with him—two accepted.

As I looked around the room, I saw mostly vacant looks, but also some skepticism as well as affirmative head nodding. The major placed his hand on the heads of the two young men kneeling before him and asked God to forgive them, perhaps in a manner similar to that of General Booth under a lighted tent in East London a hundred years prior. Meanwhile the four men sitting in front of us were engrossed in their Bibles, snickering, elbowing one another, and pointing out passages as they read from the Song of Solomon.

> Thy navel is like a round goblet . . . thy belly is like an heap of wheat set about with lilies. Thy two breasts are like two young roes that are twins. . . . How fair and how pleasant art thou, O love, for delights! . . . and thy breasts two clusters of grapes. . . . Let us get up early to the vineyards; let us see if the vine flourish, whether the tender grape appear, and the pomegranates bud forth: there will I give thee my loves.

I'm not sure how many of the words Fausto could read, but he seemed to understand the general intent. Indeed, Satan may have been in the room that day and may have been expunged by the major's sermon, as neither Mary nor I attended another—paradigms had clashed and this was, after all, the house that Booth built, not our house.

JOHNNY THE CHEF

Fausto and his friends referred to the Salvation Army as a "religious labor camp." The Protestant creed of God and work were the philosophical pillars on which the program stood. Work was considered therapeutic—in fact, it was called "work therapy." Fausto made $5 a week, and after some pleading was placed in the kitchen, since he had learned some institutional cooking skills in prison. As it turned out, getting a job in the kitchen would not be that difficult—there was a regular turnover of kitchen help and as one former kitchen worker put it, "The chef's a fucking racist. You won't last long."

A man of Irish stock and a recovering alcoholic, Johnny the Chef was known to go on a few binges a year, when he wouldn't show up to work for a few weeks. Nonetheless, he had cooked at the facility for thirty years—the kitchen was his and he wanted anyone who worked for him to recognize that fact. Fausto was eager to win his approval but Johnny was not very obliging in the beginning. On two occasions in the first month, Johnny passed Fausto and me in the facility and, despite Fausto's greeting, refused to acknowledge his presence. Undeterred, Fausto forged ahead, intent on earning Johnny's respect and approval. Fausto worked extra hours when residents didn't show up for work and eagerly displayed the skills he had learned in prison kitchens. On one afternoon, he prepared turkey salad sandwiches, using his own recipe, and later reported, "Johnny was like, hmmmm, not bad, and the guys in the chow hall, they loved it, bro." His bigger challenge was, however, engaging Johnny interpersonally and managing the chef's attitudes toward Puerto Ricans.

According to Fausto, Johnny made regular derogatory comments about Puerto Ricans—references to rice and beans, lowrider cars, street jungles, gold chains, foreigners, and the like. Often these comments were made as jokes. Fausto responded by eagerly learning the history of the Irish in the United States. He asked Mary and me frequent questions, as well as another resident who was an avid reader of history. Fausto would listen intently and prepare himself for his next "battle" with the chef, and then report the outcome to me later in the evening.

I got that motherfucker today. I went into the kitchen and I waited, and Johnny says something about Puerto Ricans being lazy and shit, so I hit him with, "Hey, Johnny, do you know how the paddy wagon got its name?" He's like, "What you talking about?" And I told him, I'm like it was because of you lazy, drunk Irish people, your people, Johnny, that's what I told him. I said, "Paddy's a name for your people and the police used to fill that truck up with your people, that's how it got its name." I had everybody in the kitchen laughing and that motherfucker didn't have nothing to say. He didn't know what hit him. I bum-rushed that motherfucker.

Similar exchanges between Fausto and Johnny became part of the daily kitchen routine—in fact, it became the connection through which Fausto and Johnny's relationship developed. It took the form of "playing the dozens," a linguistic street game in which power and respect are established through the exchange of insults—the basis of the now commonplace insult "yo momma!" The masculine under-pinnings of the game were readily apparent.

Oh man, did I get Johnny today. I been talking to Ben, you know the guy that's always sitting at the front desk, and I been ask-ing him some questions, you know, and he gave me this book. So today I says to Johnny, "Hey, Johnny, you know you're not white." So he says, "What you trying to say?" So now I got every-body listening in the kitchen and I say to him, "Johnny, you black. You ever heard of the Black Irish?" He don't know what I'm talk-ing about, so I hit him with, "Let me tell you about your history. The Black Irish come from back in the day when the Spanish people marched through Ireland and kicked your butts and raped your women. So you talk all this shit about black people, and I just wanted you to know that you black, you and your people are Black Irish."

More than a year later when Fausto was leaving the Salvation Army, he described saying goodbye to Johnny: "He had tears in his eyes when I left. He told me that I had taught him more than any other Puerto Rican he had ever met. He says to me, 'Fausto, you are differ-ent, you are a special guy, a very smart guy, a credit to your race.' Can you believe it?"

Good and Bad

Waking Up

Residents at the Salvation Army were racially and ethnically diverse, but the staff were all white, with one exception. Jamal Brock was an African American counselor at the facility whose mother had earned accolades in the community for her civil rights work. Fausto continually landed in Jamal's office for afternoon conversations until he was formally transferred to his caseload. No longer would he be asked to kneel and pray like he had during his counseling sessions with his first counselor; instead, Jamal engaged Fausto's burgeoning intellectual identity. They talked about *Lakota Woman, Makes Me Wanna Holler,* and *Always Running,* books about racial and ethnic inequality that Fausto was attempting to read. A very large man who wore his hair in long braids, Mr. Brock stood out at the facility. Moreover, he possessed a charisma that extended beyond the black and Latino men and women who lived in the facility to the white officers as well. He was professionally trained, had worked in the drug addiction field for more than twenty years, and, perhaps most important, understood the persistent legacy of American racism and its intractable, insidious effects. He regularly engaged and challenged Fausto, and, as a counselor, wanted Fausto to use his insights to his own benefit. Fausto described his approach:

> He raises good questions and he, in his own way, he's trying to explain to me how the way things are now and how to learn how to play the game, right, to start making the system work for you, right? 'Cause this system is here to stay . . . what we need to do is just learn how to play the game and become part of the system and start making the system work for us. This is what he's basically trying to teach me.

Brock was essential to making the Salvation Army work for Fausto, but there were other reasons it worked as well.

Perhaps Fausto and his friends were correct when they described the Salvation Army as a "religious labor camp," but the facility also provided structure and a space where they could develop alternative identities to the streets. Fausto met several men who, like himself, used this time to make sense of their lives and to nurture an intellectual identity. Jamal Brock institutionally anchored this process, engaging the men individually and encouraging their fellowship with one another. Fausto's mind and body were clear of heroin, so his thinking sharpened and he wrote occasionally in a journal to record his thoughts as well as to improve his writing. During one conversation I had with him, he articulated his understanding of social marginalization and drug use:

> Tim, when I got out [of prison], I felt like I didn't belong. So much of my life was gone. Julio and Sammy and you are all doing different things, you know. You've gotten on with your lives. I felt lost out there, like I was outside. Everything I knew was about life behind the wall. We had our own rules and I didn't fit into the rules everybody else was living by. That hurt, man, that hurted real bad. That's real painful, man, to feel like you don't belong. Drugs worked. I could numb myself, I could not give a fuck, you know. And I could find others who I knew behind bars going through the same thing, you know. I could feel real close to them, cop with them. Not that I trusted them, but we could do shit together. But we were doing it for the same reason, because we didn't belong in this society anymore.

Reading and discussing *Lakota Woman*, Fausto began to formulate his understanding of marginalization in more political terms. He talked about the injustices committed against the American Indians and then how social services were later set up to "help them, after they, you know the white man, had taken everything away from them." He applied his insight to contemporary racial and ethnic dynamics.

> I have a theory. I think it's good that the government is taking everything away from minority poor people. That's good. Let 'em throw us in prison, let 'em keep us poor; let 'em take away our rights; let 'em take away jobs that will let us take care of our babies. That's good, you know why? Because at some point peo-

ple will rise up. It will happen. You keep taking things away and people will rise up at some point.

Some of Fausto's friends at the facility also utilized the space it created for reflection and critical thought, and a nearby coffeehouse provided a way for Fausto and his friends to receive validation of their new identities. The coffeehouse did not serve alcohol and was organized to facilitate community across racial and class boundaries— to provide a space for people to talk, think, and reflect. Community events were posted on the wall, tables with comfortable chairs were scattered around the room, and there were regularly scheduled poetry readings, talks, and music, along with open mikes and a weekly poetry slam. Fausto and a network of friends from the Salvation Army began to attend regularly, although they ran into some problems with the management because, at times, they lacked the money to spend on coffee and pastries. Further, some of the young men began participating in the poetry slams. They would read their own narratives, often about grim lives, to an attentive and supportive group of social critics and poets. Their experiences appeared cathartic and affirming of new emerging identities.

Physically removed from the Salvation Army, the coffeehouse also provided a space for the men to openly criticize the facility— which they did frequently. Fausto's closest friend, Trevor, was an African American who read his poetry regularly. On one occasion, Trevor talked about how the Salvation Army staff reduced them to "addicts" and, in doing so, failed to understand the individual complexity of their lives. Using a metaphor similar to W. E. B. Du Bois's veil, Trevor explained that the staff could not see beneath the "mask of the addict."

It's like we wear a mask, you see, the mask of the addict. They can't see me, the me that is flesh and blood, the me that is an individual sitting there with all kinds of things, feelings, problems going on. They only see me as an "addict" who needs his work therapy and who needs to turn his life over to God. But there's more to me than that. I have turned my life over to God. I used to be a Muslim and I learned how to be human, how to respect the humanity of myself and others. But when I go in to see my counselor, he starts by asking me questions about what he has heard from others. I heard that you been doing this or that. He doesn't ask what's going on in my life, he doesn't look at me and treat me like the individual I am sitting before him. He can only see the mask and he don't know how to see beneath it.

The men also complained about "progress staff meetings," in which all Salvation Army staff involved with a resident would meet with him as a group once a month to discuss his progress. During these meetings, personal information was shared between a wide range of staff, including the officers, counselors, house managers, and warehouse, maintenance, and kitchen supervisors (including Johnny). The men felt as if they were being talked about as objects and that their personal lives were openly on display, without respect for their privacy. Consequently, the process created an atmosphere in which the residents were likely to hold back information, or to be dishonest. Fausto explained:

> I like what Jeremy [a resident] said, "Let the games begin." You know, you go in there [to the staffing] and you play games. You do what you need to do to get through the program. You can't open up and be critical of the place. You can't tell them what's going on because they go and tell everybody else. So you game 'em. And this doesn't help with our addictions, because why? Why? Because this is what addicts already know, what we already know and do good. We know how to play games, we're good at it. This is what we do on the streets. So we apply our addict minds to these people. That's not rehabilitation, you know.

Another chief complaint frequently discussed concerned the no fraternization rule. Trevor elaborated:

> I learned as a Muslim that you treat the brothers and sisters with respect. Now can you imagine that I go through the door and I open the door and say good morning to the sisters, but then I have to look down or up at the ceiling. I can't talk to them. That's

not what I've been taught is the Christian way or the Muslim way. I don't look at them as a sex symbol or like that, you know. I'm trying to say, "Here I am and there you are" and "How you doing today, sister?" but if I start doing that, they are going to kick me out of here. And they don't care who they kick out— they don't care. So many people come and go for stupid reasons that have nothing to do with their recoveries, for stupid rules. You can't run a recovery program and pretend like you care about people and then throw them out for stupid shit like expressing their humanity to the sisters.

Fausto's identity as a student deepened during this time. He began to tell people at the coffeehouse that he was a student. He carried a book wherever he went. He attended a poetry reading by Nuyorican poet Willie Perdomo at a local college with Mary and me, and inspired by the images of struggling Puerto Ricans that Perdomo eloquently and viscerally articulated, Fausto approached him afterward and left with a signed copy of his book. Fausto again embraced his desire to be a social movement leader and talked about going to college, convinced that "education should set us all free."

When I talk to everybody who I believe are beginning—getting more aware what's going around in their communities . . . now I ask people when did you wake up. . . . We are enslaved in our own minds in these communities, right, just these beliefs of, you know, we want things and we see 'em on TV . . . the dumb tool, right, and here's society promoting their products and their big corporations and how the American Dream can be achieved if you work hard and patriotism and all these things, right, but they don't tell you how to get there. They just show 'em to you. We make our own conclusions how to get there, right? Someone chooses to sell drugs or whatever to achieve the American Dream and it's a nightmare, you know . . . we don't bother to pick up a book, right? It's not mandatory in my house to pick up a book, you know, and it's mandatory in my house to pay the rent and pay the bills, right? That comes up every month, right? So, if you're fortunate enough to make it through an age, right, or to make it through after going through jails and, and DYSs [Department of Youth Services] of the world, right, and these organizations, right, 'cause . . . that's what we end up at, right? That's predicted for us, right? Then, you wake up.

Ironically, the Salvation Army provided a space for Fausto to "wake up," a space that was removed from his street routines, from his drug life, and even from the unstable existence of off-the-books work. Nineteenth-century Protestant evangelicalism with its moral value given to work may have provided the Salvation Army with historical meaning and significance, but Fausto, his small network of friends, and Jamal Brock had seized the public space provided and created their own meaningful identities. But this little insulated corner of the world was cordoned off from the daily grind of physical and psychological survival that defined their prior lives, and finding a more permanent place to ground their new identities would be extremely difficult. Other forces were at work that undermined the process, some within the Salvation Army and others outside it.

ON THE OUTSIDE

Fausto completed the rehabilitation program and was faced with the uncertainty of the next step. He had taken nine months to complete the six-month program, because after the first two months in the program, he attended his court case for shoplifting and was sentenced to thirty days in the county jail.[13] The Salvation Army officers were unhappy that he had lied on his application, but they liked Fausto and agreed to reserve his place at the facility—still, they required that he start the program over when he returned. Having completed the program, Fausto was given the option of remaining at the facility, working at minimum wage, and paying room and board. He accepted the offer, but was transferred out of the kitchen to the warehouse, where he was trained to drive a truck to pick up furniture donations.

The warehouse was much different from the kitchen. He didn't like the supervisor, whose managerial role required him to meet costs and run an efficient shop. Further, Fausto was no longer a "client" receiving services, but now a bona fide employee. During Fausto's first week of work, while attempting to turn the truck around on an unpaved country road, he got stuck and a tow truck was needed to pull him out of the mud. He was reprimanded by his supervisor and placed on probation, while his salary was docked for the cost of the tow truck. Fausto's experiences at the Salvation Army had made him more emotionally stable, but he still needed constant affirmation, and the rebuke by the supervisor stung.

> I knew that motherfucker didn't like me, I told you that! What am I supposed to do, he sends me out in the middle of bum-fuck nowhere and I got to turn the truck around. It's raining like a motherfucker and I get the wheel stuck in the fucking mud. And then the motherfucker's going to make me pay for it. Fuck him— all he cares about is his fucking truck and the fucking customers. I'm going to talk to the major.

The major did intervene and Fausto was paid his full weekly salary, but the supervisor was angry that Fausto had gone over his head and that the major had not supported him. Tensions increased, as did the temptation of the streets.

Fausto's prison friend, who had recruited him to be part of his drug operation in a central Massachusetts housing project, spotted Fausto standing in front of the Salvation Army one afternoon enjoying a cigarette. He stopped and chatted briefly, inquiring about Fausto's situation, and then returned later that night with his father-in-law, the point man behind the drug operation, who had also done prison time with Fausto. While he was on the streets, Fausto had been paid handsomely for setting up a business connection between "the old man"—Fausto's name for the father-in-law—and Alexander Rodríguez in Springfield. The connection bridged the western and central parts of the state, but the old man, like many who have done business with Alexander, was unhappy with him. They asked Fausto to set them up with Alexander's competitor, Little Acosta. Removed from the streets, Fausto assumed a critical perspective.

> They playing me. You know, they don't give a shit about me, I'm there for them to use. They come saying shit like, "We glad you clean, Fausto, that's what we like. My father-in-law want to see

you." But I know that once they get what they want that they'll be gone. That's just the way it is. [My friend's] father-in-law will protect him, because [he] is married to his daughter, but not me, he won't protect me for shit.

Fausto turned down a $1,500 offer to make the connection. "Once I take the money, then they'll come back and want me to do something else. They try to buy me." Fausto was, of course, tempted. He was working for minimum wage at the time and $1,500 is a lot of money for setting up a meeting. Moreover, the stress he was feeling in the warehouse most likely enhanced the temptation. Nonetheless, amidst a long walk in the woods with me, Fausto reached in his bill-fold and ceremoniously wadded up his friend's telephone number and threw it on the ground, but not without admitting later that he was tempted to go back and find it.

In addition to problems in the warehouse and to the temptation that Fausto's friend posed, a third incident occurred that undermined Fausto's recovery—the coffeehouse closed its door to Salvation Army residents. One of the residents had gotten into an argument with an employee of the coffeehouse. The manager took advantage of the opportunity to call the Salvation Army officers and complain. She had frequently expressed her disapproval of the young men's presence at the coffeehouse, mostly because they occupied space without spending much money, but perhaps also because they stood out in what was mostly a white college student hangout. She received a sympathetic response from Mrs. Delaney, who had also never approved of the arrangement. The Salvation Army imposed a new rule forbidding residents from attending the coffeehouse and the manager agreed to let her know if anyone broke the rule. Not only did the decision seal off public space that had helped to nurture an intellectual identity among Fausto and his friends, but it reproduced the conditions of alienation that all of them had experienced during their lifetimes. Fausto's friend Trevor, who also had completed the program and was voluntarily living at the facility, decided to move out after the rule was imposed. Fausto not only lost his hangout, he lost his closest friend.

Before leaving, Trevor wrote a poem about the incident with the hopes that someone he had met at the coffeehouse would read it at one of the weekly poetry slams. Entitled "Cold Closed Door," the poem captured the significance of the coffeehouse to Trevor, Fausto, and other residents who had found community there.

I have come to this spot for at least five months,
to express the realities I lived since childhood.
For many years I have told of dreams and desires,
cold rain and the warmth of gentle fires.
I loved this spot—'cause it helped me be free,
especially during the importance of my sobriety.
The coffee is great and the cakes were too,
the chatter of voices were all to me something new.
The younger folk talked of school, music, and crazy things to do,
the younger adults were into college exams, dating, poetry and music too.
The older crowd came to examine the changes that the generation would
*   bring,*
the experience of life, and all its challenges were the most attractive things.
So why do I have to stand outside looking into a place that gave me a
*   chance?*
I may not have spent a lot of money,
for I own twenty dollars a week.
I enjoyed spending it in your place,
because I felt as if I were at home.
I'll always walk by remembering that this door
was my entrance to a place that for five months made my dreams come true.
I will thank you for that.
All I ever asked for was a place where I could be known,
and my expression be not only heard but listened to.
So now its over, nothing I can do.

The structure that had supported Fausto's alternative identity to the streets was crumbling.

GOOD AND BAD

Since he had completed the program, Fausto was free to come and go at the residence as he pleased. He had developed a strong attraction to one of the female residents and had covertly carried on a relationship, meeting her at various public places in an effort to get to know each other better. He borrowed my car and arranged a long trip to western Massachusetts for an afternoon of horseback riding, and in the evening drove to Julio's house in Springfield, where, left alone, they consummated their mutual attraction. A few weeks later I received a call from Fausto. His routine urine test, required as a condition of residency at the Salvation Army, had turned up positive and he was being kicked out. He was incensed, insisting he had not done any drugs, but had been set up by staff who didn't like him. He suspected his supervisor and one of the house managers, who had a key to the urine storage chest, were in cahoots. When I arrived, the staff firmly dismissed Fausto's accusations and, while sympathetic, assured me that the test was infallible. "No false positives?" I queried. "None," they insisted.

Shortly thereafter, Fausto and I sat in Jamal Brock's office, behind a closed door, as I watched the master at work. Jamal stated calmly that no one had set Fausto up, that the staff at the facility all liked him, and that the tests were accurate. At the same time, he told Fausto he believed him because he had no reason to suspect that Fausto was lying. Jamal allowed the contradiction to ring in the room. He wasn't trying to force a confession from Fausto, he was gently telling Fausto that he knew the truth but still supported his recovery. He gave Fausto ample opportunity to admit his transgression, as did I in private conversations with him later. Fausto held firmly to his story— he desperately needed to. The denial made sense to me, because I recalled an earlier conversation I had taped with Fausto in which he had described relapse and the unbearable self-loathing associated with it:

> I can use, [sigh] I could stop for a while, right, and you think that one bag will not harm you . . . but it's the worse . . . you cannot pick up that one bag, 'cause that one bag is what's gonna take you back, [not] because of the drug, itself. It's what you gonna do to yourself mentally, right? This is the trap. You've been clean all these years and . . . they say that the ones that have the longest term of recovery are the ones most close to using . . . you think

you can use again and when you do, then you start killing your-self. "Fuck! How the fuck did I do that?" . . . That thing works on you! Like, "Oh fuck! This is what killed you! You're a fuckin' asshole! What the hell are you doing? Look at your family!" And all of a sudden you get all depressed . . . and it just keeps on depressing you and this is yourself doing it to you and all of a sudden you're back out there again.

Jamal Brock tried to be encouraging, identifying the progress that Fausto had made and discussing his options. He tried to assure Fausto he would be all right, but I sensed that Jamal expected the worst, and so did I.

I took Fausto to Springfield to live with Julio, but after a few weeks of unsuccessfully looking for work, Fausto began using heroin regularly. He contacted the old man in central Massachusetts and set up a meeting with Little Acosta in Springfield. His heroin use esca-lated and he moved out of Julio's apartment and in with some friends in the same housing project where his childhood friend Roberto lived. Roberto had been present at the bank robbery that had landed Fausto in prison and had moved up in Springfield's underground drug economy. Fausto binged for about two weeks. During this time I went to Springfield to find him. At two in the morning, Julio and I saw him on the streets. Fausto was closely examining a gold chain that someone wanted to exchange for cocaine when we walked up. He was clearly uncomfortable. He asked a few obligatory questions of Julio and myself before jumping in a car and leaving with a friend.

After a month on the streets of Springfield, Fausto moved back to Lynne's apartment in central Massachusetts. He enrolled in a methadone maintenance clinic, began receiving counseling at the clinic, and was referred for psychiatric care. He was diagnosed with post-traumatic stress disorder, stemming from his prison experi-ences. Fausto also began having epileptic seizures, much like his mother had suffered throughout her life. He was treated by a team of doctors and clinicians who simultaneously addressed his PTSD, drug addiction, and epilepsy. He worked off-the-books jobs, until he had a seizure on top of a house while working for a roofing company. Fausto applied to the state for assistance and received food stamps,

Medicaid, and some cash assistance. He also applied for Supplemental Security Income for his disability, but had been turned down twice. On his doctor's recommendation, he was applying a third time. Fausto's life had become a routine of going to the clinic, attending doctor's appointments, and watching television, while moving between periods of drug binging and recovery.

For a brief period in Fausto's life, at the Salvation Army, I was able to get a glimpse of what could have been. With a reasonable degree of economic stability, with supportive educational opportunities, and with a network of friends whose shared life experiences could become the basis for shared understanding, social and political critique, and mutual acceptance, Fausto might have blossomed, overcome his educational deficiencies, and, who knows, perhaps become the community leader that he wanted to be. But creating and maintaining these public spaces is difficult in a world that affords the most destitute little power, little support, and little opportunity. The Salvation Army was, thankfully, there to break the fall, but they were not an agent for social change, and sustaining what the residents, Jamal Brock, and a group of supportive patrons of a coffeehouse had created was like shoveling sand at the tide.

Keeping in touch with Fausto by phone after he returned to Lynne's, I arranged for him to speak in one of my classes at the university. Fausto was nervous and did not sleep the night before. To create a more relaxed setting, I interviewed him in front of the class, asking questions that would elicit reflections on his life. He was articulate, charming, and funny, but also serious and thoughtful—all the qualities that had drawn me to Fausto fifteen years earlier. Toward the end of the class, he drew a racetrack on the board and talked about inequality in terms of those who are privileged and have the inside track and those who have a longer distance to run to compete. He concluded:

> Some of you will go out and have good jobs, have powerful jobs, maybe working in government or something. And I hope that you will remember that there are people who are different from you, people who don't have the same skin color, maybe not as lucky as you, people who didn't have everything you had. They

may have made mistakes, but I would like you to remember, even though they aren't like you, they are still human. We are not monsters, we are human beings, and you should treat everyone like humans. So if you get a job with the government or a job where you make decisions about people, treat them like humans, that's all. Remember that despite what you may have been told, or what you see in the media, we are human too.

Fausto was stirred up by the experience. Several of the students came up after class to continue the conversation. Their responses were gratifying, but it also forced Fausto to see what he was not. He was not a student, he would not have the lives he imagined they would have, he would not have their education. On the drive back, he struggled to integrate the seemingly disparate parts of his life. He contemplated that he was a person who can "sit down with people, put a nice tablecloth on my lap, and have a good discussion about things," but at the same time, a guy who can "take a gun and stick you up." "I am both," he surmised, "*good and bad, both lives inside of me.*"

Conclusion

ON A SUMMER EVENING in 2003, I returned to the block with Julio. The warm night air brought out a large number of men, but only a few familiar faces—until I looked more closely. Alexander, Jorge, and Roberto were still there, attempting to teach a roving band of seventeen- to twenty-year-olds the ropes. I also recognized youngsters I had seen when I was hanging out six years earlier who were now searching for their place on the streets. As is common on the block, Julio and Jorge had been engaging some of the younger generation in a passionate "my boy, your boy" argument. Tonight the argument was about basketball and I was their boy. They were sure I could beat any of their boys and I, unaware of the provocation, was apparently in town that night to prove it.

On the block in the mid-1990s, we occasionally played the game of 21—the ultimate game of individualism, in which anyone can play, there are no teams, and everyone plays against everyone else. Now several years later, I slipped off my Tevas and laced up Alexander's sneakers while a portable basketball hoop was rolled out to the street. The banter escalated as an audience gathered around the hoop. Warming up, I recognized my competition as one of the kids who played 21 on the block years ago, but who now, at the age of twenty, had grown into a thin six-feet-four-inch adult body. I was trounced 11–3 and became the butt of many jokes for the remainder of the evening. A new generation of street youths had arrived, and Jorge, Julio, Roberto, Fausto, Sammy, and Alexander were becoming "old-Gs."

An old-G is a term used on the street that has a variety of different references—an old gangster, an old moneyman, an old generation,

336

an old goat, or an old game. Perhaps the best way to understand an old-G in poor urban neighborhoods is by contrasting it with the "old head" as characterized by Elijah Anderson. The male old head is a stable, employed black man who lives in black neighborhoods and derives his authority from his belief "in hard work, family life, and the church." He is "an aggressive agent of the wider society whose acknowledged role is to teach, support, encourage, and in effect socialize young men to meet their responsibilities regarding work, family, the law, and common decency."[1] The old-G is not stably employed, has spent time on the streets, often dealing drugs, but is nonetheless a moral authority in poor urban areas. He too encourages youths to stay in school and work, and stresses the importance of loyalty to family and friends.

As social-economic changes have disrupted common routes into working-class jobs, the presence and authority of the old head has diminished, while the old-G has gained more status as a moral authority. The loss of living-wage jobs and the increased role of prisons in the lives of the urban dispossessed have meant that growing numbers of inner-city men will remain on the margins of the labor force over their life course. The process of aging off the streets has slowed down and some youths will find themselves economically marginalized or obsolete as adults, in and out of prison and drug treatment, working as part of a contingency workforce on the margins of a global economy, often in under-the-table jobs, or else victims of drug overdose, HIV, or street violence. Instead of aging off, some street youths age on to another life stage on the streets—they become middle-age street guys, often in their thirties, who give the street a multigenerational presence. While old-Gs are not old heads, neither are they street thugs leading new generations of street youths into meaningless violence and amoral forays of street terror. They try to carve out moral orbits within the changing urban conditions that have occurred over the past twenty to thirty years.

Old-Gs are complicated, often contradictory, characters. On the one hand, old-Gs try to encourage young men to stay in school, go to work, get off the streets, to straighten out their lives. They often betray these admonitions, however, through their stories of "back in the day" or their behavior. Still, their hopes for the new generation and their identities as community elders are expressed in their sincere efforts to guide neighborhood kids to take advantage of opportunities that may not have been available in their lifetime or, as many will say, to not make the same mistakes they made. On the other hand, they also teach the new generation street smarts—routines to survive on the street, a code of honor and mutual respect, and the importance of loyalty. It is the random violence and crime the old-Gs abhor— meaningless street fights and shootings, robberies, street hustles— that fall outside the moral boundaries of the street.[2]

Juan Rivera is an old-G. Juan worked in many factory jobs until he developed back problems and became disabled in his late forties. He has also supplemented his income as a street mechanic and by selling small quantities of drugs whenever an opportunity arose. Since his accident he has spent more time on the streets, gambling, smoking pot, snorting cocaine, and soliciting women. He moves back and forth between Puerto Rico and Springfield. In Springfield in the 1990s, Juan hung out at a gambling house each night with a group of men, tossing dice, sharing drugs, and having some laughs. Juan's influence on his children is complex, similar to relationships between old-Gs and street youths. As we have seen, Juan has often given his sons "the lecture" about staying in school and pursuing opportunities he never had. Similarly, as a boy, when Fausto would walk into the gambling house to say something to his father, he was greeted with affectionate hugs, sincere questions, and encouragement about doing the right thing, all from a group of red-eyed men who would spend the night rolling dice, snorting cocaine, and drinking homemade rum until daybreak.

The old-Gs maintain some presence on the street, albeit a minimal one. Street life is dominated by the younger generation, but occasionally the old-Gs make an appearance, sometimes on behalf of the younger generation, and sometimes as a policing force to impose street justice themselves. When I first met Alfredo Acosta, the legendary drug dealer who had introduced Sammy to North End street life, he was sitting at a bar, looking like an old man far removed from the action of the streets. People passed by and "paid their respects."

Alfredo's status rested on stories and memories of being "out there," and occasionally he would drink too much and initiate a fight at the bar—the fading roar of a retired street player. When Alfredo Acosta took Julio aside, showed him his AK-47, and told him that if he ever had any problems on the street that he would have his back, he was asserting his reputation as an old-G. Or when a group of old-Gs reportedly showed up at a bar one evening to intervene in a street dispute, they leaned against the wall with their arms tightly folded across their chests to send a message. Sometimes old-Gs become neighborhood leaders involved in community action groups and recruit youngsters into more positive community activities, or they may intervene in hostilities between neighborhood gangs. All of these actions are folded into a moral discourse about the street, about showing loyalty and honor in standing up for one's family or one's friends, about strengthening the neighborhood, or about taking care of business.

As my book was coming to an end, the influence of Juan and his generation was passing and men like Jorge, Roberto, and Sammy, now in their thirties and with some lasting presence on the street, were becoming old-Gs. The mantle had been passed along to them to teach youngsters the importance of sharing, honor, respect, loyalty, and toughness—values that help organize and regulate street activities.

These moral codes are often resisted. On the night of the basketball game, I was introduced to Bear, the brother of Jorge's common-law wife. Bear appeared to be the leader of a younger group of men, and walking by me I heard him say to a friend, "Yo, man, I'm hungry and I ain't got no cash. I'm about to rob someone so I can get me some food, yo." Throughout the night, I watched as Jorge continued to dole out $10 and $20 bills to Bear, who drank and snorted his way through the evening. Bear acted the part of the "bugged-out" youth, down for anything, embracing friends with hugs of mutual respect, grabbing the microphone at a karaoke bar and rapping, bantering with the old-Gs, and winking at me.

During the course of the evening, I asked Julio about Bear: "Well look at his brothers. That's who he has to look up to. They both junkies. They both done all the shit he's doing. He's the leader of these young punks." Striking a more sympathetic tone, Jorge adopted an old-G posture:

I try to talk to him but he don't listen to nobody. These guys, they haven't taken it to the next level yet. They not carrying guns. When they do that, then I got to let go of 'em. But, I mean, they went into D'Angelo's the other night and robbed the place to put money in their pockets. They used knives. I try, man, I try to talk to them. I give 'em money all the time to try to keep 'em from doing shit. But I don't have that much money. I tried to teach him how to deal, but I give him some shit and he walks off, I never see him again. He doesn't come back to see me, to pay me. He don't give a shit about anything. When these guys need some cash, they steal. They walking out of a house every day with a television set.

Bear had spent much of his adolescence in and out of juvenile lockup facilities. Prison didn't scare him and he had advanced his street acuity inside these facilities. Jorge's efforts were futile and his struggle to find respect on the streets was fading as he passed from a street player to an old-G.

Earlier in the evening, Jorge had put his arm around another fresh-faced street youngster and had commented to Julio and me: "This nigga earned my respect the other night. He took it to this dude. I'm telling you, the guy was twice my nigga's height. But he fucked that dude up for trying to take his shit." Jorge was praising the youngster for standing up for himself and for his toughness; he was also attempting to establish his own moral authority as an old-G and acquire respect from the youngster.

Like most adolescents, these youngsters resisted the moral authority of their parents and their parents' generation, striking out to create their own identities, often in opposition to the old-Gs. In the same way that an old head might have fumed about the lack of discipline among youths who didn't want to work in the local factory, who called in sick on too many occasions or spent too much time at the local bar, the old-Gs express frustration as street youths defy their efforts to show them how to play the "street game" and how to deal drugs, or their efforts to direct them away from the streets on paths toward school and jobs. That same evening, both Jorge and Julio shook their heads in dismay as they talked about a fifteen-year-old high school football star who was going in the direction of the streets. "That nigga is fucking up a college scholarship." And after I had failed to live up to my challenge on the court earlier that evening, Julio, Jorge, and myself spent the next half an hour rebuking the twenty-year-old winner for choosing cigarettes, drugs, and the streets over a basketball career—all typical old-G behavior.

Shifting circumstances in poor urban neighborhoods over the past thirty years have meant that many of the same men who might have been old heads in the past are now becoming new old-Gs. Located at the margins of the economy in the mid-1990s, many of the men from the block are still at the margins as the twenty-first century unfolds, with many carrying the additional burden of being ex-felons. In their mid-thirties, they are becoming old-Gs. A few, like Julio, however, gained a foothold in the 1990s economy and have followed a path to middle-income status. They bridge the worlds between old heads and old-Gs.

A TRUCKER'S NIGHTMARE

Born in the 1970s, but becoming adults in the 1990s, the Rivera brothers' early lives span a period of pivotal political and economic change in the United States. Rising energy prices, increased global economic competition, and gains made by labor and social movements produced a crisis in economic capitalism in the 1970s, signaled by a significant loss in profits. Corporate elites responded by funding conservative think tanks like the Heritage Foundation, the Manhattan Institute, and the American Enterprise Institute, where new political and economic strategies were devised to restore profit rates and roll back social-democratic and civil rights gains made under the 1930s New Deal and the 1960s Great Society.[3] Ushered in under the presidency of Ronald Reagan, these new strategies decreased taxes on wealthy individuals and corporations, deregulated businesses, privatized public services, created deep cuts in social welfare spending, globalized industrial production, reduced trade barriers and controls on capital and finance, weakened labor unions, and used interest rate adjustment as a tool to reduce inflation and protect investments at the costs of rising un- and under-employment. In other words, the 1980s ushered in an era of neoliberalism.

These neoliberal policies are heralded as the new TINA, that "there is no alternative" if we want to compete in the global economic market, maintain international political supremacy, and preserve America's privileged way of life. These policies—now referred to by scholars and journalists as the "Washington Consensus"—continued under Democratic president Bill Clinton as if political party differences had been dulled by the apparent needs of a new global economy, and have been advanced with missionary zeal under Republican president George W. Bush. As we approach the end of the first decade of the twenty-first century, social-economic conditions could not be much worse for most of the men I have observed for the past eighteen years, despite the fact that for most of these eighteen years, our economy has been in a state of expansion.[4]

The lengthy economic recovery in the 1990s, generated largely by a boom in the information technology industry and sustained through personal and corporate debt, improved the conditions for most groups at the bottom of the labor force. Family income grew by about one-third for blacks and one-fourth for Latinos, while poverty and unemployment rates dropped precipitously. Some of the men from the block, like Julio, benefited. At the same time, the recovery revealed the bedrock of social inequality that the post-1970s economy had instituted, as social inequality continued to grow, reaching levels not seen since the 1920s. The number of U.S. billionaires tripled in the 1990s, while the gap in pay between the average CEO and hourly worker wage grew from 96 to 1 in 1990 to 458 to 1 in 2000.[5] In other words, as more people at the bottom of the labor force were going to work and earning more income due to a tighter labor market, the economy was also producing record numbers of rich Americans. It was a grand time: billionaires were buying mega- and giga-yachts and pushing the prices of art to unforeseen levels; former Enron chief executive Kenneth Lay hired a yacht and crew for $200,000 for his wife's birthday party; and Clara got a $120,000 home and a $10-an-hour job.

In 2008, however, Julio and Clara find their middle-income achievements under assault on many fronts. Like many from the working class, Julio's middle-income status is dependent on the strength of U.S. labor unions. A large part of the strategy to restore corporate profits after the 1970s was to weaken labor unions, which produced a lucrative union-busting legal industry.[6] Rising health care costs have been at the center of most labor contract negotiations over the past fifteen years, and while Julio's company was paying 100 percent of health care costs in the earlier part of the decade, in their most recent negotiations, they demanded that the union accept a two-tiered contract that favored seniority. With many of the drivers approaching retirement, the union voted to accept the offer, which undermined union solidarity and alienated younger drivers like Julio. Starting wages for newly hired employees were lowered and contributions toward their health insurance became required. Even though Julio had been employed long enough to not be affected directly by these changes, he sympathized with the younger drivers and understood that a divided workforce damaged the union's strength. "We may as well not even have a union, that's what I told them, but they was only thinking about themselves." Julio continued, "As one of the guys said, Jimmy Hoffa must be turning over in his grave right now."

A year later, Julio left the union and became an independent driver, what is known as "an owner operator." The label is, however, misleading. Julio does not own his truck, but instead leases it from the company. And he is not really independent, because he still works for the same company only under a different title. This too, as it turns out, is part of the company's strategy to dilute the power of the union. It is to their benefit to siphon off as many members as possible and encourage them to become "independent" and leave the union.[7]

Moving out on his own may not have been a prudent move for Julio in the current economic climate. Rising gas prices have become a trucker's nightmare. Julio was paying around $1,500 in fuel each week in the summer of 2008, about one-half of his total weekly pay. In addition, he has to pay income and Social Security taxes, any repairs beyond general maintenance on the truck, and $750 per week to lease the truck. Julio says that the company is not taking the $750 lease payment out of his check, but neither are they paying the 20 percent gas subsidy they had promised. In the end, Julio comes out ahead on this deal, so he hasn't said anything. The deal is an unspoken one without a paper trail. Concerned, I asked, "How do you know they won't say you owe the money later?" "I don't know," Julio responded. Clara quickly added, "That's what I was saying to him, too." Julio reasoned, "I do know that I'm not the only one. They doing the same for some other drivers. And if they wanted the $750 for the lease, I couldn't pay them. I'd give the truck back. They would probably hire me back as a regular driver, but I can't pay the lease and they know that."

In addition to the trucker's nightmare, Julio and Clara have fallen victim of another national crisis pushing the economy into recession. By the end of 2007, the home mortgage crisis had sent shocks through the finance industry and produced a record number of foreclosures. Banks and brokers recorded $43 billion in losses by the end of November 2007, with another $25 billion expected. Further, in the first three months of 2008, late payments had increased to an all-time high and people were losing their homes at the highest rate on record.[8] In the winter of 2008, Julio and Clara's subprime variable interest rate jumped from 9.9 to 11.9 percent, at around the same time that a young friend of mine and his family bought their first home in Hartford at an interest rate of 5.75 percent.

Adding to their financial stress, Julio and Clara's fifteen-year-old daughter, Iris, gave birth in 2007. She missed only six weeks of school, while the school provided in-home support immediately after the birth so she wouldn't be held back her tenth-grade year. Julio and Clara rallied around her to keep her on track to graduate from high school. As Julio put it, "Family is always there, you know what I'm saying, Tim? Family is there to pick you up when you fuck up. That's what family's for. Besides," he added, "what can I say? She didn't do anything that Clara and I didn't do." Clara left her job to take care of the child during the day while Iris completed her sophomore year, with "three honors in her last two marking periods," Clara proudly emphasized. Iris is attending Springfield's vocational school, working on a CNA, Certified Nursing Assistant, degree. Julio, who at her age had dreamed of being a doctor, injects, "She wants to go to AIC [American International College] when she graduates to get her RN

[Registered Nurse] degree. I hear they have a good program there and it is just across the street."

Clara is currently looking for a second-shift job— "something from three to eleven," she explained, "anything really, some way to help out Julio so he don't have to do it all. But I want to take care of the baby during the day while Iris is at school." Reminding me that she dropped out of school to take care of Iris, Clara states emphatically, "I don't want Iris to do what I did, you know." Clara completed her GED five years after she left school.

AN ERA OF SOCIAL INDIFFERENCE

Even before the rising gas prices and the home mortgage crisis, the first decade of the twenty-first century had little to offer Julio's two brothers, Fausto and Sammy. To address the 2001 recession, the Bush administration passed two rounds of tax cuts to stimulate the economy, which did little more than deepen social inequality. Corporate profits grew as a result of the stimulus plan, but many in 2003 were calling the expansion a "jobless recovery." Reports now show wage and employment growth during the 2001–2007 recovery to be the weakest on record since the end of World War II.[9] In her book *The War at Home,* Frances Fox Piven reports that the median tax cut wage earners received from the 2003 legislation was $217, compared to an estimated average $90,000 for each millionaire.[10] Combining the tax cuts, the escalating costs of the Iraq and Afghanistan wars, the domestic costs attributed to the 9/11 attacks, and the sputtering economic recovery, the federal deficit has spiked from a surplus of $230 billion in 2000 to a deficit of over $400 billion in 2008.[11]

The redistribution of income and wealth upward and the loss of public monies work against the Rivera brothers and others portrayed in this book. Transforming the social economic conditions in which they live would require social reform on the level of what might be called a New New Deal or an Urban Marshall Plan. Public works programs, universal health care, two-way bilingual education programs, tuition-free quality public schools and colleges, and affordable child care and housing require serious investments. However, a rising federal deficit, growing social inequality, the 2008 economic recession, and general social indifference toward poverty are not likely to get us there. Instead of social reform, the United States continues to rely largely on prisons to manage the lives of a segment of the population left behind in the post-1970s economy, even when this strategy pushes states, shouldering the majority of these costs, toward bankruptcy.

It is perhaps extraordinary to think that in seventeen of the eighteen years that I have known the Rivera brothers the economy was in a period of expansion. It is also extraordinary to consider that during this same time prisons were also rapidly expanding. In 1990 when I met the Riveras, the federal and state prison population had reached an all-time high of 743,382 inmates. In 2007 that number had more than doubled to 1,528,041, and during the 2001–2007 period of economic expansion, it increased 15 percent.[12] The other side of incarceration is the growing number of prisoners returning to communities in the United States after completing their sentences—now nearly 700,000 a year.[13] As Fausto's experiences indicate, the lack of programs to support self-determination, higher education, and civic participation in the prison, along with prison violence and continuing state penalties after release, have funneled many former inmates back onto the streets. These narrowing and dehumanizing circumstances have resulted in fewer distinctions between the streets and prison, to the extent where the streets have become like prisons and prisons like the streets.[14]

Jorge, at the center of drug-dealing activities on the block in the mid-1990s, represents one of these statistics. Released in 2003 after serving five years in federal prison, Jorge struggled unsuccessfully to find a job after his release. On the streets, he struggled with his loss of status, a place that he had occupied before with style and aplomb. At one point he hit bottom as his daily trail of empty Budweiser cans increased and he became unable to make a distinction between life inside and outside the prison walls.

> JORGE: Tim, I don't give a fuck about anything anymore. You
> know, it wasn't supposed to be this way when I got out [of
> prison]. I didn't want this, but, you know, this is what I know,
> this is all I ever knowed. Fuck it.
> TIM: How was it supposed to be?

JORGE: I was going to give this shit up, get a job, be straight, you know. Everybody keeps telling me to get a job, my girl, Mom, even my brothers. But I put in job applications all over the place when I got out and nobody called. That's the way it is.

TIM: But isn't this risky, man? You're hanging and the cops are taking notes on you, you know that. There's only one end to this story.

JORGE: Yeah, but I don't give a fuck. I really don't care. It's no different being in there than being out here—they're both bad. There's no difference. I mean, I don't get pussy in there. That's it, though. It ain't no different other than that.

TIM: Come on, man . . . you got people yelling in your face all the time. You don't have the freedom to get up when you want, to pop a Budweiser at noon if you want . . . don't give me that shit.

JORGE: No, I'm telling you, I really don't give a fuck. I know I'm going to do time and I don't care.

Jorge did eventually find a job, working in the warehouse of a department store. He has been there for three years. He derives little satisfaction or money from the job, but gets along well with his boss and is granted periodic favors from him. More important, Jorge has avoided going to prison a second time. Settling into his role as an old-G, he spends a lot of time hanging out at the block where Fausto, Sammy, and Juan now rent an apartment.

In the spring of 2008, the Rivera brothers' mother, Angela, died suddenly of a brain hemorrhage at age fifty-three. Jorge, Roberto, my wife, Mary, and I spent the night with the Rivera family and most of the next day at the hospital before they turned off her life support. It was a big loss to the family; their mother had always kept her door open to her sons, even in their most self-destructive periods. Both Fausto and Sammy were living with her at the time, and both were still struggling with drug addiction. Sammy had traded heroin for cocaine binging—a common remedy to the lethargy of methadone maintenance—which led to his separation from María. Angela's death left Fausto and Sammy without shelter. Cobbling together

Fausto's and Juan's Supplemental Security Income checks along with Sammy's unemployment check, they rented an apartment on the block—a new bachelors' pad and hangout location for Jorge, Roberto, and others.

Sitting on the couch in their new apartment on a hot summer day, I talked to Fausto about his drug addiction. Before the death of his mother, Fausto circulated between his girlfriend, Lynne's, and his mother's homes, surviving on a $550-a-month SSI check and their willingness to care for him. He spent one year on the streets engaged in urban drug warfare, where he managed to survive despite shoot-outs, several narcotics police sweeps, and an addiction that spiked to new heights. Julio and I attempted a second intervention, but Fausto had drifted far away from us as the involuntary muscular spasms and physical ticks that caromed through his body demonstrated. He refused our efforts, and it was only after a minor arrest and the loss of a friend to an overdose that he was jolted into detox and a period of relative sobriety. Sitting on the couch that day, it appeared that his body had again grown healthy, his biceps close to the same size as my thighs. "Drug treatment doesn't work for me," he said. "I been through all that. For some people it works, for me it doesn't. I need family, that's what works for me, to surround myself with family." He now goes to the gym regularly with his brothers and Roberto, and to church every Sunday with Julio and Clara. Fausto insisted that he is not using illicit drugs anymore.

> I'm working out three times a week. I'm not addicted to anything except pussy! I see the stuff, you know, but whenever I think about it my body just pulls away. It's like my body is saying why would I want to go through all that again. You know, I remember all the shit I been through, and I don't do it. We stay straight. But the pussy, damn, Tim, there are girls coming through here all the time.

These were the sunny days of July; I worried about the dark days of December.

For me, this study began by studying school dropouts, but evolved through my relationships, particularly with Fausto. Where possible, I attempted to help Fausto but, in retrospect, Fausto needed much more than an advocate or a mentor, he needed a social movement. Fausto developed a language of social critique that needed a home, a place where his reflections could be grounded and validated, and his intellectual identity could be nurtured and sustained. Ironically, the closest he came to this was at the Salvation Army, where a space for critique and self-examination was provided by a charismatic counselor, a coffeehouse, and a network of racially diverse men with biographies much like his own. These social spaces, however, are difficult to create and sustain. Community organizers struggle in all urban areas to pry open public spaces for understanding, healing, and strategizing, as they attempt to reach the millions of individuals that the Rivera brothers and other men from the block represent. But clearly, much more is needed—at minimum, a larger social movement that will no longer tolerate exacerbated social inequality, lost freedoms, and a trail of wasted lives.

Together, the post-1970s economy and the War on Drugs, along with its unprecedented prison lockup, have channeled a large proportion of poor urban minority youth into socially disabling and self-denying lives. Their choices are limited. They may work in the unregulated drug trade, where concentrated drug enforcement in urban minority areas combined with mandatory minimum prison sentencing increases their chances of spending time in prison and where the violence of the lawless drug trade limits their longevity. Or they may work in monotonous off- or on-the-books jobs that do not and are not likely in the future to afford self-sufficiency or to provide for children. Compliance with these jobs is nevertheless enforced by the threat of prison and the reduction in welfare entitlements. Some men acquiesce to the low-wage workforce, some become unemployable and receive limited governmental assistance, some take their chances in the drug trade, and many utilize combinations of these resources.

Walking back to my car after the conversation with Fausto at his new place, I thought about the three Rivera brothers. Julio was hanging on to his home and job, attempting to make the climb into the middle class. Sammy's unemployment insurance was running out and he looked ready to use his connections on the street to keep money in his pockets. Fausto appeared complacent for the time being, surrounded by his brothers and their friends, relying on and sharing his SSI check with them as well. Regardless of life outcomes, family remains at the center of their lives. The Rivera brothers protect their own—they are in it together. They symbolized this by recently agreeing to tattoo one another's names on their arms. Julio already had his brothers' full names reaching from his biceps to his wrists. Fausto had done the same but had abbreviated Sammy's name, and Sammy was not about to let it pass: "Just wait, Tim. Next time you see me, I'm going to have Julio's name here [pointing to his right arm] and a butterfly on this arm for Fausto" [laughter].

On my way to my car, I passed by another apartment that triggered a memory. About six months earlier, I had been at Julio and Clara's house. We had settled into their living room with a full plate of food and a Corona to watch a boxing match showcasing welterweight champion Miguel Cotto, the most recent pride of Puerto Rican boxing fans. I asked Julio if he had been to the block recently. "No," he replied, "but the last time I was there, there was cops all over the place, walking all around the block, you know. And those young kids—you know, Benedicto's son, Roberto's nephew, Jorge's niece—were inside their houses selling, while the cops are right outside. They crazy, bro. I guess they just don't give a fuck." A few weeks after this conversation, the apartment was busted and I watched on the nightly news as these eighteen- and nineteen-year-old nephews, nieces, sons, and daughters were led from the apartment in handcuffs. I had seen a few of them on the block ten years earlier walking around with their mothers, fighting for attention from the men on the block, or competing to get the basketball in a game of 21. I turned around before reaching my car, looked down the street to where Fausto, Sammy, and Juan were now living. I had come full circle. Juan, the aging old-G, and Fausto and Sammy, the new old-Gs, were living not far from where I had been introduced to Jorge and others on the block; only now, a new, younger generation was being led away in handcuffs.

ACKNOWLEDGMENTS

Eighteen years is a long time and I apologize in advance to those whose support I may forget to recognize. There have been many, but only one who has been involved from beginning to end. Michael Lewis was my dissertation adviser when this study began in 1990 and is still the person I call at any time of the day or night for advice. There is not enough room here to convey all that I have learned from Mike, or to express the extent of my gratitude for his wisdom, patience, insight, and friendship. In a first-year gradu-ate seminar, a discussion spilled out of the classroom and into the hallway and ended that evening when, just before Michael disappeared into his office, he extended his arm, pointed his finger at me, and said, "To be continued, Black." Indeed the conver-sation did continue—for now twenty-four years—and I would simply not be the scholar, writer, teacher, or person that I am without the guidance I have received from my friend Michael.

Three others have read the entire manuscript and provided invaluable comments. Foremost, my wife, Mary Patrice Erdmans, has lived this book with me. A far better sociologist than me and a talented writer, Mary improved this book at every stage of its development. She mastered the excruciating task of providing candid criticism with one hand while offering support with the other. I have benefited immensely from her erudite mind and her companionship, and could always count on unconditional sup-port from her, even when it wasn't deserved. Steve Valocchi and John O'Connor also read the entire manuscript and provided important feedback and support. I met with each of them occasionally at a favorite watering hole to discuss the book and each, for different reasons, became the intellectual standard-bearer of the book—I knew I had something when I got their nod of approval.

I am also grateful to many others who commented on the manuscript at different stages of its development. I would like to thank Stephen Adair, Jay Demerath, Chris Doucot, Corey Dolgon, Doug Eichar, Nilda Flores-González, Bob Forrant, Carolyn Howe, Phillip Kassel, Jerry Lembcke, Jean Malone, Steve Markson, and Deborah Mil-bauer for their thoughtful comments. I would also like to thank John Clark, Bette Decoteau, Sabine Merz, Gladys Moreno, Josiah Ricardo, Michael Shively, and Jay Stewart for their research, technical, and clerical support; Bill Ward for helping me to gain access to the Springfield public schools; and Jack Foehl, Carolyn Magnan, and Harriet Wetstone for their support over the years. My editor at Pantheon, Keith Gold-

351

smith, has seamlessly guided me through the process of publication and provided a keen eye to help me avoid the dark hole of social science jargon, all of which has been much appreciated.

Of course, no one deserves more thanks than the Rivera family. They opened their lives to me, were always willing to accommodate me, and fed me better than any researcher deserves. I am truly humbled by their generosity. I apologize in advance if anything in this book contradicts their understanding of events, or if in any way I insult or demean them. It is certainly not my intention. They gave me the liberty to tell their stories, and I take that privilege seriously. Still, while it is their life stories, it is my book, and I assume full responsibility for that.

Finally, I want to thank my mother, Jean Baker, and my two brothers, Greg and Todd Black. I marvel at the personal resiliency that each has displayed in the face of adversity, and I am fully aware that my professional accomplishments pale in comparison. You have influenced this book in ways that even I do not fully understand.

NOTES

INTRODUCTION

1. The literal translation is "faith moves mountains."
2. The term "social grooves" is taken from Mary Patrice Erdmans, *The Grasinski Girls: The Choices They Had and the Choices They Made* (Athens: Ohio University Press, 2004).
3. According to a report from the State Commission on Hispanic Affairs in 1987, 56 percent of Hispanic youngsters left school before graduation. See Marisa Gianetti, "Area Hispanics Caught Between Two Worlds," *Sunday Republican* (Springfield, Mass.), 8 March 1987, B1. About a decade earlier, in 1979, a local television documentary reported the Hispanic dropout rate to be 85 percent in Springfield. See Ruth Dankert, *Sunday Republican* (Springfield, Mass.), 4 November 1979, F1, F8. Data taken from the 1990 U.S. Census indicate that the poverty rate for Hispanics in Springfield in 1989 was 52 percent. Census CD (New Brunswick, N.J.: GeoLytics Inc., 1996).
4. Jonathon Tilone, "Commission Warned of a 'Lost Generation' of Hispanics," *Union News* (Springfield, Mass.), 18 May 1984, 11.
5. Information taken from *Hispanic Prisoners in the United States* (Washington, D.C.: Sentencing Project, October 2003), www.sentencingproject.org. See also Allan J. Beck, Jennifer C. Karberg, and Paige M. Harrison, *Prison and Jail Inmates at Midyear 2001* NCJ 191702 (Washington, D.C.: U.S. Department of Justice, Bureau of Justice Statistics, April 2002), 13, http://www.ojp.usdoj.gov/bjs/abstract/pjim01.htm.
6. C. Wright Mills, *The Sociological Imagination* (New York: Oxford University Press, 1959), 158. Mills describes the social location where individuals encounter larger structural forces as one's "milieu," or "the social setting that is directly open to his personal experience and to some extent his willful activity" (8).
7. Profit rates dropped by more than one-third between the mid-1960s and late 1970s, from an average of 10 percent net (after-tax) profit to less than 6 percent. See Bennett Harrison and Barry Bluestone, *The Great U-Turn: Corporate Restructuring and the Polarization of America* (New York: Basic Books, 1988).
8. David Harvey, *A Brief History of Neoliberalism* (New York: Oxford University Press, 2005), 23.

9. For more on the rise of neoliberalism and its effects, see Harvey, *A Brief History of Neoliberalism;* Doug Henwood, *After the New Economy* (New York: New Press, 2003); and John O'Connor, "From Welfare Rights to Welfare Fights: Neoliberals and the Retrenchment of Social Provision" (Ph.D. diss., Department of Sociology, University of Massachusetts, Amherst, 2002).

10. Thomas R. Swartz, "An Editorial Comment: The Working Poor and the Prospect of Welfare Reform 1995 Style," in Thomas R. Swartz and Kathleen Maas Weigert, eds., *America's Working Poor* (Notre Dame: University of Notre Dame Press, 1995); and Harvey, *A Brief History of Neoliberalism.* Also see Robert Pollin and Stephanie Luce, *The Living Wage: Building a Fair Economy* (New York: New Press, 1998); Richard B. Freeman and Peter Gottschalk, *Generating Jobs: How to Increase Demand for Less-Skilled Workers* (New York: Russell Sage Foundation, 1998), 1–17; Sheldon Danzinger and Peter Gottschalk, "Hardly Making It: The Increase in Low Earnings and What to Do About It," in Swartz and Weigert, eds., *America's Working Poor,* 69–85; and Beth Rubin, *Shifts in the Social Contract: Understanding Change in American Society* (Thousand Oaks, Calif.: Pine Forge, 1995).

11. Of course, white poverty and unemployment were also dropping during this period, reaching 7.4 percent and 3.5 percent respectively in 2000. See Heather Boushey and Robert Cherry, "The Severe Implications of the Economic Downturn on Working Families," *Working USA* 56, no. 2 (2003): 35–54; Doug Henwood, "Money Trickling Down," *Left Business Observer* 96, no 4 (2001); and Freeman and Gottschalk, "Introduction," *Generating Jobs.*

12. William K. Tabb, "Wage Stagnation, Growing Insecurity, and the Future of the U.S. Working Class," *Monthly Review* 59, no. 2 (2007): 20–30.

13. Thomas M. Shapiro, *The Hidden Cost of Being African American: How Wealth Perpetuates Inequality* (New York: Oxford University Press, 2004).

14. "Key Facts at a Glance, Correctional Populations" (Washington, D.C.: U.S. Department of Justice, Bureau of Justice Statistics, December 2007), www.ojp.usdoj.gov/bjs/glance/tables/corr2tab.htm. Another way of describing this increase is that the number of men and women locked up in federal and state prisons increased from 350 to 478 for every 100,000 adults living in the United States, while the total number of people under correctional supervision (in prison, in jail, on parole or probation) increased from 4.9 million to 6.4 million. Also see *2001 Sourcebook of Criminal Justice Statistcs,* Table 6.24 (Washington, D.C.: U.S. Department of Justice, Bureau of Justice Statistics, 2002), 495, at http://www.albany.edu/sourcebook/pdf/sb2001/sb2001-section6.pdf.

15. William Julius Wilson, *The Truly Disadvantaged: The Inner City, the Underclass, and Public Policy* (Chicago: University of Chicago Press, 1987).

16. Charles Murray, *Losing Ground: American Social Policy, 1950–1980* (New York: Basic Books, 1984); and Lawrence Mead, *Beyond Entitlement: The Social Obligations of Citizenship* (New York: Free Press, 1985).

17. Wilson argued that the loss of the black middle class had eliminated the social buffer that had historically provided a stabilizing function for black urban neighborhoods during economic downturns.

18. In 1965 the U.S. Department of Labor, Office of Planning and Research, issued a report titled *The Negro Family: The Case for National Action*. Daniel Patrick Moynihan, the director of the agency and primary author of the report, borrowed the term "tangle of pathology" from Kenneth B. Clark's *Dark Ghetto: Dilemmas of Social Power* (New York: Harper Torchbooks, 1965) and attributed social pathologies, such as poor school performance and high delinquency, crime, and unemployment rates among blacks, especially black males, to a weak black family structure, that is, single-parent families. The report stated that "at the center of the tangle of pathology is the weakness of the family structure. Once or twice removed, it will be found to be the principal source of most of the aberrant, inadequate, or anti-social behavior that did not establish, but now serves to perpetuate the cycle of poverty and deprivation" (30).

19. Douglas S. Massey and Nancy A. Denton, *American Apartheid: Segregation and the Making of the Underclass* (Cambridge: Harvard University Press, 1993).

20. I should note, however, that Wilson's subsequent studies did include resident interviews and ethnographic observations in Chicago neighborhoods, designed to strengthen his theory of the social isolation of the black ghetto.

21. Mercer Sullivan, *Getting Paid: Youth Crime and Work in the Inner City* (Ithaca: Cornell University Press, 1990).

22. Sudhir Alladi Venkatesh, *American Project: The Rise and Fall of a Modern Ghetto* (Cambridge: Harvard University Press, 2000). There are of course many other examples, including Venkatesh's second book, *Off the Books: The Underground Economy of the Urban Poor* (Cambridge: Harvard University Press, 2006), in which he moved outside the housing project into the surrounding community to examine how the underground economy was inextricably integrated into the economic and social fabric of the community. Wilson himself sent graduate students into poor black communities in Chicago to learn more about the perspectives of residents, which informed his book *When Work Disappears: The World of the New Urban Poor* (New York: Alfred A. Knopf, 1996). Wilson, along with Richard Taub, then launched a large Chicago-based study, in which they examined racial, ethnic, and class conflict in four Chicago neighborhoods in the 1990s. From this work Wilson and Taub published *There Goes the Neighborhood: Racial, Ethnic, and Class Tensions in Four Chicago Neighborhoods and Their Meaning for America* (New York: Alfred A. Knopf, 2006). Moreover, they trained a large number of talented young sociologists on this study, many of whom published their own books on the separate neighborhoods they were studying, including Maria J. Kefelas, *Working-Class Heroes: Protecting Home, Community and Nation in a Chicago Neighborhood* (Berkeley: University of California Press, 2003); Mary Patillo-McCoy, *Black Picket Fences: Privilege and Peril Among the Black Middle Class* (Chicago: University of Chicago Press, 2000); and Reuben A. Buford May, *Talking at Trena's: Everyday Conversations at an African American Tavern* (New York: New York University Press, 2001). Still other important books that address the issues of social and economic isolation, cultural adaptations, and community organization and conflict include Mario Luis Small, *Villa Victoria: The Transformation of Social*

Capital in a Boston Barrio (Chicago: University of Chicago Press, 2004); Mary Patillo, *Black on the Block: The Politics of Race and Class in the City* (Chicago: University of Chicago Press, 2007); and Alford A. Young Jr., *The Minds of Marginalized Black Men: Making Sense of Mobility, Opportunity, and Future Life Chances* (Princeton: Princeton University Press, 2004).

23. Mitchell Duneier, *Slim's Table: Race, Respectability, and Masculinity* (Chicago: University of Chicago Press, 1992); Mitchell Duneier, *Sidewalk* (New York: Farrar, Straus & Giroux, 1999); Elijah Anderson, *Code of the Street: Decency, Violence, and the Moral Life of the Inner City* (New York: W. W. Norton, 1999); Katherine Newman, *No Shame in My Game: The Working Poor in the Inner City* (New York: Alfred A. Knopf and Russell Sage Foundation, 1999); and Katherine Newman, *Chutes and Ladders: Navigating the Low-Wage Labor Market* (Cambridge: Harvard University Press, and New York: Russell Sage Foundation, 2006).

24. In a sense, this set of studies rushed onto the scene like the sociological cavalry to save the public image of the black urban poor that was being run through the public mill historically used to morally excoriate the unworthy poor. In fact, these studies were following sociological protocol that had been established, first, in response to the representations of the poor put forth by Oscar Lewis and the culture of poverty theorists, then by Daniel Patrick Moynihan and his conceptualization of the black family, and more recently by Wilson's characterization of a black urban underclass. Katherine Newman ("No Shame: The View from the Left Bank," *American Journal of Sociology* 107, no. 6 [May 2002]: 1577–99) said specifically, "The genesis of *No Shame* was a confrontation with the central tenets of underclass theory." As such, they entered into what anthropologist Philippe Bourgois (*In Search of Respect: Selling Crack in El Barrio* [New York: Cambridge University Press, 1995], 11) describes as the politics of representation, "where discussions of poverty tend to polarize immediately around race and individual self-worth." Bourgois agreed with liberal sociologists that the urban poor were victims of social and economic marginalization, but was concerned that "countering traditional moralistic biases and middle-class hostility toward the poor should not come at the cost of sanitizing the suffering and destruction that exists on inner-city streets" (ibid., 11–12).

Sociologist Loïc Wacquant ("Scrutinizing the Street: Poverty, Morality, and the Pitfalls of Urban Ethnography," *American Journal of Sociology* 107, no. 6 [May 2002]: 1469–70) shared Bourgois's concern, which became the basis of his vicious critique of Newman's, Duneier's, and Anderson's books, whom he accused of "celebrat[ing] the fundamental goodness—honesty, decency, frugality—of America's urban poor . . . because it resonates with the moral schemata and expectations of its audience, but at the cost of a dangerous suspension of analytic and political judgement." Both Wacquant and Bourgois objected to ethnographic work that engaged the politics of representation and not the politics of neoliberalism. Instead, they saw a symbiotic violent street and prison culture entrenched in neglected urban neighborhoods that had its roots in neoliberal capitalism and structural violence—that is, violence that occurs because of political and economic neglect. Sanitized versions of the urban poor—or versions that attempted to show that most poor racial minorities are decent, law-abiding people—failed to grasp this.

My book has been shaped by this debate. In the spirit of C. Wright Mills, I draw the analytical lines from neoliberal economic capitalism, through the social institutions that organize it, to the immediate milieus of marginalized urban minority communities. My intention is to engage the complexity and messiness of human life—to demonstrate how lives are nested in social structures and to account for processes that lead to individual change—but at the same time to show the ubiquitous power of social structures in reproducing racially and ethnically segmented poverty.

Regardless, I unavoidably enter into the politics of representation. I have known the Rivera brothers for eighteen years and my understanding of their lives is rooted in my intimate connections with them. My intention is to provide an empathetic understanding of their lives, in order to see firsthand how oppression operates, but to do so without minimizing the structural and individual violence that is inextricably embedded in the processes of economic and social marginalization.

25. Jay McLeod, *Ain't No Makin' It: Leveled Aspirations in a Low-Income Neighborhood* (Boulder, Colo.: Westview Press, 1987); Bourgois, *In Search of Respect.*

26. Bourgois, *In Search of Respect,* 12.

27. Edna Acosta-Belén and Carlos E. Santiago, *Puerto Ricans in the United States: A Contemporary Portrait* (Boulder, Colo.: Lynne Rienner, 2006).

28. U.S. Bureau of the Census, Current Population Survey, Annual Social and Economic Supplements, Table 2: "Poverty Status of People by Family Relationship, Race, and Hispanic Origin: 1959 to 2006" (Washington, D.C.: Poverty and Health Statistics Branch, Housing and Household Economic Statistics Division, 2007); and U.S. Bureau of the Census, Current Population Survey; Table 39: "Social and Economic Characteristics of the Hispanic Population, 2006," http://www.census .gov/compendia/statab/tables/08s0039.pdf. The poverty rate for stateside Puerto Ricans (25.3 percent) in 2006 was about one-half the rate for island Puerto Ricans (45.4 percent) but still higher than Mississippi, which had the highest state poverty rate in the United States (21.1 percent). Median household income for stateside Puerto Ricans in 2006 was similar to Mississippi ($33,927 v. $34,479) and about twice as high as median income on the island ($17,621). See U.S. Bureau of the Census, American Community Survey Reports, Tables 2 and 9, "Income, Earnings, and Poverty Data from the 2006 American Community Survey" (Washington, D.C.: Department of Commerce, 2007).

29. Susan S. Baker, *Understanding Mainland Puerto Rican Poverty* (Philadelphia: Temple University Press, 2002). In 2003, 55.8 percent of Puerto Ricans lived in central city areas, higher than the rates for Mexicans, Cubans, and Central or South Americans.

30. Merrill Singer, *The Face of Social Suffering: The Life History of a Street Drug Addict* (Long Grove, Ill.: Waveland, 2006), 11.

31. My entrée into the school was provided by a program evaluation study of a school dropout prevention program that sociologist Michael Lewis and I had completed the previous year in one of Springfield's schools. Working through Springfield's Private Industry Council, I was given access to Commerce High to continue our study of school dropouts by using an ethnographic method. I am grateful to Bill Ward, a member of the Private Industry Council, for helping me to gain access to the school. For more on the evaluation, see Michael Lewis and Timothy Black, *Project ACCES and Drop Out Prevention in Springfield: Assessment of Impact* (Amherst: University of Massachusetts, Social and Demographic Research Institute, 1989).

32. Prior to this, my research had focused on schools and the social marginalization of racial minority youth, which had been the basis of my doctoral dissertation.

33. Wedding godparents are honored guests at a wedding ceremony, a different role from christening godparents.

ONE: "I AM A *JÍBARO*, BUT I GET MY HAIR CUT IN THE CITY"

1. According to José Trías Monge, *Puerto Rico: The Trials of the Oldest Colony in the World* (New Haven: Yale University Press, 1997), in 1899, 15 percent of the island was used for the cultivation of sugarcane, but, by 1930, 44 percent of the land enriched the sugar exploits of absentee finance capital (83). By 1940, sugar accounted for two-thirds of all Puerto Rican exports (Gina M. Pérez, *The Near Northwest Side Story* [Berkeley: University of California Press, 2004], 35). In addition to sugar, capitalist investments also occurred in cigar production and the needle trades. See Edna Acosta-Belén and Carlos E. Santiago, *Puerto Ricans in the United States: A Contemporary Portrait* (Boulder, Colo.: Lynne Rienner, 2006).

2. At the time that Spain ceded Puerto Rico to the United States in 1898, the people of Puerto Rico enjoyed more political autonomy than in some respects they do today. For most of the four hundred years that Spain dominated the island, it was neglectful at best and brutal at worst. In nineteenth-century Spain, internal struggles between royalists and liberals fighting for a representative constitutional government largely defined politics on the island. Independence and reform movements developed as more liberal openings emerged in Spain, resulting in some progressive reform, especially in the latter half of the century. However, when the monarchy was restored in Spain, the brutally repressive arm of its militia often came down on resistant movements, while reforms were often rolled back. Finally, in 1897, Spain granted political autonomy to Puerto Rico, one year before the U.S. takeover. The first U.S. governing act, the Foraker Act, signed in 1900, however, rescinded many of the liberties Spain had granted. As Trías Monge describes: "Puerto Rico lost the right to government by consent of the governed" (*Puerto Rico*, 43). Also see Acosta-Belén and Santiago, *Puerto Ricans in the United States.*

   The colonial spirit of the Foraker Act was reinforced by the U.S. Supreme Court in the *Downes v. Bidwell* case, one of the insular cases that was decided between 1901 and 1905 to determine the relationship between the United States and its new territories. By a one-vote margin, the *Downes* case made Puerto Rico a colony of the United States, a decision that many believed was in violation of the U.S. Constitution, including Supreme Court justice John M. Harlan. In his dissenting opinion, Harlan wrote: "The idea that this country may acquire territories anywhere upon the earth, by conquest or treaty, and hold them as mere colonies or provinces—the people inhabiting them to enjoy only such rights as Congress chooses to accord them—is wholly inconsistent with the spirit and genius, as well as with the works, of the Constitution" (Trías Monge, *Puerto Rico*, 50).

3. Ibid., 83.

4. James L. Dietz, *Economic History of Puerto Rico: Institutional Change and Capitalist Development* (Princeton: Princeton University Press, 1986), 163.

5. See Acosta-Belén and Santiago, *Puerto Ricans in the United States*. Armed struggle was, however, limited to a small group of Puerto Ricans and was not endorsed by most groups fighting for independence.

6. According to several authors, Albizu Campos was tortured and subjected to radiation experiments while he was incarcerated in Atlanta. After a spate of violence on the island and the mainland in 1950, Albizu Campos was again imprisoned, but was pardoned by Muñoz Marín in 1953. He was arrested and incarcerated shortly after nationalists entered the U.S. House of Representatives and opened fire in 1954 (see note below). Albizu Campos remained imprisoned until he was again pardoned by Muñoz Marín in 1965, shortly before he died (ibid.).

7. Public Law 600 passed on July 3, 1950, in the United States, giving Puerto Rico the rights to draft a constitution and elect a government. However, the final bill also gave the U.S. government the right to annul the constitution, veto legislation, and alter the compact unilaterally. Both the House and the Senate reports made clear that "the measure would not change Puerto Rico's fundamental political, social and economic relationship to the United States" (Trías Monge, *Puerto Rico*, 113).

   Public Law 600 was approved on the island by plebiscite vote in 1951, but less than a majority (47 percent) of registered voters affirmed the measure. Groups advocating independence boycotted the election, while a small contingent of nationalists attempted to kill Muñoz Marín and President Harry Truman, and attacked towns throughout Puerto Rico. Later in 1954, nationalists opened fire from the U.S. House of Representatives' spectators gallery, wounding five congressmen. Nonetheless, Muñoz Marín's Popular Democratic Party would remain in power for the next sixteen years.

   Today, Puerto Rico's commonwealth status deprives it of full self-determination, which is in direct violation of United Nations Charter Resolution 1514, signed in 1960, which provided the conditions for decolonization and the rights to self-government. In 1972, the United Nations specifically announced that the colonial relationship between the United States and Puerto Rico needed to end and the island granted the right to full self-determination (Trías Monge, *Puerto Rico;* also see Acosta-Belén and Santiago, *Puerto Ricans in the United States*). In 1993 and 1998, nonbinding referenda were held on the status of the island. Essentially these were votes on whether island residents desired to become a U.S. state or continue their current status, since the option of becoming an independent nation at this point is not considered a viable alternative. In both instances, 46 percent of voters favored the statehood option, falling short of a majority. In 1998, led by the PDP, one-half of voters selected the option "none of the above," protesting the way in which Governor Pedro Rosselló, a statehood supporter, had conducted the referendum and indicating a dissatisfaction with both the statehood option and the status quo. See Bill Vann, "Puerto Rico's Referendum: A Vote of Social Protest," *World Socialist Website,* http://www.wsws.org/news/1998/dec1998/pr-d22.shtml.

8. To many on the island, Sánchez Vilella is remembered as the man who split the PDP and allowed the opposition party, the New Progressive Party, to take power in 1969.

9. McK Jones supported Muñoz Marín's founding of the Liberal Party in 1932 and traveled to Washington with Muñoz Marín in 1933 to protest the incompetence of U.S.-appointed governor Robert Gore. The Liberal Party consisted of the liberal wing of the old Union Party, made up of *independista* political and economic elites. More militant *independistas* broke from the Union Party in 1922 and established the Nationalist Party. In the 1932 election, both the Liberals and the Nationalists ran on independence platforms. However, when the Liberal Party evolved into the Popular Democratic Party in 1940, they dropped their call for independence and instead adopted New Deal strategies. See Dietz, *Economic History of Puerto Rico;* Trías Monge, *Puerto Rico;* and Juan Flores, *Divided Borders: Essays on Puerto Rican Identity* (Houston: Arte Público Press, University of Houston, 1993).

10. For more on Walter McK Jones and Helen Buchanan, see http://villalba_pr.tripod.com/mcjones.html.

11. Dietz, *Economic History of Puerto Rico,* 101. Also discussed by Dietz, tariff protections that had established European markets ended when Spain ceded the island to the United States and Puerto Rican coffee was never able to compete in the United States with South American varieties. The final blow occurred, so to speak, when hurricanes devastated the coffee crops in 1899, 1928, and 1935. Coffee continued to be produced, but mostly by independent farmers for domestic use.

12. Carmen Teresa Whalen, *From Puerto Rico to Philadelphia: Puerto Rican Workers and Postwar Economics* (Philadelphia: Temple University Press, 2001), 74–75.

13. Ibid., 75. Both the Puerto Rican and U.S. governments promoted labor contracts. In *Divided Borders,* Juan Flores traces this practice back to Puerto Rico governor Arthur F. Yager, who in 1914 proposed planned emigration to the U.S. mainland as a solution to unemployment and overpopulation on the island. In 1947, the Bureau of Migration and Employment was established as an integral part of Operation Bootstrap to promote labor contracts on the mainland. However, as Juan Flores explains, the problem was often described in terms of "overpopulation," which placed the focus more on fertility than economics as the cause. In response, sterilization became a viable strategy that was monitored by the Eugenics Board, which was created in 1937 (Pérez, *The Near Northwest Side Story*); as Whalen (*From Puerto Rico to Philadelphia,* 35) reports, one-third of Puerto Rican women between

the ages of twenty and forty-nine were sterilized by 1965, the highest proportion in the world. Moreover, Puerto Rico was also used by U.S. pharmaceutical companies as a test site for the birth control pill before it was marketed in the United States. See Acosta-Belén and Santiago, *Puerto Ricans in the United States*, 50.

14. Dietz, *Economic History of Puerto Rico*, 124–25.
15. Trías Monge, *Puerto Rico*, 99. Spain's educational neglect of Puerto Rico was apparent when the United States acquired the island in 1898. A secondary school system had not existed on the island until 1882 and there were no universities. Puerto Rico had the highest illiteracy rate in the West Indies, estimated at 83 percent (ibid., 15).
16. As part of the New Deal, FDR's administration also established the Puerto Rico Emergency Relief Administration in 1933 to provide temporary aid to the most destitute. See Acosta-Belén and Santiago, *Puerto Ricans in the United States*.
17. Early governing laws—the Foraker Act and the Jones Act—exempted individuals and corporations making income on the island from paying federal income tax. Further, Section 931 of the IRS tax code exempted "possession corporations"— U.S. corporate subsidiaries conducting most of their business activity within U.S. territories—from U.S. corporate taxes. Then, in 1947, the Puerto Rican commonwealth granted a "tax holiday" to targeted industries that exempted them from paying corporate income taxes on the island through 1959, as long as profits were not repatriated to U.S. parent companies. This was in addition to previously established exemptions on municipal and license taxes, as well as property and excise taxes. In 1954, the corporate tax exemption policy became permanent when the looming 1959 deadline was abolished and a ten-year exemption was granted to firms irrespective of when they began operating on the island. As a consequence, between 1950 and 1963, the number of manufacturing firms on the island grew from 96 to 910 (Francisco L. Rivera-Batiz and Carlos E. Santiago, *Island Paradox: Puerto Rico in the 1990s* [New York: Russell Sage Foundation, 1996], 9). For more on tax policies and their consequences, see Dietz, *Economic History of Puerto Rico;* Pedro Cabán, "Reworking the Colonial Formula: Puerto Rico into the 21st Century," *Radical America* 23, no. 1 (1990): 9–19; Rivera-Batiz and Santiago, *Island Paradox;* and Ronald Fernández, *The Disenchanted Island: Puerto Rico and the United States in the Twentieth Century*, 2nd ed. (Westport, Conn.: Praeger, 1996).
18. The economy grew 8.3 percent in the 1950s and then another 10.8 percent in the 1960s (even though real GDP growth—that is, growth adjusted for price increases—was an average of 5.3 percent per year in the 1950s and 7 percent per year in the 1960s). Per capita GNP more than doubled in the 1950s, and then leaped from $716 in 1960 to $3,470 in 1980, exceeding all Latin American countries except Venezuela. Social indicators reflected these changes as well, as the number of physicians per persons doubled between 1960 and 1980 so that the ratio was one for every 534 people, similar to the ratio on the U.S. mainland; life expectancy jumped from forty-six in 1940 to seventy-three in 1980; and the literacy rate improved to 91 percent in 1976. These figures are taken from Dietz, *Economic History of Puerto Rico*, 245, 307–8.

19. Ibid., 244.
20. Agricultural employment plummeted between 1950 and 1970 from 39 to 8 percent of the workforce as large numbers of Puerto Ricans relocated to urban areas (Whalen, *From Puerto Rico to Philadelphia*, 28). In the 1960s alone, the urban population grew by more than 50 percent, and by 1970, almost 60 percent of the island's population lived in urban areas (Dietz, *Economic History of Puerto Rico*, 282).
21. Whalen, *From Puerto Rico to Philadelphia*, 33.
22. During the 1950s alone, 460,826 people left the island, more than three times as many as had migrated during the 1940s (Dietz, *Economic History of Puerto Rico*, 286). Still, the population on the island continued to grow during this period, which is attributable to a stable birth rate between 1930 to 1950, and a rapid decline in mortality rates. See Acosta-Belén and Santiago, *Puerto Ricans in the United States*.
23. The period of excessive economic growth ended after the 1960s. Rivera-Batiz and Santiago (*Island Paradox*, 8) report that the economy grew, on average, a mere 1.6 percent a year between 1970 and 1990.
24. Carmen Gautier-Mayoral, "The Puerto Rican Socio-Economic 'Model': Its Effect on Present Day Politics and the Plebiscite," *Radical America* 23, no. 1 [1990]: 21–34, reports that "in 1989, 60.8 percent of net income or $10 billion, left the island as payments to U.S. capital, whereas in 1970 only 16 percent of net income was lost to absentee owners" (23). The repatriation of profits was due to policy changes made in 1976 when Section 936 of the IRS Code was amended to allow U.S. subsidiaries operating in Puerto Rico to repatriate profits directly to the mainland. Corporations operating in Puerto Rico were required to pay a 10 percent tollgate tax on repatriated profits that was reduced to as much as 4 percent if profits were left in island banks for twelve to eighteen months, while several manufacturing industries were exempted from paying the tax altogether, including apparel, textiles, and shoe manufacturers. See Cabán, "Reworking the Colonial Formula"; Dietz, *Economic History of Puerto Rico;* and Fernández, *The Disenchanted Island*. This giveaway was too much for even the Reagan administration to swallow. During the early 1980s recession, Section 936 was again revised so that one-half of the income that was reported to the IRS was subject to the U.S. corporate income tax. See Rivera-Batiz and Santiago, *Island Paradox*.
25. James L. Dietz, *Puerto Rico: Negotiating Development and Change* (Boulder, Colo.: Lynne Rienner, 2003).
26. In *Island Paradox*, Rivera-Batiz and Santiago report a decrease in poverty from 60 percent in 1980 to 57 percent in 1990 (76).
27. For sixteen- to nineteen-year-olds, the 1990 unemployment rates were reported at 54 percent for men and 62 percent for women, and for twenty- to twenty-nine-year-olds, 24 percent and 29 percent respectively (Rivera-Batiz and Santiago, *Island Paradox*, 5–6). Further, the percentage of people either unemployed or totally removed from the labor force increased from 40 to 53 percent between 1980 and 1990 (Dietz, *Puerto Rico*, 164). Dietz also illustrates that successful improvements in education have not paid off within the restructured economy. He reports that the percentage of U.S. families headed by a householder with a high school

diploma living below the poverty line in 1980 was 6 percent and with a college degree 3 percent. In Puerto Rico, almost one-half (48 percent) of families headed by a householder with a high school diploma did not earn enough to raise them above the poverty line, while slightly more than one-quarter (26 percent) of college-educated-headed families remained in poverty (165). Finally, despite efforts to increase private sector jobs, the largest job growth during the 1970s and 1980s occurred within the public sector, which by 1986 employed 23 percent of the total workforce on the island (Fernández, *The Disenchanted Island*, 249).

28. Cabán, "Reworking the Colonial Formula." Dietz (*Puerto Rico*, 161, 166) shows that public transfers accounted for around 20 percent of GNP each year after 1980. Further, he demonstrates that reductions in poverty after 1980 are attributable to public transfers rather than improvements to the economy.

29. See Trías Monge, *Puerto Rico*.

30. Community is derived from the land, or as Jorge Duany explains, the native land is seen as "the source of all moral values and the imperial power as the root of all evil." Duany, *The Puerto Rican Nation on the Move: Identities on the Island and in the United States* (Chapel Hill: University of North Carolina Press, 2002), 19.

31. Pérez, *The Near Northwest Side Story*, 55–58. Also see Arlene Dávila, *Sponsored Identities: Cultural Politics in Puerto Rico* (Philadelphia: Temple University Press, 1997).

32. Philippe Bourgois makes a similar point in his book *In Search of Respect: Selling Crack in El Barrio* (New York: Cambridge University Press, 1995).

33. The term "patrol the borders" is taken from Michelle Fine and Lois Weiss, *The Unknown City: The Lives of Poor and Working-Class Young Adults* (Boston: Beacon, 1998).

34. Migrants to Puerto Rico from the mainland also included Puerto Ricans born on the mainland. See Rivera-Batiz and Santiago, *Island Paradox*.

35. Rivera-Batiz and Santiago report in *Island Paradox* that 26 percent of all *native-born* Puerto Ricans lived on the U.S. mainland in 1990 (17). According to Acosta-Belén and Santiago in *Puerto Ricans in the United States*, of the 3.4 million Puerto Ricans residing on the mainland in 2000, only 42 percent were born on the island (83). Other metaphors have been used to describe these patterns of migration and return migration, including "the commuter nation," "the revolving door," and "the air bus" (*guagua aérea*), coined by writer Luis Rafael Sánchez (Acosta-Belén and Santiago, *Puerto Ricans in the United States*, 2–3).

36. By 1960, approximately two-thirds of Puerto Ricans residing on the mainland lived in New York City, where most were hired as a source of cheap labor in garment factories and assembly plants—or as Clara Rodríguez put it, "New York's claim to be the garment capital of the world rested upon Puerto Rican shoulders." Clara Rodríguez, *Puerto Ricans Born in the U.S.A.* (Boston: Unwin Hyman, 1989), 99. Most of the Puerto Rican garment factory workers were women, following the pathways of Jewish and East European women before them, even though as Acosta-Belén and Santiago point out (*Puerto Ricans in the United States*, 55), most Puerto Rican garment workers found it difficult to gain membership in the International Ladies' Garment Workers' Union.

37. Marixsa Alicea, " 'A Chambered Nautilus': The Contradictory Nature of Puerto Rican Women's Role in the Social Construction of a Transnational Community," *Gender and Society* 11, no. 5 (1989): 597–626; and Dávila, *Sponsored Identities.*

38. Duany, *The Puerto Rican Nation on the Move,* however, goes on to argue that this cultural identity—of the *jíbaro* from the highlands—embraces the experiences of a light-skinned segment of the population hailing from the rural center of the island whose history fails to give voice to the experiences of many other Puerto Ricans, such as black Puerto Ricans, the urban working and professional classes, women, and gays and lesbians (22). Similarly, Acosta-Belén and Santiago, *Puerto Ricans in the United States,* describe racism on the island as being "camouflaged" and, drawing on the title of an article written by Samuel Betances, assert that Puerto Ricans suffer from "the prejudice of having no prejudice" (17).

39. Marvette Pérez, "La 'Guagua Aérea': Política, Estatu, Nacionalismo y Ciudadanía en Puerto Rico," in Daniel Mato, Maritza Montero, and Emanuele Amodio, eds., *América Latina en Tiempos de Globalización: Procesos Culturales y Transformaciones Sociopolíticas* (Caracas: CRESALC, 1996), 192, quoted in Duany, *The Puerto Rican Nation on the Move,* 29.

40. Duany, *The Puerto Rican Nation on the Move,* 31–32. See also Flores, *Divided Borders.* For more recent ethnographic studies on the negotiation of transnational identities within Puerto Rican communities, see Elizabeth M. Armanda, *Emotional Bridges to Puerto Rico: Migration, Return Migration, and the Struggles of Incorporation* (Lanham, Md.: Rowan & Littlefield, 2007); and Pérez, *The Near Northwest Side Story.*

41. Brent Staples, "Yonkers Shows How Not to Desegregate a School District," *New York Times,* 18 January 2002, A22.

42. This turned out to be a much easier goal to accomplish than the housing desegregation order, which required scattered-site housing to be built on the white east side. See Rodríguez, *Puerto Ricans Born in the U.S.A.* Also see Lisa Belkin's book *Show Me a Hero* (New York: Little, Brown, 1999), in which she vividly portrays the fierce white resistance to Judge Sand's housing order and the tragedy that followed as Mayor Nicholas Wasicsko attempted to implement the order. The struggle is seen through the lives of several characters in Belkin's book and displays the moral agony that remains so central to racial politics in America.

43. Most Puerto Ricans in the United States made their homes in either Brooklyn or the South Bronx in the 1970s. These boroughs alone accounted for more than 80 percent of all housing units that were eliminated in the United States in the 1970s due to housing destruction and abandonment. See Arthur Yong and F. Hohn Devaney, *Sheltering Americans: New Directions of Growth and Change* (Washington, D.C.: U.S. Census Bureau, 1982); and Rodríguez, *Puerto Ricans Born in the U.S.A.*

44. Staples, "Yonkers Shows How Not to Desegregate a School District," 18.

45. *United States v. City of Yonkers,* No. 80 CIV. 6761(LBS), 1989 WL 88698 (S.D.N.Y. Aug. 1, 1989), appeal dismissed, 893 F.2d 498 (2d Cir. 1990); *United States v. City of Yonkers,* No. 80 CIV. 6761(LBS), 1992 WL 176953 (S.D.N.Y. July 10, 1992).

46. The phrase "places and spaces make races" was inspired by Carlo Rotella, who in

his book *Good with Their Hands: Boxers, Bluesmen, and Other Characters from the Rust Belt* (Berkeley: University of California Press, 2002) writes about how the filming of urban chase scenes in cinema provides an "implicit account of the city and its history," and about how 1971's *The French Connection* was emblematic of a series of films that portrayed the deterioration of the urban ghetto. The phrase he uses to describe this is "chases in spaces make places" (119).

TWO: THE LOST GENERATION

1. One of the informants in Jay Demerath and Rhys Williams's study of religion and politics in Springfield explained that Dimauro's election was possible because there were no viable Irish candidates at the time, but also quipped that "it didn't hurt that his wife was Irish." N. J. Demerath III and Rhys H. Williams, *A Bridging of Faiths: Religion and Politics in a New England City* (Princeton: Princeton University Press, 2002), 65.

2. Median family income in Forest Park was nearly three times greater than in Brightwood— $18,185 compared to $6,838. These data were reported by the Springfield *Union News* in 1988, taken from Springfield Planning Department documents and the 1980 U.S. Census, and are presented in Demerath and Williams, *A Bridging of Faiths,* 175.

3. Mark Jaffee, "Puerto Rican Population Doubles," *Sunday Republican* (Springfield, Mass.), 8 September 1974, 16.

4. Francisco L. Rivera-Batiz and Carlos E. Santiago, *Island Paradox: Puerto Rico in the 1990s* (New York: Russell Sage Foundation, 1996), 139. They document that in 1980, over one-half of all Puerto Ricans resided in New York City, Chicago, Philadelphia, or Newark. By 1990, this figure had dropped to 41 percent as Puerto Ricans migrated to smaller cities like Springfield (133–35).

5. Information taken from Census CD (New Brunswick, N.J.: GeoLytics, Inc., 1996). Citing U.S. Census data, Edna Acosta-Belén and Carlos Santiago report that 56 percent of Puerto Ricans living in the Springfield Metropolitan Statistical Area in 1990 lived below the poverty line (*Puerto Ricans in the United States: A Contemporary Portrait* [Boulder, Colo.: Lynne Rienner, 2006], 137).

6. Robert Forrant, "Roots of Connecticut River Deindustrialization: The Springfield American Bosch Plant, 1940–1975," *Historical Journal of Massachusetts* (Winter 2003). Robert Forrant is both an insider and outsider of Springfield's industrial past—he worked as a machinist at the American Bosch plant before becoming a historian and writing extensively about the rise and decline of the Connecticut River Valley's industrial legacy. My historical understanding of Springfield is much indebted to his scholarship.

7. The nickname "Industrial Beehive" is derived from a four-volume history of industrial development in Massachusetts written by Orra L. Stone and published in 1930. The title of Chapter 26 in the first volume is "Springfield: The Industrial Beehive of Massachusetts and the Habitat of Almost Four Hundred Manufacturing Enterprises." Orra L. Stone, *History of Massachusetts Industries: Their Inception, Growth and Success* (Boston: S. J. Clarke, 1930).

8. Robert Forrant, "Greater Springfield Massachusetts Deindustrialization: Staggering Job Loss and Grinding Decline," *New England Journal of Public Policy* 20, no. 2 (2005): 67–88. See also Michael Best and Robert Forrant, "Community-Based Careers and Economic Virtue: Arming, Disarming and Rearming the Springfield, Western Massachusetts Metalworking Region," in Michael B. Arthur and Denise M. Rosseau, eds., *The Boundaryless Career: A New Employment Principle for a New Organizational Era* (New York: Oxford University Press, 1996), 314–30.

9. The roots of Springfield's manufacturing legacy can be traced back to the Revolutionary War when General Henry Knox and company transported a cannon through Springfield en route to Boston. Noting the desirable location of Springfield, Knox and George Washington recommended in 1777 that the federal arsenal be located here. On the eve of the Civil War, Springfield was already home to seventy-three machine shops (Forrant, "Greater Springfield Massachusetts Deindustrialization," 75). The war increased gun manufacturing at the armory and enhanced the reputations of private companies in Springfield, like Smith & Wesson. After the war, the metalworking industry in Springfield produced the machinery that gave birth to New England's nineteenth-century manufacturing legacy in textiles, jewelry, furniture, typewriters, bicycles, paper, and shoes. In the early twentieth century, Springfield became home to the nation's first gasoline-powered automobile factory and first motorcycle manufacturing company—the Stevens-Duryea Car Company and the Indian Motorcycle Company—as well as to prominent foreign companies like Rolls-Royce and Bosch Magneto. Springfield's economy was not limited to only industrial invention. The Merriam-Webster dictionary can trace its roots back to Springfield, as can the popular magazine *Good Housekeeping*, and prominent insurance companies also thrived in Springfield as far back as the nineteenth century, including Mass Mutual Life Insurance. In keeping with its reputation for invention—and closer to my own heart—Springfield is also where James Naismith created the game of basketball in 1891. Forrant, "Roots of Connecticut River Deindustrialization."

10. Robert Forrant, "Too Many Bends in the River: The Decline of the Connecticut River Valley Machine Tool Industry, 1950–2002," *Journal of Industrial History* 5, no. 2 (2002): 75.

11. German Jews migrated mostly after the collapse of the March Revolution in Germany in 1848 and the harsh counterrevolution of 1850. See James A. Gelin, *Starting Over: The Formation of the Jewish Community of Springfield, Massachusetts, 1840–1905* (Lanham, Md.: University Press of America, 1984).

12. Forrant, "Roots of Connecticut River Deindustrialization."

13. The new century began auspiciously in Springfield when William P. Hayes, a Democrat, was elected as the first Irish Catholic mayor in the city in 1899. Still, Yankee Republicans remained in control of city politics for several more decades. Throughout New England, the 1928 presidential campaign of prominent Catholic Al Smith marked the turning of the tide in ethnic politics and the rise of the Irish within the Democratic Party. In 1932 in Springfield, Catholic Democrats won

seven of the eight seats on the City Council and shared power with an "Irish-friendly" mayor. By the 1950s, Catholics in Springfield, led by the Irish, had created the foundation for machine politics. See Demerath and Williams, *A Bridging of Faiths.*

14. The Irish stranglehold on the city seemed to have changed in the 1990s. In 1996, Italian Michael Albano was elected mayor. Albano's coalition reached a wider ethnic population that included Puerto Ricans. The first Puerto Rican to ever sit on the City Council, José Tosado, was the first runner-up in the 2001 election, but was selected to the City Council when one of the council members resigned to become election commissioner. In an interview I conducted with a local political activist who asked to remain anonymous, she strongly stated that Albano "would not have gotten elected without people of color." However, in 2004 the city collapsed into near bankruptcy and was placed into state receivership and overseen by the state-appointed Finance Control Board. Two years later the city resurrected former Irish stalwart Charles Ryan, who had served as mayor of Springfield in the 1960s, returning the mayor's office to a member the "old Irish guard."

15. The new city charter, referred to as the Plan A Charter, was voted in by referendum in 1959 and implemented in the 1960 election of the mayor and City Council, who took office in 1961 (Demerath and Williams, *A Bridging of Faiths,* 63–64).

16. The shifting focus from the neighborhoods to the downtown business community was particularly noticeable as federal grants for urban renewal were commandeered by political and economic elites to build new towering office buildings downtown while the neighborhoods screamed about resource drain.

17. Even though the elections were nonpartisan, by the 1960s, city politics in Springfield were controlled by the Democratic Party. For all intents and purposes, it had become a one-party town.

18. One black pastor, in Demerath and Williams, *A Bridging of Faiths,* put it this way: "there's no difference between New England's indigenous blacks and whites. They hold their 'Yankeeism' in common, and both tend to have an insider's viewpoint" (178).

19. Demerath and Williams in *A Bridging of Faiths* tell the story about a group of black clergy referred to as the Covenant that did attempt to rock the boat in the 1980s by refusing to back an established black candidate for office, by requesting an audit of the city's use of federal funds, and by demanding economic development in a poor black area of the city. Most of the members of this group were relative newcomers, but despite their moral legitimacy as clergy, their success was ultimately curtailed by the maneuvering of the white power structure and the lack of support from the black middle class.

20. Due to the lack of Spanish-speaking census workers, early census counts were poorly conducted and estimates among different groups in Springfield varied considerably.

21. The survey was conducted by the Forest Park Civic Association. See Lee Ham-

mel, "Spanish-American Families Said to Pay More Rent," *Union News* (Springfield, Mass.), 8 August 1969.

22. Nikki Finke, "Hispanics Here Find Jobs Too Hard to Locate," Springfield *Daily News,* 2 February 1977, 1, 9.

23. Jaffee, "Puerto Rican Population Doubles," 16.

24. "101 White Children in Riverview Apartments," *Union News* (Springfield, Mass.), 4 July 1964.

25. "NAACP to Take School Protest to U.S. Agency," *Union News* (Springfield, Mass.), 4 June 1964.

26. Information acquired from the Springfield Public School Department, Springfield, Massachusetts.

27. Carol Schultz, "Fenton Should Apologize," Springfield *Daily News,* 1 May 1975, 12C.

28. "Chief's 'Communist' Claims Disputed," *Union News* (Springfield, Mass.), 24 April 1975.

29. Finke, "Hispanics Here Find Jobs Too Hard to Locate," 1, 9.

30. Robert Forrant and Erin Flyn, "Seizing Agglomeration's Potential: The Greater Springfield Massachusetts Metalworking Sector in Transition, 1986–1996," *Regional Studies* 32, no. 3 (1998): 209–22.

31. Jaffee, "Puerto Rican Population Doubles," 16.

32. The study, released in October 1978, was commissioned by the Spanish American Union and designed by University of Massachusetts sociologist Peter Rossi. See Penny Filosi, "Demographic Study of Hispanics Reveals Economic, Educational Gaps," *Union News* (Springfield, Mass.), 31 October 1978, 13, 19.

33. Ibid.

34. Forrant, "Greater Springfield Massachusetts Deindustrialization."

35. Jonathon Tilone, "Commission Warned of a 'Lost Generation' of Hispanics," *Union News* (Springfield, Mass.), 18 May 1984, 11.

36. The Mill River, which is just north of the row houses, marks the neighborhood boundary, but the neighborhood boundary and the census tract boundary are not the same in this area. The street the Riveras lived on is included in a census tract that extends from the Six Corners neighborhood, which is demographically similar to the residents living on the Riveras' street in the 1980s (36 percent Latino, 31 percent black, 40 percent below the poverty line).

37. Marisa Giannetti, "Area Hispanics Caught Between Two Worlds," Springfield *Republican,* 8 March 1987, B1.

38. Michelle Fine, *Framing Dropouts: Notes on the Politics of an Urban Public High School* (Albany: State University of New York Press, 1991), 33.

39. Richard Sennett and Jonathan Cobb, *The Hidden Injuries of Class* (New York: W. W. Norton, 1972).

40. The middle schools in Springfield included the ninth grade until the late 1990s, when the policy was changed.

41. Information acquired from the Springfield Public School Department, Springfield, Massachusetts.

42. Nilda Flores-González, *School Kids/Street Kids: Identity Development in Latino Students* (New York: Teachers College Press, 2002), 12.

THREE: BILINGUAL EDUCATION AND THE SCHOOL DROPOUT

1. Pat Delo, "City's Bilingual Plan Shows Way for Hispanics," *Daily News* (Springfield, Mass.), 31 May 1977, 1, 3. The public schools in New York did not provide transitional bilingual classes at the time, but only an English as a Second Language class. All other subjects were taught in English.

2. I draw extensively from Carlos J. Ovando, "Bilingual Education in the United States: Historical Development and Current Issues," *Bilingual Research Journal* 27, no. 1 (2003): 1–24, to characterize the U.S. history of bilingual education. These policies varied across states in the nineteenth century. In 1900, approximately 4 percent of all elementary school students were receiving some instruction in German, mostly in Midwestern states. Still, as early as 1889, English-only school laws had been passed in the heavily German populated states of Illinois and Wisconsin. Anti-Semitic and anti-Catholic reactions toward Eastern and Southern European immigrants and "cultural cleansing" practices on Indian reservations prompted more coercive forms of assimilation in the early twentieth century. By the end of World War I, most school districts had eliminated German foreign language programs altogether.

   First- and second-generation European immigrant groups largely embraced the Americanization movement, especially after World War II, when economic opportunities reshaped the labor force and paved the way for class mobility. European ethnic groups shed their ethnicity by anglicizing names, adopting white racial identities that redefined their privileges and social status, and by endorsing English language as a marker of citizenship. As ethnicity gave way to whiteness, legitimate questions about the educational efficacy of English immersion strategies were subverted. English immersion became inseparable from the Americanization movement and, as such, became an integral part of white ethnic moral tales of success. Meanwhile, immigrant families who became victims of inflexible English language policies in the public schools were largely invisible as they were absorbed by burgeoning manufacturing industries where entry-level work for a lower-educated population flourished throughout much of the first half of the twentieth century. English immersion programs—popularly referred to as the "sink or swim" method—remained dominant during the assimilationist era reaching into the 1960s.

3. For more on the opposition to bilingual education, see Rosalie Pedalino Porter, *Forked Tongue: The Politics of Bilingual Education* (New York: Basic Books, 1990); Rosalie Pedalino Porter, "The Case Against Bilingual Education," *Atlantic Monthly* 281, no. 5 (1998): 28; Christine H. Rossell, "Nothing Matters? A Critique of the Ramírez et al. Longitudinal Study of Instructional Programs for Language-Minority Children," *Bilingual Research Journal* 16, nos. 1 & 2 (1992): 159–86; Christine H. Rossell and Keith Baker, "The Effectiveness of Bilingual Research," *Research in the Teaching of English*, 30 (1996): 7–74; Keith Baker, "Structured

English Immersion: Breakthrough in Teaching Limited-English-Proficient Students," *Phi Delta Kappan* (November 1998): 199–204; B. J. Roche, "Lost in Translation: Will the Fight Brewing over Bilingual Education Be the Salvation of Spanish-Speaking Students?," *Commonwealth Magazine* (2002), http://www.massinc.org/index.php?id=356&pub_id=1186; and Laura Pappano, "Sink or Swim: Immersion Is Now the Way Non-English-Speaking Students Are Taught. But Are They Learning the Language—Or Other Subjects—Any Better?," *Commonwealth Magazine* (2006), http://www.massinc.org/index.php?id=497&pub_id=1795.

4. The difference between these two approaches is that TBE programs provide Spanish instruction in all classes while students are being transitioned into mainstream courses. In ESL programs, like the one the Rivera brothers attended in Yonkers, students learn English in an isolated class—an ESL class—but all other classes they attend are taught in English (math, science, history, and so on). The latter is more consistent with the English immersion approach.

5. Wayne P. Thomas and Virginia P. Collier, "A National Study of School Effectiveness for Language Minority Students' Long-Term Academic Achievement" (Santa Cruz: University of California, Center for Research on Education, Research, and Diversity, 2002).

6. Interestingly, after the launching of Sputnik in 1957, the U.S. government established a national defense agenda that increased funding for foreign language programs in U.S. schools, but these funds targeted English-speaking students. The Cuban program evoked debates pertaining to immigrant language educational strategies that had been all but buried in the earlier part of the twentieth century. Ovando, "Bilingual Education in the United States."

7. Ibid.

8. Ibid.

9. Thomas and Collier have assessed bilingual programs for more than two decades in twenty-three different school districts spanning fifteen states. They are supportive of both one-way and two-way language enrichment programs. The one-way model differs in that the target population is a specific ethnic group with differing levels of proficiency in the first and second languages. These programs are especially appropriate in border areas where school districts are ethnically concentrated—e.g., Mexican students along the southern U.S. border, French students along the northern border, or American Indian students in reservation areas. These students learn both languages simultaneously in all subjects and their varying levels of proficiency at the time of school entry provide an atmosphere of mutual support, without preferencing one language over the other. Two-way language programs adopt a similar philosophy, only English-speaking students are integrated with English Language Learners (ELLs) toward the same objectives. See Virginia P. Collier and Wayne P. Thomas, "The Astounding Effectiveness of Dual Language for All," *NABE Journal of Research and Practice* 2, no. 1 (Winter 2004): 1–20.

In 2002, Thomas and Collier issued "A National Study of School Effectiveness for Language Minority Students," a report on a sixteen-year longitudinal study of ELLs entering kindergarten or first grade with little to no proficiency in English in five school systems in three different areas of the country—northern Maine; Houston, Texas; and Salem, Oregon. The authors concluded that one-way and two-way developmental bilingual and dual language immersion programs were the only programs that assisted students in reaching and maintaining the fiftieth percentile on national standardized reading tests. These programs also had the fewest dropouts.

Students in ESL content classes did not fare well. These students had received ESL instruction for two to three years before being mainstreamed into the English curriculum. Reading scores for these eleventh graders averaged at the twenty-third percentile. Students in TBE, Transitional Bilingual Education programs like the one in Springfield that emphasized mainstreaming students usually within three years, also did not fare well when compared to developmental or bilingual immersion programs.

Thomas and Collier emphasized in their report that ELLs are only likely to excel if they receive quality instruction in their *first language*, since high academic achievement in their first language is the best predictor of student achievement in a second language.

10. See Donna Christian, "Two-Way Immersion Education: Students Learning Through Two Languages," *Modern Language Journal* 80, no. 1 (1996): 66–76, for a summary of the research literature in the late 1980s and first half of the 1990s. Christian concludes that two-way immersion programs "promise to expand our nation's language resources by conserving the language skills minority students bring with them and by adding another language to the repertoire of English-speaking students. Finally they offer the hope of improving relationships between majority and minority groups by enhancing crosscultural understanding and appreciation." See also Jim Cummins, "Beyond Adversarial Discourse: Searching for Common Ground in the Education of Bilingual Students," in C. J. Ovando and P. McLaren, eds., *The Politics of Multiculturalism and Bilingual Education: Students and Teachers Caught in the Cross Fire* (Boston: McGraw-Hill, 2000), 126–47; Stephen D. Krashen, *Under Attack: The Case Against Bilingual Education* (Culver City, Calif.: Language Education Associates, 1996); James Crawford, *At War with Diversity: U.S. Language Policy in an Age of Anxiety* (Buffalo: Multilingual Matters, 2000); and R. R. Rumbault, "The New Californians: Comparative Research Findings on the Educational Progress of Immigrant Children," in R. Rumbaut and W. Cornelius, eds., *California's Immigrant Children* (San Diego: University of California, Center for U.S.-Mexican Studies, 1995), 17–69. For a summary of studies examining school dropouts among ELLs, see Stephen D. Krashen, *Condemned Without a Trial: Bogus Arguments Against Bilingual Education* (Portsmouth, N.H.: Heinemann, 1999).

11. Today, few dual language programs exist and even TBE programs are under fire

as the English-only movement has reemerged, which has occurred historically in every period of heavy immigration. California eliminated its transitional bilingual programs in 1998, when millionaire Ronald Unz led the "English for the Children" campaign that replaced bilingual programs with short-term English language learning programs. More recently, the California Board of Education eliminated its bilingual and cross-cultural language credentials for teachers, which provided training in how to constructively work with non-English-speaking students in making the transition to an English curriculum. The irony is, as Susan Katz and Herbert Kohl ("Banishing Bilingualism," *The Nation* 9 [December 2002], 7) point out, "when 45 percent of the students in California public schools will [soon] be living in non-English-speaking homes, these credentials will be phased out," essentially leaving scores of teachers unprepared to work effectively with the growing non-English student body. Unz's movement has been busy in other states as well. In 2002, Massachusetts joined two other states to pass an English-learning referendum, which passed by a three to one margin. English Language Learners in Massachusetts are now provided "sheltered English Immersion" where they are exposed to intensive English language classes for one year before being mainstreamed into the English language curriculum.

At the federal level, the Bilingual Education Act of 1968, the cornerstone of linguistic rights for non-English-speaking populations, was eliminated in 2001 and replaced by the No Child Left Behind legislation, which only provides funds for English acquisition efforts. As Katz and Kohl put it, "the words 'bilingual education' have been excised from the federal government's lexicon."

12. The 1965 Immigration Act eliminated the quota system established in 1924 that had privileged white European immigrant groups, and thereby opened the floodgates to Asian and Latin American immigrants, producing an era of immigration not seen in the United States since the turn of the twentieth century. Large-scale immigration together with the civil rights movement created the momentum to reopen the case for bilingual education in the public schools. In 1968 the Bilingual Education Act was passed (Title VII of the Elementary and Secondary Education Act).

At stake was whether bilingual education programs would value minority languages and build educational literacy programs around the development of both minority and English languages as the Cubans had done in Florida, or whether a minority language would be viewed as a problem or a barrier to educational achievement that needed to be dispensed with in the cultivation of English as rapidly as possible. A compromise emerged. The "sink or swim" paradigm of the earlier era was rejected while the education theory that stressed the importance of providing language and educational instruction in the first language as a means of becoming literate in a second language became widely accepted. Still, the primary goal of bilingual programs was English acquisition rather than educational literacy, and instruction in a first language was used only as a means for learning English and transitioning students into the mainstream English-speaking curriculum. In this regard, bilingual education defined minority languages as deficits—

as something to be overcome—rather than a resource to be developed. Programs became transitional and indistinguishable from remedial educational strategies, particularly as these programs targeted poor Puerto Rican and Mexican families. Embracing this compromise, Massachusetts passed the first Transitional Bilingual Education policy in 1971 and other states followed suit. See James Crawford, *Bilingual Education: History, Politics, Theory, and Practice*, 4th ed. (Los Angeles: Bilingual Education Services, 1995).

Despite these legislative victories, policy implementation was poorly funded and there was little oversight. Programs developed unevenly throughout the United States and the bilingual education movement turned to the courts. The 1971 *Lau v. Nichols* case provided the legal pillar to advance the movement. The Supreme Court in *Lau* found that students sitting in classes unable to comprehend or participate in educational practices were being denied their equal educational opportunity. However, as Sandra Del Valle ("Bilingual Education for Puerto Ricans in New York City: From Hope to Compromise," *Harvard Educational Review* 68, no. 2 [Summer 1998]: 193–217) pointed out, *Lau* did not interpret this educational neglect in terms of the Equal Protection Clause of the Fourteenth Amendment, which would have raised the case to the status of 1954's *Brown v. Board of Education of Topeka*, which found racially segregated public schools in violation of the right of racial minorities to an equal education. Instead the case was decided on the basis of Title VII of the 1964 Civil Rights Act, which precluded discrimination on the basis of national origin and defined equal education as providing access to English language instruction. In so doing, the right to an equal education was surrendered to the right to English language instruction, and minority languages were once again defined as a deficit that school districts were obliged to assist students in overcoming. While *Lau* did not mandate any specific remedies, it was nonetheless used by the courts to impose "consent agreements" on nearly five hundred school districts, mostly in the Southwest, between 1975 and 1981. These "Lau plans" laid the groundwork for a court-ordered requirement that the Carter administration standardize *Lau* remedies, but they also required school districts to demonstrate effectiveness.

Growing resistance to bilingual education became part of the white political backlash that was mounting in the late 1970s toward civil rights legislation and the War on Poverty. Critiques of bilingual education invoked white immigrant mythologies of "self-made success" that stemmed from the earlier assimilationist period, while high Latino dropout rates and poor test scores opened the door to reform. Soon after Ronald Reagan's election as president, he dispensed with the *Lau* remedies developed at the end of President Carter's term, while Secretary of Education William Bennett authorized English immersion programs as a legitimate option for school districts to adopt.

13. José Trías Monge, *Puerto Rico: The Trials of the Oldest Colony in the World* (New Haven: Yale University Press, 1997), 15.

14. Penny Filosi, "Demographic Study of Hispanics Reveals Economic, Educational Gaps," *Union News* (Springfield, Mass.), 31 October 1978.

15. U.S. Bureau of the Census, 1990 Census of Population and Housing, Summary Tape File 3: "Population: School Enrollment and Educational Attainment."
16. Trías Monge, *Puerto Rico,* 120.
17. Sonia Nieto, "Puerto Rican Students in U.S. Schools: A Brief History," in Sonia Nieto, ed., *Puerto Rican Students in U.S. Schools* (Mahwah, N.J.: Lawrence Erlbaum, 2000), 20.
18. Project ACCES was a public-private initiative established under the Job Training Partnership Act (JTPA), the law, co-authored by Senators Edward Kennedy and Dan Quayle in 1982, that replaced the Comprehensive Education Training Act (CETA). The JTPA reflected the priorities of the Reagan administration by increasing the involvement of private industry in publicly funded job training programs.
19. Buffy Spencer, "Jordan Calls for Hispanic on Council," *Daily News* (Springfield, Mass.), 23 July 1982, 13C.
20. Mary Ellen O'Shea, "Good Balance Predicted for High Schools," *Daily News* (Springfield, Mass.), 13.
21. Michael Lewis and Timothy Black, *Project ACCES and Drop Out Prevention in Springfield: Assessment of Impact* (Amherst: University of Massachusetts, Social and Demographic Research Institute, 1989).
22. The policy gave the Springfield schools national recognition. At the time the new rule went into effect, 41 percent of students at Commerce lost eligibility to participate in extracurricular activities. Also, it was revealed that, in 1984, over a quarter of high school graduates in the Springfield public schools maintained a D average.

FOUR: THE TAIL OF THE DRUG TRADE

1. These estimates take into account seizures and additional losses. United Nations Office on Drugs and Crime, *World Drug Report 2005* (Vienna, Austria: UNODC, June 2005), 127.
2. Alfred McCoy reports that by 1975 Mexico was providing 90 percent of heroin to the United States, but that its inferior grade contributed to a decline in the market in the mid-1970s. A precipitous increase in opium production in Afghanistan in the 1970s, in heroin processing in Pakistan, and in the involvement of the Sicilian Mafia as intermediaries meant, according to McCoy, that by 1981 Pakistani laboratories were providing 60 percent of U.S. heroin and a greater share in Europe. Alfred W. McCoy, *The Politics of Heroin: CIA Complicity in the Global Drug Trade* (Chicago: Lawrence Hill, 2003).
3. The cartel's expansion into cocaine processing and distribution occurred with the collapse of the farming and mining economies in Peru and Bolivia and was facilitated by the infrastructure that had already been created by the Colombian marijuana trade. The Medellín Cartel also militantly took control of the cocaine trade from the Cubans in South Florida in 1978, an important port of entry; see Paul B. Stares, *Global Habit: The Drug Problem in a Borderless World* (Washington, D.C.: Brookings Institution, 1996).

4. Stares explains that the increased demand for cocaine in the United States in the early 1980s turned the Medellín Cartel into a sophisticated business "integrating and subcontracting various logistical functions, establishing large-scale processing laboratories, acquiring their own security forces, using advanced technologies for smuggling, and developing sophisticated money-laundering operations" (ibid., 32–33). The U.S. cocaine market also made the careers of some of the most notorious drug warlords, like Pablo Escobar and the Ochoa brothers. However, Stares argues that the U.S.-supported crackdown on the Medellín Cartel, resulting in the incarceration of high-level figures and eventually the death of Escobar, would result in the control of the market shifting to Colombia's Cali Cartel, which by the mid-1990s would control around 80 percent of the world cocaine market.

5. Information taken from a grant proposal submitted by the Springfield Housing Authority on August 8, 1991, for a "Zero Tolerance Program" located in public housing developments. The proposal cites the state's Department of Public Health Food and Drug Laboratory as its source of information. The current Web site for the State Laboratory Institute is http://www.mass.gov/dph/bls/.

6. See *2001 Sourcebook of Criminal Justice Statistics*, Table 6.24 (Washington, D.C.: U.S. Department of Justice, Bureau of Justice Statistics, 2002), 495, at http://www.albany.edu/sourcebook/pdf/sb2001/sb2001-section6.pdf.

7. The tests were multiple-choice exams that did not require that he write. His biggest improvement was in number sequencing, an exercise Fausto had never done before the exam. He went from getting none of them correct on the first exam to all but two correct on the second exam.

8. The conversation presented here is based upon field notes that I recorded immediately after the meeting.

9. Carol Stack's book *All Our Kin: Strategies for Survival in a Black Community* (New York: Harper & Row, 1974) is the sociological classic on this topic.

10. Robin Kelley argues that minority street youths transcend the polarity of work and play that is central to working-class lives in a capitalist culture. Working in the underground economy allows for creative forms of playful work, according to Kelley, in which masculinity (and femininity), sexuality, power, and pleasure are creatively produced. See Robin D. G. Kelley, *YO' Mama's disFunktional: Fighting the Culture Wars in Urban America* (Boston: Beacon, 1997).

11. Census CD (New Brunswick, N.J.: GeoLytics Inc., 1996).

12. Joseph T. Howell, *Hard Living on Clay Street: Portraits of Blue Collar Families* (Garden City, N.Y.: Anchor, 1973).

13. Bruce Western cites research showing that drug use surveys of high school seniors have repeatedly shown higher use of illicit drug use among white students, compared to blacks. Similarly, he cites study data from the Drug Abuse Warning Network that indicate whites are two to three times more likely to use emergency room services for drug-related problems than blacks in twenty-one cities. See Bruce Western, *Punishment and Inequality in America* (New York: Russell Sage Foundation, 2006), 47–48.

14. Elijah Anderson, *Code of the Street: Decency, Violence, and the Moral Life of the Inner City* (New York: W. W. Norton, 1999), 33–34.

15. Of course, some of our most valued regulated commodities, such as oil, are secured through geopolitical networks that control and obviate international law and regulatory institutions, and that use violent means to maintain their privileged positions in controlling the extraction, production, and distribution of the resource.

16. Sudhir Venkatesh, *Off the Books: The Underground Economy of the Urban Poor* (Cambridge: Harvard University Press, 2006).

17. In his book *Islands in the Streets: Gangs and American Urban Society* (Berkeley: University of California Press, 1991), Martín Sánchez Jankowski identifies a defiant individualist character among gang members he studied. Jankowski's observation can be applied more broadly to the streets, where a culture of resistance, rooted in a lack of material and social resources, fosters both intense defiance and shrewd individualism. The premium on respect needs to be understood in this context, for it can be acquired only through competitive struggle for limited resources necessary to overcoming material deprivation and the self-loathing discourses of internalized failure. The culturally projected images of success are defiantly individualistic. Having "heart" on the streets requires the courage to embrace this identity in its extreme—to stop at nothing. In Philippe Bourgois's book *In Search of Respect: Selling Crack in El Barrio* (New York: Cambridge University Press, 1995), the author demonstrates how a defiant individualist character is rooted in the colonial identity of rural Puerto Rican culture and subsequently reproduced in an urban street culture of resistance. In Puerto Rico, defiance to U.S. colonial power is symbolized by the *jíbaro,* as discussed earlier, the self-reliant peasant farmer whose integrity is defined through his resistance toward a plantation economy and his honor through patriarchal forms of sacrifice and resilience. In the postindustrial urban economy, defiance is manifested on the street where an emasculated service sector economy is resisted through street culture and the reconstituted urban *jíbaro.* Both Jankowski and Bourgois emphasize the centrality of defiant individualism as it is reproduced through a culture of resistance, and both articulate the challenge that Manny Torres is faced with in organizing his drug business.

18. Manny was later arrested on a domestic violence charge and was then prosecuted for the prior drug arrest, among other charges. He is currently serving a lengthy prison term that was apparently lowered because of his willingness to cooperate with authorities in apprehending others involved in his drug operation.

19. On corporate drug gangs, see Sudhir Alladi Venkatesh, *American Project: The Rise and Fall of a Modern Ghetto* (Cambridge: Harvard University Press, 2000); Steven D. Levitt and Sudhir Alladi Venkatesh, "The Financial Activities of an Urban Street Gang," *Quarterly Journal of Economics* 115, no. 3 (2000): 755–89; and Sudhir Alladi Venkatesh and Steven D. Levitt, "Are We a Family or a Business? History and Disjuncture in the Urban American Street Gang," *Theory and Society* 29, no. 4 (2000): 427–67.

FIVE: THE BLOCK

1. Jonathon Tilone, "Commission Warned of a 'Lost Generation' of Hispanics," *Union News* (Springfield, Mass.), 18 May 1984, 11.

2. Stephanie Kraft, "Warning Signs," *Springfield Advocate,* 22 June 1995, 8–11.

3. Later in the 1990s, another street gang, Ñeta, also organized in Springfield and joined forces with the Latin Kings and La Familia.

4. Julio received assistance from the New England Farm Workers' Council in securing the new job, assistance that was available because he had done farmwork for more that a year at the Connecticut nursery.

5. RICO is the Racketeer Influenced and Corrupt Organizations Act, which is Title IX of the Organized Crime Control Act of 1970. Its intention is "the elimination of the infiltration of organized crime and racketeering into legitimate organizations operating in interstate commerce." S.Rep. No. 617, 91st Cong., 1st Sess. 76 (1969), http://www.usdoj.gov/usao/eousa/foia_reading_room/usam/title9/110mcrm.htm.

6. For a full account of these demographic changes, see Paul A. Jargowsky, *Stunning Progress, Hidden Problems: The Dramatic Decline of Concentrated Poverty in the 1990s* (Washington, D.C.: Brookings Institution, May 2003). See also Paul A. Jargowsky, *Poverty and Place: Ghettos, Barrios and the American City* (New York: Russell Sage Foundation, 1998).

7. *Springfield and Its Neighborhoods* (Springfield, Mass.: Springfield Planning Department, May 1993).

8. These data characterize the census block group where the block was located. The information was taken from the 1990 Census, on Census CD (New Brunswick, N.J.: GeoLytics, Inc., 1996).

9. Paul Willis, *Learning to Labour: How Working Class Kids Get Working Class Jobs* (New York: Columbia University Press, 1977), 29.

10. Sitting in a holding cell in a local jail in Hartford the morning after a group of us had closed down the federal building in protest of the Iraq War, we were confronted by a number of young street men also waiting for their cases to be called. They greatly approved of George W. Bush's sentiments. "We should blow those motherfuckers off the map," one man insisted, or "Nuke the whole fucking country," another one chimed in. And as if to emphasize the masculine world they shared with the president, one of them commented, "What are you guys, a bunch of pussies or something?"

SIX: LEAVING THE STREETS

1. Robert Pollin and Stephanie Luce, *The Living Wage: Building a Fair Economy* (New York: New Press, 1998).

2. From 1969 to 1979, earnings for the bottom one-fifth of wage earners increased 18 percent, while earnings for the top one-fifth increased 22 percent, and for the top 5 percent, 17 percent. See Thomas R. Swartz, "An Editorial Comment: The Working Poor and the Prospect of Welfare Reform 1995 Style," in Thomas R.

Swartz and Kathleen Maas Weigert, eds., *America's Working Poor* (Notre Dame: University of Notre Dame Press, 1995).

3. Richard B. Freeman and Peter Gottschalk, "Introduction," in Richard B. Freeman and Peter Gottschalk, eds., *Generating Jobs: How to Increase Demand for Less-Skilled Workers* (New York: Russell Sage Foundation, 1998), 1.

4. U.S. Department of Labor, Bureau of Labor Statistics, "State and Area Employment, Hours and Earnings," http://data.bls.gov/servlet/SurveyOutputServlet, and "Local Area Unemployment Statistics," http://www.bls.gov/eag/eag.ma _springfield_mn.htm. See also Paul N. Foster, "Summary of a Demographic and Economic Analysis of the City of Springfield" (West Springfield, Mass.: Regional Information Center, Pioneer Valley Planning Commission, September 2006), http://www.springfieldcityhall.com/planning/fileadmin/Planning_files/Market _Study_ppt_v3.pdf.

5. U.S. Department of Labor, Bureau of Labor Statistics, "State and Area Employment, Hours and Earnings," http://data.bls.gov/servlet/SurveyOutputServlet.

6. U.S. Department of Commerce, Bureau of Economic Analysis, Regional Economic Accounts, "Personal Income by Major Source and Earnings by Industry," http://www.bea.gov/regional/reis/. This decline could have been more dramatic if it wasn't for changes made in the metalworking sector in Springfield, whose tradition reaches back to the early 1900s. At the end of the twentieth century, there were still more than 350 small metalworking firms in Springfield. Due to the Machine Action Project, a public-private initiative begun in 1986, and continuing inter-firm organization provided largely by the National Tooling and Machining Association, the metalwork sector of the Springfield economy has held on, even as the manufacturing sector, more broadly, has declined. See Robert Forrant and Erin Flynn, "Seizing the Agglomeration's Potential: The Greater Springfield Massachusetts Metalworking Sector in Transition, 1986–1996," *Regional Studies* 32, no. 3 (1998)."

7. Sheldon Danzinger and Peter Gottschalk, "Hardly Making It: The Increase in Low Earnings and What to Do About It," in Swartz and Weigert, eds., *America's Working Poor.*

8. David Kotz, "Neoliberalism and the U.S. Economic Expansion of the '90s," *Monthly Review* 54, no. 11 (2003): 15–33.

9. Between 1995 and 2000, wages for the average worker rose nearly 10 percent, with wage growth particularly strong for the lowest wage earners. The poorest quintile of households saw an income gain of over 16 percent between 1993 and 1999, which was almost as much as the 17 percent gain that occurred among the richest 5 percent of households. For blacks, the poverty rate in 1999 dropped to a historic low of 23.6 percent and the black unemployment rate fell beneath 10 percent to 7.3 percent for the first time since the Bureau of Labor Statistics began reporting unemployment rates by race in 1972. Meanwhile, unemployment for Hispanics reached a low of 5.7 percent. Of course, white poverty and unemployment were also dropping during this period, reaching 7.4 percent and 3.5 percent, respectively, in 2000. See Heather Boushey and Robert Cherry, "The Severe Implica-

tions of the Economic Downturn on Working Families," *Working USA* 56, no. 2 (2003): 35–54; Doug Henwood, "Money Trickling Down," *Left Business Observer*, 96, no. 4 (2001); and Freeman and Gottschalk, "Introduction," in *Generating Jobs*.

10. The police had rushed through their investigation, had taken Julio and Juan in on charges without taking their statements, and had not searched for a third party to the event for an unbiased perspective on what had occurred. While Julio and Juan lingered in police custody, my now former wife's law firm took the case pro bono. She and I found the third-party witness and secured Julio's and Juan's release. The tragedy in this case was averted—Julio and Juan might have remained in prison for a long time if competent counsel was not provided—but the costs of the Hartford PD's mistake were still considerable, especially for Julio, who lost valuable time in his diesel mechanic's program and eventually dropped out.

11. This is, of course, technically welfare fraud. According to Kathryn Edin and Laura Lein, virtually all welfare-supported families resort to some type of fraud, though usually minor in scope. They do so to maximize self-interest and to make ends meet when state resources are insufficient. In short, welfare fraud is generated by a system that fails to meet the needs of poor families, and thus fraudulent practices such as the one Julio and Clara engaged in are normative—they are part of the system. See Kathryn Edin and Laura Lein, *Making Ends Meet: How Single Mothers Survive Welfare* (New York: Russell Sage Foundation, 1997).

12. The Eno Foundation for Transportation estimated that the total value of trucking services accounted for 4.76 percent of GDP in 1997. In that same year, 2.4 percent (just over three million) of all workers reported "truck driver" as their primary occupation, and trucks pulling at least one trailer or semi-trailer accounted for 12 percent of petroleum consumed. See Steven V. Burks, Kristen Monaco, and Josephine Myers-Kuykindall, "How Many Trucks, How Many Miles: Trends in the Use of Heavy Freight Vehicles in the U.S., from 1977 to 1997," working paper, Trucking Industry Program, February 15, 2004, http://www2.isye.gatech.edu/tip/HowManyTrucks-HowManyMilesForDistribution2-15-04.pdf.

13. My understanding of the trucking industry is greatly indebted to Michael Belzer. Teamster president Jimmy Hoffa decreased the disparity in wages for drivers across the country in the 1950s and 1960s so that regional differences would not undermine union solidarity. The first National Master Freight Agreement was negotiated in 1964 and produced interregional protocols. At its peak in the mid-1970s, it covered between 300,000 and 500,000 workers. See Michael H. Belzer, *Sweatshops on Wheels: Winners and Losers in Trucking Deregulation* (New York: Oxford University Press, 2000).

14. Fly-by-night operators were pawns used by manufacturers and truck dealers to push rates and wages down. Essentially, these drivers acquired a truck on loan and then negotiated rates that were well below costs to undercut the market until they defaulted on the truck loan. See Dorothy Robyn, *Braking the Special Interests: Trucking Deregulation and the Politics of Policy Reform* (Chicago: University of Chicago Press, 1987); and Ellis W. Hawley, *The New Deal and the Problem of Monopoly* (Princeton: Princeton University Press, 1966).

15. The Motor Carrier Act of 1935 divided for-hire carriers into three groups. Common carriers set rates collectively through rate bureaus approved by the ICC; posted tariffs, routes, and schedules for the public; and hauled a wide variety of commodities. Contract carriers hauled similar products but rates were set through for-hire contracts with shippers and mostly consisted of full truckload hauls. Tariffs were not publicly posted and carriers were not liable for the load. Carriers were limited by law to contracting with a maximum of eight shippers. Finally, carriers that hauled specific goods (e.g., newspapers, agricultural goods), that hauled within designated urban commercial zones, and that were intrastate and part of air freight lines were exempted from federal regulation. See Belzer, *Sweatshops on Wheels*.

16. The Motor Carrier Act of 1980 provided easy entry into the industry for new carriers, limited the capacity for carriers to collectively negotiate prices under rate bureaus (which were eventually phased out altogether), eliminated controls on routings, and removed restrictions on the number of shippers that a carrier could contract with as a private carrier. Deregulation of the industry served its purpose of lowering costs and there were many winners as a result. Belzer estimates that 80 percent of the savings passed along to consumers was derived from wage reductions. Large shippers also benefited from "destructive competition" where carriers negotiated rates that were below costs in order to capture market share. These losses were then made up by passing costs along to smaller shippers. Distributors and manufacturers also benefited from lower rates. Of course, there were also losers, particularly carriers and their employees. In 1995, deregulation of the industry was completed when it was extended to intrastate trucking. For more, see Belzer, *Sweatshops on Wheels*.

17. Less Than Truckload (LTL) protocols follow more closely the old system established by the ICC, in which drivers pick up from several different contractors and deliver to terminals where dockworkers and warehouse handlers unload and sort the merchandise for distribution to local vendors. Shipments vary considerably, anywhere from 50 to 48,000 pounds, but average around 1,200 pounds, while a load is likely to be made up of around thirty shipments. See Belzer, *Sweatshops on Wheels;* and Burks, Monaco, and Myers-Kuykindall, "How Many Trucks, How Many Miles."

18. Truckload (TL) shipments range from 10,000 to 48,000 pounds, with an average of 26,000 pounds, and often fill the truck. See Belzer, *Sweatshops on Wheels;* and Burks, Monaco, and Myers-Kuykindall, "How Many Trucks, How Many Miles."

19. Donald V. Harper and James C. Johnson, "The Potential Consequences of Deregulation of Transportation Revisited," *Land Economics* 63, no. 2 (May 1987): 137–46. The authors also state that bankruptcies for intercity carriers were nearly thirteen times greater in 1985 than in 1978.

20. Belzer, *Sweatshops on Wheels*.

21. While declining revenues and increased bankruptcies illustrate the consequences that deregulation has had on carriers, and while declining wages and increased driving hours document the costs to trucking employees, Belzer identifies a third

loser in the mix as well—the public. Market regulation of the industry has increased the need for social regulations or, in other words, public spending on the negative consequences of market regulation. Decreased wages usually paid by the mile and long hours of road time create conditions that can compromise public safety on the roads. According to Belzer, a 1992 study revealed that drivers routinely misreported driving hours in logs, regularly exceeded legal hourly limits, and that one-third reported dozing or falling asleep at the wheel during the thirty days prior to the survey. Similarly, declining working conditions led to more lost workdays between 1992 and 1996 due to occupational illnesses and injuries than any other occupation—a 5 percent increase for drivers compared to 20 percent decreases in other leading occupations. Concerns with public safety have led to a flurry of new social regulations since the industry became market-regulated in the 1980s. These include, but are not limited to, requiring Commercial Driver's Licenses, mandating driver training and safety programs, specifying and enforcing civil and criminal penalties for failure to maintain driving logs, and requiring regular alcohol and drug testing of drivers. The costs of social regulations have increased considerably since the 1980s—drug testing alone was estimated by the Federal Highway Administration to cost $1.6 billion in 1992 when this legislation took effect. As Belzer (*Sweatshops on Wheels,* 73) states, "Economic deregulation may have compromised public safety even as social regulation made it more costly and complicated for carriers to comply with safety rules."

22. Burks, Monaco, and Myers-Kuykindall, "How Many Trucks, How Many Miles."

23. U.S. Department of Labor, Bureau of Labor Statistics, Table 22: Employed Civilians by Detailed Occupation, Sex, Race, and Hispanic Origin, 31, nos. 1–6 (Washington, D.C., January–June 1984), 182; and Table 11: Employed Persons by Detailed Occupation, Sex, Race, and Hispanic Origin, 50, nos. 1–3 (Washington, D.C., January–March 2003), 174. In 2003, the Bureau of Labor Statistics refined their category further to measure "Industrial Truck and Trucker Operators." Hispanics accounted for 29 percent of these drivers. See Table 11: Employed Persons by Detailed Occupation, Sex, Race, and Hispanic or Latino Ethnicity, 51, nos. 1–3 (Washington, D.C., January–March 2004), 214.

24. According to Burks, Monaco, and Myers-Kuykindall ("How Many Trucks, How Many Miles," 11), for-hire trucking firms contracted to haul freight drove 38 percent more in total miles compared to companies that move their own freight (private carriers), but did so with about half as many trucks. They also show that from 1977 to 1997 the proportion of vehicles that for-hire firms used for long hauls nearly doubled, from 32 to 62 percent of their fleets (13).

25. Employees of trucking companies regulated by the Motor Carrier Acts of 1935 and 1980 are exempted from the Fair Labor and Standards Act, which means that rules pertaining to the forty-hour workweek and paid overtime do not apply to employees working for motor carriers, including drivers, mechanics, and platform workers. Belzer estimates that 1.3 million employees are exempted from the FLSA. The Hours-of-Service Rules were revised by the Department of Transportation and took effect in January 2004. But the changes were marginal (e.g., instead of drivers

being able to drive ten hours after being off duty eight hours, they can now drive eleven hours after ten hours of being off duty) and did not institute an overtime pay requirement. See www.fmsca.dot.gov for the specific changes.

26. Chirag Mehta and Nik Theodore, "Paying the Price for Flexibility: Unemployment Insurance and the Temporary Staffing Industry," *Working USA* 56, no. 2 (2002): 84–110.

27. Ibid.

SEVEN: TRANSITIONS

1. Newman defines "high flyers" as workers whose hourly wage increased by an average of at least $1.25 a year (in 2000 dollars) between 1993 and 2000. In her sample, 22 percent met this threshold. However, when she examined a panel of workers from 1995 to 2000, taken from the Survey of Income and Program Participation, and applied the same threshold, the percentage reaching this "high flyer" status was much less (11 percent of men and 13 percent of women). Katherine Newman, *Chutes and Ladders: Navigating the Low-Wage Labor Market* (Cambridge: Harvard University Press, and New York: Russell Sage Foundation, 2006).

2. Philippe Bourgois, *In Search of Respect: Selling Crack in El Barrio* (New York: Cambridge University Press, 1995).

3. Julio and Clara also socialized with Edgar and his wife before they moved to Pennsylvania in 2003. Julio and Edgar's friendship deepened during this time and was organized around work, relationships with their spouses, and fathering. This void was not, however, filled until 2007 when Julio and Clara began to socialize regularly with another couple.

4. Merrill Singer, *The Face of Social Suffering: The Life History of a Street Drug Addict* (Long Grove, Ill.: Waveland, 2006); and Elliott Currie, *Reckoning: Drugs, the Cities, and the American Future* (New York: Hill & Wang, 1993).

5. In *The Unknown City*, Michelle Fine and Lois Weiss note that many of the Latinas in their study were strategic in combining welfare resources with educational and employment opportunities to protect and advance their families. Using a concept from the work of Rina Benmayor, Ana Juarbe, Celia Alvarez, and Blanca Vázquez, *Stories to Live By: Continuity and Change in Three Generations of Puerto Rican Women* (New York: Centro de Estudios Puertorriqueños, 1987), they referred to these women as "resource strategists."

6. Mark Robert Rank, *One Nation, Underprivileged: Why American Poverty Affects Us All* (New York: Oxford University Press, 2004).

7. Ibid., 59.

8. The term "structurally unemployed" refers to the segment of the population that is necessary to hold down wages and inflation in a capitalist economy. In other words, the concept acknowledges that some percentage of the population will need to be unemployed and/or underemployed for the market to profit and endure. Mark Rank has a good discussion of this in his book in which he uses the game of musical chairs to illustrate his point. Ibid., 75–77.

9. Bourgois, *In Search of Respect*.

10. Rank, *One Nation, Underprivileged.*

11. This is a common strategy among landlords to maximize on rental income. Section 8 requires that tenants pay 30 percent of their income toward rent, while the government subsidizes the remainder. Although landlords have to meet housing codes and regulations to be approved for the program, Section 8 is often an appealing option for them because it provides reliable rental income in poor areas and allows landlords to increase the rent to the maximum allowable amount within the area.

12. Thomas M. Shapiro, *The Hidden Cost of Being African American: How Wealth Perpetuates Inequality* (New York: Oxford University Press, 2004).

13. Thomas Shapiro points out that for working-class and poor families, wealth is seen as a form of security, something to fall back on during hard times. He writes, "In our conversations about the power of assets, working-class and asset-poor families dream that assets will give them freedom from a situation, ease a difficulty, relieve a fear, or overcome a hardship. Middle-class and asset-wealthy families see assets as power and freedom to leverage opportunities" (ibid., 35).

14. Ibid. See also Douglas S. Massey and Nancy A. Denton, *American Apartheid: Segregation and the Making of the Underclass* (Cambridge: Harvard University Press, 1993).

15. Rusk defines poor neighborhoods as census tracts in which at least 20 percent of households are poor. David Rusk, *The 'Segregation Tax': The Cost of Racial Segregation to Black Homeowners* (Washington, D.C.: Brookings Institution Center on Urban and Metropolitan Policy, 2001).

16. Ibid. This measure is called the index of dissimilarity. It measures the extent to which racial and ethnic groups are distributed unevenly across a geographical area. If a racial minority population in a metropolitan area is 30 percent, then the index of dissimilarity shows how evenly that population is distributed across neighborhoods—i.e., do 30 percent of racial minorities live in all neighborhoods. The index indicates the percentage of the indexed group (racial minority group) that would have to move to achieve an evenly integrated geographical area. So in the Springfield metropolitan area, 63 percent of Hispanics would have to move for this population to be perfectly integrated. For more on the index, see Massey and Denton, 1993, *American Apartheid.*

17. Efforts have been made to remedy barriers to first-time home buying for racial minorities, and many city mayors throughout the country have made home ownership the centerpiece of neighborhood renewal and crime fighting efforts. The 1977 Community Reinvestment Act provides the tool through which lending in lower- to moderate-income neighborhoods has increased. The CRA was an attempt to remedy redlining by requiring that banks and savings institutions provide loans in lower-income areas within their service areas. The term "redlining" refers to geographical assessment procedures conducted by lending institutions in which areas are rated for loan risk. Massey and Denton, *American Apartheid,* explain that these rating procedures became institutionalized by federal government programs that had been created to assist families at danger of defaulting on

mortgages during the Great Depression or in helping families who had defaulted acquire low-interest loans. Using four categories to rate neighborhoods, the fourth and highest risk category was coded red, and loans were rarely, if ever, provided for buying or refinancing homes in these areas. Race was part of the criteria for determining risk and thus racial minorities disproportionately lived in redlined areas. These discriminatory loan practices contributed to the deterioration of urban neighborhoods with large concentrations of urban minorities.

There are still debates about whether the CRA has successfully eliminated redlining. Studies that focus on the process of mortgage approval have found little evidence of continuing practices of redlining, but outcome-based studies that focus on aggregate patterns of lending in lower-income neighborhoods continue to show evidence of redlining, even when controlling for a wide range of variables. See John Yinger, *Closed Doors, Opportunities Lost: The Continuing Costs of Housing Discrimination* (New York: Russell Sage Foundation, 1995); and Stephen Ross and John Yinger, *The Color of Credit Mortgage Discrimination, Research Methodology, and Fair-Lending Enforcement* (Cambridge: MIT Press, 2002). Steven L. Ross and Geoffrey M. B. Tootell, "Redlining, the Community Reinvestment Act, and Private Mortgage Insurance," *Journal of Urban Economics* 55, no. 2 (2004): 278–97, show that one determining factor for loan approval in low-income areas is whether the applicant is approved for Private Mortgage Insurance (PMI). They argue that lenders meet their CRA obligations by issuing loans in low-income areas when their underwriting risks are offset by PMI.

In the past ten years, loans to black homeowners have increased 80 percent and to Hispanics 186 percent, compared to a 30 percent increase for whites. Moreover, the National Community Reinvestment Coalition estimates that $1.7 trillion in new loans has been made in urban communities since the act was passed (See Charis E. Kubrin and Gregory D. Squires, "Build Homes, Not Jails," *Dollars and Sense* 255 [2004]: 11–12). Still, these efforts have fallen short of reducing racial segregation. Home buying in low- to moderate-income urban neighborhoods may help to stabilize the neighborhood and, as everyone hopes, may even increase the value of homes in these areas, but these neighborhoods are likely to remain predominantly black, while wealthier suburban neighborhoods enjoy white middle-class privileges.

18. Shapiro, *The Hidden Cost of Being African American*, 142.
19. Reynolds Farley, Charlotte Steeh, Maria Krysan, Keith Reeves, and Tara Jackson, "Segregation and Stereotypes: Housing in the Detroit Metropolitan Area," *American Journal of Sociology* 100 (1994): 750–80; and Reynolds Farley, Elaine Fielding, and Maria Krysan, "The Residential Preferences of Blacks and Whites: A Four-Metropolis Analysis," *Housing Policy Debate* 8 (1997): 763–800.
20. The inverse pattern, notably gentrification, is also largely driven by a color-coded housing market. In this case, whites move back into the city, when it is proven to be relatively safe, which raises housing prices and pushes poor and working-class minority residents into other neighborhoods, unevenly affecting the appreciation of housing values across the city.

21. While lenders argue vociferously that race and ethnicity do not matter in loan assessment, several studies challenge their claim. In John Yinger's 1995 classic, *Closed Doors, Opportunities Lost,* he shows that even when controlling for economic characteristics, housing location, and lender, black and Hispanic applicants still face higher denial rates. In Shapiro's more recent review of Steven Ross and John Yinger's 2002 book, *The Color of Credit*—what he refers to as "the most exhaustive treatment yet published of mortgage discrimination that weighs evidence and critics"—Shapiro states that while the authors caution against overstating discrimination, "grave levels of racial discrimination are still alive in financial mortgage markets." Shapiro, *The Hidden Cost of Being African American,* 110.

22. As Shapiro, *The Hidden Cost of Being African American,* claims, home ownership is the cornerstone of middle-class status, and wealth in the United States is much more unequally distributed than income. Using data from the 1999 Panel Study of Income Dynamics, Shapiro shows that black and Hispanic households make about three-fifths of the income of white households, but typically have around one-tenth of the wealth of a white family. The differences in the distribution of wealth and income can also be seen by comparing the share of the wealth and income obtained by the top 20 percent of households. In 1998, the top 20 percent earned 42 percent of total income in the United States but possessed 84 percent of all household wealth and 93 percent of all financial wealth. Moreover, as Shapiro points out, while the economic boom of the 1990s improved average income and wealth for all social groups, it nonetheless increased wealth inequality to the point where it was more unequal in 1998 than at any point since 1929. If this were not enough, from 1998 to 2001, the net worth of the top 10 percent of households increased by 69 percent, while three in ten households in the United States continued to have no wealth at all.

EIGHT: THE PRISON PIPELINE

1. See *2001 Sourcebook of Criminal Justice Statistcs,* Tables 6.24 and 6.25 (Washington, D.C.: U.S. Department of Justice, Bureau of Justice Statistics, 2002), 495–96, at http://www.albany.edu/sourcebook/pdf/sb2001/sb2001-section6.pdf.

2. Bruce Western, *Punishment and Inequality in America* (New York: Russell Sage Foundation, 2006), 50.

3. The 1968 Omnibus Crime Bill, passed the year before Nixon took office, had weakened Miranda rights and expanded the use of phone tapping and office bugging. In fact, as Christian Parenti, *Lockdown America: Police and Prisons in the Age of Crisis* (New York: Verso, 2000), points out, the legislation allowed police to intercept communications without a warrant for up to a period of twenty-four hours if they considered the situation to be an emergency. The 1970 crime bill passed under the Nixon administration added the so-called no-knock warrants to the growing list of civil liberty restrictions, which allowed police to enter dwellings without warning. In 1970, the Nixon administration also passed the Racketeering Influenced and Corrupt Organizations Act (RICO), in which secret special grand juries were legalized. The grand juries gave law enforcement

unprecedented powers to interrogate anyone, without immunity, under the threat of imprisonment.

4. Ibid.

5. Marc Mauer, *Race to Incarcerate* (New York: New Press, 1999), 68.

6. States were required to pass "truth in sentencing" laws in order to compete for the $8.8 billion in new prison construction money made available in the legislation. Truth-in-sentencing required convicted felons to serve at least 85 percent of their sentences behind bars.

7. See *2001 Sourcebook of Criminal Justice Statistcs,* Table 6.51 (Washington, D.C.: U.S. Department of Justice, Bureau of Justice Statistics, 2002), 512, at http://www.albany.edu/sourcebook/pdf/sb2001/sb2001-section6.pdf.

8. Nixon's racial strategy is traced back to the 1964 presidential campaign of Republican candidate Barry Goldwater, who despite losing the election by a landside, demonstrated that Republicans could win the Deep South by using coded racist language that emphasized conservative principles. See Michael Goldfield, *The Color of Politics: Race and the Mainsprings of American Politics* (New York: New Press, 1997); and Kenneth J. Neubeck and Noel A. Cazenave, *Welfare Racism: Playing the Race Card Against America's Poor* (New York: Routledge, 2001).

9. Neubeck and Cazenave in *Welfare Racism* draw heavily on Martin Gilen, *Why Americans Hate Welfare: Race, Media and the Politics of Antipoverty Policy* (Chicago: University of Chicago Press, 1999), in making this point.

10. Erol R. Rickets and Isabel V. Sawhill, "Defining and Measuring the Underclass," *Journal of Policy Analysis and Management* 7, no. 2 (1988): 316–32. See also Isabel V. Sawhill, "The Underclass: An Overview," *Public Interest* (Summer 1989); and Ronald B. Mincy, Isabel Sawhill, and Douglas A. Wolf, "The Underclass: Definition and Measurement," *Science* 248 (April 1990).

11. Douglas Glasgow, *The Black Underclass: Poverty, Unemployment, and Entrapment of Ghetto Life* (San Francisco: Jossey-Bass, 1980), 104.

12. Mauer, *Race to Incarcerate,* 74–75.

13. Sasha Abramsky, *Hard Time Blues: How Politics Built a Prison Nation* (New York: St. Martin's, 2002).

14. Vijay Prashad, *Keeping Up with the Dow Joneses: Debt, Prison, Workfare* (Cambridge, Mass.: South End, 2003).

15. Paige M. Harrison and Allan J. Beck, *Prison and Jail Inmates at Midyear 2004* NCJ208801 (Washington, D.C.: U.S. Department of Justice, Bureau of Justice Statistics, April 2005), 2, http://www.ojp.usdoj.gov/bjs/pub/pdf/pjim04.pdf.

16. Western, *Punishment and Inequality in America,* 48. Western also calculates the cumulative risk of incarceration for black men without a high school education born between 1965 and 1969 as 59 percent, compared to 11 percent for white men without a high school education. Further, illustrating the consequences of the post-1980s War on Drugs era, Western shows that black men without a high school education born earlier, between 1945 and 1949, had a much lower risk of imprisonment—17 percent (25–28).

17. In the summer of 2003, I interviewed five criminal defense attorneys in Springfield, three of whom were public defenders.

18. Angela F. Davis, "Incarceration and the Imbalance of Power," in Marc Mauer and Meda Chesney-Lind, eds., *Invisible Punishment: The Collateral Consequences of Mass Imprisonment* (New York: New Press, 2002).

19. Mauer, *Race to Incarcerate*, 152; and William N. Brownsberger, *Profile of Anti-Drug Law Enforcement in Urban Poverty Areas in Massachusetts* (Boston: Harvard Medical School, 1997), 21.

20. Information taken from *Hispanic Prisoners in the United States* (Washington, D.C.: Sentencing Project, August 2003), www.sentencingproject.org.

21. Information taken from Census CD (New Brunswick, N.J.: GeoLytics Inc., 2005).

22. Sammy had been arrested on Franklin Street for possession ten years earlier at the age of eighteen.

23. Patrick A. Langan and David Levin, "Recidivism of Prisoners Released in 1994," NCJ193427 (Washington, D.C.: U.S. Department of Justice, Bureau of Justice Statistics, June 2002), 3, http://www.ojp.usdoj.gov/bjs/pub/pdf/rpr94.pdf.

24. Shawn D. Bushway, "The Problem of Prisoner (Re)Entry," *Contemporary Sociology* 35, no. 6 (2006): 562–65.

NINE: REBEL WITHOUT A CAUSE

1. Sasha Abramsky, *Hard Time Blues: How Politics Built a Prison Nation* (New York: St. Martin's, 2002). The state of Washington was the first to enact three-strikes legislation, which passed by referendum in 1993 after a horrific case in which a convicted rapist, released from prison, murdered a thirty-year-old woman. Three-strikes legislation was also passed by referendum in California, following the tragic death of Polly Klaas, a twelve-year-old who was abducted, raped, and strangled by a released sex offender. By 1996, twenty-four states and the federal government had enacted "three strikes and you're out" legislation. See James Austin and John Irwin, *It's About Time: America's Imprisonment Binge*, 3rd ed. (Belmont, Calif.: Wadsworth/Thomson Learning, 2001).

2. John Irwin, Vincent Shiraldi, and Jason Ziedenberg, *America's One-Million Nonviolent Prisoners* (San Francisco: Justice Policy Institute, 1999), 12.

3. The prison rate increased from 132 per 100,000 residents the year before Weld took office in 1991 to 248 in 1997, the year he left.

4. Joan Petersilia, *When Prisoners Come Home: Parole and Prison Reentry* (New York: Oxford University Press, 2003), 75. Also see Robert Worth, "A Model Prison," *Atlantic Monthly* (November 1995).

5. See *2001 Sourcebook of Criminal Justice Statistcs*, Table 6.24 (Washington, D.C.: U.S. Department of Justice, Bureau of Justice Statistics, 2002), 495, at http://www.albany.edu/sourcebook/pdf/sb2001/sb2001-section6.pdf.

6. Information taken from *Hispanic Prisoners in the United States* (Washington, D.C.: August 2003), Sentencing Project, www.sentencingproject.org.

7. Carlos Torres Irriarte became a martyr for the Ñeta prison movement in 1981 when he was murdered by members of a rival gang, known as Group 27. Ñeta continued to develop and became the largest prison association in Puerto Rican prisons in the 1980s. Several chapters of Ñeta were established in the late 1980s in Brooklyn and the Bronx, and by the 1990s, the organization extended up to New Jersey, Connecticut, and Massachusetts. On the mainland the gang became increasingly involved in drug dealing and street violence. For a brief history, see http://www.gangsacrossamerica.com/profiles_neta.php.

8. According to John Irwin, *The Warehouse Prison: Disposal of the New Dangerous Class* (Los Angeles: Roxbury, 2005), transfers and the use of supermax prisons have effectively decreased gang membership and activities in prisons.

9. Phillip Kassel, "The Gang Crackdown in Massachusetts Prisons," *New England Journal on Criminal and Civil Confinement* 24, no. 1 (1998): 37–63. Attorney Kassel also points out that it is important to remember that Fausto's description of gang activity and the prison environment is influenced largely by his gang involvement. Kassel argues that the existence of gangs in prison and the extent to which they threaten institutional security are often exaggerated. Further, he states that the abiding reality of prison life for most prisoners is tedium and boredom rather than gang violence (personal correspondence).

10. The Internal Perimeter Security team is comprised of officers responsible for conducting internal investigations, especially concerning gangs, drugs, and sexual assaults.

11. The prison in Walpole is a maximum security facility, and until the 2003 construction of a supermax prison in Shirley, it housed many prisoners with life sentences and, prior to the Massachusetts ban on the death penalty in 1984, prisoners on death row. With a history of violence and brutality, Walpole is perhaps best known for the brief period in 1973 when guards went on strike and prisoners ran the facility through an interracial organization, the National Prisoners' Reform Association. To learn more about this event, see the documentary *Three Thousand Years and Life,* and for a review of the film, Brooks Berndt, "History Behind Bars," *Znet,* 6 January 2003, http://www.zmag.org/content/showarticle.cfm?ItemID=2832. See Jamie Bissonette, *When the Prisoners Ran Walpole: A True Story in the Movement for Prison Abolition* (Cambridge: South End, 2008).

   Walpole also received attention in 1981 and 1982. S. Brian Willson, a former aide to Massachusetts state senator Jack Backman, Democrat of Brookline, spent a year documenting more than one hundred prison brutality complaints, one-half of which were reported from Walpole. Because of the governor's neglect of the issue, a report was submitted to Amnesty International by Senator Backman and Rose Vivano, director of Families and Friends of Prisoners, in Dorchester, Massachusetts. The report cited torture and other forms of abuse that guards were using against inmates in segregated units at Walpole. S. Brian Willson submitted the cover letter in Backman's behalf and it can be read at http://www.brianwillson.com/awolwalpole.html. According to Willson, Amnesty International followed up in 1982, reporting that, on March 6, 1981, inmates at the facility had been "allegedly clubbed, beaten, kicked and tear gassed at close range." Willson states that no action was ever taken and that shortly after the report was submitted and after receiving threatening phone calls, he took a leave of absence from Backman's office as "a personal safety precaution."

Because of Walpole's reputation, local residents petitioned to have the name changed in the mid-1980s, and it is now referred to as Massachusetts Correctional Institution–Cedar Junction.

12. Phillip Kassel, "The Gang Crackdown in the Prisons of Massachusetts: Arbitrary and Harsh Treatment Can Only Make Matters Worse," in Louis Kontos, David Brotherton, and Luis Barrios, eds., *Gangs and Society* (New York: Columbia University Press, 2003), 228–52.

13. Ibid.

14. Fausto's claims are similar to the prison brutality measures that are described in Jamie Bissonette's book *When the Prisoners Ran Walpole,* and documented by State Senate aide S. Brian Willson, in segregation units at Walpole in the early 1980s. See footnote 11 for more on this.

In his book *The Warehouse Prison* (61–64), criminologist John Irwin describes the hostility that guards and prisoners harbor toward one another under normal prison conditions. Prisoners' disdain for the guards stems from pre-prison experiences with police, but is exacerbated by conditions of extreme deprivation. Guards, on the other hand, must deal with angry prisoners in these conditions and, according to Irwin, develop derogatory attitudes toward them, generally viewing them as "worthless, untrustworthy, manipulative, and disreputable deviants." Moreover, Irwin argues that guard unions have made it difficult for management to punish misbehavior among guards, "which in turn enables individual guards and groups of guards to get away with rule violations, even illegal activities."

15. Extractions were filmed to protect the guards against charges of cruel and unusual punishment.

16. At the time of the sweep, Walpole was undergoing renovations. Gang members were placed in the East Wing of the prison and for five months denied any time outside their cells—the lockdown was twenty-four hours. *Haverty v. Department of Corrections* began as a case to challenge the lockdown but grew into a case that addressed Department of Corrections' practices during the lockdown and claimed racial discrimination against Latino prisoners. The court challenge filed in 1995 did end the twenty-four-hour lockdown and as described earlier prisoners were granted one hour of time outside their cells, four out of every five days. Kassel, "The Gang Crackdown in Massachusetts Prisons."

17. The *Haverty* decision also stated that the Department of Corrections' claim denying racial discrimination was "limited" and was admitted as "material fact to be resolved at trial." Massachusetts Corrections Legal Services Legal Notes, "Long-Awaited Decision in *Haverty* and *Gilchrist*," http://www.mcls.net/newsletter/archives/mcls_notes/991102NE.htm.

18. According to attorney Kassel, the Department of Corrections has "largely

rescinded its racist gang policy in the wake of the decision," and has converted solitary confinement cells to be used by the general population. See Phillip Kassel, "Good and Bad News in *Haverty* Aftermath: No Good Time for Ad-Seg Placement," *Prison Legal News* 15, no. 3 (March 2004).

19. The hole was the first stage of integrating the inmates back into the population. Conditions at Norfolk were indeed much different from Walpole. Norfolk was built in the 1930s and, according to Jamie Bissonette in *When the Prisoners Ran Walpole* (17–18), was considered to be the first male "community prison" in the United States: "During a period in which corrections aimed to make 'gentlemen' out of criminals, the DOC built Norfolk State Prison. Norfolk was designed to replicate a small town with industry, school, and government (administration). It was to be a place where prisoners could practice the responsibilities they would shoulder after their release. It was a place where men could better themselves by attending classes, learning a trade, and participating in the running of the institution through an active inmate council." The idea of "community corrections" was particularly strong in Massachusetts in the 1970s. Both Republican governor Francis Sargent and his commissioner of corrections, John O. Boone, attempted to implement the model. Boone, an African American from Georgia, had grown up when chain gangs in the Southern prisons were common, and had an uncle who experienced the worst of this for possession of a handgun. When Boone was commissioner, his penal philosophy was that "prisons must be fair; prisons must not be harsh; staff must not abuse power and must model nonviolence; problems must be resolved through conflict resolution; and most important, the prisoners know their own paths to liberty" (Bissonette, *When the Prisoners Ran Walpole*, 46). Bissonette tells a fascinating story about Boone's and other reformers' efforts to establish community corrections practices in the prison. Boone's removal in June 1973 was symbolic of the end of serious prison reform in Massachusetts. Contrasting this initiative with Governor William Weld's "circles of hell" penal philosophy demonstrates the distance we have come since then.

20. Quote is from Deputy Director Joanne Miller. For a summary of the report, see "Rape Crisis in U.S. Prisons: First-Ever National Survey Finds Widespread Abuse, Official Indifference," www.hrw.org/press/2001/04/usrape0419.htm.

21. Robert Weisberg and David Mills, "Violence Silence: Why No One Really Cares About Prison Rape," *Slate*, slate.msn.com/id/2089095.

22. Parenti, *Lockdown America*.

23. Jamie Fellner, "Prisoner Abuse: How Different Are U.S. Prisons?," Human Rights Watch, www.hrw.org/english/docs/2004/05/14/usdom8583.htm.

24. Fox Butterfield, "Mistreatment of Prisoners Is Called Routine in U.S.," *New York Times*, 8 May 2004.

25. Fellner, "Prisoner Abuse," 2.

26. Hazel Trice Edney, "Experts Say U.S. Prisoners Are Subjected to Iraqi-Style Abuse," *Wilmington* (Del.) *Journal*, 8 June 2004, http://www.commondreams .org/headlines04/0608-09.

27. Ibid.

28. Scott Christianson, "Prisoner Abuse Starts at Home," Capital Hill Blue, www .capitalhillblue.com/artman/publish/article_4670.shtml.

29. These incidents are reported in Parenti, *Lockdown America*.

30. Sean P. Murphy, "Geoghan Report Faults Prison: Officials Blamed in Fatal Transfer," *Boston Globe*, 4 February 2004, B1.

31. Thomas Farragher, "In Death, Geoghan Triggers Another Crisis," *Boston Globe*, 30 November 2003, A1, A30–31.

32. The guards made the fatal mistake of opening all twenty-four cells at once for lunch, a practice that contradicted the policy of opening only two cells at a time. The autopsy revealed chest trauma, broken ribs, and a punctured lung in addition to the ligature strangulation. See Michael S. Rosenwald and Stephen Kurkjian, "Monthlong Plot to Kill Geoghan, DA Describes Inmate Attack, Romney Orders Correction Probe," *Boston Globe*, 26 August 2003, A1; Anne Barnard and Sean P. Murphy, "Governor Sets Review of Prisons, Seeks to Solve 'Systemic' Woes," *Boston Globe*, 18 October 2003, A1; and Raphael Lewis and Sean P. Murphy, "Governor to Fire Safety, Prison Chiefs; Aide Describes Changes as Part of Wide Overhaul," *Boston Globe*, 2 December 2003, A1.

33. In response to Geoghan's death, Governor Mitt Romney ordered an internal review, appointing three members to the investigation. Initial findings indicated that the problem went much further than a few deviant guards and represented systemic problems. Romney then appointed a fifteen-member panel, headed by Scott Harshbarger, former president of Common Cause and former state attorney general, to investigate three issues: prisoner discipline, classification, and internal prison investigations. As the investigation went forward, Romney vowed to end the "get-tough" strategy that had begun in 1995, when Fausto was transferred to Walpole, and to instead reorganize the prison system with a focus on rehabilitation and parole. See Murphy, "Geoghan Report Faults Prison," B1.

34. Sean P. Murphy, "Report Seen Ripping Prison Management," *Boston Globe*, 11 December 2003, A1.

35. Murphy, "Geoghan Report Faults Prison," B1.

36. Kassel, "The Gang Crackdown in the Prisons of Massachusetts."

TEN: WHEN A HEART TURNS ROCK SOLID

1. Jeremy Travis, *But They All Come Back: Facing the Challenges of Prisoner Reentry* (Washington, D.C.: Urban Institute Press, 2005).

2. Joan Petersilia, *When Prisoners Come Home: Parole and Prisoner Reentry* (New York: Oxford University Press, 2003), 3.

3. Travis, *But They All Come Back*, 32.

4. Susan Tucker and Eric Cadora, "Justice Reinvestment," *Ideas for an Open Society* 3, no. 3 (2003): 2–5, http://www.soros.org/resources/articles_publications/ publications/ideas_20040106/ideas_reinvestment.pdf.

5. Blackmun's statement is taken from his majority opinion in *Mistretta v. United*

States (1989). See Vijay Prashad, *Keeping Up with the Dow Joneses: Debt, Prison, Workfare* (Cambridge: South End, 2003), 94.

6. Travis, *But They All Come Back*, 3.

7. Along with indeterminate sentencing, the use of parole boards has declined significantly over the past twenty-five years. The number of states using parole boards to oversee community supervision declined from thirty-one in 1966 to ten in 2000. Only one-fourth of current prisoners are released by parole boards. Instead community supervision has been largely transferred to Department of Corrections employees, who, according to Jeremy Travis (*But They All Come Back*, 46), "have far more discretion and far less accountability for the exercise of that discretion than judges and parole board members." See also Petersilia, *When Prisoners Come Home*.

ELEVEN: GOOD AND BAD

1. The following description of the intervention is based upon my recollections recorded in field notes. I developed an outline in the evening and wrote notes after I dropped Fausto off at a detox facility the next afternoon. The intervention was too important and too personal to tape-record.

2. The agency's Temporary Support Service program was full, so even if Fausto had completed the detox program, there were no available placements for him—a common problem in state-supported drug programs. He had already been encouraged to go to the Salvation Army upon completing the program because of the lack of space.

3. *Improving Substance Abuse Treatment: The National Treatment Plan Initiative* (Washington, D.C.: U.S. Department of Health and Human Services, Substance Abuse and Mental Health Services Administration, November 2000), 16.

4. Lillian Taiz, *Hallelujah Lads and Lasses: Remaking the Salvation Army in America, 1880–1930* (Chapel Hill: University of North Carolina Press, 2001), 107.

5. William Booth commissioned a group of seven women (lasses), under the leadership of George Scott Railton, who reached New York in March 1880, to advance the mission of the Salvation Army in the "new world." Followers of Booth, however, had already set up missions before the officially sanctioned group landed in New York. James Jermy, emigrating from England in 1872, established two missions in Cleveland, Ohio, although they were abandoned after he returned to England in 1875. Shortly thereafter, Eliza Shirley, a former lieutenant of Booth's, and her mother began ministering to the poor from an old chair factory they rented in Philadelphia in 1879. It was the success of the latter that led Booth to send his delegation of eight to the United States to oversee the expansion of the Army in America. See Diane Winston, *Red-Hot and Righteous: The Urban Religion of the Salvation Army* (Cambridge: Harvard University Press, 1999).

6. Edward McKinley, *Marching to Glory: A History of the Salvation Army in the United States, 1880–1980* (San Francisco: Harper & Row, 1980), xi.

7. Taiz, *Hallelujah Lads and Lasses*, 19.

8. McKinley, *Marching to Glory*.

9. This information was provided by *The Chronicle of Philanthropy* (2006) and displayed in a table entitled "U.S. Charities Receiving Highest Donations in 2005," http://www.infoplease.com/ipa/A0770757.html.

10. Smith's passion for social justice would later lead him to part ways with the Army's founder, William Booth, who considered Smith's political activities unpalatable. See Taiz, *Hallelujah Lads and Lasses.*

11. Ibid., 105.

12. James Price, "Random Reminiscences, 1889–1899," Record Group 20.27, Salvation Army Archives, quoted in Taiz, *Hallelujah Lads and Lasses,* 164. The integration of the Salvation Army into the social mainstream was signified in November 1954 when President Dwight Eisenhower declared National Salvation Army Week and then again in the Army's centennial year, 1965, when a commemorative stamp was issued by the federal government.

13. Fausto received a lenient sentence largely because of the two months he had invested in his sobriety. I submitted testimony to that effect and my presence in the courtroom was pointed out to the judge. But just as the judge was about to sentence him, he called both attorneys to the bench and expressed concern about Fausto's violent record. As a result, a nine-year suspended sentence was tacked onto his thirty-day jail sentence.

CONCLUSION

1. Elijah Anderson, *Streetwise: Race, Class, and Change in an Urban Community* (Chicago: University of Chicago Press, 1990), 3. Anderson's use of the "old head" concept draws on the theoretical insights of William Julius Wilson, who argued in *The Truly Disadvantaged* (Chicago: University of Chicago Press, 1987) that concentrated urban poverty was mostly a consequence of job loss in the inner city and the migration of stable working-class families out of the black ghetto. Wilson added that the loss of the stable black working class in the inner city resulted in the loss of a "social buffer" that maintained normative stability during periods of macroeconomic crisis. Old heads were the stalwarts of the social buffer.

The loss of old heads reflects changing conditions in urban areas, especially in the old manufacturing areas of cities in the Northeast and Midwest, where living-wage jobs have declined and where urban sprawl has spatially divided privileges along racial, ethnic, and social class lines. Anderson laments that old heads—both male and female—have either left the ghetto or have lost their status and become disengaged with youths in areas where an underground economy thrives. Drug dealers become the "new old heads" and model success through displays of material self-aggrandizement. Anderson describes the new old head as "young, often a product of a street gang, and at best indifferent to the law and traditional values. . . . If he works at the low-paying jobs available to him, he does so begrudgingly. More likely he makes ends meet, part time or full time, in the drug trade or some other area of the underground economy" (ibid.). As new old heads age, they become old-Gs.

Of course, both male and female old heads still exist in black ghettos and in the barrios, just as grassroots community organizations regularly attempt to confront problems in these areas. It would be a grave oversimplification to assume that the loss of the stable black and Latino working class or of old heads has left residents in urban ghettos or barrios bereft of moral codes to live by or without normative routines that reinforce social decency. The majority of residents in areas of concentrated black and Latino poverty work and have internalized mainstream working-class norms and expectations. In Philippe Bourgois's study of crack dealers in Spanish Harlem (*In Search of Respect: Selling Crack in El Barrio* [New York: Cambridge University Press, 1995]), he emphasizes that the majority of residents in the barrio are law-abiding citizens who have nothing to do with drugs. Only a small minority of residents are drug dealers or street-involved. And as Elijah Anderson documents in *Code of the Street* (New York: W. W. Norton, 1999), a large proportion of mothers and fathers living in urban ghettos obey the law, want their children to excel in school, want to live in safe, stable neighborhoods, and want to find loving and supportive partners. These desires have, however, been increasingly difficult to attain for many reasons: poor job opportunities, increased social inequality, organized inner-city drug cartels, welfare retrenchment, decreased city resources and institutional decay, and an aggressive prison and police strategy for managing the black and Latino urban poor. As Anderson demonstrates, the moral authority and relevance of male and female old heads have been undermined by these changes. Like Wilson, he is demonstrating how changes in community status and authority reflect changing job opportunities in poor urban areas and how the erosion of a stable working class has intensified the economic and cultural struggle for control of public spaces in these areas.

2. The "code of the street" that Elijah Anderson expounded upon, in which the strongest prevail through predatory actions, by "punking down" the weak, taking their possessions, their women, their self-respect, does not represent the moral codes articulated and modeled by old-Gs. On the contrary, the code of the streets Anderson described is an element of street culture that has been shaped largely in prisons and by the lawless drug trade. Old-Gs also exist in prisons and in organized street gangs as well. Old-Gs in this context are like the inmate who introduced Fausto into the street gang Ñeta in Chapter 9; they articulate the gang's philosophy and its efforts to create a moral order (to eliminate unnecessary violence, rape, and mistreatment of others in prison, to share resources, and to create ways for people to live with dignity and respect in dehumanizing conditions). These old-Gs are likely to refer back to the golden years, when gang behavior presumably reflected more of these principles and to lament a new generation of inmates who resist the codes, engage in unnecessary violence (gang-banging), and do not know or appreciate the history of the gang.

3. Frances Fox Piven, *The War at Home: The Domestic Costs of Bush's Militarism* (New York: New Press, 2004).

4. When I met the Rivera brothers in 1990, the United States was entering an economic recession. In 1991, the recession ended and from 1993 until March of 2001 the economy heated up, creating a prolonged period of economic expansion. After

a brief recession in 2001, the economy again expanded from 2001 to 2007. In other words, with the exception of nine months, the economy has been in a state of expansion, however modest, from 1991 to 2007. Of course the prolonged expansion glossed over important facts like the loss of U.S. jobs overseas and the decline in long-term investment everywhere that has led to dangerous levels of debt and financial bubbles.

5. Robert Perrucci and Earl Wysong, *The New Class Society: Goodbye American Dream?*, 2nd ed. (New York: Rowan & Littlefield, 2002), 54. The number of U.S. billionaires increased from ninety-nine in 1990 to 298 in 2000. In 2006, the *Forbes* list of the four hundred wealthiest Americans were all billionaires and the total number in the United States had reached a record number 482. See Hollie Sclar, "Billionaires Up, America Down," McClatchy-Tribune News Service, 18 October 2007, http://www.ms.foundation.org/wmspage.cfm?parml=559; and Glen Elert, ed., "Number of Billionaires," *The Physics Textbook: An Encyclopedia of Scientific Essays*, http://hypertextbook.com/facts/2005/MichelleLee.shtml.

6. Art Levine, "Union Busting Confidential," *In These Times*, http://www.alternet.org/workplace/63438/. Also see Beth Rubin, *Shifts in the Social Contract: Understanding Change in American Society* (Thousand Oaks, Calif.: Pine Forge, 1995); and see Chapter 2, Rick Fantasia and Kim Voss, *Hard Work: Remaking the American Labor Movement* (Berkeley: University of California Press, 2004).

7. There are other strategies that the company has employed as well to disaffect union solidarity. They own two trucking subsidiaries, or different companies, that are not located far from each other, but they negotiate separate labor contracts with each. Drivers at Julio's plant carry multiple loads in their trucks, drop off and count the deliveries while they are unloaded, before they proceed to the next location. Much of their time is spent in warehouses while deliveries are separated from the larger load in the trailer, removed, and counted. The other company, however, does what is referred to as "hook and drop" deliveries, where they take one large truckload to a given location, drop it, and pick up another load. There is less involved in this process—there are no warehouse waits and no need to organize multiple drops in the trailers as they deliver and pick up. They simply pick up, drop off, and get back on the road. For this service, they are paid less than the drivers in Julio's plant and have to make a larger contribution to their health insurance. However, recently the company opened another subsidiary that hires nonunion drivers. They have given the hook-and-drop business to the nonunion drivers and forced the other drivers to do the same work as the drivers in Julio's plant—in fact, they have moved several of them into Julio's plant. In other words, in the plant where Julio works, the company has placed two different groups of drivers from two different companies to do the same work, but at different wages. Tensions have mounted. To add insult to injury, the company has more recently moved some of the nonunion drivers into the plant, a third company. Anger at the managers has surfaced, but status differences have also generated animosity among the drivers, satisfying the company's divide-and-conquer strategy.

8. According to UBS (Union Bank of Switzerland) research, worldwide losses are

projected to reach $480 billion. See Julia Werdigier, "HSBC's Mortgage Losses Are Spreading," *International Herald Tribune,* 14 November 2007, http://www .iht.com/articles/2007/11/14/business/hsbc.php. An Associated Press article also indicated that the average homeowner's housing debt now exceeds what they own in equity. See Jeannine Aversa, "Foreclosures Hit a Record High—And More Coming," Associated Press, http://biz.yahoo.com/ap/080605/home _foreclosures.html?printer=1.

9. Employment grew a mere 0.9 percent during the 2001–2007 recovery, compared to an average 2.5 percent for all other expansions since World War II. Real wages grew 1.9 percent, half of the average of 3.8 percent. Corporate profits on the other hand averaged 10.3 percent across the 2001–2007 recovery compared to a post–World War II expansion average of 7.4 percent. See Aviva Aron-Dine, Chad Stone, and Richard Kogan, "How Robust Is the Current Economic Expansion?" *Center on Budget and Policy Priorities,* April 22, 2008, http://www.cbpp .org/8-9-05bud.htm.

10. Piven, *The War at Home,* 46, 41. Piven explains that the more highly touted average tax cut of $1,126 publicly promoted by the White House was misleading because the average included huge tax cuts being disproportionately given to the wealthy. By instead focusing on the median tax cut, this skewing effect was eliminated, and the figure dropped to $217 per taxpayer, a more accurate reflection of the tax cut given to middle America. In addition to the average $90,000-per-millionaire tax cut estimated in 2003, Piven writes, "the federal estate tax on large inheritances was phased out, the rate of capital gains was cut from 20 percent to 15, and the top rate on dividends was slashed from 39.6 percent to 15 percent" (41). Corporations also fared well from the legislation, as write-offs on investments were expected to reduce the public coffers by $175 billion. Further, according to Piven, the 2001 tax cuts passed by the Bush administration will cost the public an estimated $1 trillion over ten years and the 2003 cuts that followed are expected to cost another $850 billion. Already in 2004, tax cuts had decreased public monies by $270 billion, and as Piven points out, only 11 percent of the cuts are scheduled to take effect before 2008 (41, 45).

11. *The Huffington Post* reports that legislation passed in 2008 would raise the present costs of the two wars to $850 billion. Ben Feller, "War Costs for Iraq and Afghanistan Hit $850 Billion," *Huffington Post,* July 16, 2008, http://www.huffingtonpost .com/2008/06/30/war-costs-for-iraq-and-af_n_110109.html?view=print. In a *Washington Post* article, Linda Bilmes and Joseph Stiglitz estimate that, after the interest is figured into the massive loans that have been acquired to pay for the Iraq war, the total costs for the war will exceed $3 trillion. Linda J. Bilmes and Joseph E. Stiglitz, "The Iraq War Will Cost Us $3 Trillion, and Much More," *Washington Post,* 9 March 2008, B1. Bilmes previously wrote that once the costs of the war reached $1.3 billion, it would cost each household in the United States $11,300, suggesting that current projections may cost U.S. households well over $20,000 each. Linda Bilmes, "The Trillion-Dollar War," *New York Times,*

20 August 2005, http://www.nytimes.com/2005/08/20/opinion/20bilmes.html
?_r=1&pagewanted=print&oref=slogin.

The mounting federal deficit has long-term costs to public policies and social programs that have traditionally been used to support the un- and under-employed, the sick, the impaired, the elderly, and the disadvantaged. Piven, in *The War at Home*, reports that only one in seven needy families was receiving child care subsidies in 2003. Moreover, she explains that as states scramble to pay for the increasing costs of public assistance and for unfunded federal mandates (like homeland security and the No Child Left Behind policies), the Bush administration is targeting what they call the states' "creative bookkeeping ploys" to get more federal Medicaid money. More recently, in 2007, the president vetoed legislation passed by Congress to expand the popular State Children's Health Insurance Program (SCHIP). Meanwhile, nearly 43 million Americans remain uninsured, while the escalating costs of health insurance are crippling businesses and families alike. Along with the 2008 government bailout of Wall Street it now appears that the deficit will exceed $1 trillion.

12. The number of state and federal prisoners increased from 1,324,465 in 2001 to 1,528,041 in 2007. If we include inmates in jails throughout the nation, the prison population increased an average of 2.6 percent each year between 2000 and 2006, reaching nearly 2.3 million (2,299,116) in 2007. William J. Sabol and Heather Couture, "Prison Inmates at Midyear 2007," NCJ221944, and William J. Sabol and Todd D. Minian, "Jail Inmates at Midyear 2007," NCJ221945 (Washington, D.C.: U.S. Department of Justice, Bureau of Justice Statistics, June 2008), at http://www.ojp.usdoj.gov/bjs/prisons.htm. For 1990 data, see "State and Federal Prisons Report Record Growth During Last 12 Months," U.S. Department of Justice press release, 3 December 1995, http://www.ojp.usdoj.gov/bjs/pub/pdf/pam95.pdf.

13. Bruce Western, "Reentry: Reversing Mass Imprisonment," *Boston Review* (July/August 2008), http://bostonreview.net/.

14. See Loïc Wacquant, "Deadly Symbiosis: When Ghetto and Prison Meet the Mesh," *Punishment and Society* 3, no. 1 (2001): 95–134.

INDEX

Numerals in *italic* refer to maps.

399

A NOTE ON THE TYPE

Pierre Simon Fournier *le jeune,* who designed the type used in this book, was both an originator and a collector of types. His services to the art of printing were his design of letters, his creation of ornaments and initials, and his standardization of type sizes. His types are old style in character and sharply cut. In 1764 and 1766 he published his *Manuel typographique,* a treatise on the history of French types and printing, on typefounding in all its details, and on what many consider his most important contribution to typography—the measurement of type by the point system.

Composed by North Market Street Graphics, Lancaster, Pennsylvania
Printed and bound by Berryville Graphics, Berryville, Virginia
Book design by Robert C. Olsson
Maps by Mapping Specialists, Ltd.